Generative Art and Computer Vision

A Comprehensive Guide for Artists

James Parker

Apress®

Generative Art and Computer Vision: A Comprehensive Guide for Artists

James Parker
Rockyview County, AB, Canada

ISBN-13 (pbk): 979-8-8688-2147-9　　　　　ISBN-13 (electronic): 979-8-8688-2148-6
https://doi.org/10.1007/979-8-8688-2148-6

Copyright © 2025 by James Parker

This work is subject to copyright. All rights are reserved by the Publisher, whether the whole or part of the material is concerned, specifically the rights of translation, reprinting, reuse of illustrations, recitation, broadcasting, reproduction on microfilms or in any other physical way, and transmission or information storage and retrieval, electronic adaptation, computer software, or by similar or dissimilar methodology now known or hereafter developed.

Trademarked names, logos, and images may appear in this book. Rather than use a trademark symbol with every occurrence of a trademarked name, logo, or image we use the names, logos, and images only in an editorial fashion and to the benefit of the trademark owner, with no intention of infringement of the trademark.

The use in this publication of trade names, trademarks, service marks, and similar terms, even if they are not identified as such, is not to be taken as an expression of opinion as to whether or not they are subject to proprietary rights.

While the advice and information in this book are believed to be true and accurate at the date of publication, neither the authors nor the editors nor the publisher can accept any legal responsibility for any errors or omissions that may be made. The publisher makes no warranty, express or implied, with respect to the material contained herein.

　　Managing Director, Apress Media LLC: Welmoed Spahr
　　Acquisitions Editor: Spandana Chatterjee
　　Editorial Assistant: Gryffin Winkler

Cover image designed by Freepik (www.freepik.com)

Distributed to the book trade worldwide by Springer Science+Business Media New York, 1 New York Plaza, New York, NY 10004. Phone 1-800-SPRINGER, fax (201) 348-4505, e-mail orders-ny@springer-sbm.com, or visit www.springeronline.com. Apress Media, LLC is a Delaware LLC and the sole member (owner) is Springer Science + Business Media Finance Inc (SSBM Finance Inc). SSBM Finance Inc is a **Delaware** corporation.

For information on translations, please e-mail booktranslations@springernature.com; for reprint, paperback, or audio rights, please e-mail bookpermissions@springernature.com.

Apress titles may be purchased in bulk for academic, corporate, or promotional use. eBook versions and licenses are also available for most titles. For more information, reference our Print and eBook Bulk Sales web page at http://www.apress.com/bulk-sales.

Any source code or other supplementary material referenced by the author in this book is available to readers on GitHub. For more detailed information, please visit https://www.apress.com/gp/services/source-code.

If disposing of this product, please recycle the paper

For my friend Gadget

Table of Contents

About the Author xiii

About the Technical Reviewer xv

Chapter 1: Art, Vision, and Computers 1

    Biological Vision Systems 3

    Electronic Vision Systems – Images 6

    Visual Response 8

        Brightness 8

        Color 8

        Resolution 9

    Coding and Images 11

    Set an Image to Green 15

    Drawing Things 17

        Lines 17

        Circles 18

        Ellipses 18

        Rectangles 18

        Examples 19

    The Drawing Surface 20

    Randomness 21

    Generative Art 23

        Algorithms in the Arts 25

        Generative Art Design 25

    Summary 28

    Library – Code Provided for You 28

TABLE OF CONTENTS

Chapter 2: Line **29**
   Drawing Vertical Lines Using Pixels 31
   Drawing General Straight Lines Using Pixels 33
   The DDA Algorithm for Drawing Lines 38
      Other Forms of Straight Line 40
   Curved Lines 52
      Arcs 52
      Example: A Vase 59
   Simulating Human Drawn Lines 64
   Identifying Lines – Vision or "Undrawing" 71
      Brute Force – Tracing Lines 72
      Extracting Curves from Pixels 73
   Thick and Thin Lines (Again) 76
   What Use Is This? 78
   Summary 81
      Tools and Examples 82
      Library – Code provided for you 82

Chapter 3: Value **85**
   Pixel Values 86
      The Gray-Level Histogram 88
      Contrast 91
   Thresholding 97
      Thresholding: Select a Value 99
      Local Thresholds 102
   Regions and Boundaries 104
   Smoothing 107
      Mean and Median 108
   Boundaries 111
   Edges 113
      Sobel Edges 115
      Canny Edges 116

Shading	117
Bi-Level Display of Values	118
Halftones	119
Dithering	121
Quantization: Changing Number of Levels	124
Marilyn	126
Filled Contours	132
Summary	134
Tools and Examples	134
Library Code	135

Chapter 4: Color 137

Color Representations	137
Hue, Saturation, and Brightness	141
Paint and Subtractive Mixing	144
The RYB Color Model	144
The CMYK Color Model	148
Color from Value	153
Pseudocolor (False Color)	153
Space Images	155
Colorization	156
Color Temperature	156
Variations on a Color	158
Tints	159
Shades	160
Tones	161
Color Pairings	162
Complementary Colors	163
Split Complementary Colors	163
Triadic Colors	164
Analogous	165
Transparency	166

TABLE OF CONTENTS

- Restricting the Number of Colors (Quantization Again) 167
  - Equal Distance Between Colors 168
  - Median Cut 169
- Smoothing 172
- Color and Edges 173
- Color Psychology 175
- Finding Color Regions 177
  - Example: Orange Tree 179
- Example: Sepia Toning 180
- Summary 182
  - Tools and Examples 182
  - Library Code 183

Chapter 5: Shape 185

- Geometric Shapes 186
  - Polygons 187
  - Circles 188
  - Ellipses and Ovals 191
- Shapes – Closed Curves 195
  - Organic Shapes 197
  - Example – Blobs 197
  - Example: Spatter or Splat 199
  - Example – Natural Organic Shapes 200
  - Example – Invented Shapes (Midcentury Modern) 202
- Identifying Patterns 206
  - Extracting Shapes from Images 207
  - Using *Features* of Shapes 209
- Convexity 214
  - Convex Hull 214
  - Template Matching 218

Example: Ghosts	219
Summary	219
Library Code	221

Chapter 6: Texture 223

Applying Textures	224
Traditional Texture Mapping	227
Natural Textures	229
Tiled Textures	230
Synthetic Textures	232
Controlled Randomness – Value Noise	233
Cubic Noise	236
Controlled Randomness – Perlin Noise	239
Shading	242
Using Characters	243
Grunge Textures	248
Identifying Textures	251
Local Binary Patterns	252
Summary	253
Library code	254

Chapter 7: Form 257

Coordinates in 3D	259
Coordinate Systems	260
Shapes in Object Coordinates	261
The Digital Perspective Transform: What Do We Need?	262
Drawing a Cube – Using *Processing*	267
The Most Basic Perspective Projection	274
One-Point Perspective	275
Geometric Transforms in 3D	280
Translation	280

TABLE OF CONTENTS

- Scale 280
- Rotation 280
- Parallel Coordinate Projections 282
  - Orthographic 282
- Finding the Vanishing Point in an Image 284
- 3D Viewing 286
  - Disparity 286
  - Image Pairs 287
  - Anaglyphs 289
- Textures in 3D 290
  - Making a Building 293
  - Texture Mapping Triangles 295
- 3D Models 296
  - .OBJ Files 297
- Illumination Models 299
  - Ambient Light 300
  - Diffuse Reflection 300
  - Flat Shading 301
  - Gouraud Shading 301
- Example: Cubism 303
- Summary 306
  - Library Code 307
  - Stand-Alone Demo Programs 308

Chapter 8: Space 309

- Empty Canvas 310
- Positive and Negative Space 314
- Three-Dimensional Space 315
- Deep and Shallow Space 317
- Digital Image Space 318
  - Digital Image Space is Inaccurate 319

    Digital Images Are Distorted for Convenience 320

    Digital Image Space Is Malleable 321

    Digital Image Space Is Relative 322

    Digital Image Space Can Be Imaginary 322

    Digital Image Space Is Outside of Time 326

Space and Vision – The Rendering Process 326

    Visual Response 327

Space in Abstract Composition 332

    Cruciform Composition 332

    Asymmetrical or Unbalanced Composition 334

    Horizontal Composition: High and Low 334

    Vertical Composition 335

    Overlapping Frames 335

    Curvilinear Composition 336

    Constellation or Group Mass Composition 337

    Diagonal Composition 338

    Golden Section or Golden Ratio 339

    Centered Composition 340

    Radiant or Radiating Composition 341

    Balanced Composition 342

    3-Spot or Triangular Composition 343

    Tunnel Composition 344

    L or Rectangular Composition 345

    Pattern Composition 346

    O or Circular Composition 347

    S or Compound Curve Composition 348

Compositional Rules That Make Sense 349

Summary 352

Library Code 353

TABLE OF CONTENTS

Chapter 9: Dynamism 355

    Animation 355

    Time 357

        Frame-by-Frame Animation 359

        Creating Animation Frames 360

        Procedural Animation 363

    Chroma-Key 367

    Responsive Art 368

        Color 370

        Speed 371

        Shape 371

        Video Cameras 372

    Summary 372

        Stand-alone Demo Programs 373

Appendix I: Math for Generative Art 375

Appendix II: Programming in Processing 389

References 413

Index 421

About the Author

**James R. Parker** has a BSc in Mathematics, an MSc in Computer Science, and a PhD in Informatics (with greatest distinction) from the State University of Gent. He was a professor of computer science for 27 years and has been a professor of art for 14 years. He teaches a generative art course at the University of Calgary (as well as programming for artists, electronics for artists, and game design).

He specializes in computer vision and has published multiple books on that subject. James has participated in many art exhibitions and sold works. He is a juried member of the Alberta Society of Artists for professional artists.

James has written and published 16 books on subjects like computer vision, video game creation, generative art, and others. He also writes fiction, was the original bass player for the band Detour, and is a pretty fair cook.

About the Technical Reviewer

Kritika is a dynamic and experienced interdisciplinary researcher. With a substantial portfolio of scholarly publications and keynote engagements, her insights have been widely recognized across various academic and industry platforms. In addition, she also serves as a technical reviewer for academic conferences, peer reviewer for top journals, and book chapter reviewer.

CHAPTER 1

Art, Vision, and Computers

It seems obvious that to be a visual artist, one should be able to *see*. But what does that really mean? *Seeing* is more than simply detecting light or being able to form images on a film or retina or computer chip. Seeing is about being able to use images to make decisions or draw conclusions. For that to happen, we have to be able to discern shapes and *objects* in an image. An object is something that we have a label for, and so we must not only have encountered it previously, but we must be able to characterize it somehow, not only with respect to visual characteristics but also concerning its function or *class* of object.

A cat is an object. It has a range of visual appearances but has a set of features that allow us to identify it as a cat. Once we have that label, we can now place it within classes of objects: it is an animal, it is a mammal, it can be a pet, it is among objects we could find in a home, it is a carnivore. How do we visually identify something as a cat? That turns out to be a very hard question. But once we do, we can now abstract it and generalize it. These are among the things that artists do.

When looking at a cat, we can only see it from one side at any moment. Our brain can integrate multiple views to build a model, in three dimensions, that an artist can use to create an interpretation of the object. We have a model or archetype cat object, perhaps multiple ones, that we can use, but at any moment we can see the cat from only one place. It is interesting that we can still recognize a cat from the fourth image in Figure 1-1, where we are seeing the cat from behind, even though we can't actually see many of the features that we associate with a cat. Things that are cats have a set of characteristics that we can think of as "cat-ness," and these can be exaggerated, focused on, modified, or abstracted as we choose.

CHAPTER 1   ART, VISION, AND COMPUTERS

Figure 1-1. *The same cat seen from multiple points of view. Each one shows distinct parts of the cat that might not be visible from other places, yet we always know this is a cat.*

An artist could decide to paint a cat as it appears to the eye or camera. Another might focus on one part of the cat: the face or a paw. One might abstract the cat, either creating a model cat with a few extra features or exaggerating cat shapes or colors. It depends on what the artist wishes to say about the subject (Figure 1-2). The important thing here is that *the artist knows that it is a cat*. If that is known, then we only need to see one part of the cat to imagine the rest. We can place the cat in a normal environment doing what cats do, or knowingly do the opposite. The ability to recognize objects is critical to making art. But we don't know how we do it, only that we can.

In order for us to write a computer program to recognize something, we must have a good idea of how the recognition process works. The goal of the field of computer vision is to be able to interpret visual scenes, to break them into identifiable objects so that it is possible to interpret what is going on. For example, is this a farm scene? A factory? Is it summer or winter? And so on.

In some cases this is easy, because the scene has been artificially constructed to be easy to understand. We often use a computer vision system for inspecting things, and the scene is usually very sparse: the objects being inspected and a blank background, or parts on a conveyor belt, for example. In this way, anything that is not the color of the background is probably something we need to look at, and the system knows what those things are and what their shape and color should be.

CHAPTER 1 ART, VISION, AND COMPUTERS

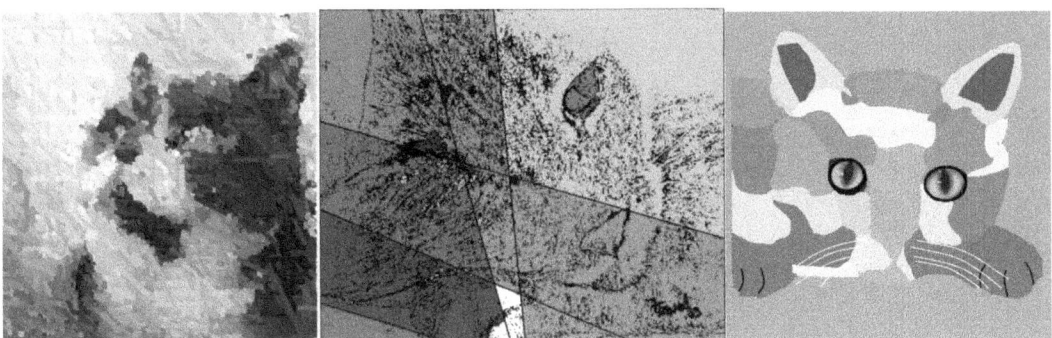

Figure 1-2. *Artistic variations on "cat." Each requires that we undertstand what a cat looks like.*

Life for an artist is not that simple. Often the complexity of a scene is the interesting aspect of it. It could be the interplay of colors, or the textures, or any number of other values. We nonetheless need to know what the individual objects are in the scene if only to ensure that we treat them appropriately. A cow is rarely purple and does not fly, and there are very few situations where it would be appropriate to portray that, so we must understand the components of the subject.

The visual system is only a part of the overall recognition scheme but is important because it defines the basic parameters. It provides data to the system, and the nature of those data gives the rest of the system, the perception system, and its character. Animal vision systems vary quite a bit, but all of them can be modeled at least partly by lenses, digital cameras, and acquisition devices. This means that one digital system could be more flexible in many ways than any one biological system, although the perceptual part, which is the most difficult, remains relatively mysterious.

Biological Vision Systems

The vision system of mammals has a physical, optical portion and a bioelectric sensor and transmission portion. The optical portion is typical of what one might see in cameras and does not really influence how or what we see – only that we can see. Of course, damage and disease can change the image that we can form, and this could impart a specific perspective to any artworks.

CHAPTER 1   ART, VISION, AND COMPUTERS

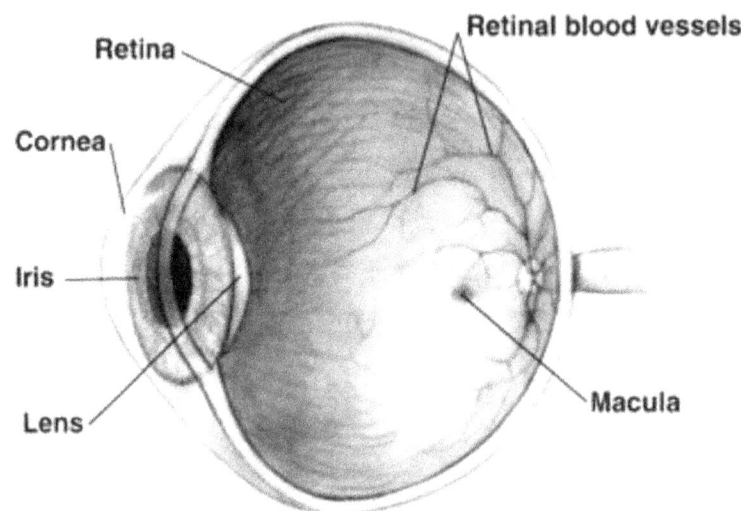

Figure 1-3. *The human eye (by NIH National Eye Institute, Public Domain,* `https://commons.wikimedia.org/w/index.php?curid=267708`*).*

The iris, lens, and cornea (Figure 1-3) will direct light and focus an image on the retina, which is the light sensor. The retina contains cells that convert light into chemical signals and then into nerve impulses that are sent to the brain. The thing is that the cells are not arranged in a grid, which is how they are in a camera. They are arranged along a curved surface at the back of the eye and are denser in some places than others. The brain must sort out these irregularities when it receives the signals.

The cells in the retina that detect light are of two basic types: rods, which are quite sensitive to light intensity, and cones, which detect color. In the human eye there are three types of cones. One type is most sensitive to green light, one type is most sensitive to blue light, and one type we call red, although it is sensitive only to red, yellow, and some shades of green. Cones are not as sensitive to the amount of light, though, which is why we cannot see colors in the dark. Humans perceive all the colors that we do as combinations of the red, green, and blue signals coming from the cones. We perceive yellow light as a combination of signals from the red and green cones, for example.

Dogs and cats have fewer cones and of a different sort and can see only a limited range of colors, generally in the blue frequencies. Chickens have no rods and only cones and can see the colors humans do but are essentially blind at night. Whales have two cone types and can see shades of grey and a few colors. Interestingly, turtles have five distinct types of cones, including ultraviolet-sensing cones, and so can see colors we cannot. We can't even imagine the colors they could perceive (Figure 1-4).

CHAPTER 1   ART, VISION, AND COMPUTERS

Perception, of course, happens in a brain, and we don't understand how. What we perceive to be red is impossible to describe except in terms of other things that are red and as feelings that redness gives us. It's not possible to compare one person's experience of red with someone else's. The word that best describes this is "qualia," which is an individual instance of a subjective conscious experience. This is one thing that makes art an individual enterprise.

The combination of red, green, and blue sensors in the human eye gave rise to the normal color system used on computers. Each color in a display or an image consists of a red, a green, and a blue component, represented as numbers. The numbers represent the amount of that component as a fraction of what is possible, usually from the least intense color value to the more. The normal numbers used on a computer are either 0.0-1.0 or 0-255.

Why not use light frequencies or wavelengths like they do in physics? Red is a range of wavelengths from 780 nm to 620 nm (nanometers). Why not use such numbers? Partly because they are only indirectly connected to our perception of color. 780, 770, and 650 nm light is all red, and defining exactly HOW red would be complex and relative to the viewer. All of these red components could appear as simply red to various viewers.

There is no frequency defined for some colors. Brown is not one color by frequency but is a combination of frequencies. Using red, green, and blue components (RGB), we could define brown as red = 0.64, green and blue = 0.17 with many shades with a slight variation in each color component, or as a combination of two light sources with frequencies between 564 nanometers and 534 nanometers. Combining frequencies is tricky.

Figure 1-4. *(a) A scene as seen by a human. (b) The same scene as seen by a dog. (c) As seen by a whale (if that were possible).*

5

Computer vision is all about identifying objects within an *image* using a computer. Humans and other animals can do this with apparent ease using their brains and eyes, but because computers are human-engineered machines, we must devise a mechanism that converts an image or a scene into a form that computers can use, and we need to be able to create algorithms for examining those images and identifying objects. We don't really know how humans recognize objects, and even if we did, it is not at all clear that a computer could use the same method. A brain and a computer are very different things.

Electronic Vision Systems – Images

We are going to be using computers to do art, and so we have to understand the limitations that they have in this context. A computer can only manipulate data that is in the form of numbers, and so we must have a way to represent an image as a collection of numbers. Such a representation has existed for many decades now. Relatively few people understand it, and even fewer understand how we capture images; that is, how a real 3D scene becomes a digital image using electronics. We do need to understand that process because it affects the images that we'll be using.

Artists often, but not always, begin with a scene, which they see as an image as perceived in their brain. They render what they see, filtered through their perception, interpretation, and purpose, onto paper or canvas. The visual impression of the scene image is reflected in the resulting rendered image. Similarly, a generative artist often begins with a digital image and then manipulates it according to a plan to produce a final rendered result, so we need to understand digital images.

We'll define an image as a two-dimensional array of color values. Each value is called a *pixel*, or picture element. An image, for the purposes of this book, was captured using a camera of some kind from a real scene, which could be as simple as a scanned document or as complex as a large, high-resolution, full-color photograph. In all cases, the image is in a form that the computer can process and display; this means that the pixels must be stored as numbers, because a computer can only process numbers. It is usually stored in a computer file in a format like GIF, JPG, or PNG, which should be familiar to most people because of images on the Internet. Most common cameras will save images in the JPG format, which is not very good for reproduction but results in small files. A JPG image often contains distortions (artifacts) that result from reducing its size.

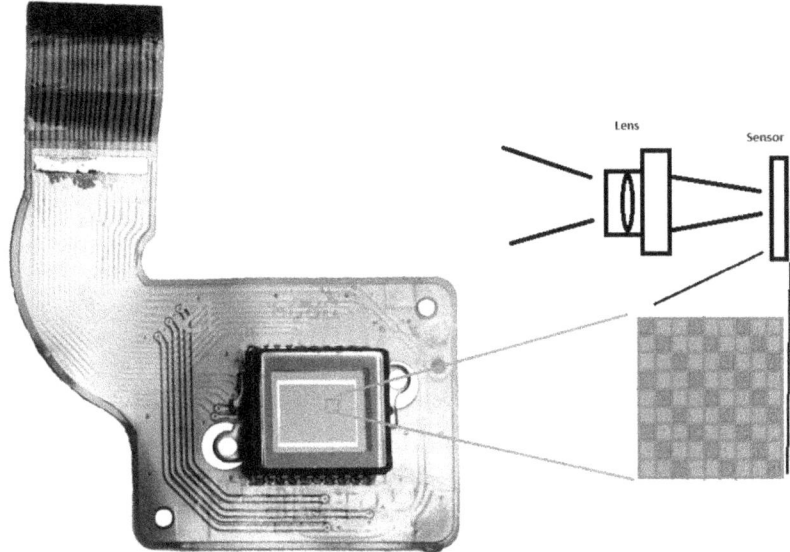

Figure 1-5. *A digital image capture device. It is a two-dimensional array of light sensors frequently covered by a color filter (*`https://commons.wikimedia.org/wiki/File:Ccd-sensor.jpg`*).*

A digital camera, which is to say one that can create an image that a computer can use, is mostly the same as an older, film-style camera except for how it creates the image. A digital camera possesses a two-dimensional array of light sensors on which the light from the scene is focused (Figure 1-5). These sensors have a color filter in front of them, either red, green, or blue, so that the color vision of a human is simulated. The image thus obtained is a two-dimensional array of red, green, or blue values. The physical nature of the sensors and the filters significantly influences the values (numbers) stored in the array. The digital image is not the same as the scene, nor is it the same as what a particular viewer might see.

The individual light sensors are very tiny electronic devices that are like photocells – they measure the amount of light that strikes them and convert that into an electric current. The more light that hits a sensor, the larger the current it generates. This current is converted into a number that is recorded by the computer.

Visual Response

There are some terms that we need to understand here even if we avoid mathematics. These concepts turn out to be important in understanding vision and perception. Any system has limits. In a system for capturing images, the limits involve *brightness* (the range of brightness that can be represented or collected), *color* (what colors can be captured?), and *resolution* (what level of detail can be seen?).

Brightness

A brighter light causes a larger current (or voltage) to be generated by a sensor, and there must obviously be an upper limit **J** to the current that can be produced. Beyond that, the device cannot respond to brighter lights. Similarly, the smallest current the device can produce is zero at a light intensity **I**, and any amount of light smaller than that won't be detected. Different devices have different minimum and maximum light levels and different amounts of current they can produce.

Another important question concerns the degree to which a change in light intensity is reflected in a change in current or voltage. What is the smallest change in light intensity that causes a change in current? Is that change in intensity the same at low light intensities as it is at high ones?

Figure 1-6 shows a graph of light intensity vs. voltage for a device. What it shows is that there is a range of illumination for which the device is designed to function properly. Less light than that and the result is no response (black), and more light means that the maximum value will be recorded (white), which is called *saturation*. This response changes from device to device depending on the purpose for which they are designed. The response also changes due to external factors such as temperature, although this is rarely important except in special-purpose devices.

Color

Most cameras are designed to produce images for human beings, and so they are designed to produce a red, green, and blue brightness value for each pixel location. A color value will be represented as a percentage of the maximum possible red, green, and blue value, in which case it's usually a value between 0.0 and 1.0, or as a number between 0 and the maximum possible value, which is often 255. The number 255 was chosen because the numerical values between 0 and 255 fit into one byte of storage (8 bits). The three color components together thus amount to 24 bits in total. There is a fourth color component (transparency, which we'll deal with later) that makes the total 32 bits, hence the term *32-bit color*.

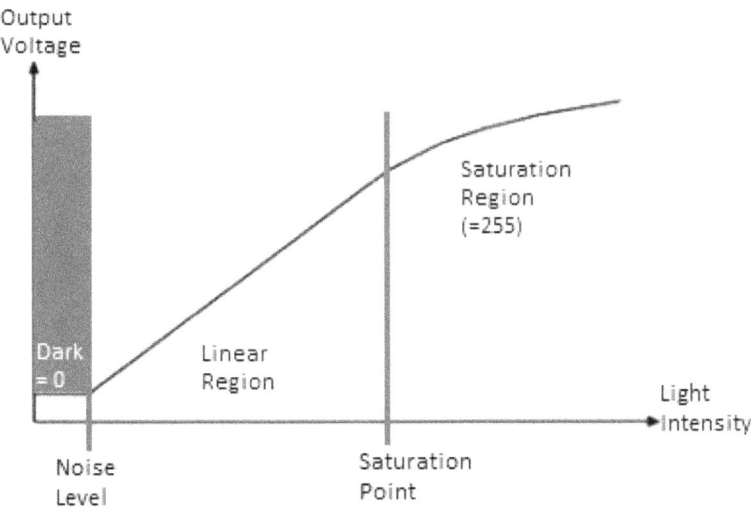

Figure 1-6. *The response curve of a sensor. Light can be too bright or too dark to sense, and specific devices differ in these respects.*

24 bits allows a total of 2^{24}, or 16,777,216, different numerical values (distinct colors), but there are still colors that can't be represented. Colors form a continuum – a color is a frequency of light, and between any two colors there is another. This means that any image is an approximation of reality, a fact that artists already know. The number of distinct colors or grey values that are possible in a particular system is referred to as the quantization level and is often given in *bits*. An 8-bit quantization gives 256 different levels (2^8), for example, and a 4-bit quantization gives 2^4 or 32 levels. For human vision, 8 bits is sufficient.

Resolution

This term is used in confusing ways. To many it means the size of the image in pixels – a *megapixel*, or 1000x1000 pixels, is an example. More properly, it refers to the level of detail available in the image, or the minimum distance that can be observed between two points. An image with more pixels might or might not have more detail – it may simply be larger.

CHAPTER 1   ART, VISION, AND COMPUTERS

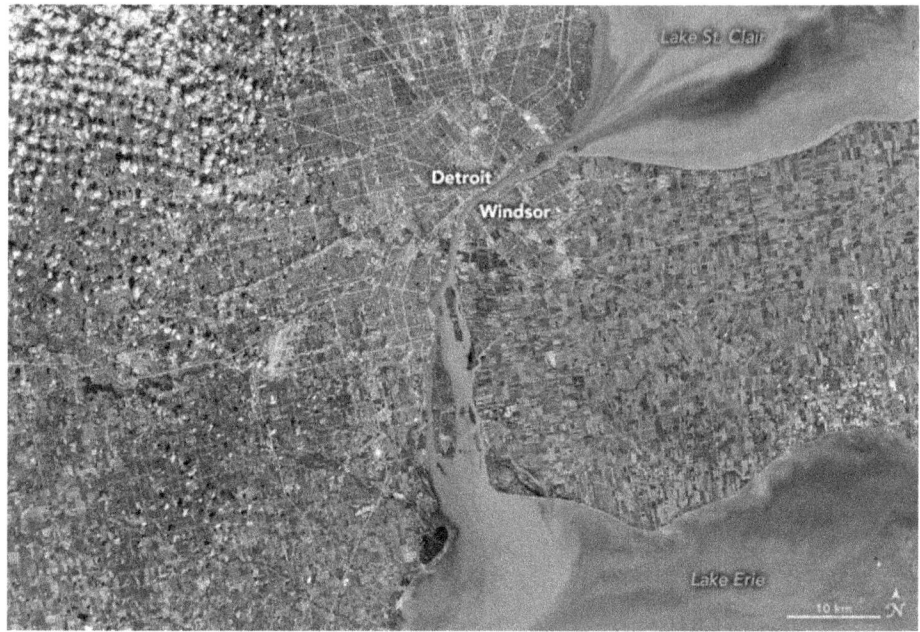

Figure 1-7. *A Landsat 9 image of Windsor and Detroit (NASA)*

As an example, a satellite image from Landsat 9 has a pixel size (resolution) of 49 feet, meaning that a single pixel contains about 2400 square feet. All of the detail within that area is averaged into one color or value (Figure 1-7). The size of the image is 5000x5000 pixels. The same applies to images of small things – resolution could be measured in millimeters or microns. When speaking of resolution in a display or printed version, the term "resolution" refers to the number of pixels per inch (PPI) and is less ambiguous.

Once an image is acquired, the resolution can't be improved. A blurry image can be sharpened, but the sharper image is an estimate of what the actual pixels might have been. Sharpening is done for visual improvement, not to gain more data.

If an image is made larger, what happens is that we make the existing pixels bigger. Increasing the size from 500x500 pixels to 1000x1000 pixels really means that each pixel in the original becomes four pixels in the new image. We can't know exactly what the real scene contained. We can only expand what we already have. And if that's not confusing enough, resolution can be the *density* of pixels – the number of pixels per inch (*PPI*).

CHAPTER 1   ART, VISION, AND COMPUTERS

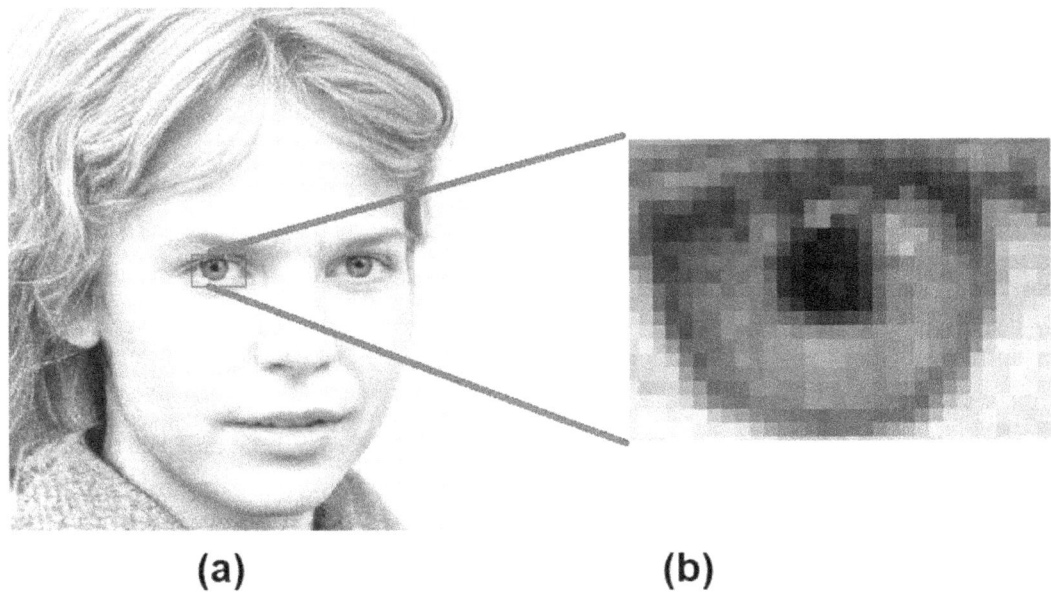

Figure 1-8. *(a)* **An AI-generated face.** *(b)* **The** *right eye expanded 50 times, allowing individual pixels to be seen.*

Let's look at this using a small image. In Figure 1-8a, we see a black and white (monochrome) image of a girl. The portion of this image surrounded by the yellow rectangle was expanded 50 times and is shown in Figure 1-8b. We can see in the expanded image that the pixels are squares and that each square has a uniform grey value. If the entire original image were expanded in the same way, it would be 45000 x 22500 pixels, giving a total of 1.5 billion pixels (gigapixels). The original is about 150 pixels per inch; the expanded one would be about 3 PPI or would require 25 inches to print at the original resolution.

Printing and scanning processes make it hard to determine resolution sometimes. For example, the image of Figure 1-8 is not the same physical size as the image that was generated, and the grey values will differ a bit from the original as well.

Coding and Images

Appendix II summarizes the syntax of the *Processing* language that will be used wherever code is given. This language was designed specifically for artists and automatically opens a drawing area whenever it executes. We assume that you will read through this appendix, because a programming language is a very precise way to specify an algorithm.

Programming is not as complex a task as many believe; it simply requires that you, the artist, specify your task in detail using a set of rules defined by someone else. English is a terrible language for giving precise instructions, since most words have multiple meanings and the syntax can be ambiguous. This is true of most human languages. Indeed, many jokes are based on this idea. Consider the sentence "We saw her duck." Is "duck" a noun or a verb? How about "The chicken was ready to eat." This has the same problem. A computer language is designed to be unambiguous.

In the remainder of this chapter, we'll explain the code quite thoroughly, but in the remaining chapters you should refer to Appendix II when you have difficulty with the code.

The computer language *Processing* has a built-in type for an image: **PImage**. We can state that a particular name (variable) will contain an image in a *declaration*:

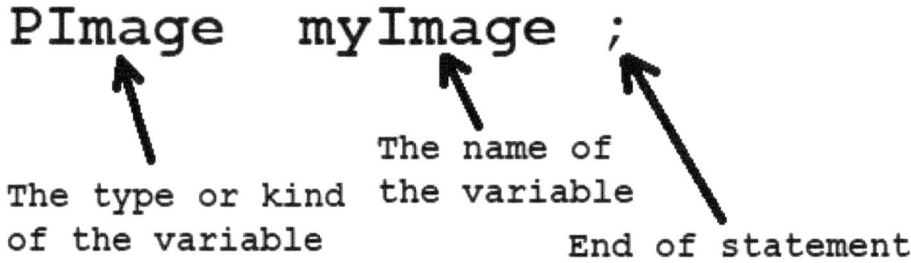

This says that the name **myImage** represents an image and contains all pixels and supplementary information. This name is called a *variable*, and most computer languages have them. A variable is simply a name that a programmer gives to some value that is important. An image is just a two-dimensional collection of pixel values, and most languages allow us to define a 2D *array* of numbers that would work for this purpose. *Processing* understands that a **PImage** contains pixels and offers operations that are specifically intended for images, such as reading from a file, displaying them on the screen, and so on.

We can read an image from a file as follows:

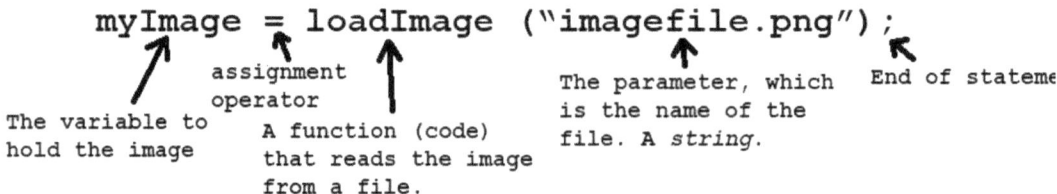

where the image being read in has the name "imagefile.png." The loadImage operation can read most common types of images and identifies them using the suffix. We can also save an image in a file:

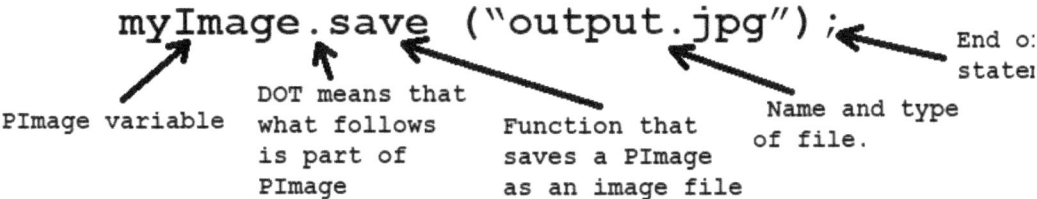

where the suffix (.jpg, .png, etc.) defines the type of image file that will be created.

Accessing individual pixels is done by specifying the x and y coordinates of the pixel using the **get** operation:

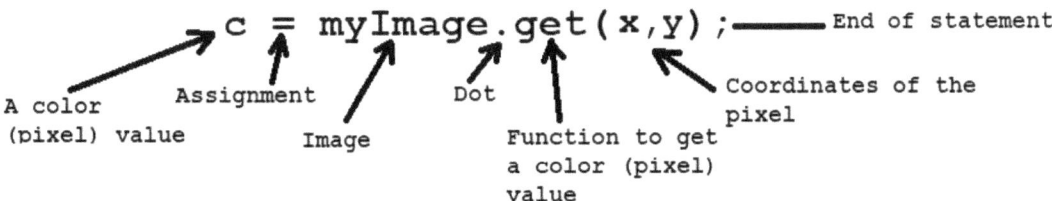

The name **c** represents a variable that has the *type* color:

color c;

because a pixel is a color. It is represented as a number, and a color is another name for an integer. Setting a pixel value is done using **set**:

set (x, y, c);

where **(x,y)** is the location of the pixel and **c** is the color.

Displaying an image on the screen is also simple:

image (myImage, x, y);

will display the image with the upper left corner placed at location **(x,y)** in the display area.

CHAPTER 1 ART, VISION, AND COMPUTERS

A complete program that reads and displays an image is:

Code: file 'I01display.pde'	Algorithm: *display1* – Display an image.
`PImage myImage;`	Create a *PImage* named **myImage**.
`myImage=loadImage("imagefile.png");`	Read the image from a file named "imagefile.png"
`image (myImage, 0, 0);`	
	Display the image.

Figure 1-9a shows the result of this program. The image displayed is a window that is too small, because we did not specify what it should be. The default is 100x100 pixels. Adding a size specification allows us to draw into arbitrary canvases:

Code: file 'I02display.pde'	Algorithm: *display2* – Display an image, correct size.
`PImage myImage;`	Create a *PImage* named **myImage**.
`size (474, 314);`	Set the drawing area size to 474 by 314, which is the size of the image.
`myImage=loadImage("imagefile.jpg");`	Read the image from a file named "imagefile.png"
`image (myImage, 0, 0);`	
	Display the image.

The result of this program is Figure 1-9b. We can see that the image of oranges is much larger and is, in fact, the full size of that image.

The following operations (functions) are provided and are very useful when using images:

```
myImage.width()      - The width in pixels if the image.
myImage.height()     - The height in pixels of the image.
```

CHAPTER 1 ART, VISION, AND COMPUTERS

Figure 1-9. *(a) A program to display an image, in this case of oranges. (b) The display area was too small to show the whole image, and we can see all of it when we expand it using the size operation.*

```
createImage (x, y, RGB) - Create a new RGB image of size x by y pixels.
red(p)                  - Where p is a pixel (color) give the value of the
                          red component, between 0 and 255.
green(p)                - Where p is a pixel (color) give the value of the
                          green component, between 0 and 255.
blue(p)                 - Where p is a pixel (color) give the value of the
                          blue component, between 0 and 255.
brightness(p)           - Where p is a pixel (color) give the value of the
                          Grey level or brightness, between 0 and 255.
color(r, g, b)          - Give a pixel (color) value having the color
                          values red=r, green=g, and blue=b where each
                          value is between 0 and 255 inclusive.
```

Set an Image to Green

This example assumes you can do *some* coding and/or have examined Appendix II.

15

Setting an image to one color means changing each pixel, one by one, to that color. Each pixel is accessed using a horizontal index **x** and a vertical index **y**. We can set one pixel at (x,y) to green using the code:

```
myImage.set(x,y, color(0,255,0));
```

The color represented by (0,255,0) has *only* green in it and the maximum possible amount of green. We could set each pixel this way:

```
myImage.set(0,0, color(0,255,0));
myImage.set(0,1, color(0,255,0));
myImage.set(0,2, color(0,255,0));
     ...
```

And so on. This would be tedious, so we use what programming languages call a *loop*:

```
for (x=0; x<myImage.width; x=x+1)
  myImage.set(x,0, color(0,255,0));
```

This specific loop steps through all values of x between 0 and the width of the image and sets the pixel at (x, 0) to green. That's only the first row, though. We need to do all rows:

```
for (x=0; x<myImage.width; x=x+1)
  for (y=0; y<myImage.height; y=y+1)
    myImage.set(x,y, color(0,255,0));
```

Now all pixels in the image are green. If we display it, we can see that is true. The complete program is:

Code: file '**l03setgreen.pde**'	Algorithm: *setgreen* – Set all pixels in an image to green
PImage myImage;	Create a *PImage* named **myImage**. Set all pixels in **myImage** to green.
int x, y;	**X** is the horizontal pixel index; Y is the vertical index.

(*continued*)

`myImage = createImage (200,200, RGB);`	Create a new image 20x200 and assign it to **myImage**.
`for (x=0; x<myImage.width; x=x+1)`	For each horizontal pixel (column)
`for (y=0; y<myImage.height; y=y+1)`	and for each vertical pixel (row)
`myImage.set(x, y, color(0,200,0));`	
`image (myImage, 0, 0);`	Set that pixel to green, in this case 0,255,0 Display the image.

Drawing Things

Drawing something in an image pixel by pixel is both tedious and non-intuitive. Individual pixels are too small; they make sense as an object only as a collective. Also, artists use basic shapes when constructing a scene. It makes sense that *Processing* (or any computer graphics code library) would have drawing operations for shapes in addition to pixels.

Lines

A *line* is drawn between two pixels.

`line (x0,y1, x1,y1)`

draws a line between pixels (**x0,y0**) and (**x1,y1**) by setting the pixels between them to a specified color. The default color is white. The color used to draw lines is set using the function **stroke**. For example,

`stroke ( color(200,0,0) );`

sets the line color to red, in this case. The thickness of the line, in pixels, is set using:

`strokeWeight ( k );`

where **k** is the line thickness.

Circles

A *circle* is drawn from the location of its center and its width and height, which will be the same and which are double the circle's radius (diameter):

```
circle (x, y, 5);
```

draws a circle at location (x,5) with a diameter of 5 pixels using the current stroke color and thickness. There is a fill color that is used to color the inside of objects, and that is set using **fill**:

```
fill ( color(0,200,0) );
```

will result in all following circles and other objects with the specified color, in this case green. The default is to have white as the fill color, and we can have *no* fill color using the call:

```
noFill();
```

There will be a line drawn around the circle if the stroke color is set, or not if it is not set. The call:

```
noStroke();
```

will result in no line drawn around objects.

Ellipses

An ellipse can be thought of as a variation of a circle. It has a center and a width and height, but the width and height can differ:

```
ellipse (x, y, wid, ht);
```

Again, it can be filled or not and have an outline or not.

Rectangles

We all know what rectangles are. They have a location, which in this case is the upper left corner of the rectangle, and a width and height. Again, it can be filled or not and have an outline or not.

Examples

In Figure 1-10, we can see examples of all of the basic shapes we've described. The program that draws them is:

Code: file 'l04shapes.pde'	Algorithm: *shapes* – Draw all of the shapes in Figure 1-10
`size (900, 600);`	// Set the drawing area to 900x600 pixels
`stroke (0);`	// Black line
`line (100,100, 150, 100);`	// Draw a horizontal line from x=100 to x=150.
`line (100,120, 150,170);`	// Draw a 45-degree line from (100,120) to (150,170)
`stroke (0,200,0);`	// Change line color to green = (0,200,0)
`strokeWeight (2);`	// Change line thickness to 2 pixels
`line (100,150, 150,200);`	// Draw 2-pixel-wide green line from (100,150) // to (150,200), or 45 degrees
`strokeWeight (4);`	// Change thickness to 4 pixels
`line (100,200, 150,250);`	// Draw 4-pixel-wide green line from 1(00,200) to // (150,250), or 45 degrees.
`circle (250, 100, 50);`	// Draw a green circle, default fill, at (250,100) radius 25.
`noFill ();`	
`circle (250, 170, 50);`	// Draw green circle, no fill, at (250,170) radius 25.
`fill (0,0,200);`	// Fill with blue
`noStroke();`	// Turn off stroke (outline) drawing
`circle (250, 250, 50);`	// Draw a blue filled circle at (250,250) radius 25
`rect (300,100, 100, 50);`	// Draw a blue rectangle width=100 height=50 with upper left // at (300,100) line thickness 4
`stroke (0);`	// Set line color to black.
`noFill ();`	// Turn off filling.
`strokeWeight (1);`	// Set line thickness to 1 pixel
`rect (300,160, 50, 50);`	// Draw a rectangle (a square) width=height=50 pixels where // the upper left is (300,160), unfilled.

Processing is a fully featured programming language, and it offers a lot of specific functionality for creating art: it creates a region of the screen where drawing is done, displaying and saving images is easy, drawing shapes and colors anywhere in the drawing area is simple, it offers 3D graphics, and there are libraries for video and sound. The program that draws a circle is only one single line of code, which is remarkable.

The Drawing Surface

The drawing surface is very much like an image – it consists of pixels, but these are always being displayed in a window on the screen. This is where your final artwork will be drawn. You will want to store this as a file, and that's easy:

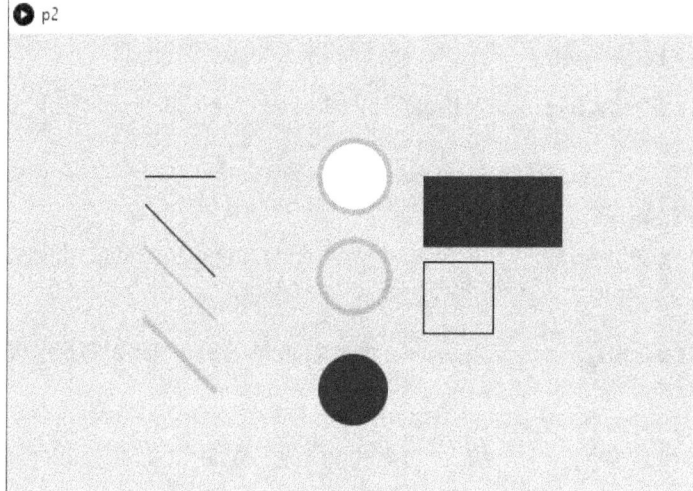

Figure 1-10. Some shapes we can draw using processing.

CHAPTER 1 ART, VISION, AND COMPUTERS

Figure 1-11. *Images created by the generative AI tool Midjourney using the prompt "candle in the wind."*

save ("filename.png");

will do that. This is the same as the way we saved an image but does not have the image name prepended to it. The surface has RGB pixels drawn by default, but this can be changed.

Randomness

Art involves a great degree of *random* activity. A human guides a pencil or brush, but the path is never perfectly straight or curved, and the unpredictability in the lines and strokes created is random. What does that mean? Randomness means, essentially, *unpredictability*. Trees appear randomly in a forest. Yes, there can be statistical measures that we can use to characterize them: they may be ten feet apart on average, for example. But if they are exactly ten feet apart in all cases, then it does not seem realistic. A program designed to draw a forest must not draw all the trees the same distance apart, or the same height, or with the same number of branches. They must vary in separation and height by reasonable amounts, which is to say they should look like a real forest. The distance between trees should be random within a reasonable range, as should the heights. We use *randomness* in art to give the appearance of reality.

When we produce random numbers by rolling dice, each number is unpredictable. The numbers can have a well-defined range (for a pair of dice this is 12) and average value (7). In a generative artwork, random numbers are compositional elements, and their parameters should normally agree with those observed in the world. Let's say that trees have an average height of 13 feet and are between 10 and 15 feet in general. There are many ways to create a collection of trees that have these characteristics. Only some actually look right. When using a computer, we need to be able to generate numbers that are random, in the sense of being unpredictable.

When using a computer, a sequence of numbers having the randomness property is generated by a *random number generator*. These numbers can be used to do things that a programmer would find unpredictable, and so they are used to simulate complex things (e.g., the location of cars on a freeway or raindrops falling on a window) and the action of intelligent agents, like animals and people. People's behavior is complex enough that it can seem random to other people.

The random number generator in *Processing* is named **random**. The expression **random(100)** will generate a real number at random between 0 and 100, but less than 100. The expression **random (10, 20)** will return a real number between 10 and 20, but less than 20. Based on these definitions, a random (call it *unpredictable*) x position within the sketch window would be generated by the expression **random (0, width)**, and a random **y** position would be **random (0, height)**.

How these numbers are generated is less important than that they seem to be random, according to statistical tests. How do we test them? Well, we could generate many die rolls and ensure that each number between 1 and 6 was generated the same number of times, more or less. If we generated 6000 die rolls, we would expect each number to appear around 1000 times (not exactly because, you know, *random*).

How can we use this in a drawing? We could, for a start, draw a circle in a random position. This could be done as follows:

```
ellipse ((int)random(0, width), (int)random(0, height), 5, 5);
```

The code as presented would always draw a circle of size 5 pixels. Randomizing size and color and drawing a collection of them would complete an artwork:

```
for (i=0; i<50; i++)
{
  fill ((int)random(0,256),(int)random(0,256),
            (int)random(0, 256),60);
```

```
    siz = (int)random(5, 40);
    ellipse ((int)random(0, width), (int)random(0, height),
                     siz, siz);
}
```

The value of **(int)random(0,256)** is a number between 0 and 256 (not including 256), which is a value we can use as a color component. The random values this created can be used as pixel coordinates, lengths, diameters, angles – any geometric component of an artwork.

Generative Art

The term "generative art" refers to art that is created using an *autonomous* (usually non-human) system under the *algorithmic* control of the artist. That's quite a mouthful, but it almost always means that an idea developed by an artist is broken down into methodological steps (an *algorithm*), and then a computer (autonomous system) is programmed to perform those steps. The human effort involved occurs in the design of the work, while the "autonomous" part occurs during the rendering process.

There is confusion between this and *generative AI*, unfortunately. An AI system is not really under the control of the artist, nor does the artist define an algorithm. AI systems such as *Midjourney* and *NightCafe* only allow the user to specify a request by using a simple phrase. This is essentially what someone might do when *hiring* an artist but is certainly not an algorithm. The images in Figure 1-11 were generated using the phrase "candle in the wind." The images are very pleasant, but not necessarily what the artist had in mind, and were certainly not under the control of the artist and so are less interesting to artists specifically.

Generative art is not a *movement* or a *style*. A style would permit a positive assessment of a work as belonging or not to a particular class or genre on inspection. It would involve visual elements, for example, and characteristic image transformations that would allow works to be classified. Generative art is more about how it is made. In that sense it can be thought of as *constructivist*. Constructivist art was about how materials behaved. How is plastic different from steel and glass distinct from stone? In *constructivism,* the form taken by an artwork is defined by its materials and not the reverse. An artist often takes materials like oil and tints and creates painted renderings, transforming the raw material into a painting or drawing or sculpture.

The basic ideas around generative art are as follows:

1. Generative art is the ***art of the algorithm***. The artist must define how the work is constructed, in careful and very specific terms. The description can include a random component, but one that has been designed into the algorithm so as to enhance some aspects of the work, rather than to have the machine "create" something. In other words, randomness must be very specifically applied to some aspects of the creation of the work.

2. The machine (computer) is relegated to the role of renderer, not creator. The artwork is defined well enough by the artist that their view is the one being visualized.

3. The computer is used as a tool, but in such a way that there is an autonomous, programmable element. This precludes drawings made using *Paint*, *Illustrator*, or *Photoshop* from being classed as generative.

4. Generative art can be interactive (responsive to the viewer) and/or dynamic (changing with time) but does not have to be. A computer can "see" or "hear" the environment using sensors and adapt the visual result to those inputs.

5. Randomness in a generative work is under the control of the artist. The ultimate work is not completely random but can use randomness (as is the case in reality) to make variations in the rendering. No two drawings by the same artist are the same, but they have similar characteristics.

6. Two artists may have the same idea in mind, but their algorithms may differ in places so that the results differ too. Both may be satisfied with the result, even though the visual result differs.

A generative artist does not need to be a programmer, but it certainly helps. The ability to specify what the artwork should look like and how to create it ultimately must be specified in terms that a computer or like device can execute. That's why we need to know about pixels, and computer-defined (RGB) colors, and randomness. Visual artists have not traditionally used algorithms in their work. They have often used design components like visual studies, but that's very different.

Algorithms in the Arts

Musicians are somewhat used to algorithms: written music is an algorithm. It's true that you can try to play a musical piece precisely as written, but generally each performance will be a variation on the score. That's why there are so many recordings of the same musical piece. For example, the best performance (instance) of Beethoven's Symphony No. 7 is said by some to be DG E471 4902 by the Berlin Philharmonic conducted by Claudio Abbado. The second best could be Decca 478 3496 by the Leipzig Gewandhaus Orchestra conducted by Riccardo Chailly. They are the same symphony (algorithm), but the two instances are distinct from each other in their realization or performance. There is a degree of randomness in the performances.

Hamlet is an algorithm. The words are all there and mean the same thing to most of us, but there are thousands of different performances. We can ask; *who is the best Hamlet*? Richard Burton? Laurence Olivier? Benedict Cumberbatch? The fact that this question is even asked means that there are differences between them, and they are differences in execution. There is a degree of randomness in the performances.

Visual art has not historically had the use of algorithms in this way. A painter can have a *process*, but that's individual to a painter and is not really an algorithm. For one thing, a process is more like a style in that it is not about a specific artwork but is in fact about the artist. All of the works by an artist show the same process at work: individual pieces are not described by the *process*.

Generative Art Design

There are many ways to think about the creation of art, and specifically the creation of generative art. A key question is "Where do we begin." Here are some ideas.

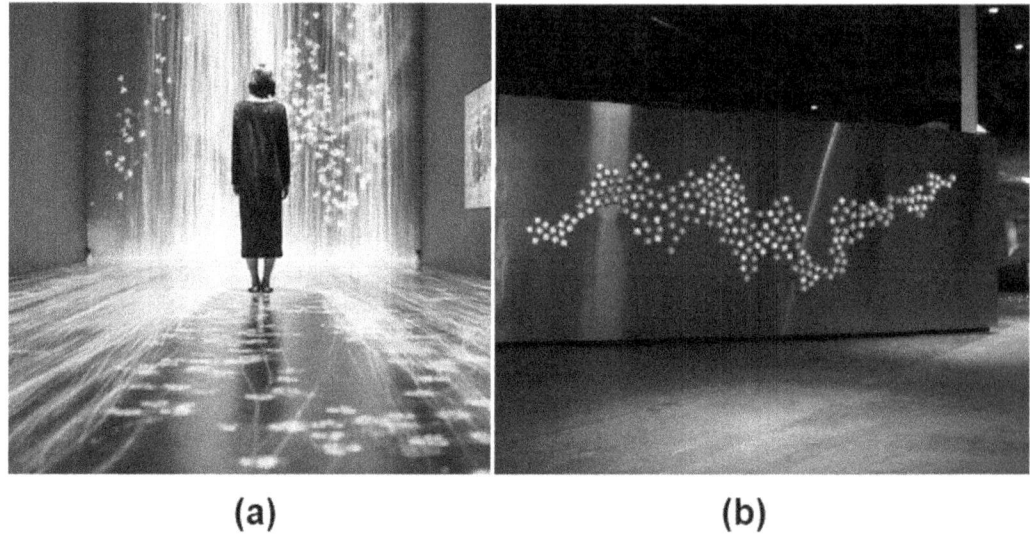

Figure 1-12. *(a) The interactive work transcending boundaries by teamLab (`https://aesthesiamag.wordpress.com/2017/05/30/immersive-interactive-installation-in-an-art-gallery-in-london/`). (b) The interactive work six-forty by four-eighty by the design intelligence lab at MIT (`https://designintelligence.mit.edu/work/sixforty`), with permission.*

The artist begins with an actual image. This is what happens when someone takes an easel into the mountains and paints what they see. For a generative artist, it means starting with an image captured using a camera or like device. The artist wishes to modify the image to become what *they* see or feel about it.

The artist has a detailed image in their mind. This is often how an artist begins an abstract work. Shapes and colors appear in the artist's mind, and they then devise a method for rendering it.

The artist wonders what would happen *if*. This is like the two in Figure 1-12, but in generative art experimentation is much more part of the design process. Often the idea fails; sometimes it succeeds. Experimenting with a generative work is faster than with painting, for example. We can restart a generative process partway through, and we can change colors and modify shapes and sizes quite easily and then assess the visual result.

The artist can take a static idea and make it dynamic. We can take the image of a candle and cause it to flicker and move like a real candle. We can cause objects in a scene to move and change color. In this sense, generative art includes things like animation and video.

CHAPTER 1   ART, VISION, AND COMPUTERS

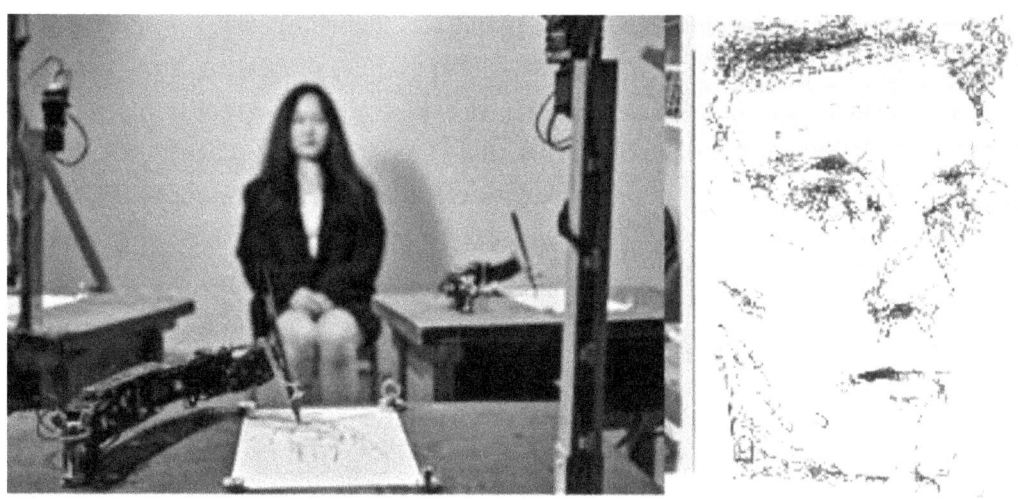

Figure 1-13. Human Study #1, an example of human/robot collaboration in art. Patrick Tresset (2102).

The artist can allow the viewer to contribute. Computers can sense their surroundings using cameras, microphones, and various sensors. An artwork can change as a function of what it sees and hears. If movement is used as interaction, it is called *motion-based interactive art*.

For example, the piece *Flowers and People* by Teamlab shows flowers growing and blossoming and then withering and fading (Figure 1-12a). The distance of the view from the work determines whether the blossom blooms or dies and falls. The piece *Six-Forty by Four-Eighty* by artists Zigelbaum + Coelho is a two-dimensional lighting installation with 220 pixels that respond to touch by changing color (Figure 1-12b).

The artist can merge multiple forms, like sounds, touch, and colors. In the absence of user interaction, multiple media can be used to communicate with the audience. A simple example is the music visualizations that accompany some PC-based MP3 players. Musical notes can be made to correspond to motion and shapes and colors.

The artist can use robotic and mechanical devices. The output device does not have to be paper or a computer screen, at least not directly. The artist Van Arman uses a robot arm to paint with real paint and brushes; Sougwen Chung, who presented abstract paintings, sculpture, video, and performance made in collaboration with robots during her exhibition *Entangled Origins*; and Patrick Tresset devised ways to have robots sketch a human being in real time (*Human Study #1*, 2012, Figure 1-13).

Generative art is definitely art in the usual sense of the word. Art is a way that humans communicate feelings to each other. The artist has complete control over the final work, and at a detailed level. Machines have assisted artists in rendering, and really that's what a computer does for us. Because generative art is still art, the usual characteristics of art still apply. In particular, the traditional seven elements that we learn in art school are still essential: *line, value, color, shape, form, texture, and space*. We will discuss each of these in the context of generative art and then add an *eighth* element: *motion*.

Summary

The use of computers forms a new medium for artists. As such, an artist should know as much about this medium as possible, both the advantages and limitations. To use a computer, we need to *capture* or *sample* data such as images and represent it as numbers. This changes it from a continuous, real-world form into a discrete virtual form. We should also know about the process of sampling, because it introduces distortions in images.

Once the image has been sampled, we can manipulate it using computer programs. If we write our own programs, then we have complete control over the artwork. In *generative art* we define the artwork completely as a sequence of steps used to create it – this is an *algorithm* and is the work of the artist. The algorithm is then converted into a computer program, which does the drawing. Generative art is not the same as AI art, because the generative artist has complete control over the work, whereas when using AI, one simply says what you want in a general sense.

Library – Code Provided for You

l01display	– display image without size
l02display	– display image with size
l03setgreen	– set all pixels to green
l04shapes	– draw the shapes in Figure 1

CHAPTER 2

Line

All elements of a computer image consist of *pixels* (picture elements), which are to say small areas, dots, spots, or however one wishes to describe them. A pixel is the smallest *addressable* unit in an image. That is, it can be uniquely located using a horizontal coordinate value **X** or **i** and a vertical coordinate value **Y** or **j**. We usually specify these values as integers, precisely because they are the smallest addressable unit, and so there can be no pixel between two adjacent pixels. Note that computer graphics typically use a coordinate system where (0,0) is at the top-left corner, with Y values increasing downward, which differs from standard mathematical coordinate systems.

A human artist would not do this. The *line* element in art is used to define overall shape, delimit boundaries, create textures, and generally render visual aspects of any scene. It has been defined by artists as a *point moving in space*. 20th-century artist Paul Klee is quoted as saying, **"A line is a dot (a** pixel**) that went for a walk."** Of course, the "dot" leaves a copy of it behind in each previous position and must (in the computer context) move from one pixel coordinate to an adjacent one. This gives us a clue concerning how to make a line out of pixels but also creates some interesting visual conceptions.

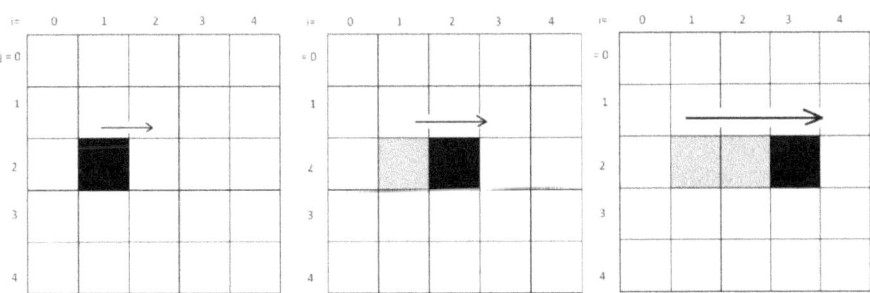

Figure 2-1. *A pixel at (1,2) going for a "walk" to the right, which is the positive X direction, setting pixels (1,2), (2,2), (3,2), and so on.*

CHAPTER 2 LINE

Consider a pixel at some location specified by coordinates (i,j). If it is "walking" to the right, we get the situation seen in Figure 2-1, where each square represents a pixel location on the display grid. The coordinates shown indicate the precise addressing system used to locate each pixel. The line will end up being horizontal, starting at (i,j) and proceeding to (i+1,j), (i+2,j), and so on (Figure 2-1).

A human artist would express this differently and execute it differently too. This is a horizontal line and is accomplished by using an instrument like a pencil or brush, touching the surface at some location, and then moving the instrument to the right (Figure 2-2). An artist uses no coordinates (a computer must) and describes the action rather vaguely.

Figure 2-2. *A human draws a line using an instrument and drags it across the drawing surface (paper, canvas)*

The result is a horizontal line that is continuous (not digital/discrete) but less perfect; a human line is never perfectly straight. This gives human art part of its visual character.

A line can be straight or curved. A straight line can have any orientation or direction, and this is often indicated as an angle. It is a set of pixels where the next pixel is a fixed direction from the last one. A curve is more difficult to define and draw but essentially does not have that property. All other types of lines are just variations of these two. Jagged lines, for example, are really just collections of regular lines of different angles joined end to end. Broken lines are straight lines with a common direction and a fixed-sized gap between them (Figure 2-3).

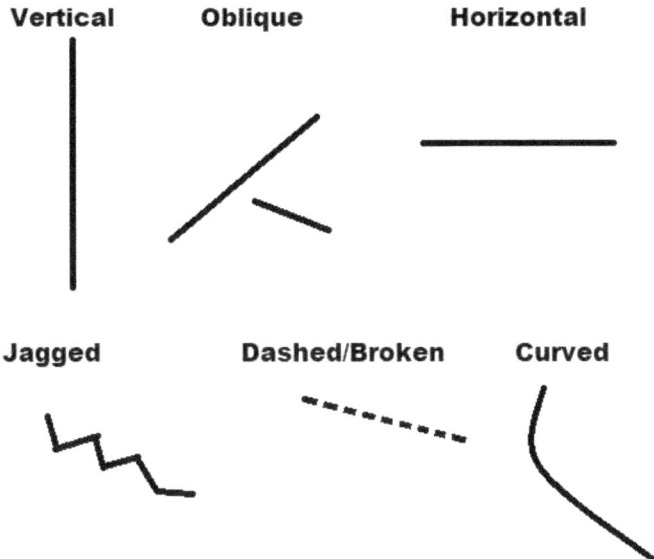

Figure 2-3. *Type of lines*

Let's first look at how lines are drawn using a computer and programs.

Drawing Vertical Lines Using Pixels

Let's write a bit of code that will draw a vertical line. It will be called **vline** and will be passed a starting point (x,y0) and an end point (x,y1). Of course, because this draws only vertical lines, we don't need to pass both x values: On a vertical line all, pixel x values are the same, so the call:

vline (100, 100, 200)

could mean use **x=100** and draw a vertical line between y_0=**100** and y_1=**200**. The function would be defined as **vline (x, y0, y1).**

When we draw such a line, we can draw the start and end points first; by that we mean set them to black, given that the background is white. A first step in this program would be:

drawPixel(x, y0)
drawPixel(x, y1)

CHAPTER 2   LINE

where the operation **drawPixel(a,b)** sets the pixel at location **(a,b)** to black. Now begin at the start point and draw adjacent vertical pixels until we get to the end point, as in Figure 2-4. For example:

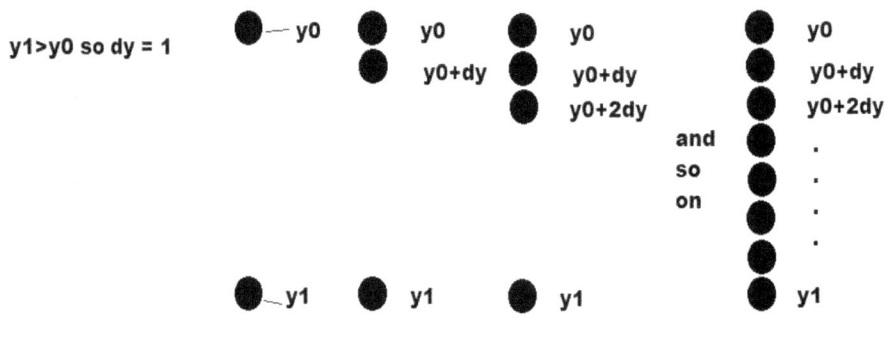

Figure 2-4. *Drawing a vertical line*

```
1 y = y0              // Starting Y coordinate
2 d = y1 - y0         // Number of pixels between y₀ and y₁
3 if d>0 let dy=1     // Line goes DOWN from y0
4 if d<0 let dy=-1    // Line goes UP from y0
5 y = y + dy          // Next pixel from y
6 drawPixel (x, y)    // Set this pixel to black
7 y = y + dy          // Next pixel
  . . .               // repeat the process
```

We can now turn this into a *loop,* and we have a program!

The algorithm is a description that could be followed by a non-programmer. It is not precise enough to *be* a computer program, though. The names **x, y, y₀,** and **y₁** are variables, and in a program would need to be given a *type* in a declaration. What kind of variables are they? The sentence "repeat again from step 6 until y=y1" is something that a computer would have trouble with. Loops in a language have a specific syntax. The **if** is also something that each language implements in a specific syntax.

The code and algorithm for this are:

Code: **code** vline.pde	Algorithm: *vline* – Draw a vertical line from (100, 100) to (100, 200)
	The operation drawPixel(x, y) sets the pixel at (x,y) to black. It's really just set(x,y,color(0)) dy is the change in y on each pixel. Y is the current vertical pixel position being drawn.
`int dy, y, y0=100,` `y1=200, x=100;`	Y0 is the starting vertical position. Y1 is the end vertical position. X is the horizontal position. Distance between 200 and 100 (=100)
`size (300, 300);`	Set the drawing area to 300x300 pixels
`dy = y1-y0;`	In this example y1-y0 is positive, meaning we are drawing *down*.
`if (dy > 0) dy = 1;` `  else dy = -1;`	This tests to see if we go down or up from y0.
`for (y=y0; y != y1; y = y + dy)` `    drawPixel (x, y);`	Set pixels to black starting at y0 and moving one pixel at a time to y1.
	Changing y0 and y1 will change the start and end pixels for the line.

The syntax of the **if** and the **for** statements in *Processing*, the language we'll be using here, can be found in Appendix I. Figure 2-4 shows how consecutive pixels are set in this method. The drawPixel (x,y) operation sets the pixel value at coordinate (x,y) to black. Horizontal lines are drawn in an analogous way, this time fixing the y value and drawing between x0 and x1.

Drawing General Straight Lines Using Pixels

Algorithms for drawing general straight lines, which is to say *between any two points P0 and P1*, use some mathematics that should be vaguely familiar. It's basically high school level, but for some it may have been some years since we looked at it. We will be setting

CHAPTER 2 LINE

pixels between the points (x0,y0) and (x1,y1) as before, but the orientation is arbitrary. The equation of a line is a mathematical relationship that tells us when a point lies on a line: if the equation is *true* (left side = right side) for some value of x and y, then (x,y) is on the line.

Mathematically, a *straight line* is a set of points (which we can think of as *pixels*) that satisfy (i.e., result in a value of 0) an equation that defines a line. One such equation is:

$$y - y_0 = \frac{y_1 - y_0}{x_1 - x_0}(x - x_0)$$

where P_0 is the point (x_0, y_0) and P_1 is the point (x_1, y_1). Any values of (**x, y**) that satisfy this equation are said to be *on the line*. If we know a value of **x**, then we can find the corresponding **y**, and vice versa. If $x_1 = x_2$, then this equation fails (we can't divide by zero), but we do know that in this case the line is vertical; the equation reduces to

$$x = x_0$$

The other commonly used equation for a line is the *slope-intercept* form, which is (of course) a variation of the two-point equation. Let's let:

$$m = \frac{y_1 - y_0}{x_1 - x_0}$$

The variable **m** is called the *slope* and is related to the angle the line makes with the X axis. When we substitute **m** for the more complex expression, the two-point equation becomes:

$$y - y_0 = m(x - x_0)$$

CHAPTER 2   LINE

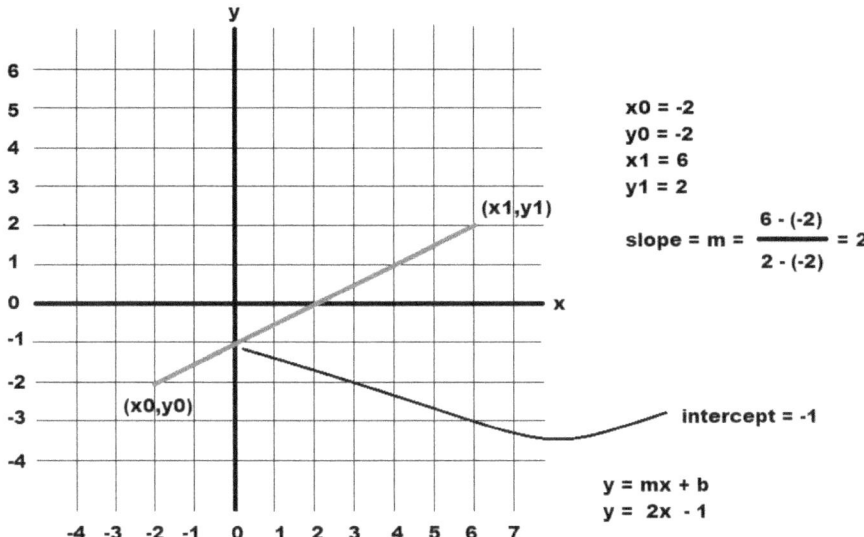

Figure 2-5. *The slope-intercept equation of a line*

Solving for **y**, we get:

$$y = m(x - x_0) + y_0 = mx - mx_0 + y_0 = mx + b$$

where **b = -mx₀ + y₀**. The *intercept* represents the **y** value of the line equation when **x=0**; this is also called the *y-intercept*. The slope is not really an angle but represents the ratio of the number of steps the line makes horizontally compared to the steps made vertically. In Figure 2-5, the slope is 2, meaning that there are two horizontal steps for each vertical step. Roofers and carpenters would recognize this value. These equations relate the x and y values to each other: *for any* x *we specify, there is exactly one* y *value that is on the given line.*

We have these two variations of the equation of a line, where one requires a slope and intercept and the other requires two points. In mathematics, there is a value **x** between any two values x_0 and x_1, and this is what makes mathematical lines *continuous*. In an image this is not true, and coordinates **x** and **y** are integers. If $x_1 = x_0+1$, there can be no value between x_0 and x_1, and this makes these pixel coordinates *discrete*.

Drawing a line in a computer program usually means specifying the endpoints of the line and setting the pixels between them, so the two-point version could be the most useful. We need to draw pixels where the **(x,y)** coordinates satisfy the equation. A problem is that it will rarely happen on a raster grid, because the coordinates have to be integers, but the solution to the equation might not be. On a raster grid like a computer

35

CHAPTER 2 LINE

screen, we select the pixels that are *nearest* to being actually on the line rather than a perfect solution. The lines will be a bit jagged, but at high enough resolution the line will look fine. For the line of Figure 2-5, the pixels that will be set are the gray ones in Figure 2-6.

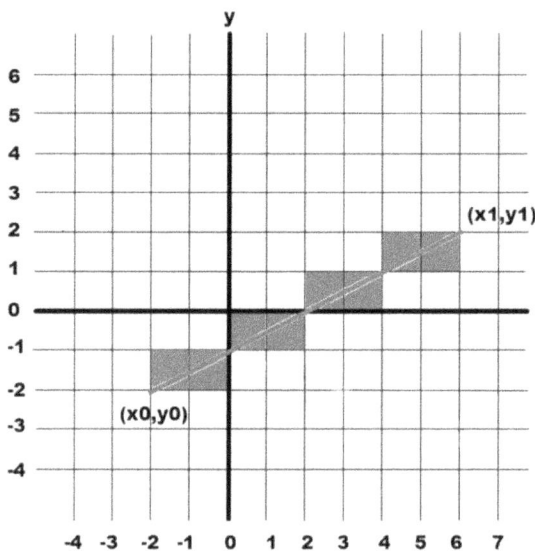

Figure 2-6. *Which pixels are set when drawing a line?*

The pixels chosen are those having a distance to the line less than or equal to 0.5. By distance to the line, we mean a perpendicular distance: Draw a line **Z** between the target point (**x,y**) and the line being drawn **L** so that the angle between **L** and **Z** is 90 degrees. Then if the length of **Z** is less than 0.5, set the pixel (**x,y**) to black. The perpendicular distance between **L** and (**x,y**) (i.e., the shortest distance from the point (x,y) to the line L) is:

$$\frac{\left|(x_2-x_1)(y-y_1)-(x-x_1)(y_2-y_1)\right|}{\sqrt{(x_2-x_1)^2+(y_2-y_1)^2}}$$

You can check this on the Internet, but don't need to remember it to use it.

A program and algorithm that does this is:

Code: file **dumb.pde**	Algorithm: *dumb* - Draw a general line
| ```
void dumb (int x0, int y0,
          int x1, int y1)
{
float z, zz;
int a, b, c, d;
float m, bb=0;
``` | This syntax (see Appendix I) defines an operation named dumb that draws a line between (x0,y0) and (x1,y1).

Define variables that we'll need for this calculation. |
| ```
a = (int)min(x0,x1);
b = (int)max(x0,x1);
c = (int)min(y0,y1);
d = (int)max(y0,y1);
``` | Range of x values is a .. b
Range of y values is c .. d |
| ```
if (abs(x0-x1) > 0)
{
  m = ((float)(y0-y1)
      /(float)(x0-x1));
  bb = y0 - m*x0;
}
``` | Is the slope of this line defined (not infinite)? If so, the slope m is
The change in y divided by the change in x. We can not compute the intercept bb using this slope and either (x0,y0) or (x1,y1) |
| ```
else
  m = 1000;        // Vertical
for (int i=a; i<=b; i+=1)
  for (int j=c; j<=d; j+=1)
  {
    if (m > 900) zz = abs(i-x0);
``` | Otherwise the slope is infinite. Just make it really large = 1000.

Examine all pixels (i,j) where x is between a and b and y is between c and d. |

(continued)

CHAPTER 2 LINE

```
        else zz = abs((m*i)+bb-j);
      if (zz <= 1)
        set (i, j, color(0));
    }
}
```

If line is vertical and (i,j) is near the line, then set pixel (i,j).

If the line is not vertical, then compute m*i+b-j. If smaller than 1, then set pixel (i,j) to black.

We are allowing the distance between a pixel and the line to be 1 at most, which is what we would get if we rounded to the nearest integer. If the value is increased, the thickness of the line drawn increases too as pixels more distant from the mathematical line are included. This is one not very good example of a *line generation algorithm*. It's slow because it examines far too many pixels. The method used by most software to draw a line is a *digital differential analyzer* (DDA), and while the idea is pretty simple, the algebra can get complex.

The DDA Algorithm for Drawing Lines

The situation is: draw a line on a raster grid between **(x1,y1)** and **(x2, y2)**. Start by setting the pixel **(x1, y1)**.

We can see how a simple DDA works in Figure 2-7. The line is drawn from **(x, y)** to **(x+3, y-2)** in screen coordinates. If we set **(x,y)**, the next pixel is **(x+1, y)** or **(x+1, y-1)** – the actual line will pass between those locations. In deciding which pixel to set, we ask *which of these pixels is closest to the actual line*; that is, the line represented by the equation. Visually, that would appear to be **(x+1, y+1)**, so we set that pixel. Now look at the next pixel, which is at **(x+2, y-1)** or **(x+2, y-2)**. The pixel nearest to the line is **(x+2, y-1)**, so we set that pixel, and so on.

CHAPTER 2 LINE

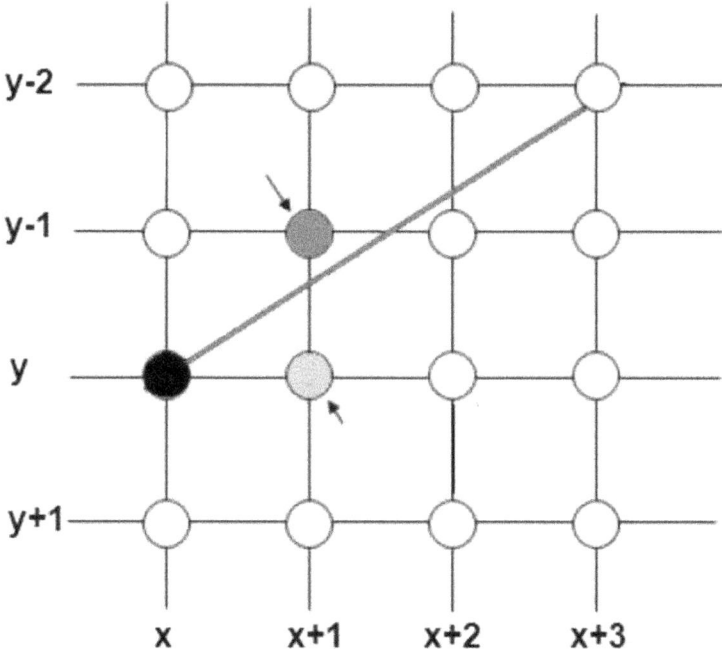

Figure 2-7. *How a digital differential analyzer draws a line. Starting at (x, y), a DDA algorithm sets the points that are nearest to a line as defined by an equation.* https://www.gatevidyalay.com/dda-algorithm-line-drawing-algorithms/.

We begin at **(x0, y0):** let **x = x0, y = y0**. The number of pixels that will be set in total will be the maximum of the change in **x** and the change in **y**, so if the value **x1-x0** has a magnitude greater than **y1-y0,** we will change **x** by 1 in each step (=**dx**) and change **y** by **(y1-y0)** divided by the length of the line; otherwise, let **dy = 1** and **dx = (x1-x0)** divided by the length of the line.

Now let **x=x+dx** and **y=y+dy**. Let's assume that **dx=1**. Then this means that **x=x+1**, and **y = y + dy** where **y<=1**. If the value of **y** has a fractional part that is < 0.5, then set **(x, (int(y)))** to black; otherwise, set **(x, (int)(y+1))** to black. Repeat until x >= x0. This is known as *Bresenham's* algorithm to computer programmers and is also implemented by the function **line()**, which is built into the *Processing* language.

CHAPTER 2   LINE

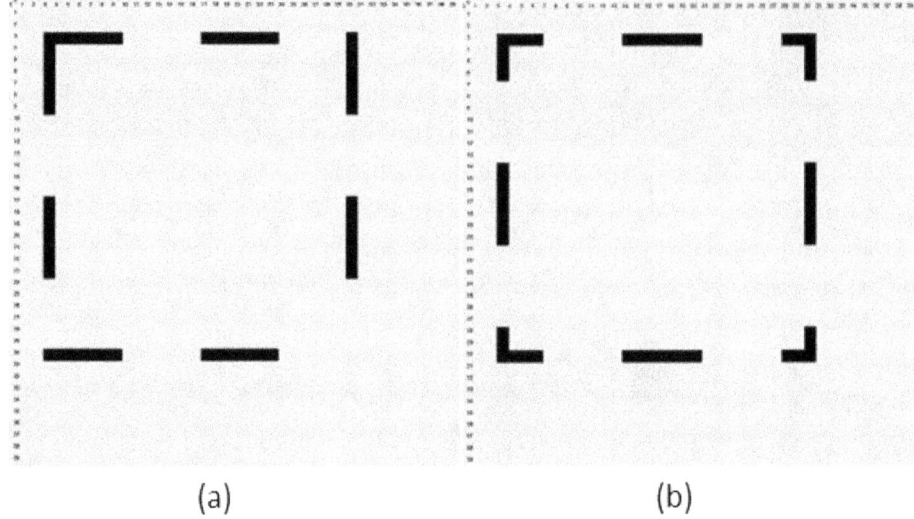

Figure 2-8. (a) A square drawing using dashed lines could have gaps that make things hard to interpret. (b) Beginning a dashed line in the middle of a dash can solve this.

Other Forms of Straight Line
Dashed lines

There are many ways to draw a dashed line, and an easy one is to keep a count of how many pixels we have drawn, and when a number indicating the length of a *dash* is reached, we set a flag to turn off drawing. This flag is **true** at the beginning of the line. Each time a pixel is drawn (i.e., black), we count it, and when the count exceeds the number of pixels in a dash, then set the drawing flag to **false** and reset the count.

This method can, unfortunately, sometimes not draw the end pixels of a line if the final stage is one with drawing turned off. Consider drawing a square as four (dumb) lines:

```
a = 3; b = 3; c = 30; d = 30
dumb (a, b, c, b)
dumb (c, b, c, d)
dumb (c, d, a, d)
dumb (a, d, a, b)
```

If we're not careful, there could be gaps at the end of the lines, and the square could look like the one in Figure 2-8a. We'd line the beginnings and ends of a dashed line to be set pixels.

To ensure that there are no gaps at the ends, we first find how many dash/gap pairs there are in each line. Let **L0** be the number of pixels in a gap or dash, and **L** be the length of the line in pixels, which is **dist(x0,y0,x1,y1)**. Then **lox = L/(2*L0)** is a fraction that tells us how many pixels are left over at the end of the line – these will be black pixels if we started with black pixels. If **lox > 0.5** then the final stage of the line will be gap, or white, pixels and we don't want that. In that case begin the first dash part way through by setting the initial count to, let's say **L0/2**. The result is as shown in Figure 2-8b.

Code: file **dumbdash.pde**	Algorithm: dumbdash - draw a dashed line

`void dumbDash (int x0, int y0,`
`              int x1, int y1, int`
`              L0)`	

`{`	Define slope, intercept, and other variables we need:
`  float m, bb=0, z;`	L0 is the length of a dash
`  float L, lox; // For aligning ends`	L is the length of the line
	lox is number of dashes
`  int pcount = 0;`	on = true is we are drawing, =false otherwise
`  boolean on = true;` `  int a, b, c, d;`	NOW lox is number of partial dashes.
`  L = dist (x0, y0, x1, y1);`	
`  lox = (L/(2*L0));`	
`  lox = lox - floor(lox);`	
`  if (lox > 0.5) pcount = L0/2;` `  else pcount = 0;`	If lox>0.5 then there will be a gap, so start counting pixels half way through instead of at 0.
`  a = (int)min(x0,x1);`	X extent of the line is a..b
`  b = (int)max(x0,x1);`	Y extent of line is c..d
`  c = (int)min(y0,y1);`	
`  d = (int)max(y0,y1);`	

(continued)

CHAPTER 2 LINE

```
  if (abs(x0-x1) > 0)
  {
    m = (float)(y0-y1)/
        (float)(x0-x1);
    bb = y0 - m*x0;                         Equation is y = m*x+bb
  }
  else
    m = 1000;
  for (int i=a; i<=b; i+=1)                 Vertical line has slope= m= 1000 when x0=x1
  {
    for (int j=c; j<=d; j+=1)
    {                                       Examine all pixels (i,j) where x is between a and b
                                            and y is between c and d.
      if (m >= 1000) z =                    If line is vertical and (i,j)is
abs(i-x0);                                  near the line then set
                                            pixel (i,j).
      else z = abs((m*i)+bb-j);
      if (abs(z) <= 1)                      If line not vertical then
      {                                     compute m*i+b-j. If smaller than then:
                                            set pixel (x, y) to black if
        if (on)                             drawing is turned on.
          drawPixel (i,j);
        pcount= pcount + 1                  count drawn pixels.
```

(continued)

42

```
            if (pcount >= L0)
            {
               on = !on;
               pcount = 0;
            }
         }
      }
   }
}
```
If count is >= than the size of a dash, reset the count and turn drawing on if it's off and off if it's on.

Thick Lines

We could define a *thick line* as any line that is more than one pixel wide. The easy way to draw such a line is to draw larger circles at each pixel on the line: change the code **circle(i, j, 1)** to **circle(i, j, 5),** for example, making the line 5 pixels thick. In the code we have been writing the function **drawpixel()** or **set(i,j,color(0))** sets a pixel black, so we could simply modify this so that it would draw an circle of size **t** where **t** was the desired line thickness in pixels.

```
void drawPixel(int x, int y, int t)
{
  noStroke();
  fill (0);
  circle (x, y, t);
}
```

In fact, when using languages like *Processing* we can have multiple functions with the same name that depend on the number of type of the parameters, so both **drawPixel(x,y)** and **drawPixel(x,y,t)** can exist at the same time. The function

```
void lineThick(int x0, int y0, int x1, int y1, int thickness)
```

will draw thick lines in this way.

Jagged Lines

A *jagged* or *zig-zag* line consists of a set of short line segments connected end to end at alternating fixed angles to the direction of the main line. The collection of lines begins and ends at a specified point and has that general direction, but none of the short lines that comprise the line point exactly in that direction. A jagged line will usually have a fixed size for the small line segments and will have a specific angle these line segments make with the (imaginary) straight line between the start and end points, or a specified distance between the line and the peaks of the zig-zag line.

This is confusing, so look at Figure 2-9, where we define the parameters of such a line. As usual, the line **L** is drawn between two specified end points **(x0,y0)** and **(x1,y1)**. This method of drawing jagged lines specifies the distance between *jogs* **D1** and the distance from the peak of the jog to the line **L**, **D2**. We can see that the line has **N = length(L)/D1** jogs altogether, alternating between the left and the right side of the line.

Starting at **(x0,y0)**, the position of the first jog is **(x0+deltaX, y0+deltay)** where **deltax = (x1-x0)/N** and **deltay = (y1-y0)/N**. We can compute the position of each jog point on the line from the previous point in this way. So far the code is:

```
x = x0; y = y0;            // Start point
L = dist(x0, y0, x1,y1);   // Length of the line
dx = x1-x0;                // Total change in X
dy = y1-y0;                // Total change in Y
N = (int)(L/d1);           // Number of jogs
deltax = dx/N;             // X distance between jogs
deltay = dy/N;             // Y distance between jogs
```

CHAPTER 2 LINE

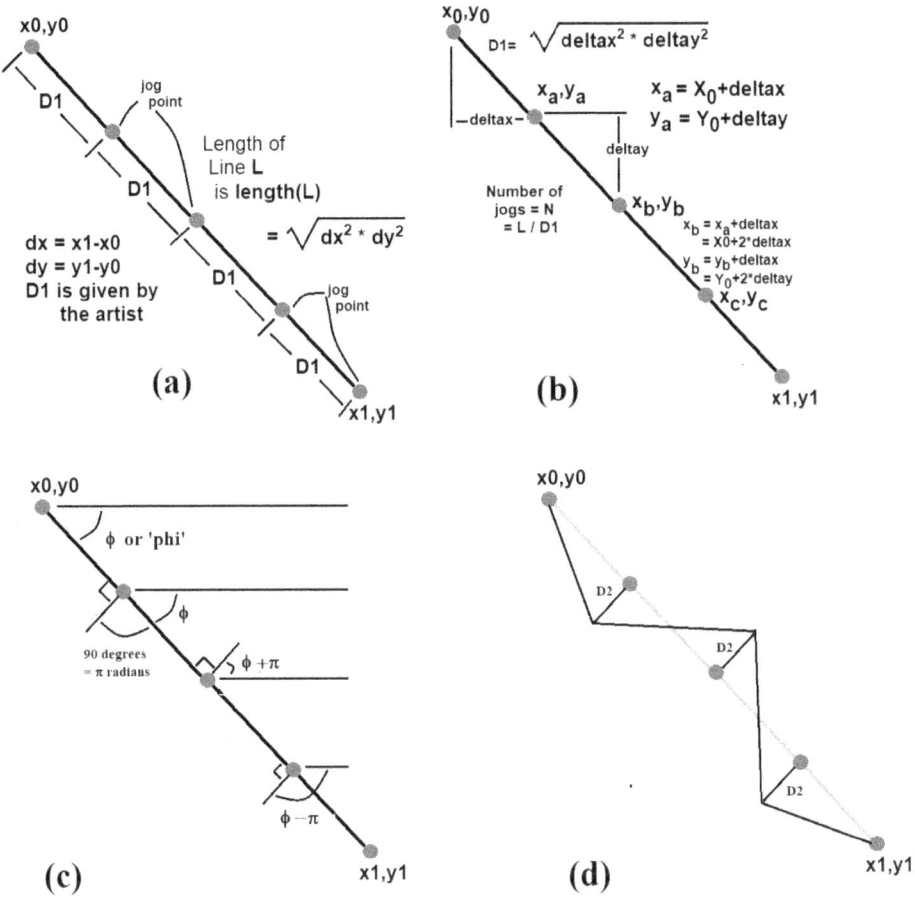

Figure 2-9. *Drawing a jagged line. (a) The artist specifies how wide the jobs are = D1 (pixels). (b) Divide the line into sections D1 pixels long and determine the height (vertical) and width (horizontal) of a jog. (c) Determine the perpendicular to the line, as an angle. (d) Determine the distance D2 perpendicular to the line and then draw it.*

The first jog point is at (**x0+deltax, y0+deltay**), the second is at (**x0+2*deltax, y0+2*deltay**), and so on. At each jog point we construct a line (but do not draw it) through that point at 90 degrees (perpendicular) to the line **L**. The we find a point that is distance **D2** from **L** along this perpendicular, where the artist has specified the value for **D2** as the height of the jog. The angle the line L makes with the X axis is ϕ = **atan2(y1-y0, x1-x0),** the inverse tangent function (If your trigonometry has been forgotten, then you'll have to trust me). The perpendicular line to this has angle ϕ+**90** degrees or ϕ+π radians, an angle we'll call γ (gamma).

45

CHAPTER 2 LINE

```
phi = (atan2(y1-y0, x1-x0));   // Angle of the line
gamma = phi + (PI/2);          // Perpendicular
```

Of course, the angle or $\phi-\pi$ radians ($\phi-90$ degrees) is also perpendicular to **L** and indicates the other side of the line. Now we can begin drawing the jagged line, starting at **xb=x0** and **yb=y0**. There are N jogs, so for each jog:

```
// For each step, find the point on the line and the one 90
// degrees from it distance d2.
  xb = x0;
  yb = y0;
  for (int i=1; i<N; i++)
  {
```

Find the coordinates of the next jog point:

```
x = x0+i*deltax;
y = y0+i*deltay;
```

Determine the angle of the perpendicular line:

```
// PI/2 is 90 degrees. This makes Zeta perpendicular to phi
zeta = phi + sign*(PI/2);
```

The value of **sign** will be +1 or -1, as we'll see. Now find the point that is distance **D2** from the jog point and that lies on this perpendicular. We need a bit of the most basic trigonometry for this:

```
dx = cos(zeta)*d2;
dy = sin(zeta)*d2;
xa = x+dx;
ya = y+dy;
```

The point (**xa,ya**) is the point we need. Now draw a line from the previous drawn point to this one:

```
  line (xb, yb, xa, ya);
```

The end of this line will be the beginning of the next one:

```
xb = xa;
yb = ya;
```

CHAPTER 2 LINE

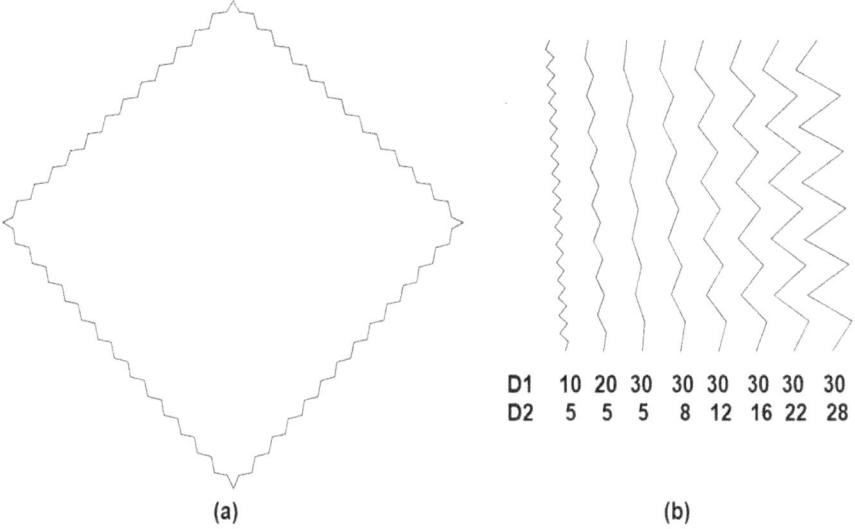

Figure 2-10. *(a) A rectangle with jagged lines. (b) Different lines having different parameters.*

Change the sign. This will result in the perpendicular points being on opposite sides of the line, making the jagged shape.

```
    sign = -sign;
}
```

And finally complete the line L, since it is unlikely that the final jog will end exactly on (**x1,y1**):

```
  line (xb, yb, x1, y1);
```

As an example, Figure 2-10 shows a rectangle drawn using jagged lines having **D1=15** and **D2=5**, and also the results obtained by varying those parameters.

Textured Lines

The following sections describe types of lines that we simply can't draw without using your own line drawing code. That's because each pixel in the line can vary in some way from the others – in brightness, color, size, and so on. Typical line drawing primitives allow lines of various colors and thickness, but not on a pixel-by-pixel basis.

47

A textured line does not use a solid color but instead uses some pattern that we'll call Chapter 6, "Texture." A good example is a pencil line. When drawing with a pencil the resulting line is not a uniform degree of black or gray but varies according to the nature of the surface that we are drawing on (paper?) the pressure of the pencil to the surface, and perhaps other parameters. This can be hard to simulate and would use some mathematics that is unknown to most of us. We have other choices, though.

Let's stay with the pencil example. How can we draw a line as if we had drawn using a pencil? Here's a thought: create a pencil texture – an image created using a real pencil to shade an area on paper – and then use pixels from that image instead of using a specific line color. Take a pencil and create a shaded area, then scan that image. This creates an image as shown in Figure 2-11. This specific image has a size of 517x286 pixels.

When we draw a line using this texture, we simply copy pixels from this image into the line as we draw it. If we are drawing a line from (100,100) to (400,300) we use a different version of the **drawpixel** function, one that sets pixels according to values it finds in the image, rather than to a fixed value. If we draw a pixel at (**x,y**), we use the pixel at (**x,y**) in the pencil texture image. If that pixel is outside of the texture image we can simply map the pixel coordinates onto the texture using the **mod** operation, which is **%** in most programming languages. So if drawing a pixel at (1031, 853), we use the texture pixel at **(1031%w, 853%h)**, where **(w,h)** are the maximum coordinates in the texture image.

Figure 2-11. *A pencil texture made by an artist*

Drawing a rectangle with upper left corner at (100,100) and lower right corner at (900, 600) means sampling pixels from the pencil image rather than setting them to black, and can be accomplished, assuming an existing texture image named **texture**, using:

```
void drawtpixel(int x, int y, int t)
{
  color p;

  for (int i=-t/2; i<t/2; i++)
    for (int j=-t/2; j<t/2; j++)
    {
      p = texture.get((x+i)%texture.width,
                      (y+j)%texture.height);
      stroke(p);
      point (x+i,y+j);
    }
}
```

The parameter **t** is the line thickness. This function copies pixel values from a texture image and draws them into a **t/2** by **t/2** sized area in the target image. The function

```
void tLine(float x1, float y1, float x2, float y2, int t)
```

uses this function to draw the pixels. An example can be seen in Figure 2-12.

Lines of Variable Thickness

A typical computer drawn line has a fixed thickness, often specified by calling a function. In *Processing*, the function **strokeWeight(t)** sets the line thickness to **t** pixels. What if we want the thickness to vary a little along the line? That would seem more realistic, in the sense that humans draw lines using pencils that vary in thickness, and don't exert constant pressure as they draw.

There is no function in *Processing* that would allow us to draw such lines, but because we now have an understanding of how lines are rendered pixel by pixel we could adapt some of the line drawing we have to do this. In principle it's pretty simple: whenever a pixel is drawn, set the thickness of the line to some desired value.

CHAPTER 2 LINE

What is the desired thickness? How should it vary? That would be up to the artist and should be simple to specify. SO: should the line thickness be random? Should it follow a predefined pattern? Should it depend on some other aspects of the artwork? To draw a line of variable thickness that is random, we call the function **drawpixel(x,y,t)** whenever we draw on of the pixels in the line, whichever line drawing method we're using and specify the thickness value **t** using a random number. Like so, perhaps:

```
drawpixel (x,y,round(random(1,t)));
```

This should draw a line having a completely random thickness of between 1 and **t** pixels (Figure 2-12).

```
// Random
int thick(int t)
{
  float x, r;

  x = random (1, t);
  if (x<=0) x = 1;
  else if (x>t) x = t;
  return (int)x;
}
```

Figure 2-12. A rectangle with random thickness lines

This should draw a line having a regular sine/cosine variation in thickness (Figure 2-13):

```
//Cosine
float _z = 0;
int thick(int t)
```

```
{
  float x, r;
  x = abs(cos(_z)) * t;
  _z += 0.1;
  if (x<=0) x = 1;
  else if (x>t) x = t;
  return (int)x;
}
```

Figure 2-13. *A rectangle with cosine thickness lines*

This thickness function averages two random values (moving average), the previous and current, to provide a thickness (Figure 2-14):

```
// Random Average
Float prev = 2;
int thickavg(int t)
{
  float x, r;

  r = random (-1, 1);
  x = t/2 + r;
  x = (x + prev)/2;

  if (x<=0) x = 1;
  else if (x>t) x - t;
  prev = x;
  return (int)x;
}
```

CHAPTER 2 LINE

Figure 2-14. *A rectangle using a moving average thickness*

Any thickness function based on any random or periodic function can easily be implemented based on the examples here.

Curved Lines

So far we have looked only any straight lines and collections of straight lines. Obviously, curves exist too. Some are quite specific, such as those based on mathematical functions like an ellipse or parabola, and some are designed by the artist by specifying a set of points.

Arcs

An *arc* in Processing is a *portion* of an ellipse. The start and end point of the arc is specific, as are the beginning and ending angles and the size of the ellipse in X and Y. The call to a *Processing* function that draws an **arc** is:

arc (a, b, c, d, start, stop)

where:
(**a,b**) are the coordinates of the center of the ellipse
(**c, d**) are the ellipse width and height, respectively
start is the angle at which to start drawing the arc, in radians
stop is the angle at which the drawing of the arc ceases, in radians.

Let's start explaining this rather hard to characterize shape by beginning with the problem of drawing an ellipse as four arcs. Consider the ellipse (Figure 2-15):

ellipse (300, 200, 100, 80);

52

CHAPTER 2 LINE

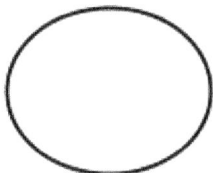

Figure 2-15. *An ellipse*

Now select a part of this ellipse to be drawn using arc: from 0, to 90 degrees, the lower right part. Draw this in gray. 0 degrees is down, and 90 degrees is to the left. So (Figure 2-16)

```
stroke (128);
arc (300, 200, 90, 80,
   radians(0), radians(90));
```

Figure 2-16. *Lower right of an ellipse*

radians(x) converts the angle **x** degrees into radians.

Now try the lower left section by itself (Figure 2-17):

```
arc (300, 200, 90, 80,
    radians(90), radians(180));
```

Figure 2-17. *Lower left of the ellipse*

This curve starts at the bottom and curves upward - *up* corresponds to 180 degrees. Next the upper left (Figure 2-18):

```
arc (300,200, 90,80,
   radians(180), radians(270));
```

53

Figure 2-18. Upper left of an ellipse

Moving upwards, the curve arc to the right, which is 270 degrees. The final section (upper right) is (Figure 2-19):

```
arc(300, 200, 90, 80,
  radians(270), radians(360));
```

Figure 2-19. Upper right of an ellipse

Putting these four arcs together we get the entire ellipse. The idea here was simply to show how the angles are used to define the curve.

Connecting Arcs

Imagine that we wish to draw two different arcs, with one continuing from the other. There are many reasons to want this. Perhaps we are drawing a vine, or a snake, or a leaf. We can connect line segments easily, because we know the start and end coordinates of the line. An arc does not require that we know the coordinates of the start and end, only the angles and the parameters of the ellipse. What we need is the ability to find the endpoints of an arc given the parameters. This must be possible, because the *Processing* system must do it in order to draw the arc

We will need to find the point on an ellipse that corresponds to the start and end angle parameters of the **arc** function. This is so we can continue different arcs from the same point. How do we do this using the material we just learned?

We know the equation of an ellipse, so for any given x value the y values of pixels on the ellipse are known. Given the point (x_c, y_c) at the center of the ellipse, we wish to know what the pixel coordinates are at an angle of θ degrees from that point. A way to picture this is to draw a line from (x_c, y_c) having an angle θ and see where it intersects the ellipse. Figure 2-20 illustrates the situation.

The calculation that will give us the point (x,y) that we're looking for is the intersection of the line and the ellipse in the figure. To find that, we must solve the equation of the line AND the equation of the ellipse to find a point that satisfies both equations at the same time. This results in some ugly algebra, which fortunately we don't actually have to do here. It is encapsulated within the function **startPoint** that can be found in the file **startPoint.pde** which is provided in the library on the web site. The code is defined as:

```
float[] startPoint (float xc, float yc,
          float w, float h, float angle)
```

where:
(xc,yc) is the center of the ellipse.
w is the width
h is the height
angle is the angular position of the end point from 0 degrees. (radians)

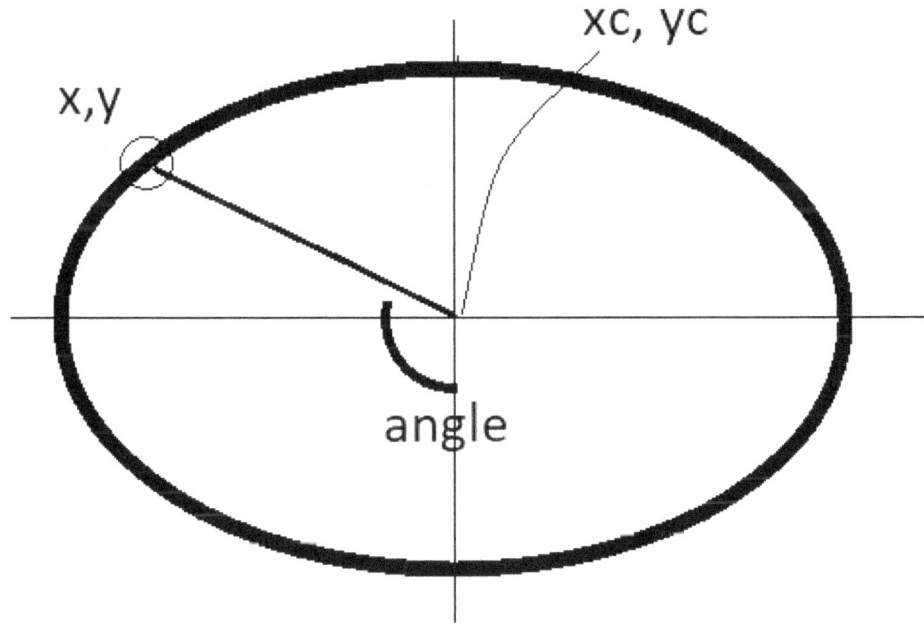

Figure 2-20. *Defining an arc*

CHAPTER 2   LINE

Using the **arc** function zero degrees is down, 90 degrees is left, and so on as we discovered above. When drawing lines, zero degrees is horizontal and to the right. We have to adapt to this change of coordinates within the function.

To find the endpoint of

arc (x, y, w, h, a);

we call:

pts = startPoint (x, y, w, h, a);

and the point (**pts[0], pts[1]**) is the location we are looking for.

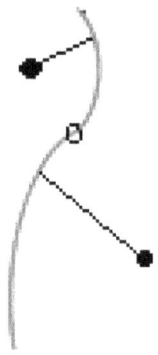

Figure 2-21. Joining two arcs

Now what? We want to continue the curve from that point in some direction to somewhere else (Figure 2-21). As a practical example, let's use a section of the vase. To top left curve in the vase was drawn by:

arc (65, 75, 33, 64, radians(295), radians(360+65));

The parameters of the next section were found using graph paper.

arc (80,190, 87,172, radians(135), radians(258));

The parameters to the **arc** function were determined manually. Can we do better? Perhaps, but it is probably not worth trying. *Processing* has the ability to draw a curve that follow any specified set of points.

CHAPTER 2 LINE

General Curves - Splines

We can think of a *curve* as a smooth line drawn through a set of points. An **arc** draws a part of an ellipse through a pair of points, but when using **curve** we can specify many points. The line drawn by a spline will pass smoothly through all of them.

Mathematically speaking *Processing* computes what is called a *Catmull-Rom spline*. That's not crucial to understanding it, but it allows the keen people to look it up on the Web. In drafting, back when it was done using pencils, a spline was a bendable strip that could be used to position at certain points along its length and create a smooth curve (Figure 2-22). One then slid the pencil along the strip to draw that curve.

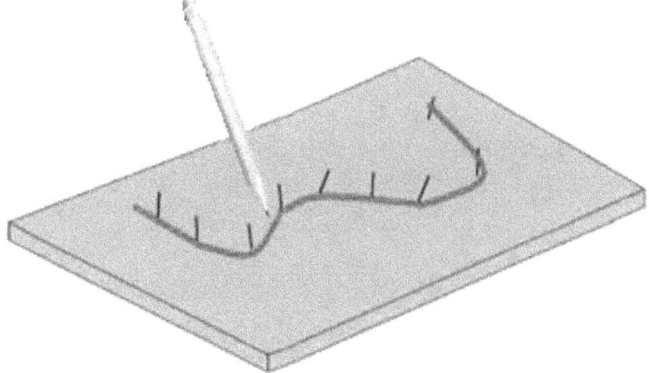

Figure 2-22. *A spline as used in drafting*

A spline can connect any set of points with a smooth curve. Some sets will be difficult, especially of there are a great many sharp changes in direction, but the result will be a smooth as one could hope for.

As an example, imagine the points that represent the corners of a square: (100,100), (110, 130), (140,160), (200, 100), (230, 90), (250, 110), and (280, 130). We can draw a smooth curve through these points using the following *Processing* code:

```
beginShape();
  curveVertex(100, 100);
  curveVertex(110, 130);
  curveVertex(140, 160);
  curveVertex(200, 100);
  curveVertex(230, 90);
```

CHAPTER 2   LINE

```
    curveVertex(250, 110);
    curveVertex(280, 130);
  endShape();
```

The **beginShape()** says to begin drawing a shape made of points. Each **curveVertex()** specifies one point to be drawn that is a part of the curve, in the order they appear on the curve. The process stops when **endShape()** is seen. We could expect this code to draw a smooth curve between 7 points. Not quite. In order to draw a curve we need to know something about the shape of the curve at every point, and we get that information from the preceding and successive points on the curve. The first point does not have a preceding point, though, and can be used only to provide shape context for the second point. A similar situation applies at the final point (Figure 2-23a). A simple way to solve this is to repeat the first and last points in the sequence, making the code:

```
beginShape();
   curveVertex(100, 100);
   curveVertex(100, 100);
   curveVertex(110, 130);
   curveVertex(140, 160);
   curveVertex(200, 100);
   curveVertex(230, 90);
   curveVertex(250, 110);
   curveVertex();
   curveVertex(280, 130);
endShape();
```

So to connect a set of points using a spline, we simply place them in sequence in **curveVertex()** calls between a **startCurve()** and **endCurve()**, duplicating the first and last pixels. We can draw any set of points this way. We can adjust the shape of the start and end by adjusting those coordinates until the shape looks OK. Figure 2-23 illustrates this idea, of connecting specific pixels using a smooth curve.

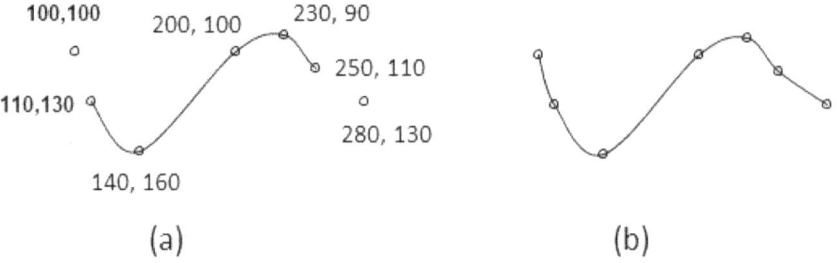

Figure 2-23. *(a) Pixels that define the points on the curve (b) The result with the defining points circled*

Example: A Vase

Vases come in many shapes, but the one pictured at the right is pretty typical. There are multiple curves that have to meet just in the right way if the rendering is to look correct.

Figure 2-24. *Drawing of a vase*

Vases come in many shapes, but the one pictured in Figure 2-24 is typical. There are multiple curves that must meet just in the right way if the rendering is to look correct. There is no mathematical way to describe the vase, at least not an arbitrary one. This means that there is no right way to construct the curves. There are easier ways and harder ones, but the idea is to create a computer graphic that looks like what we want, and that has the lines and curves all joining up properly. Unless you possess a digitized set of points for a particular object, or have created a 3D model, there's no automatic way to program the rendering of a vase. Or any arbitrary shape.

CHAPTER 2   LINE

A good idea would be to sketch the vase on some graph paper or in a drawing program. Then the endpoints of the lines and curves can be found using the grid by assigning coordinates to key points. The endpoints of curves and lines have been identified on the sketch in Figure 2-25. There are five curves, an ellipse, and two straight lines which need to joined seamlessly (Figure 2-26).

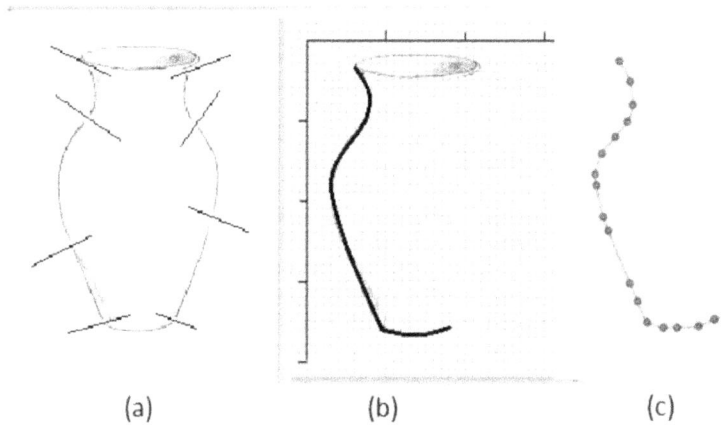

(a)   (b)   (c)

Figure 2-25. *(a) Select places where curves will join up. (b)The left side of the drawing an graph paper. (c) Selected points*

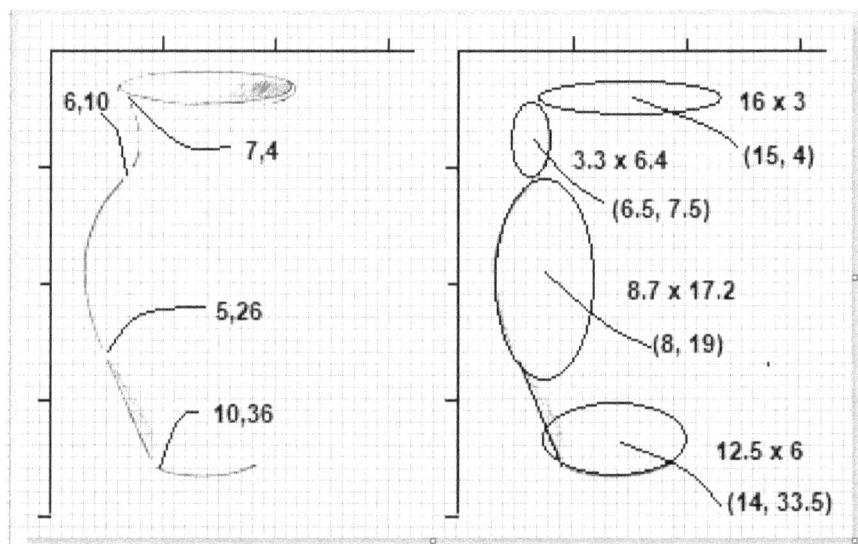

Figure 2-26. *(a) Pixel locations of join points, with coordinates. (b) Sketch of the result with estimated ellipse sizes*

At this point, note that the vase is not symmetrical. It probably should be. A solution is to divide it in two vertically and choose which half to draw. When this is complete simply redo the same curves as a mirror image.

Creating the grid allows us to determine coordinate values, at least approximately. For this example, we require the dimensions of each ellipse and the coordinates of the center. With the first guess a preliminary view can be created by just drawing the ellipses and the lines.

```
ellipse (150,40, 160,30);
ellipse (65,75, 33,64); ellipse (80,190, 87,172);
ellipse (140,335, 125,60);
line (55, 270, 90, 350);
```

This is a fair approximation for a first guess (Figure 2-27). Now we must estimate the angles from which to subtend the arcs and then draw those instead of ellipses. The first estimate can be eyeballed or measured with a protractor.

Figure 2-27. *Initial try using arc*

The first four parameters of the call to **arc** will be the same as the ones passed to **ellipse**: the center coordinates and the size. The start and end angles are estimated as:

```
stroke (255, 0, 0);
arc (65,75, 33,64, radians(295),radians(405));
arc (80,190, 87,172, radians(110), radians(250));
arc (140,335, 125,60, radians(45), radians(135));
line (55, 270, 90, 350);
```

CHAPTER 2 LINE

Because the arcs must be drawn in a clockwise fashion, the first curve runs from 295 degrees (a little past the top right) to 405 degrees, which is 360+45 or simply 45 degrees. The line coordinates have been adjusted a little as well.

We're not quite there yet. There are some small adjustments to be made to close the gaps and smooth things. The first two curves seem OK. The third one fails to meet the second correctly, so the first step would be to adjust the angles. Extending the ends of both curves works pretty well, and the height of the third is increased just a bit so that they meet relatively smoothly.

The third curve extends too far at its beginning and is shortened by increasing the start angle. The line must be lengthened so as to meet the new starting point.

Finally, when this is done the bottom of the vase does not quite meet the straight line. The line end coordinate is changed slightly, and the bottom curve is moved a pixel to the left.

The new code is:

```
ellipse (150,40, 160,30);
arc (65,75, 33,64,
radians(295), radians(360+65));
arc (80,190, 87,172,
radians(135), radians(258));
arc (149,335, 150,70,
radians(45), radians(135));
line (49, 250, 93, 358);
```

CHAPTER 2 LINE

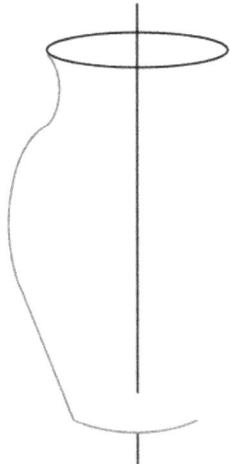

Figure 2-28. *Smoothed left side and axis of symmetry*

The vertical line in Figure 2-28 is the *axis of symmetry*. The vase should look the same on both sides of this line. It is not obvious how to do this. The vertical line is at X=150, so it would be possible to copy the individual pixels from the left side to the same distance from the symmetry axis on the right. This method works but is not interesting. Isn't it better to know how to manipulate the curves geometrically?

So, first consider the arc near the mouth of the vase. Its location is (65, 75) and the vertical axis is x=150, so the center coordinates of the symmetric version of the arc would simply be (150-65+150, 75) or (235, 150). The size will remain the same.

The angles also follow a symmetry that is simple to compute once it is understood. Simply put, angles can be expressed as negative or positive. -45 degrees is simply 360+ (-45) or 315 degrees. The -45 representation tells us how far in a counterclockwise direction the same amount of rotation 45 degrees is. Each angle on the left should be replaced by the same, negative, angle drawn on the right of the axis of symmetry. THEN it should be rotated by 180 degrees. The function that returns the angle on the right given the angle on the left (or vice versa) is:

```
a = -a+180;
```

Finally, the start and stop angles need to be swapped. If they are in clockwise order on the left, then they will be counterclockwise on the right. The corresponding pixels are:

```
arc (300-65, 75, 33, 64,
 radians(-425+180),
 radians(295+180));
```

63

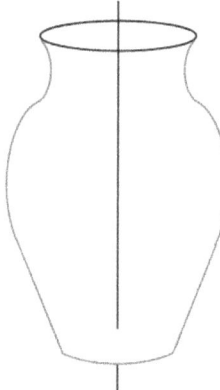

Figure 2-29. *Reflecting the left to the right side*

After an adjustment of a few pixels at the bottom, the image is in pretty good shape (Figure 2-29). Of course, this has been a highly interactive process, with manual adjustments taking place at many stages. That's because this shape does not have a specific mathematical description. One of the problems that needs to be solved when using curves is how to continue from the end of one curve directly to the next and how to create a curve that connects two or more points.

Simulating Human Drawn Lines

Of course, lines drawn by a computer tend to be quite straight and uniform, and not at all like lines drawn by a human artist. Let's look at ways to make lines more human. A generative artist must spend some time programming and must have an understanding of what the computer and the language can accomplish. But an artist will also spend a lot of time thinking about *how* to accomplish something. We need to develop systematic ways of achieving our goals. There is no method for devising a new *algorithm*, so that's where a degree of creativity comes in. The problem we are trying to solve in this case is drawing lines that are not perfectly straight or regular, so that they look like hand-drawn lines. There could be many ways to do this. It seems a first step might be to either measure hand-drawn lines to see how they differ from perfect ones, or to suggest (guess) as to how to do it and refine that process as we see what it creates and how the algorithm's lines differ from human ones. An artist might prefer the second choice; a "computer scientist" might prefer the first.

CHAPTER 2 LINE

Figure 2-30. *Three rectangles. Which one is drawn by a human?*

Figure 2-30 shows three rectangles. Two were drawn freehand using *Paint* and a mouse on a PC and one was drawn by a Processing program that was written for this book. Which is which? How is a human drawn line different from a perfectly straight line? We are about to embark of a rather complex method that involves both artistic vision and algorithms.

First, the rectangle in the middle was drawn by a computer. The process for designing the method is not a long and tedious one: we'll measure some lines drawn by humans and try to do the same. A human can't connect two points that are far apart with a perfect line but perhaps can connect nearer points. If true, this means that a long human line is a set of smaller quite straight lines. How small? We don't know, but could guess and then see how it looks, then guess again. And we'll use random numbers.

Let's say that the variable named **lthresh** will hold a number that indicates how long a typical straight line is that is drawn by a person. Any line to be drawn will be broken into smaller sections that are about this long, but in fact have random lengths *averaging* this value. Let's draw a line from (x0,y0) to (x1,y1). The length of this line is $\sqrt{(x1-x0)^2 + (y1-y0)^2}$ (called Euclidean distance) as we learned in high school math, or in Processing it would be:

```
llength = sqrt ( (x1-x0)*(x1-x0) + (y1-y0)*(y1-y0));
```

65

CHAPTER 2   LINE

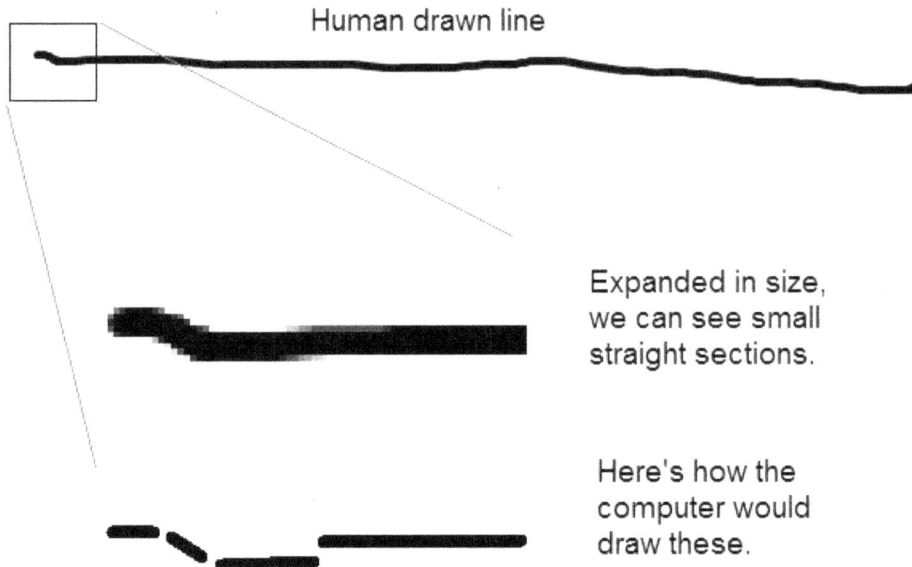

Figure 2-31. *Analysis of a human drawn line*

If this is less than **lthresh** then we'll simply draw it; otherwise, split the line into two parts: one will be a random length larger than **lthresh** and the other part will be the rest of the line. The rest of the line will be broken into smaller length for drawing later. We know this because of looking at actual human drawn lines (Figure 2-31).

How long should each piece be? Let's start at some length between **lthresh** and **2*lthresh**:

```
newLength = random (lthresh, 2*lthresh);
```

How do we split up a line? Consider the line in Figure 2-32.

The problem is that we need the actual coordinates of the split point, because that's how *Processing* draws lines: from one known point to another. How can we find those coordinates? We do know the ratio of the lengths of the short part to the long part and to the entire length, but that's all. It happens to be good enough. The fraction of the whole line that we're drawing this time is **newlength/llength**. This should also be the fraction of the vertical and horizontal parts of the line we're drawing. So, the X coordinate of the split point should be at a point **newlength/llength * (x1-x0)** from the start point x0, and ditto for the Y coordinate. Or:

```
nx = xx+(int)((xe-xx) * fraction);
ny = yy+(int)((ye-yy) * fraction);
```

66

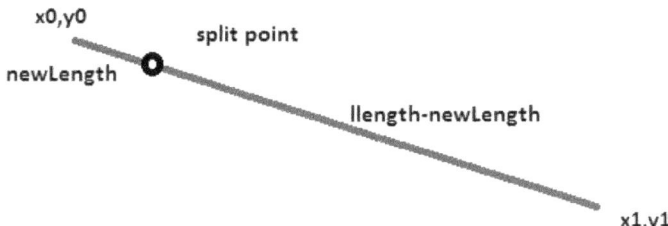

Figure 2-32. *How to split a line to make it seem human drawn*

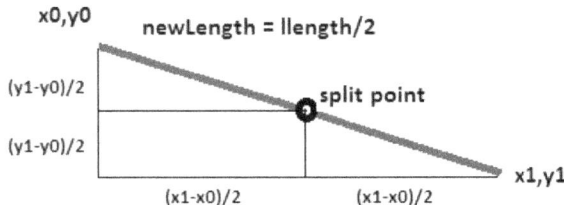

Figure 2-33. *Where to split the line*

If the split point were in the middle of the line, then Figure 2-33 shows the geometry. In this case, **nx** is halfway between **x0** and **x1** and **fraction** is 0.5.

If this is all that we did, then the lines drawn would still be perfectly straight. To add a random variation, we change the values of **nx** and **ny** from what they should be (perfect) to a small variation. How small **nx** and **ny** should be is up for grabs, but we can experiment with the value.

There will be a change in **nx** and/or **ny** at random after each line is drawn. This will happen if a random number is less than the value **vpct** (variation percent), which is between 0 and 1. 0.2 would be a 20% chance of a change.

We need to break here to examine likelihoods a bit. When we toss a coin we expect it to land with either the heads side up or the tails side up. We expect that the chance of each outcome will be the same, which we call 50-50. As a probability this would be 0.5. Something that will never occur has a probability of 0.0, and something that must occur has a probability of 1.0. Sometimes a weather forecaster will say "The probability of rain today is 25%", meaning that there is a 0.25 (or 25/100) chance of rain.

The variable **vpct** represents probability that the line endpoint will change in one of the four possible ways: increase **nx**, decrease **nx**, increase **dy**, or decrease **dy**. The value of **random(1)** is a random number between 0 and 1, so, if **random(1) < vpct** then add 1 to **nx**. In fact:

CHAPTER 2　LINE

```
if (random(1) < vpct) nx = nx + 1;
    else if (random(1) < vpct) nx = nx - 1;
if (random(1) < vpct) ny = ny + 1;
    else if (random(1) < vpct) ny = ny - 1;
```

These are the four ways the endpoint can change, and this code makes it happen. The value of **nx** can either get bigger or smaller, as can **ny**. Now we draw the line from (x0,y0) to (nx,xy).

This is not the end, because we've only drawn one small section of the line. The remainder of the line is from (**nx,ny**) to (**x1,y1**). Next, we break that part of the line into two pieces as was done before, find a new (**nx,ny**), draw that piece, and continue until the end of the line is reached (Figure 2-34).

Code: File **human.pde**'	Algorithm: *human* – Draw a line that looks like a human might have drawn it.
	See text for these parameters.
`// Draw a line from (x0,y0) to (x1,y1)`	Draw left to right.
	(xx,yy) will be the pixel we are drawing from. Start at (x0,y0).
`float lthresh=4, vpct=0.49;`	
`Void hline (int x0, int y0,`	
`           int x1, int y1)`	
`  int xx, yy, nx, ny;`	
`  float len, newLength, fraction;`	
`  if (x0>x1)`	
`  {`	Loop until xx>=x1, which means that we reach the end of the line being drawn.
`    xx = x0; x0 = x1; x1 = xx;`	
`    yy = y0; y0 = y1; y1 = yy;`	
	Pick a length (**newlength**) for the section of the line that will be drawn this time.
`  }`	What fraction of the remaining line is this?
`  xx = x0; yy = y0;`	What is the x endpoint coordinate of this shorter line segment? Use fraction.

(continued)

`len = sqrt ( (x1-x0)*(x1-x0) +` `            (y1-y0)*(y1-y0));`	Vary it a little at random, + or - 1
	Same for y: what is the new y endpoint? Also vary it by 1 pixel at random.
`while (xx<x1)`	The variable **len** is the length of the remaining line.
`{`	Draw shorter lines until the end (x1,y1)

`  newLength =`
`       random(lthresh,2*lthresh);`
`  fraction  = newLength/ll;`
 	
`  nx = xx+(int)((x1-xx)`
`  *fraction);`
 	
`  if (random(1)<vpct) nx=nx + 1;`
`  else if (random(1)<vpct)`
`  nx=nx-1;`
 	
`  ny = yy+(int)((y1-yy)*fraction);`
`  if (random(1)<vpct) ny=ny+1;`
`    else if(random(1)<vpct)`
`    ny=ny-1;`	

`  line (xx, yy, nx, ny);`	Now draw this short line segment (xx,yy, nx, ny)
`  xx = nx; yy = ny;`	The starting point for the next segment is the end point for this one, (nx,xy)
`  len = sqrt ((x1-xx)*(x1-xx) +` `            (y1-yy)*(y1-yy));`	

(continued)

CHAPTER 2 LINE

```
if (len <= lthresh)
{
   line (xx, yy, x1, y1);
   xx = x1+1;
}
}
}
```

What is the length of the remaining part of the line
If this length is small, just end the line by drawing to the end point.

The parameters that will make these lines change to be more like human ones are **vpct**, and **lthresh**. As **vpct** gets smaller the likelihood of each component of the line being changed gets smaller, and so the line becomes straighter. As **lthresh** gets larger the length of the line a human can draw gets longer, and so the line appears straighter. If **lthresh** becomes very large or **vpct** gets very small, then the lines become perfectly straight. If **lthresh** gets too small or **vpct** gets too close to 1.0 then chaos could result (Figure 2-35).

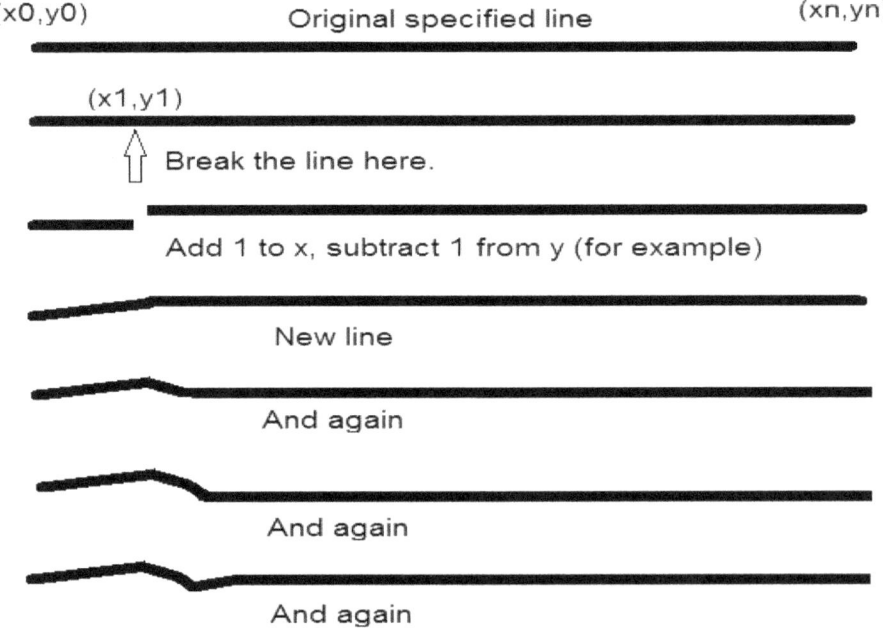

Figure 2-34. *Repeat the splitting process from the previous point until the end of the line*

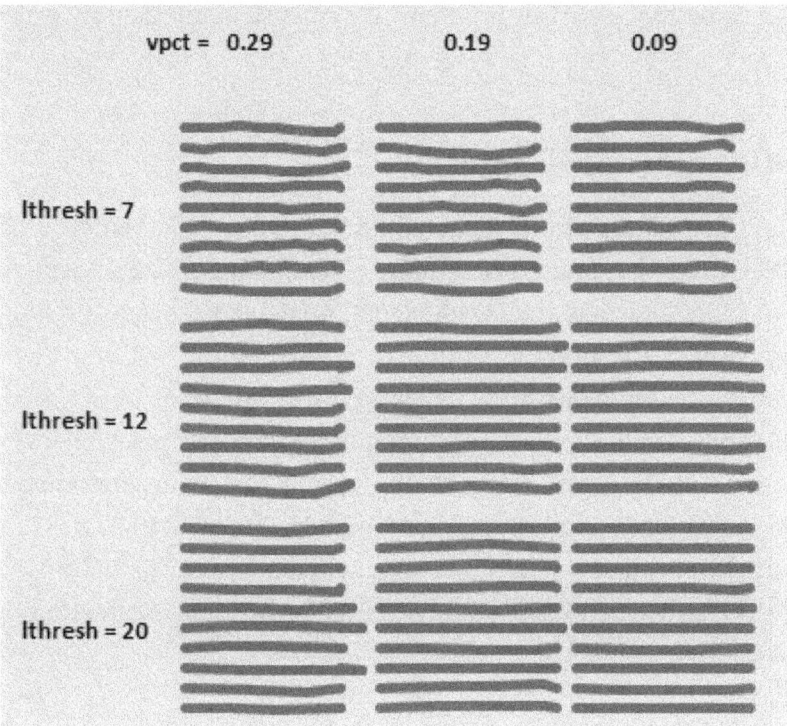

Figure 2-35. *How the lines look as parameters change*

Identifying Lines – Vision or "Undrawing"

We know how to draw lines now. Can we use this information to find them? What we want to do is determine which pixels in an image belong to lines and group the pixels that are on the same line into the same class (i.e., the same line). That is, recognizing a line means finding all pixels that belong to it.

This happens to be a much more difficult problem than drawing them. A pixel may not belong to any line. A pixel may be at the intersection of many lines and so belong to all of them. There are a great many pixels in a typical image, and it could be very time-consuming to try to find all of the lines that might pass through all the pixels. One advantage we had when drawing the lines in the first place is knowing where the endpoints were; in an image we don't know that. And finally, images acquired in the real world (photos, for example) contain lines from the real world and not from the discrete world of the computer. A DDA did not create those lines.

How can we possibly solve this problem? We can use mathematical trickery or brute force.

Brute Force – Tracing Lines

Why not simply find a black pixel and then follow connected pixels in the direction they seem to go? We could draw lines having many different angles and measure how the next pixel affects the line. We can then develop a method that adds pixels to a line until that measurement exceeds the "normal" value.

Given that idea, we wrote a program that drew lines at angles from 0 to 359 degrees. We tested the residual value, which is the amount that the new pixel differs from what the line equation would suggest. For example, let's say that we've computed the slope and intercept of a line that we are building as **m** and **b**. The next pixel we want to add is (**x, y**). We compute **residual = y-m*x + b**, which for a perfect line will be 0. For all of the lines that we drew and tested, none of the pixels had a residual greater than 1. This is the method we'll use.

The method is:

1. Find a starting black pixel (**a,b**). Starting at (0,0), scan horizontally and then vertically until we find a black pixel.

2. Find a neighboring black pixel (**aa, bb**). Note that there are really only four directions that the line can go (Figure 2-36). This defines the direction of the line we're building. Because of how we scanned for the start pixel, there can only be 4 directions the line can have (the upper and left pixels must be white). So the situation must be one of the ones in Figure 2-40. For each of these, the possible directions (pixels) the line can continue are shown by the gray pixels, and for each direction, there are only three of these.

3. Place (**a,b**) and (**aa,bb**) into a collection (set) of pixels called **S**.

4. For each of the three possible next pixels to (**aa,bb**), if that pixel is black, then do the following: (If no black pixels, then go to step 10.)

5. Let this specific pixel be at (**x0, y0**).

6. Assume that (x0, y0) is the endpoint of a line, and calculate the slope **m=(b-y0)/(x0-a)** and **y = y0-m*x0**. The line we are testing has the equation **y=m*x+b**.

7. Calculate **r = y - m*x+b** for all pixels (**x,y**) in the collection **S**. If r > 1 for any pixel, then reject it as a possibility.

8. We now have at most three residual values. Select as the next pixel the one having the smallest value of **r**. Add this to the set **S**. If all residuals are > 1 or there is NO next black pixel, go to step 10.

9. Let **aa=x0** and **yy=y0** and continue from step 4.

10. The line we are tracing is (**a, b**) to (**aa, bb**).

This works pretty well, but it should be remembered that images we capture using a camera don't have perfectly drawn lines in them, and that's what this method is looking for. Thick lines will be drawn in different ways, and lines that intersect will cause a break in one of the lines, which will split it into two lines. There are other artifacts caused by noise, scale issues, and other factors accompanying real-world images.

Extracting Curves from Pixels

Straight lines, if they are digital straight lines, can be identified in an image. What about curves? In a digital image we know which pixels are black and which are white, and we collect them into sequences of connected pixels that could be part of a curve. Then we can draw them again using a spline, if they *do* form a curve, to recreate the original curve. A measure of how well this process has worked is a measure of how similar the original image is to the one that is drawn.

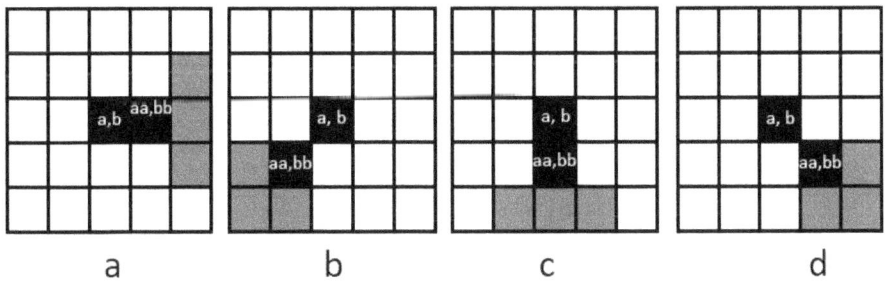

Figure 2-36. *The four directions in which we can trace a line*

CHAPTER 2   LINE

One algorithm for identifying a sequence of pixels that belong to a curve is the *chain coding* algorithm. We trace pixels along a curve one at a time, starting at some obvious place: either a pixel that is connected to only one other pixel or a pixel that is connected to two pixels on opposite sides. The method uses the neighbors of each pixel in a line or curve and steps through them while recording the direction that was used in each step. We obviously must use the same directions all the time. Each pixel has 8 neighbors, so there are eight directions, and they are numbered as seen in Figure 2-37a. There's no reason for this numbering except that it is commonly used by others. Figure 2-37b shows how this set of black pixels would be traced.

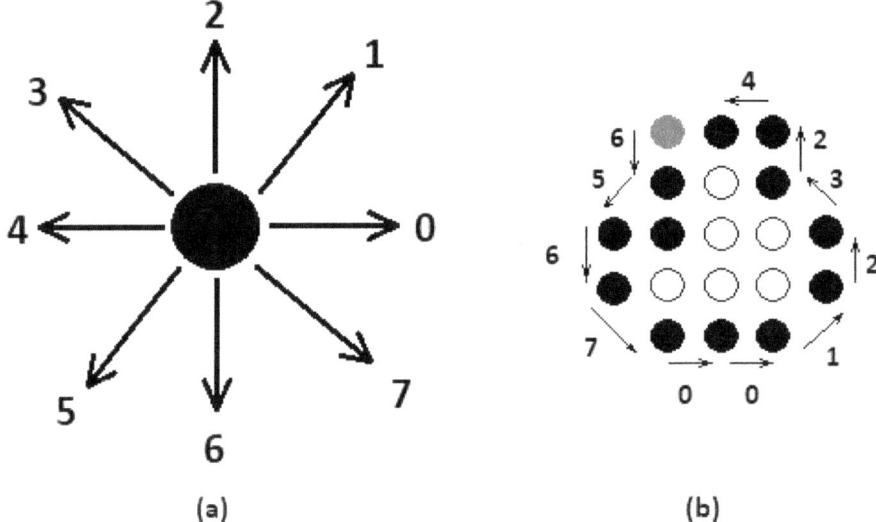

Figure 2-37. *(a) Pixel directions commonly used. (b) The pixels used by a chain code of a simple shape*

The chain coding algorithm is:

1. Choose a direction (clockwise or counterclockwise). We chose *counterclockwise*.

2. Select a starting pixel in the image (in Figure 2-41, it is the red pixel). If we wish to reproduce this curve in its original location, then we have to save these coordinates.

3. Choose a starting direction **D** to look for a neighbor. We choose 5 because we looked at the row above and the previous column already in our search for a start pixel and found no black pixels.

4. Is the neighbor in direction D black?

5. If not:

   5a. Select the next direction for D, which is D+1. If D=7, next is 0.

   5b. If we have tried all eight neighbors, then go to step 7.

   5c. Continue from step 4.

6. If so:

   6a. Save the value D as the next element in the code.

   6b. Continue from step 4.

7. Quit

Figure 2-38. *(a) A line drawing from an unknown artist. (b) The chain code of that drawing is extracted and then drawn as individual pixels. The drawing was from* https://www.boredart.com.2017.07/best-examples-of-line-drawing-art.htm#google_vignette

CHAPTER 2　LINE

In the example of Figure 2-38b, the code will be "656670012324" and would continue forever because the curve ends where it begins. To prevent this, we could set the pixels to white in step 6a.

Drawing from a chain code means simply beginning at any pixel **P**, setting it to black, moving in the direction of the first code value to find the next pixel, setting it to black, and so on until all code values are used.

Let's see how that works for curve extraction. Figure 2-42 shows a line drawing (left) and the chain code reconstruction (right), which has 39 sections. That means that each section is a distinct curve that can be manipulated independently from the other parts.

Thick and Thin Lines (Again)

If an image consists of lines, the digitized version could have those lines represented as an arbitrary thickness depending on the optics of the process. An original image with one-pixel-thick lines could have three-pixel-thick lines in the captured version, for example, or vice versa. This could cause problems when processing the image later. Also, sometimes we take a photograph and wish to make a line drawing using existing boundaries and lines. Again, these might not be one pixel thick. We saw in a previous section how to draw thick lines. If we have an image with thick lines in it, can we make them thinner? To some degree, yes.

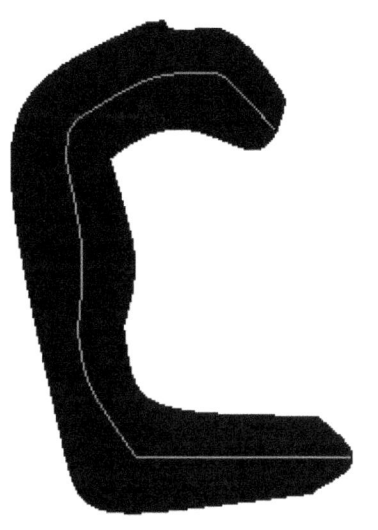 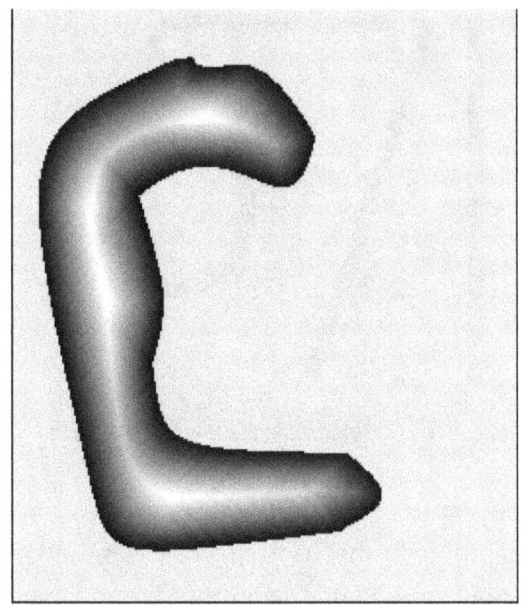

Figure 2-39. *(a) The letter "C," a thick line showing the skeleton. (b) The distance transform – white pixels are farthest from the boundary, and black ones are nearest to it*

A thick line is one that is more than a single pixel wide. To be a line, it must also be much longer than it is thick. Figure 2-39a shows an object and the corresponding thin line, also called the *skeleton*. Identifying the pixels that form the skeleton is not as easy as it may appear. A *skeletal pixel* is equidistant from the opposite sides of the shape, and opposite sides can be a tricky business to compute. The skeleton will be continuous, having no gaps. And it will be one pixel thick.

There is no known perfect method for finding skeletal pixels, but methods for doing so – called *thinning* algorithms – all of them strip pixels from the outline one layer at a time, making certain that the skeleton remains a single continuous set of pixels. The pixels having distance 1 from the background are removed first, then those with distance 2, and so on, never removing any pixel that would break the skeleton into two parts. Figure 2-39b shows these distances are gray values – the dark object pixels are nearest to the background, and the light ones are farthest away. This image is called the *distance transform* of the original object. It's not the skeleton, but it's a start.

CHAPTER 2   LINE

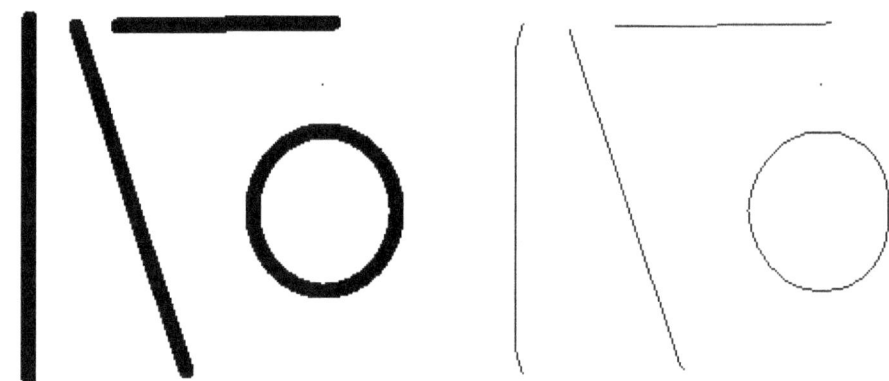

Figure 2-40. *(a) A collection of thick lines. (b) The skeletons of these lines*

The details of any good thinning algorithm are a bit specialized and ugly. There are known problems that have special cases that are handled using specific functions. Ugh. A thinning method that seems pretty good generally is given as thin in the code for this chapter for everyone to use. It assumes that the input image consists only of black or white pixels and yields a connected skeleton of the objects in the image. An example of input to and output from this program is in Figure 2-40.

What Use Is This?

The utility of any individual algorithm is limited by the imagination of the person using it. And an artist would rarely say to themselves "How shall I use a thinning algorithm today?" and more than an electrician would say, "How shall I use my pliers today?". These are tools to be used when the opportunity requires.

This is only this chapter, and all we really know about formally are things to do with black and white pixels and lines, so the choices are limited by that experience. On the other hand, lines are used by artists to draw things. We might be able to do a simple drawing from a scene (image).

CHAPTER 2 LINE

Figure 2-41. *A painting of Quorra from Tron*

Imagine that we have an image of a pencil or ink drawing, such as that shown in Figure 2-41. This is an unusual starting point, but in later chapters we'll discuss how to convert an arbitrary photographic image into such a thing. It was created from a human artwork (an India ink painting by the author). Here are a few simple processes we can apply to it that can produce interesting visual effects.

1. Find the *outline* of the image. Based on the methods seen so far, this is not difficult: keep all black pixels that have a non-black neighbor, and set the result to white. More will be said on this in the next chapter. The result is Figure 2-42a.

2. We could now vectorize the outline and draw it as vectors. Since we have endpoint coordinates, we can draw the vectors at different sizes (*scales*). For example, to draw it at ½ the original size, simply multiply all of the endpoint coordinates by ½ before drawing them. Figure 2-42b shows the result of this for 20 repetitions of scaling and drawing using a 5% reduction (multiply by 0.95) each time.

79

CHAPTER 2   LINE

3. Using the scaling idea, we can scale in the X and Y axes differently (Figure 4.42c). (Some of the "background" lines were made lighter using *Paint*.)

Depending on the image we use, there are many things we could try. An advantage of generative art is that we can make many changes in the method very quickly and keep the ones we like the most.

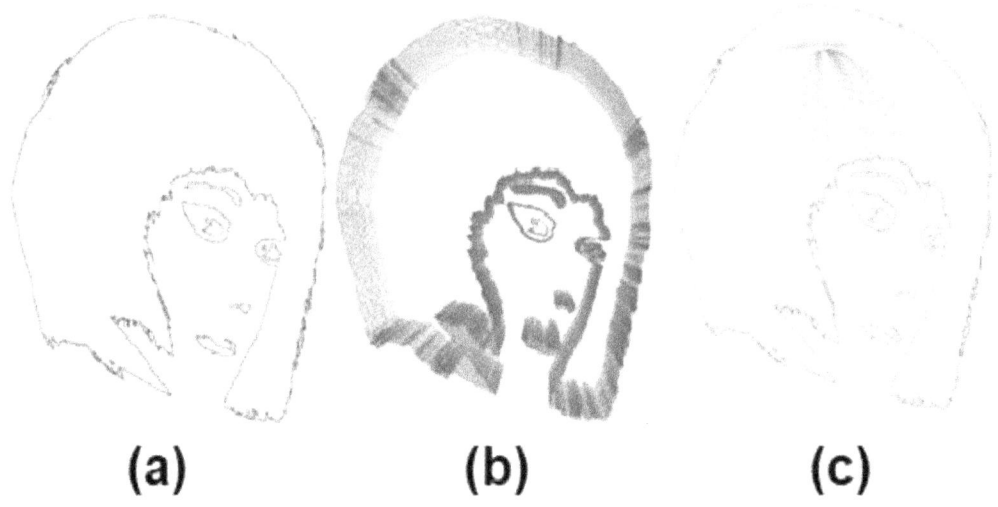

Figure 2-42. Possible manipulations of the drawing of Figure 2-41

We can also use other digital or traditional tools applied to a generative result. The image in Figure 2-43 is the result of coloring the background of the 2-46a image using *Paint* and then drawing the extracted edges over top of that image. This could have been done with programs and algorithms without using *Paint*, as we'll see in the next chapters. We could use lines of varying thickness, textured lines, or simulated human-drawn lines, or thousands of other variations.

Figure 2-43. *One possible result*

Summary

The first of the seven elements of art is the *line*. Lines are essential for outlining shapes, defining regions, and even shading. A line in art differs from a line in the digital space in that the digital line consists of connected points called *pixels*. When programming, we use a function to draw lines between two specific points.

Lines have multiple forms: dotted, dashed, thick or thin, jagged, textured, or colored, and they can have variable thickness and changing color. Lines do not have to be straight: curved lines can follow a circular or elliptical path or can be defined by a set of points. Humans can't draw the same line twice in precisely the same way, so when simulating a human artist, we have to introduce known random variations in a line.

Identifying pixels that comprise a line in an image can be very useful, and we can do that by tracing them pixel by pixel. Thick lines in digital images can be made (approximately) thin so they can be traced.

CHAPTER 2   LINE

Tools and Examples

arc	- Examples of **ellipse** and **arc**.
fig223	- Code that draws Figure 2.23 using splines
quorra.pde	- Generative art example – drawing of Quorra
human	- System for drawing human-style lines
startPoint	- Animation of ellipse/line intersection
vase	- Drawing the vase example

Library – Code provided for you

bresenham	- DDA line drawing
chain	- Chain code extraction
ChainCurve	- Chain code class
chord	- Chord property vectorization
drawPixel	- Draw one pixel
dump	- Slow, obvious way to draw a line
dumbdash	- Dashed lines
llibrary02	- Main program for testing
lineThick	- Thick lines
newline	- Line tracing
slopeint	- Slope-intercept lines
startPoint	
texture	- Textured lines
thin	- Line thinning
vAverage	- Variable thickness lines, moving average

(*continued*)

CHAPTER 2 LINE

vCosine	- Variable thickness lines, cosine-based thickness
vNoise	- Variable thickness lines, uses noise
vRandom	- Variable thickness lines, random thickness
vline	- Vertical line
zig	- Zig-zag line

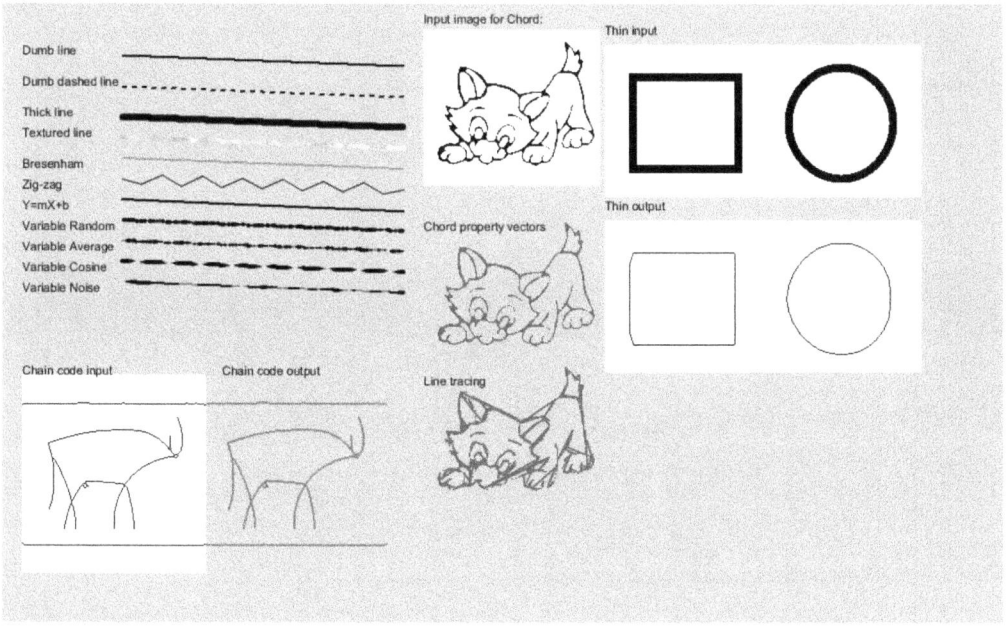

*The result of executing the program **library02**, which tests the library for this chapter*

CHAPTER 3

Value

The second of the seven elements of art that we'll deal with is *value*. This concerns how light or dark things are. Value can be an overall aspect of a work, or it can vary from place to place, but in all cases the scale we use is from the darkest value, which is black, to the lightest, which is white. Value underlies *line* and *color*, and getting the values correct might be more important than getting the colors correct.

Works that consistently use dark values we call *low key*. Such work can seem brooding, or mysterious, or even frightening. Rembrandt was famous for low-key paintings, and Yousuf Karsh used low-key lighting for many of his famous photographs. Figure 3-1 shows two examples.

Figure 3-1. (*Left*) *Low-key photograph.* (*Right*) *A Rembrandt painting typical of his low-key style*

On the other hand, work that uses light, bright values is called high key. We tend to see this as cheerful and happy, but in excess the images are washed out, and little remains except color or whiteness. Figure 3-2 shows examples of high-key imagery. In this chapter, we'll start by discussing the nature and representation of value in computers.

Figure 3-2. (Left) High-key photograph. (Right) A Monet painting in a high-key style

Pixel Values

In the context of a line, we have seen that a *pixel*, the basic element of an image, is a *color* value that is black or white. In fact, it contains a red, green, and blue component, and the *value* of a pixel is the *brightness* or intensity of the pixel, irrespective of the color it represents. While in Chapter 2, "Line," a pixel could have two levels (black or white), now let's think of it as a gray level, and it will have a value typically between 0 and 255. Normally 0 represents black, and 255 represents white, but both the range and the value associated with any number can differ. Values in between represent various intensities of gray.

The number 255 represents the largest number that we can represent in a single byte (8 bits), which is a standard unit of memory on a computer: one byte can store a single character. Some images use more than one byte to store a gray value, and the range of possible values is normally a multiple of the range possible for the pixel size: 2 bytes **per** pixel can store 65536 different levels. Without really being too restrictive, let's assume that 0-255 (256 levels) is what we are dealing with, because most humans

CHAPTER 3   VALUE

can't detect more levels than that anyway (Figure 3-3). Extensions to larger ranges are straightforward and are usually meant to handle very specific devices and data sets, such as medical and astronomical data.

Using a programming language, we can get the value of a pixel at any point (**x,y**) in an

```
p = im.get(x, y;
```

where **p** is the pixel color and **im** is the image we are looking at. Since we said that a pixel **p** has a red, green, and blue component that we can get using functions like **red(p)**, **green(p)**, and **blue(p)**. Question: What is the *value* associated with **p**? The most common way to compute this is by taking the average of the three color values; that is:

```
value = (red(p) + green(p) + blue(p))/3;
```

This makes a lot of intuitive sense, but it presumes a basic equality of the sampled colors—that there was no bias when the pixels were created. This is not often true, although this average is very commonly used and is good enough. When does this not represent a true brightness value? For example, a common source for images is television in some form. Video recordings use specific encoding schemes, and they are not unbiased. In North America we use a standard named NTSC. The formula for finding the value from an NTSC pixel is:

```
value = 0.299*red(p) + 0.587*green(p) + 0.114*blue(p);
```

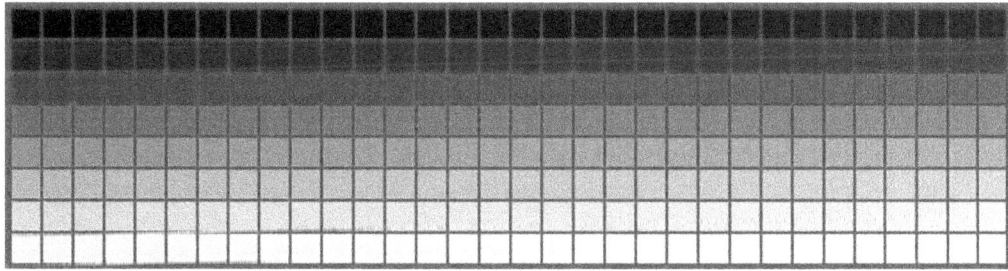

Figure 3-3. *All 256 values or gray levels that generally used in computer vision/graphics (1 byte per pixel)*

CHAPTER 3 VALUE

We call this a *weighted average*. Note that the multipliers sum to 1.0. The implication of this formula is that NTSC will favor blue values at the expense of green ones when computing the brightness, and so to get a reasonable gray from a pixel, we have to weigh the green part higher. Television is a *biased* sample of colors. In Europe and other places they use a different system called *PAL*. The formula for a PAL pixel would be:

```
value = 0.299*red(p) + 0.587*green(p) + 0.114*blue(p)
```

Any specific device may vary in its response to different colors. For most purposes, the method of the equation above is probably good enough. In *Processing*, there is a function named **brightness()** that yields a gray-level value based on another color scheme, not RGB. From now on, when we use the term "value" or "gray level" of a pixel **p,** we are referring to **brightness(p)** (Figure 3-4).

The Gray-Level Histogram

A histogram in general is a kind of graph and is used to show how a set of numerical values are distributed. A gray-level histogram shows which gray values are most common, which are least common, and what ranges of values are more populated. Since there are 256 possible values, then building a gray-level histogram begins with creating 256 distinct *bins*, one for each possible value, and initially setting them to 0. Then we look at every pixel and increment the bin associated with it: finding a value of 20, for example, causes us to add 1 to bin 20.

Figure 3-4. *Finding the value from a color image. (a) Original. (b) Mean of the colors. (c) NTSC. (d) PAL*

When we have examined all pixels, the result is a collection of bins where bin i contains the number of pixels in the image that have the value **i**. We only know how many there are, not *where* they are. That alone can tell us a lot about the image. Figure 3-5 shows the histogram for the image of Figure 3-4b, the values of the windsurfer image. From this, we can see that there is a large number of pixels around the value 149 and lesser peaks around 80, 100, and 200. The mean is shown as a red line, and we can see that there are more pixels greater than the mean (i.e., lighter) than there are smaller, making the image a bit on the bright side. A darker image, the right image of Figure 3-5, has a peak nearer to the 0 value. A high-key image will have a lot of pixels in the upper values of the histogram (rightmost, white), and a low-key image will have a lot of dark pixels (leftmost, black).

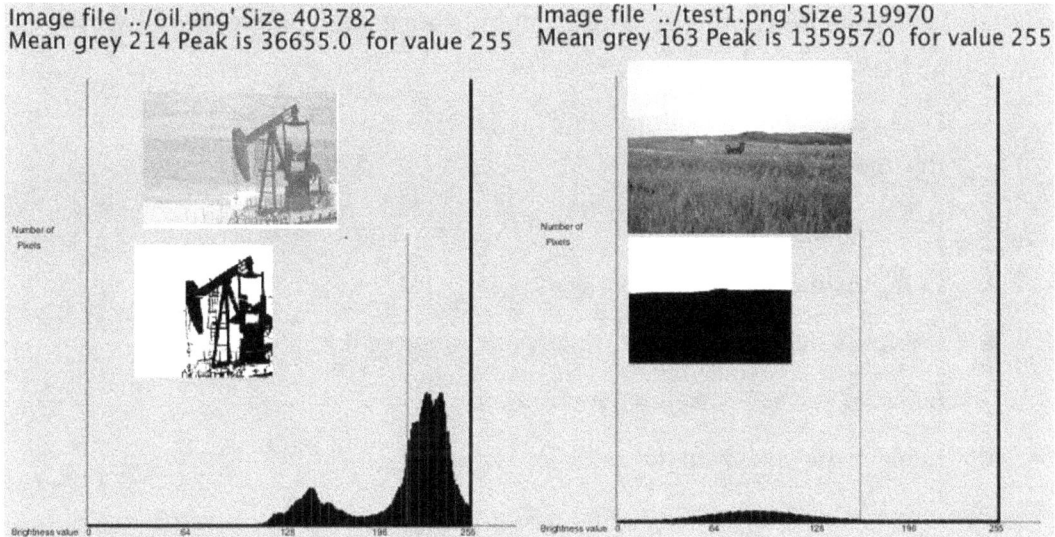

Figure 3-5. *Histograms. (Left) Pump jack image and histogram. (Right) Dog in field image and its histogram*

An image of text would ideally have two peaks: one near the background value (usually around 255) and another near the text value, which will be near 0. Depending on how the image was created, the two levels will not be the only ones. *Noise* and illumination effects creep into real images, causing values that are unwanted. (Code: ch2/acrange)

We can find out if certain values correspond to certain physical areas by selecting only those pixels to draw and setting all other pixels to white. In the case of an image of a pump jack (Figure 3-6a), there is a peak in the histogram at about 140. What does that represent? When we draw only those pixels, we find that they represent the pump jack itself, not by position but by levels being associated with that object. In the case of the

CHAPTER 3   VALUE

dog and field image (Figure 3-5b), the broad peak between 0 and 155 represents the field (grass), along with the dog; the rest (>160) is sky. We can use this kind of information when trying to compose works based on images.

Example: Contouring

The idea of selecting value ranges for display leads to an idea: why not break up the image by value into a collection of range values and select one value to represent the entire range? Pixels with a specific value are likely to be physically near to other pixels with similar values. Not always, of course, but this similarity would naturally define areas that belong to the same kind of objects in the scene. The result should be a set of regions or layers that flowed from one level to another but with greater differences between regions than in the original. What we would do is:

1. Select a number of distinct value ranges N that we wish to break the image into.
2. Examine each pixel in the image and
3. Compute the value V for that pixel
4. Compute the number of values in each range as R = 256/N
5. Let W = (V/R*R) using integer arithmetic
6. Replace the pixel with the value W

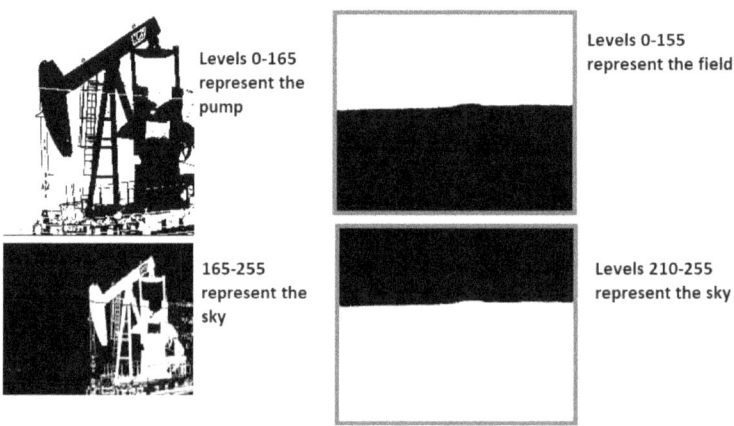

Figure 3-6. *Regions of pixels having similar value. (Left) The pump image pixels having values between 0 and 165 represent the pump. (b) Pixels in the field image having values between 0 and 155 represent the grass area*

90

Integer arithmetic is the trick for a simple solution here. When using integers, there are no decimal points or fractions, so while 4/2 = 2, 4/3 = 1. The result of I/J is the number of times J goes into I with no fraction or remainder.

As an example, let's suggest a value of N = 10. This means that the final image will contain just 10 distinct values. In this example, R = 256/N = 256/10 = 25, so each value in the final image represents 25 values in the original. When transforming the values, we see that a value of 128 in the original becomes (128/25)*25 = 5*25 = 125. In fact, values of 127, 126, 130, and 134 all have a value of 125 in the final image. Figure 3-6 shows the result for the two images (pump jack and field) that we've been using. The contours are very clear in these images.

In a technical sense, what we've done is *resampled* the pixels so that there are fewer distinct levels. This can be of advantage in art creation. We can use this method to make cartoon-like images, create pointillist works, and create an illusion of distance, just to suggest three applications.

Figure 3-7. *(Left) Original dark and low-contrast image. (Center) Image brightened by adding 128 to each pixel. We can see more detail, but contrast is still low. (Right) Each pixel multiplied by 2, showing a much higher contrast*

Contrast

Contrast is the range of gray levels that are occupied (i.e., have pixels with that level) compared with the total number of levels possible. The idea is that there may be gray values at the bottom or top of the possible range that have no pixels belonging to them, and the fraction of the range that *does* have pixels is a measure of how much contrast is in the image. An image with *low* contrast can be either bright or dark, but the range of pixels is compressed into a smaller range than it needs to be. There are no pixels at the low and/or the high ends of the range. We could stretch the histogram by moving the lowest actual pixel values to the lowest possible ones and doing that iterative up the brightness levels.

CHAPTER 3 VALUE

Brightening and Contrast Expansion

A low-contrast image has some number of values that are not being used. These frequently occur at the low end (0) or high end (255) of the possible range. It is also possible that all the values are used, but most are at one end of the histogram.

If the image is dark, as in Figure 3-7, we could add a number to all the pixel values. This *brightens* the image but does not improve contrast as such. Alternatively, we could multiply all pixels by a numeric factor, which actually *does* change the contrast. If the image was too bright, we could subtract a value from each pixel or divide them by some number. In both cases, some values will be changed so they are outside of the range 0-255 and so would be lost.

Figure 3-8. *(Left) Logarithmic transformation of the low-contrast image. (Right) Gamma transformation for g = 1.6*

These are linear changes in the values: values are changed by the same amount regardless of their magnitude. We could use other functions to modify the contrast. A logarithmic transformation is defined by finding the ratio **z** of the maximum *possible* value to the maximum value *actually used* in the image:

z = 255/log(max_value+1).

Now change every pixel by replacing each value **v** by **z * log(a+1)**. Figure 3-8 shows the result of this.

A commonly used enhancement in photography is called the *gamma* (**g**) *correction* or *gamma transformation*. This raises each pixel to the **g** power: that is, for a pixel **p,** new pixel is **p^g**. The value of **g** should usually be close to 1, or else the image quickly deteriorates. This was devised to correct for the fact that cameras and displays are often not able to capture or display values *linearly*; that is, the lighter values may be brighter than they should be, and the darker ones darker. Figure 3-8 shows the result of a logarithmic transformation and a gamma transformation on the low-contrast image.

These alterations of an image can be used to modify source images or a generative work to suit the artist, improving the visual quality.

Histogram Equalization

There is an automatic level adjustment that we call *histogram equalization*, which is an attempt to make each brightness level have nearly the same number of elements. A completely flat histogram for a 256x256 image having 256 brightness levels would have 256 bins, each containing a value of 256. It is unlikely that any real image will have a histogram like this, but the histogram equalization process attempts to make one by deciding how many pixels should be in each bin and then changing their values to make that happen.

In general, if there are N possible levels, then each bin in the histogram would contain 1/N of the pixels in the image. For example, if an image has 16 rows and 16 columns and 8 possible levels, then each bin should have b=(16*16)/8, or 32 pixels in it. In addition, we'll enforce the rule that the total number of pixels, a value of **k** or less will not be less than the value **k*b**. The number of pixels with value less than k is the *cumulative sum,* which we find from the histogram by:

$$cum_i = \sum_i h_i$$

In English this expression is the sum of the histogram values from bin 0 to bin i. For all possible values of **i**. Imagine an example having the following histogram:

Actual number of pixels	6	28	34	94	40	48	2	4
Actual cumulative sum	6	34	68	162	202	250	252	256
Ideal number of pixels	32	32	32	32	32	32	32	32
Ideal cumulative sum	32	64	96	128	160	192	224	256

The first step in equalizing the number of pixels in each bin is to move pixels from bin 1 to bin 0, since the number of pixels in bin 0 is less than the ideal number of 32 found using the cumulative sum. Note that we cannot split up a bin arbitrarily: either all of the pixels are moved or none are. In this case, the new bin 0 will have 6+28, or 34,

CHAPTER 3   VALUE

pixels, and the new bin 1 will have 0 pixels. Now bin 1 has too few pixels, and so we move (all) pixels from bin 2 into bin 1, making bin 2 empty. Continuing, bin 2 has too few pixels, and we move pixels from bin 3 into bin 2. There are far too many, but we have to move them all, making bin 2 far too large and bin 3 empty. Should we move pixels from bin 4 into bin 3? No. The current situation is:

Gray level	0	1	2	3	4	5	6	7
Actual number of pixels	34	34	94	0	40	48	2	4
Actual cumulative sum	34	68	162	162	202	250	252	256
Ideal number of pixels	32	32	32	32	32	32	32	32
Ideal cumulative sum	32	64	96	128	160	192	224	256

We are looking at bin 3 – we don't move pixels from bin 4 because the cumulative sum for bin 3 is 162 and the ideal is 128, which is less than 162. This says that there are already enough pixels having a value of 3 or less, so we leave bin 3 empty and move to bin 4. The ideal number for bin 4 is 160, and it is still smaller than that actual cumulative sum of 162, so we leave bin 4 empty also. Finally, bin 5 will take the pixels from bin 4, bin 6 will take those from bin 7, and 7 will take all of the pixels from bins 6 and 7. The final histogram is:

Gray level	0	1	2	3	4	5	6	7
Actual number of pixels	34	34	94	0	0	40	48	6

Why would we care about the contrast enhancement process? Because good art often has vibrant colors and separation between distinct areas and objects. A dingy and dark artwork might sometimes be desired but would generally not be an attraction. Images that are too bright seem *washed out* and, again, need some adjustment to make them interesting. In any case, we can now adjust the levels to make the contrast more even (Figure 3-9).

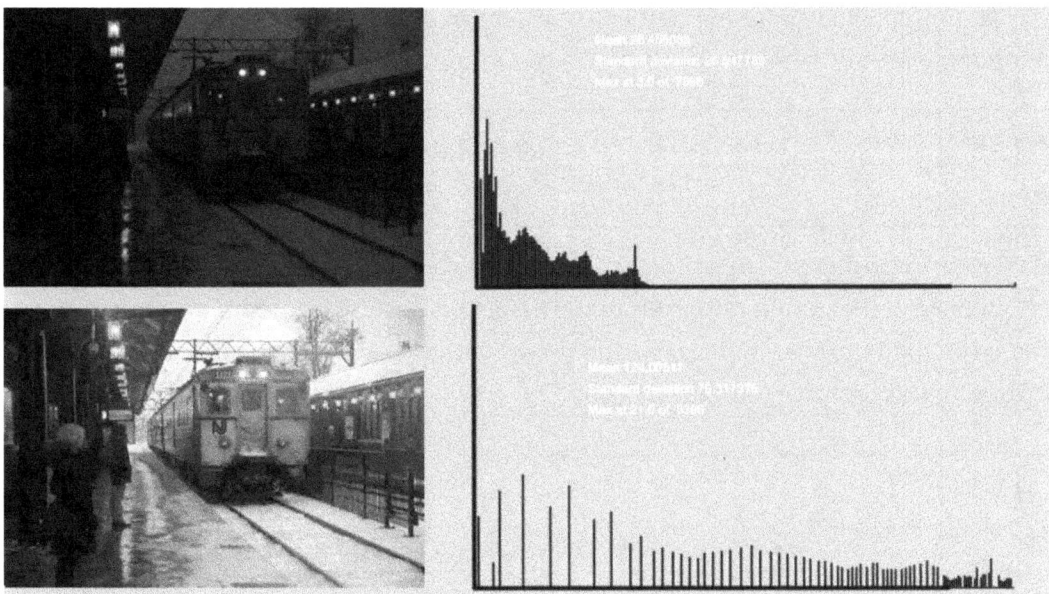

Figure 3-9. *Histogram equalization. (Top) A low-contrast image and its histogram. (Bottom) After histogram equalization, the histogram is far from perfectly distributed, but the image does show improved contrast*

Histogram Specification

Histogram equalization is a way of forcing the pixel values of an image to have a specific histogram: one that is as flat as possible. It should be possible to force pixel values into other histogram shapes, and it is. Indeed, we can change the pixels of most images to have any specific histogram we choose.

Imagine that we have an image histogram **H** for the original image **X** and a histogram that we want to impose on it, **T**. For purposes of discussion, let's make these very small, just 7 levels as before, so we can see what is going on. So **H** is:

Gray level	0	1	2	3	4	5	6	7
Actual number of pixels	34	34	94	0	40	48	2	4

CHAPTER 3   VALUE

Let's impose a histogram **T** that has one peak in the middle of the range, let's say at 3. An example is:

Gray level	0	1	2	3	4	5	6	7
Size	.05	.1	0.15	.4	0.15	.1	0.5	0

We are imposing a histogram on some unknown image, as a rule, so the size values are fractions of the number of pixels in the image being transformed. The image that created histogram **H** has 256 pixels (add up the values in **H**). To convert size into number of pixels in this case, we multiply by 256:

Gray level	0	1	2	3	4	5	6	7
Size	12.8	25.6	38.4	102.4	38.4	25.6	12.8	0

The size values add to 256.8 because of rounding errors and are floating-point numbers. They must be integers. If we round, we get:

Actual number of pixels	13	26	38	102	38	26	13	0

which sums to 256. If we truncate (throw away the fractional part), we get:

Actual number of pixels	12	25	38	102	38	25	12	0

which sums to 252. It should sum to 256 in both cases, of course. It's hard to decide which would be better in all cases, although rounding in this specific example gives a number closer to the actual number of pixels. That won't always be true, and it's not the most important aspect of the method anyway. It will be close, as we can see.

Now we can start figuring out how to change the pixel values in the original so they have the histogram given by **T**. We are going to change the pixel values in image **X**, the original, so they have the histogram **T**. Pixel values in a new image Y will be assigned from smallest value to largest using the histogram **H** as a basis; we want the image **Y** to look like **X**, so dark pixels in X should be dark pixels in **Y**, and so on.

This process can be used to force a collection of images to have a similar histogram (brightness and contrast qualities) to some standard image (Figure 3-10).

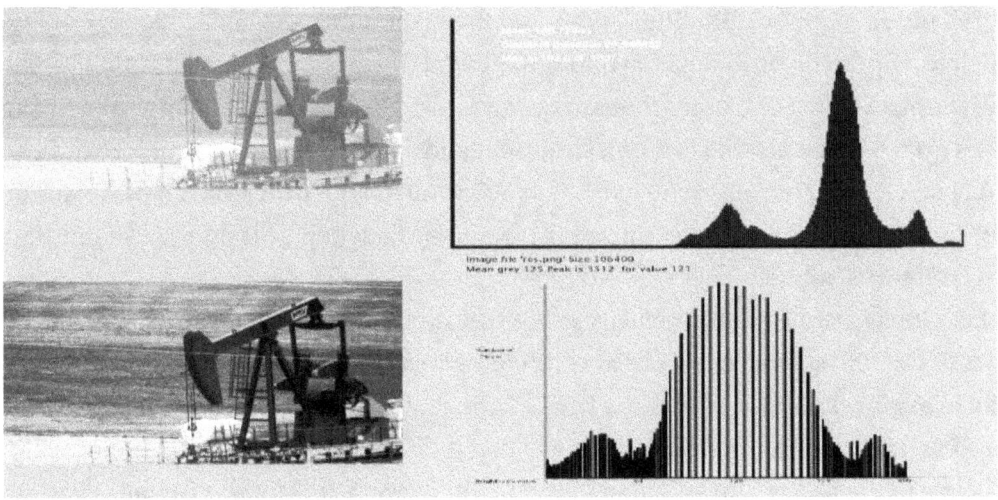

Figure 3-10. *(Top) Original image and its histogram. (Bottom) After fitting a histogram with one peak in the center*

Thresholding

One of the first things we might think about when processing a text image is to select a range of hues that would represent the text well. One might imagine that text is black, but the numerical values for black can vary, because the process of converting a document into an image is not constant or precise. The smallest possible pixel value is 0, but a scanned image has a black value in the smallest numerical range that is actually in the image and involves multiple levels. Setting the pixels with the smallest value to black and all other pixels to white is *thresholding*, where we collect pixel values above or below a certain specified value into one class and assign a single color. The common example of this in image analysis and vision is to threshold brightness values to create an image that is bi-level, meaning black and white only.

The brightness value of a pixel represents a level of gray, and we can use that value to threshold an image into black and white. We would commonly do this for images that were primarily bi-level in principle, like printed text or line drawings. Scanners and photos create images that have multiple gray values or color pixels. A first step in the processing of a text image is to *threshold* it so as to easily find the characters (black pixels) and the background (white pixels).

CHAPTER 3 VALUE

The problem in thresholding is not to set the pixel values, because that is very straightforward. The problem is to find the value of the threshold to be used that best allocates pixels into the classes that are wanted. In a typical image the brightness value ranges from 0 (black) to 255 (white), so a threshold value for an entire image would be a value between 0 and 255 inclusive. But *which* value? What threshold gives a black and white image that still shows the important features? That depends on what features we want, as it turns out.

Let's look at two images as examples for thresholding; these are shown in Figure 3-11. Both seem like excellent candidates because they are mostly black and white to begin with. If we look at the pixels, though, we'll see a variation in values caused by variations in illumination, noise, slight differences in ink color, imperfections and stims in the paper, and so on. In addition, images in JPEG format frequently have artifacts caused by the compression algorithm used in that file format, and these artifacts tend to be more prominent around edges and boundaries. The problem in thresholding is choosing the value for the boundary between black and white.

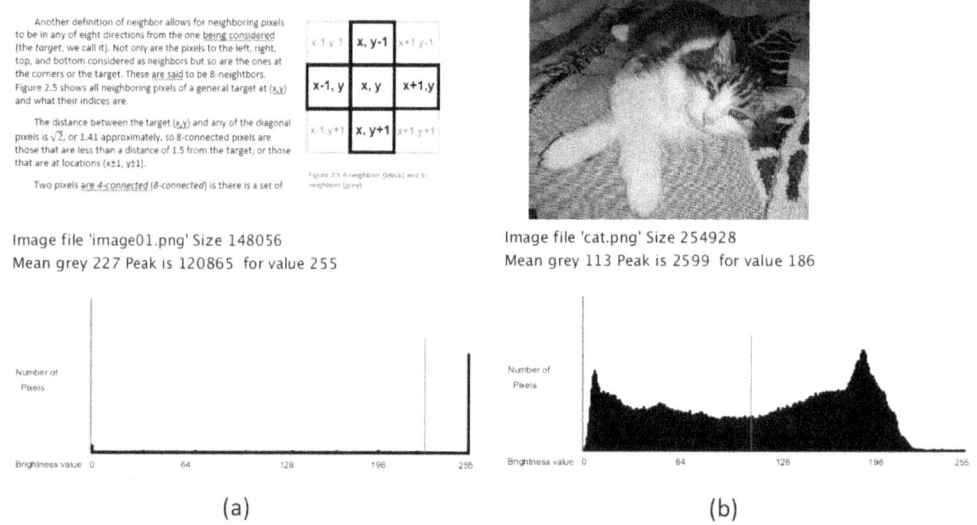

Figure 3-11. *Images for testing the thresholding methods. (a) A text image (part of a page taken from this book). (b) Image of a cat and its histogram*

Thresholding: Select a Value

As a first try we could use the middle pixel value, which, because the range here is from 0 to 255, would be 128. In this case all pixels with a brightness value less than 128 would be set to black, and those greater than or equal to 128 would become white. The principle here is that the middle value will separate the pixels into two equal groups, but that is only true in some cases. Also, it's not always true that we want half of the pixels to be black. Still, it works better than we would expect for what is a random value.

Using the Mean

The mean value of the brightness values is more likely to be in the middle of the range of gray levels than is any guess we might make. The median is actually the middle value, but it's time-consuming to calculate. Using the mean means first finding the mean level of all pixels, then thresholding the pixel values as before using that mean as the threshold.

Code: thrMean.pde	Algorithm: *thrMean* – find the mean gray level and set pixels smaller than that to black.
| ```
PImage img;
color white = color (255,255,255);
color black = color ( 0, 0, 0);
color c;
float sum = 0.0, mean = 0.0, threshold=0;
for (int i=0; i<img.width; i++)
  for (int j=0; j<img.height; j++)
    sum = sum +
        brightness( img.get(i,j));
mean = sum/( img.width * img.height);
``` | Image to be thresholded<br>White pixels are > threshold<br>Others are black.<br><br><br><br>Compute the mean by looking at all pixels in the image **img** and summing the brightness values. Then divide by the number of pixels. |

(continued)
```

`threshold = mean;` `// threshold = 128;`	Setting the variable **threshold** to 128 uses 128 as the threshold (previous discussion).

`for (int i=0; i<img.width; i++)`
`   for (int j=0; j<img.height; j++)`
`{`
	Now look at all of the pixels again.

`   c = img.get(i,j);`
`   if (brightness(c) < threshold)`
`      imgset(i,j,black);`
`   else`
`      img.set (i,j,white);`
`}`
	Get each brightness value.
	
	If the brightness is less than the mean, set the pixel to black; otherwise, set it to white.

Using the Gray-Level Histogram

A gray-level histogram is a graph of the number of pixels of each possible brightness level. There is a histogram for each of the test images given in Figure 3-13. There are two major peaks in each because there are two levels that form most of the image: black and white. These peaks are near 0 and near 255. Threshold selection will choose a numerical value for brightness that is in *between* two peaks in the histogram, if two peaks exist. This is because two peaks in the histogram are likely to represent the two pixel classes that we wish to identify. If there is one peak or more than two peaks, then that idea fails, but we nonetheless need to select a threshold that distinguishes two pixel classes. The threshold could be the value exactly between the two peaks.

CHAPTER 3 VALUE

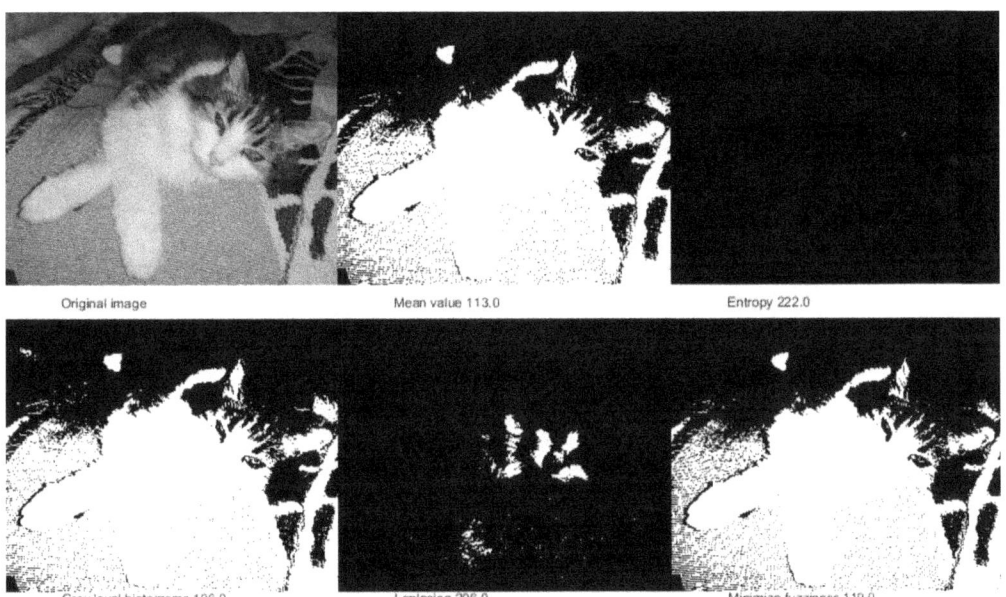

Figure 3-12. *The results of various thresholding methods applied to the cat image*

Two Pixel Classes

The goal of thresholding is to create two classes of pixels: black and white. Without knowing what kind of image we're looking at, optimizing the process of picking a threshold cannot be done. Nonetheless, many have tried, and the number of published algorithms is large (e.g., Figure 3-12).

There are multiple threshold selection methods that use the histogram, and one that is easy to understand is the *Iterative Selection* algorithm. Using this method, we select a threshold at the outset. It is common to use **T = 128**. We now group the pixels into black and white using this threshold. Now calculate the average value of the black pixels (call this **Tb**) and then do the same for the white ones (call this **Tw**). Find the average of these two values: **(Tb+Tw)/2**. Use this as the threshold, and recalculate the black and white pixels using this value as **T**. Keep repeating this process until T does not change between two iterations, and the final value of **T** is the threshold.

101

CHAPTER 3   VALUE

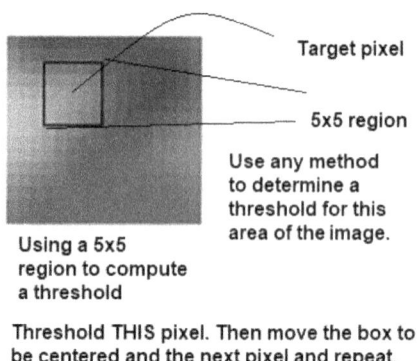

Figure 3-13. *Using a local threshold for each pixel, in this case using a 5x5 region*

This method allows the pixel values to select their own threshold. We start with a known one, but if the resulting black pixels have a mean that is very low, then it means we might have overestimated the threshold, and in the next iteration it will use a smaller value, for one example.

Code for all of these is provided in the library. We can't consider any of them to be the *best*. We can use any threshold value between 0 and 255, though, and so when creating an artwork, perhaps one good idea is to try all possible thresholds and then use the one that gives the best-looking image for the purpose. A tool such as *Photoshop* or *Gimp* can do this for you.

Local Thresholds

Scanned images and photographs and problems with noise and variable illumination. Illumination can cause the image to be brighter on one side of the image than the other, and one single threshold for the whole image simply won't work. In many cases the illumination changes from one part of the image to another, and using the same threshold applied to all of the pixels can result in a result that is too dark in some places and too light in others. When a single threshold is used on these images, a part of the resulting image will be far too dark, and another part will be too light.

A solution to that problem is to calculate *one threshold per pixel*, where we use a small region surrounding each pixel to calculate that threshold. Any method of finding a threshold will work; simply visit every pixel in the image, use a set of pixels centered at each one to compute a threshold using a thresholding method (mean or or other method), and apply that threshold to the pixel (Figure 3-13). We must use a second image to hold the thresholded pixels; otherwise, the previously thresholded pixels will affect the threshold calculation in later regions.

Figure 3-14 also shows example images as thresholded using the mean and iterative selection, showing that the methods fail to produce a good image in these instances, and shows the result of using a local threshold on these images. The results are not perfect but are obviously much better. Note that as the region size increases, the method becomes less local and looks more like the global image thresholding methods. If the size is too small, then tiny artifacts and noise can affect the threshold and result in many small regions being classed as black.

Any threshold selection method **T** can be used as a local (one pixel) thresholding method simply by taking a small section of the image centered at the target pixel and applying algorithm **T** to it, then looking at a small region about the next pixel, and so on. Methods that use a histogram need to use a larger region than those that don't because small histograms don't provide much information.

Given any thresholding algorithm, such as selecting the mean value, the local thresholding method works as follows:

1. Select the first pixel (x,y).

2. Apply the thresholding algorithm to the NxN region centered at (**x,y**), and determine the threshold **t**.

3. If the pixel at (**x,y**) has a value < **t**, then set it to black; otherwise, set it to white.

4. If (x,y) is the final pixel in the image, then stop.

5. Let (x,y) become the next pixel

6. Continue from step 2.

Figure 3-14 shows this method applied to the cat image, using a selection of basic thresholding methods as the base.

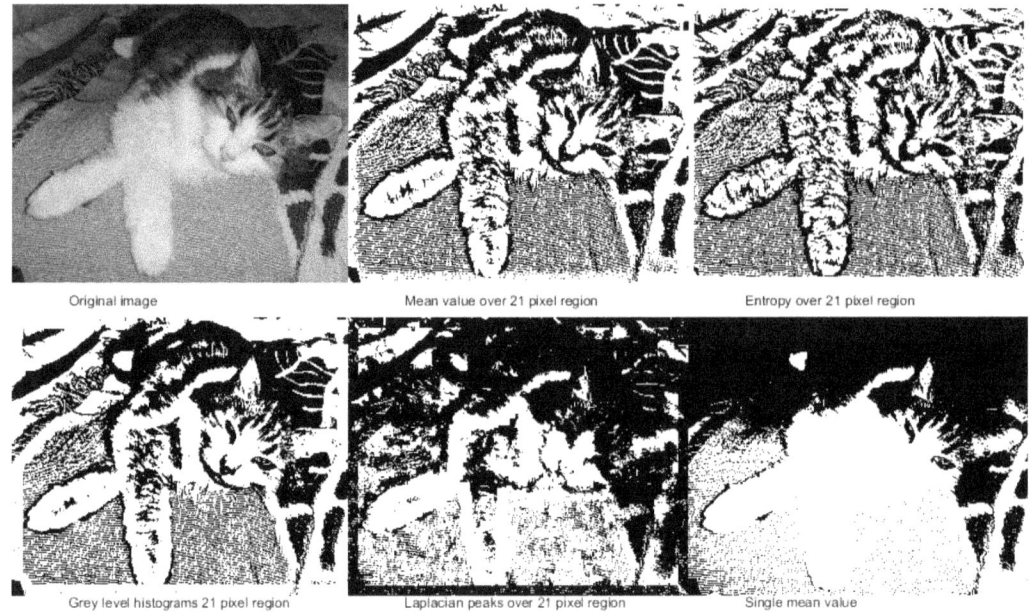

Figure 3-14. *The results produced by the local thresholding algorithm for a selection of underlying thresholding methods*

Regions and Boundaries

A region is an area having a similar gray value. It frequently represents a particular object in the image and so is something that we want to treat as a single thing. The locations where this object merges into another are called *boundaries* and usually represent lines and curves that an artist would draw to mark where one object ended and another began. These are important places.

A region is a set of contiguous pixels of the same or similar value. It is possible to have multiple regions with the same value that are separate, which makes finding regions a little more difficult.

In some images, like cartoons and others with clear, distinct gray or color areas, identifying a region is simple: we start with any pixel **P** with value **V** and *mark* it with a number or code that identifies what region it belongs to. We could use integers, starting with **mark=0**. Then we mark all pixels adjacent to it that have the same value **V** with the same code **mark** and then mark all pixels adjacent to any marked pixel having the value

V until we find no more such pixels. Then we increase the value of the mark (**mark = mark + 1**) and repeat the process using the next unmarked pixel we find until there are no more marked pixels.

In more detail, then:

1. We have an image **X** that consists of gray values on a white background. Figure 3-15 is an image of a map of the western United States that we'll use as an example. Create an array of marks **M** that is the same size, with one element corresponding to each pixel in **X**. If **M[i][j] = 1,** then the pixel **X(i,j)** is marked, and if **M[i][j] = 0,** it is unmarked. This makes the process of marking a pixel very simple. Set all marks to 0 at the beginning.

2. Find a pixel **P=(i,j)** that has a gray, not white, value. This is the start of our region, and we call this the *seed* pixel. In Figure 3-15a, this pixel has crosshairs through it. Mark this pixel (set **M[i][j] = 1**). Set **V** to its gray value: **V = X.get(i,j)** and then change its value to white.

3. Scan the image **X** for a marked pixel **P$_m$ = (a, b)**. Initially the only marked pixel will be the start pixel **P**, but this will change as the algorithm proceeds.

4. For each of the eight neighbors **Q$_i$** of **P$_m$**. If **Q$_i$** has a value of **V**, then mark it and set its value to white.

5. Repeat from step 3, continuing from pixel **P$_m$** until we find no more marked pixels.

6. Repeat from step 2, rescanning the entire image for marked pixels, until we don't mark any new ones.

7. At this point, all marked pixels belong to one region.

CHAPTER 3 VALUE

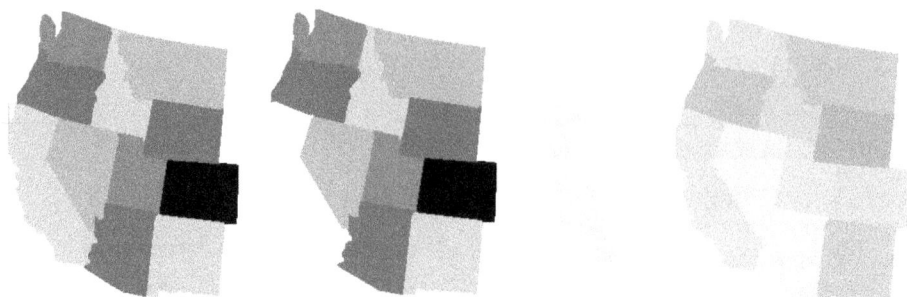

Figure 3-15. *(Left) Map of the Western United States. (Center) After the first region has been identified. (Left) Final result with all regions identified and values replaced by colors*

If the image has multiple regions of interest, then just do the whole process again after saving and clearing the marked pixels.

This algorithm is useful on ideal data, where the gray values are uniform. Sadly, this never happens. The data in Figure 3-15 was constructed for this example, and each region has nearly perfect values, which is to say exactly the same at all points. A *real* image, one captured using a camera or scanner, would have slight variations in level at different pixels caused by dust on the lens, or variations in illumination, or noise in the electronics. In that case, the algorithm we described would create regions that had missing pixels where the values did not agree with the value of the start pixel. There are a few ways to deal with this.

The first idea is to use the gray level of the start pixel as an approximate value. We could modify step 4 of the algorithm to be:

4. For each of the eight neighbors Q_i of P_m. If Q_i has an approximate value of V, then mark it and set its value to white.

How close does Q_i need to be to V? This depends on the image. It seems obvious that there should be no overlap in values between neighboring regions, or else they will be merged into a single region or two regions that do not correspond to the desired ones.

Smoothing

Pixels in a region can have varying values because of noise, which is random, or because of distortions in illumination due to other reasons. One major reason would be the use of the JPG image format, which causes changes in value due to its compression method. Pixels near the outside of a region have their values changed in what seems like a random way. If we apply the region-finding program that produced Figure 3-15 to the same image of the western United States, but this time saved as a JPG, then we get an awful collection of regions as seen in Figure 3-16.

The regions have irregular shapes that don't correspond to the original map because only the largest area in the center of each region has been left uncorrupted. The pixels between regions do not form contiguous areas, and so between 1 and 4 pixel regions are created that have the same value, but this is a spurious result of random changes generated by the JPG compression method. A lesson here is to never use JPG to store images that you want to use for art.

How does our new idea handle this? Not perfectly, but much better than before. Figure 3-16b shows the output when we allow gray values in a region to vary by 15. To determine the value of 15, we had to try a few other numbers and select the one that gave the best result, and even then it's not perfect. Regions are pretty good, but there are many tiny regions where the method failed.

We can think of the value 15 as a kind of threshold. It specifies how close in value pixels need to be to be connected to the same region. It will often have to be determined manually, by running the program with different values until a nice image results. Not all images will be able to be processed automatically in this way, and leftover issues will remain to be edited by hand. However, we can still improve on this.

CHAPTER 3 VALUE

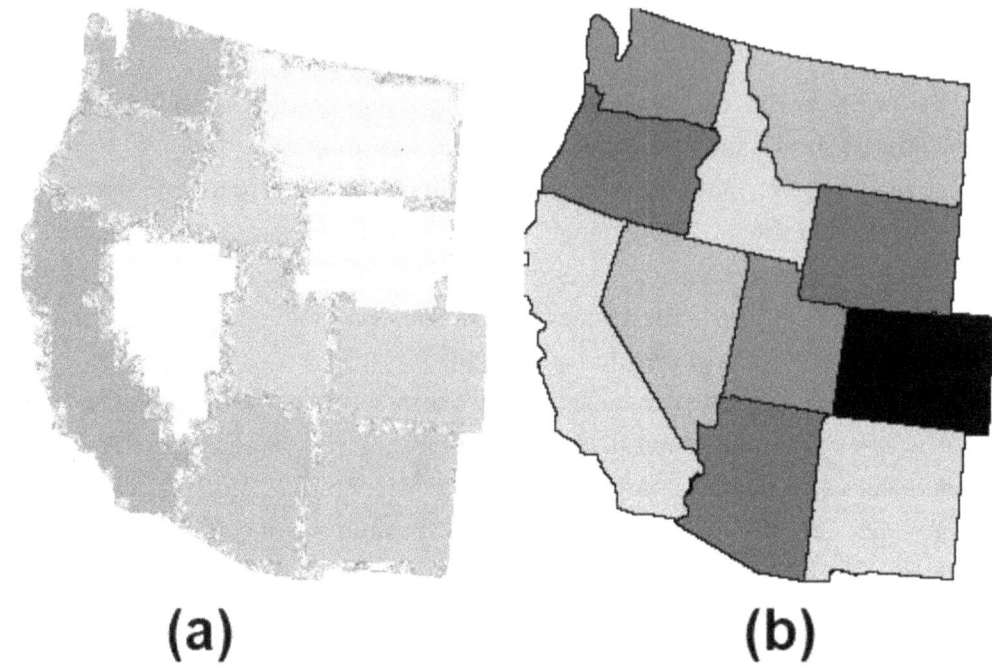

Figure 3-16. *Boundaries located in a JPEG image. (a) Simple. (b) Threshold*

Mean and Median

Pixels in images are almost never completely random. There is a basic value for the region, and a pixel may vary some amount from this, larger or smaller. Thus, we have some idea of what the pixel ought to be.

The simplest way to smooth an image is to use the average of the pixel values in a small region surrounding each pixel to replace the original value. It's easy to calculate, and we could use regions of various sizes; if one size does not work very well, we can increase it. A negative to this method is that the mean of a set of pixels might not actually be a pixel value in that region. One pixel that is very bad can cause the mean to be outside the range you want. Also, the mean is a real number, and pixels are integers, so again, the mean might not be a real pixel value.

A better choice is the *median*, which is the value in the middle of some set of values. There are eight pixels surrounding any pixel, and nine altogether counting the center pixel. Computing the median means gathering these values, sorting them, and replacing the center pixel with the middle value, the fifth one in the sorted collection. This pixel value absolutely *is* one of the values in the region. It is certainly harder to calculate the median, since it involves a sort, and the program is slower than the one that finds the mean. Is it better? Yes, as shown in Figure 3-17.

Figure 3-17. (a) Regions after using a mean filter on the original image. (b) Regions after a median filter

---

Code: medianFilter

Algorithm: *medianFilter* – Replace each pixel with the median value of a region around it.

```
int medianValue (int a, int b,
          PImage im, int d)
{
  int n=0;
  int p[] = new int[4*d*d];
```

Compute the median value.

d will be the number of pixels in the region

The array p will hold all pixel values seen, for sorting

(*continued*)

CHAPTER 3 VALUE

```
  for (int i=-d; i<=d; i++)
```
Examine all pixels in a dxd area centered at (a,b). Make sure that the pixels are part of the image (coordinates are legal).

```
  {
    if (i+a<0 || i+a >=im.width)
        continue;
    for (int j=-d; j<=d; j++)
```
Distance d from the center gives a circular region radius d.

```
    {
      if (j+b<0||j+b>=im.height)
        continue;
      if (dist(i,j,0, 0) <= d)
      {
        p[n] =
          (int)brightness
            (im.get(i+a, b+j) );
        n = n + 1;
```
Sample all values within, saving in the array p.

```
      }
```
There will be n elements in this array.

```
    }
  }
  P = sort (p);
```
Sort them.

```
  return p[n/2];
}
```
Select the middle value as the result (the median).

```
void medianFilter (PImage img,
int size)
```

(continued)

```
{
  for (int i=0;i<img.width; i++)    For each pixel in the image, replace it by the median
                                    of the pixels in a small region centered at that pixel.
    for (int j=0; j<img.height;
                    j++)
      img.set(i,j,
        color(medianValue
            (i,j,z, size)));
}
```

Boundaries

A boundary occurs at pixel locations where one region ends and another begins. We can identify these locations because there is a change of value on two or more sides of the pixel. Using the western US map image of Figure 3-12a, let's consider the pixel along the border between California and Oregon, as in Figure 3-15. The target pixel (i.e., the pixel we're examining at the moment) has a value of 184 and is part of the California region. Some of the neighboring pixels are in California (pixel value = 184), and some are in Oregon (value = 100). This is a boundary pixel because it has California on one side and Oregon on the other. In the context of our digital analysis, it is a boundary pixel because it has pixels with a value of 100 *and* pixels with a value of 184 as neighbors. A non-boundary pixel will have neighbors that all have the same value.

We can easily write some code that identifies boundary pixels and identifies them with a specific value. For example, the following sets all boundary pixels to black:

CHAPTER 3 VALUE

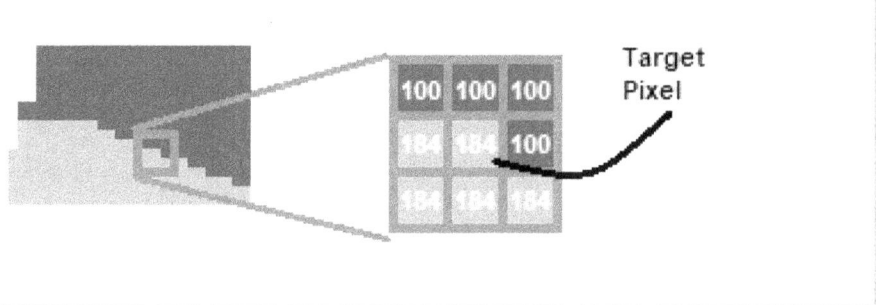

Figure 3-18. *Expanded view of a small image region around an edge pixel*

`void boundary (PImage im)`	// Enhance a boundary
`{`	
`int value;`	
`z = im.copy();`	z is a copy of the original
`for (int i=0; i<im.width; i++)`	For each pixel (may be color)
` for (int j=0; j<im.height; j++)`	
` {`	
`  value = (int)brightness(z.get(i,j));`	Convert v to a value (gray) of (i,j)
`  for (int n=0; n<8; n++)`	For each of the 8 neighbors,
`    if (neighbor(i,j,n,z) != value)`	if the neighbor differs from v, then we have a boundary pixel.
`    // If any neighbor differs`	
`      im.set(i,j,BLACK);`	So make it black.
`      // in value from target`	
` }`	
`}`	Neighbor (l,j,n,z) returns the color of neighbor n of pixel (l,j) in z.

Figure 3-19 shows the boundaries. Note that the program makes a copy of the image. This is critical and is a common mistake when writing programs to manipulate images. The program uses the values in the copy but changes the pixel values to draw the boundaries in the parameter image **im**. We must not modify pixels in the same image in which we are changing them, because modifications can be used by later iterations to make further changes, and so on. In this case, if we both modify and test pixels in **im**, the result is a completely black image. The black pixels we draw will become boundaries for adjacent pixels, causing further pixels to be considered boundaries when in fact they were not.

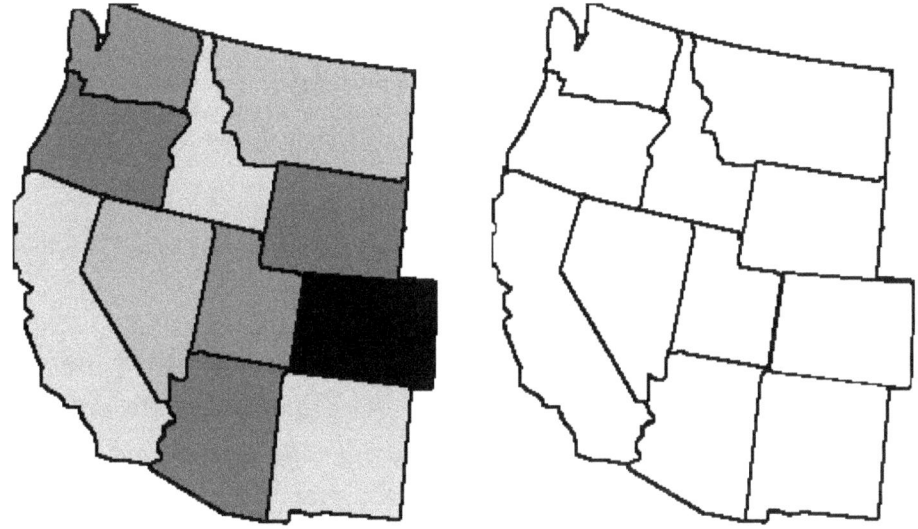

Figure 3-19. Enhancing boundaries between regions of different values

Edges

A boundary is a pixel on the outline of a region; an *edge* is a pixel that marks a change in value for any reason, especially if that pixel forms an extended feature like a line. Boundary pixels are edges, to be sure, but edges can be found inside regions or where there are lines. Since an edge is found where pixels change in value, that's how we find them: look at the pixels that are neighbors of the target pixel and see how they vary. If they vary by a large enough value, then the target is an edge. It might also be a boundary, but we don't know that for certain.

CHAPTER 3   VALUE

We have used the values of neighboring pixels before when looking for boundaries. The eight neighbors of the pixel (i,j) are shown in Figure 3-20 along with the code that identifies them. Now we'll use them to find edges. The most common methods for locating edge pixels use a template or 2D computational pattern around each pixel.

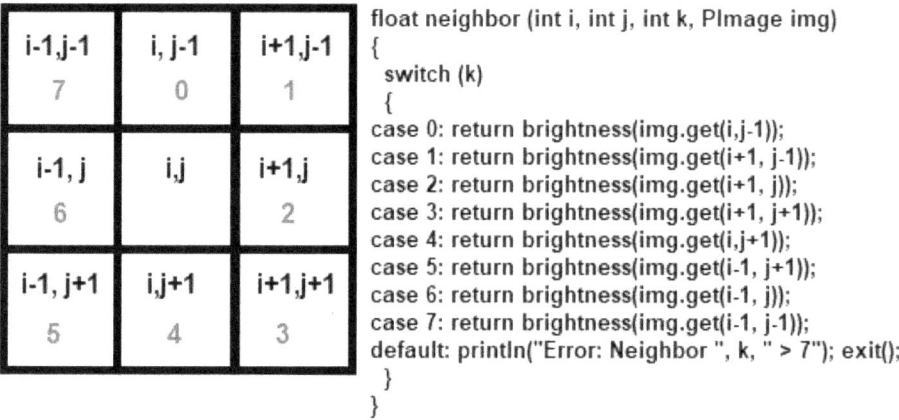

Figure 3-20. The eight neighbors of a pixel and a scheme used to label them, from 0 to 7

When looking for a boundary, we looked only at how much the target pixel varied from all of its neighbors; when looking for edge pixels, it matters where the different pixels are with respect to the target. In other words, edges have a *direction*. A vertical edge is one that has similar values above and below the target but varies in value on the left and/or right. That being the case, a pixel that lies on a vertical edge has its *1-2-3* neighbors with differing values from the *5-6-7* neighbors. This is easy to identify: simply add the values of the *1-2-3* neighbors and the values of the *5-6-7* neighbors and subtract the two sums. The target pixel is a vertical edge pixel in proportion to the size of this difference. Similarly, a horizontal edge has the *7-0-1* neighbors different from the *3-4-5* neighbors, and we find such edge pixels by the same mechanism.

Figure 3-21 shows both kinds of edge pixels. The darkness of the pixels indicates the degree to which the pixel is an edge. Note that it varies even when the edges are clearly present. That's because the actual values being used vary: the edge between values of 30 and 40 is considered less distinct than an edge between values of 30 and 200. Using neighbors in this manner is not how we usually find edges in an image. Instead, we often use a computational template. This is a 2D array of numbers that we center at the target pixel; we multiply the corresponding template values by the pixel values and sum them. For a vertical edge, the template would be:

114

CHAPTER 3 VALUE

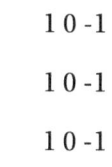

1 0 -1

1 0 -1

1 0 -1

Figure 3-21. *Edges are found by calculating the difference in value between adjacent pixels. (Left) Vertical edges. (Right) Horizontal edges*

The sum of the product of the pixel values and these coefficients gives an edge pixel value, the larger values indicating a stronger likelihood of an edge (*edge response*). We can now define a wide variety of edge detection schemes by specifying different computational templates. Many such have already been defined and tested and are often named after the person who devised them.

Sobel Edges

A commonly used set of templates is the Sobel edge detection method, which uses the specific templates:

```
        -1 -2 -1              -1  0  1
H =      0  0  0       V =   -2  0  2
         1  2  1              -1  0  1
```

We compute **H** and **V** as:

```
H = -(neighbor(7) + 2*neighbor(0) + neighbor(1)) +
    (neighbor(3) + 2*neighbor(4) + neighbor(5));
V = -(neighbor(7) + 2*neighbor(6) + neighbor(5)) +
    (neighbor(1) + 2*neighbor(2) + neighbor(3));
```

CHAPTER 3 VALUE

These are the horizontal and vertical parts of the edge. The magnitude (edge response) is $\sqrt{H^2 + V^2}$ and the direction is $\tan^{-1}\frac{V}{H}$, so we can get a rough idea about the direction of the edge. The angles are crude because we're only using a 3x3 region, and because we can't distinguish between angles 180 degrees apart: a 45-degree angle will be the same as a 125-degree angle. Figure 3-22 shows the Sobel edge response and angles.

Figure 3-22. *Sobel edges. (Left) Magnitude. (Right) Direction, as indicated by color*

Canny Edges

Edges are critical, but staring at the different algorithms gets boring after a while. Which one is the best? That's a matter for intellectual discussion, but there are a few methods that people consider very important. One is the *Canny* algorithm, named after the person who devised it. It's not especially recent, but people have been using it for many years with great success. It has the same essential quality of edge detection, which is that it uses the difference in value between adjacent pixels (differentials). It also performs noise reduction and other special methods that allow edge detection in realistic circumstances.

The algorithm is too complex to describe here, but we provide an implementation in the library as **canny.pde** so that anyone can use it in their artworks. There are a few parameters that we can adjust, but the basic method that we implemented works pretty well in most circumstances (i.e., many different images). Figure 3-23 shows some examples using a couple typical captured images from photos. These could be used to begin an artwork based on lines, areas, colors, or even more sophisticated abstractions like cubism and shading using linear features.

CHAPTER 3 VALUE

Figure 3-23. *The Canny edge detector applied to various images*

Shading

The talk of edges ignores certain aesthetic and artistic issues. In the discussion so far we've been speaking of *hard* edges, which involve a rapid change in value across a short distance. A boundary between the sea and the sky or the boundary of a shadow would be a hard edge. A *soft* edge involves a gradual change in value over a larger area. It conveys a curved or rounded surface, smoothness, or softness.

The way that value changes over a region (object) determines the *form* of an object, which will be discussed in detail in Chapter 8, "Space." In short, this variation is what makes a sphere look like a sphere rather than a circle. Figure 3-24 shows a circle on the left filled with a constant value and a circle on the right filled using a value gradient. The circle on the right has the visual appearance of a sphere.

A value gradient can be created by starting at some (x, y) location with a value V and modifying the value as a function of distance from (x, y) in a specific direction. In Figure 3-24, the value begins at V=128 and increases with increasing x from the center of the circle and decreases with decreasing x. Although the circle is two-dimensional, this shading gives the appearance of a 3D object because it mimics what we expect to see from a 3D object.

117

CHAPTER 3 VALUE

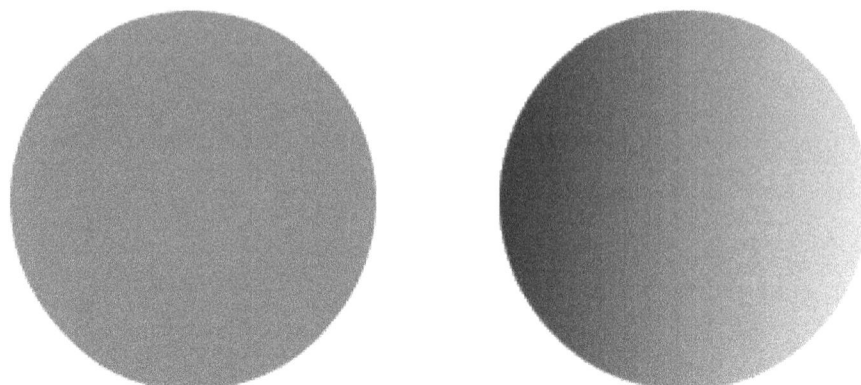

Figure 3-24. *(Left) A circle filled with value 128. (Right) Value gradient applied to the circle makes it look like a sphere*

Gradients are often used in artworks as backgrounds, rather than using a solid color. The result has more impact that way (Figure 3-25).

Figure 3-25. *(Left) Image of a laptop. (Center) Value gradient. (Right) Combining the two for a more dramatic effect*

Bi-Level Display of Values

We can visualize different values using only black and white pixels. This is an interesting effect, and in the past, when printers only had black ink, it was used to simulate levels of gray. The basic idea is to replace each pixel in the gray image with a small set of black and white pixels arranged in a pattern that, from a distance, has the appearance of gray. A white pixel in the gray image will be a small region of all white pixels; a black pixel will be a region of all black. A gray value will have an increasing number of pixels set as the value gets darker. The common methods of implementing this are *halftones* and *dithering*.

CHAPTER 3   VALUE

Halftones

This is how pictures used to be displayed in newspapers, which used only black ink. Each pixel in the original image will be drawn as a square region of pixels in the result, and those regions will have black pixels arranged in a pattern or *template*. This can't display all 256 values while also maintaining the content of the image, because it would require a template of size 16x16: the final image would be much larger than the original, or a lot of detail would be lost.

A 3x3 region is good enough for most purposes, which gives 9 pixels, or 10 possible values: zero set pixels to nine set pixels. There are 256 possible gray levels, so each region will represent a range of 25.5 values. Figure 3-23 shows the templates that we'll use and gives the range of values assigned to each one. Identifying the template to be used for any pixel is simple: divide the value by 25.5. The algorithm is:

`void half3x3 (PImage im)`	For every third pixel P: in the image
`{`	
`int n = 0;`	
`color WHITE = color(255);`	
`color BLACK = color(0);`	
`float v;`	
`for (int x=1;x<im.width-1;x=x+3)`	
`{`	
`  if (x >= im.width-1) continue;`	Let V = its value
`  for (int y=0;y<im.height-1;y=y+3)`	Let n = V/25.5
`  {`	Replace the 3x3 region centered at P with
`    if (y >= im.height-1) continue;`	template n
`    v = brightness(im.get(x,y));`	
`    n = (int)(v/25.5);`	

(continued)

CHAPTER 3   VALUE

```
  im.set(x-1, y-1, template[n]);
 }
}
}
```

The templates are stored in ten image files, which are read into the **template** array (Figure 3-26).

Another method that has been used to create artistically interesting images is to replace a small region of the original image with a filled circle. The diameter of the circle increases as the value increases, making the area darker and darker. This is the *classical* method. Again, the size of the region defines how many levels we can represent. If we select a region size of 5, meaning that a 5x5 set of pixels will be replaced by a circle, then the number of levels is 6 (sizes of 0, 1, 2, 3, 4, and 5). The number of values represented by each diameter is 255/5, or 51. The radius used for any specific value **V** will be **(255-V)/51** – brighter values have smaller diameters, so we use **255-V** instead of the value. We draw such a circle every 5 pixels vertically and horizontally.

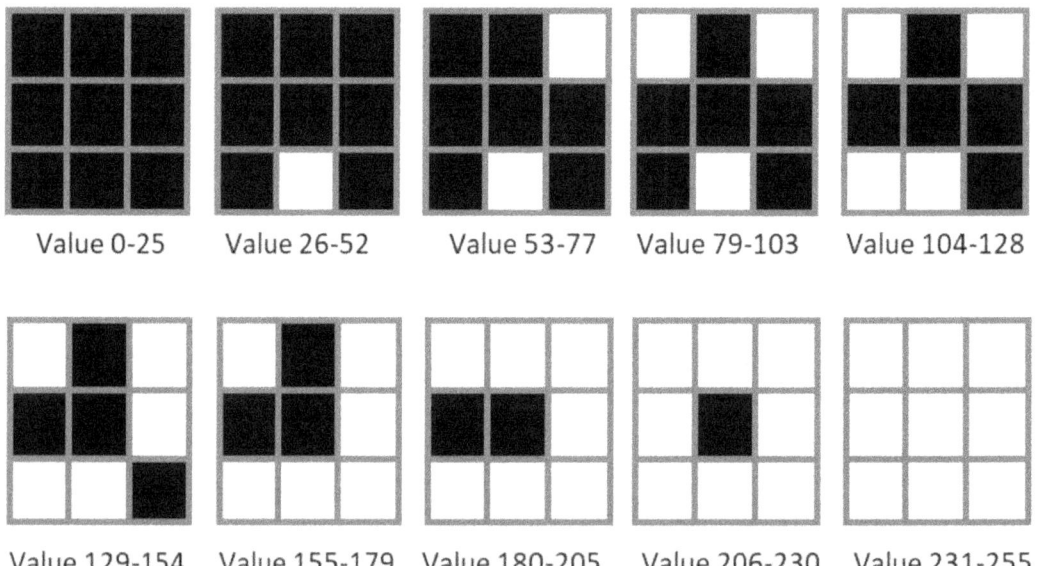

Figure 3-26. Templates used for halftone creation using a 3x3 region

`z = (int)(255/size);`	Pixels per diameter, which are integers
`for (int x=2; x<im.width-1; x=x+(int)size)`	For every **size** of pixel in each direction
`  for (int y=2; y<im.height-1; y=y+(int)size)`	
`{`	
`n=(int)((255-brightness(im.get(x,y)))/z);`	Compute the diameter as (255-V)/z
`circle (x, y, n);`	Draw the circle
`}`	

This will draw the result on the screen rather than in the image itself, in this case.

The results of both halftoning methods are shown in Figure 3-27. The classical method seems not to do very well, but a big advantage of it is that it is possible to change the size easily, and for large sizes the result can be very interesting sometimes, as we will see.

Dithering

Some definitions of "dither" include "to be unable to make a decision about doing something", and "to be very nervous, excited, or confused." It implies a kind of disordered behavior. Indeed, the origin of the word is the Middle English verb *didderen*, meaning "to tremble." This is the best description of what we are going to explain here. A *dithering* algorithm can randomly (or seemingly) place black pixels near pixels of specific values so as to visually simulate the grays. There are many dithering methods out there, but we will describe just one: the Floyd-Steinberg method.

CHAPTER 3   VALUE

Figure 3-27. (Left) Original image. (Center) 3x3 regions using templates. (Right) Classical, using size = 5

The goal is to use only black and white pixels to display grays, and black has a value of 0, and white is 255. Start with some pixel at **(x, y)** that has a value **V**. We want this pixel to become 0 or 255, so pick the value nearest to V and set the pixel to that. If **v=32**, set the pixel to black; if **V=190**, set it to white: call this thresholded value **T**. Now compute the *error* involved in this change by setting **D = V-T**. This difference between the old and new value will now be shared between neighboring pixels. The normal way to scan an image pixel-by-pixel is across rows from left to right and down columns, so the pixels above and to the left have already been determined and should not participate. There are four pixels to the right and down: (x+1,y), (x-1, y+1), (x, y+1), and (x+1,y+1). We will distribute the error **E** between them.

The creators of the method figured out the weighting for sharing the error. I'm sure they tried many times, but here is what they settled on:

```
Pixel(x+1, y) = Pixel(x+1, y) + E * 7. / 16.
Pixel(x,y+1) = Pixel(1,y+1) + E * 3. / 16.
Pixel(x,y+1) = Pixel(x,y+1) + E * 5. / 16.
Pixel(x+1,y+1) = Pixel(x+1,y+1) + E * 1. / 16.
```

Then we move to the next pixel. Its value will have been changed by this process acting on previous pixels, so its value could be greater than 255 or less than 0. This pixel is set to 0 or 1, and we share the new error as before. This is very simple to implement:

```
for (int y=1; y<im.height-1; y++)
  for (int x=1; x<im.width-1; x++)
  {
    old = pix[x][y];
    nw = nearest(old);
    pix[x][y] = nw;
    error = old-nw;

    pix[x+1][y] = pix[x+1][y] + error * 7. / 16.;
    pix[x-1][y+1] = pix[x-1][y+1] + error * 3. / 16.;
    pix[x][y+1] = pix[x][y+1] + error * 5. / 16.;
    pix[x+1][y+1] = pix[x+1][y+1] + error * 1. / 16.;
  }
```

Figure 3-28. *(Left) Dithered version of Rubic image. (Center) Original Max image. (Right) Dithered Max image*

Pix is an array of pixels, but in floating-point form, because the values could exceed the normal limits and we'll be adding fractional portions of the error. This will have to be converted back into an image, but at the end of the process all of the values will be either 0 or 255. The results are remarkable, as seen in Figure 3-28.

CHAPTER 3 VALUE

Quantization: Changing Number of Levels

The term "quantization" refers to the number of discrete values that a real image has been sampled at to create a digital image. A typical image has 256 distinct values, and a thresholded image has 2. Remember, thresholding changes some values to 0 and some to 255. But why not have 3 levels? Or 6? We can do that.

The simple way to convert an image into N levels is to find T=255/N and then map the values between 0 to T to 0, T to 2*T to T, 3*T to 3*T to 2*T, and so on. This does not always produce a good result, because the values may not be distributed in a uniform manner. It does a fair job on many images. The method for N levels is:

```
void threshn (PImage im, int n)
{
  int v, y;                              Set X to be 256/N = size of each range
  float x;                               Set Y to be 256/(N-1) = larger range
  color c;
  x = 256/n;                             For each pixel
  y = 256/(n-1);
  for (int i=0; i<im.width; i++)
    for (int j=0; j<im.height; j++)
    {
      c = im.get(i,j));
      v = (int)(c/x)*y;                  Get the pixel value V
      im.set(i,j,color(v,v,v));          Change its value V to (int)(V/X)*Y
    }
}
```

The value of Y is needed to make sure that the entire range 0-255 is used; it stretches the contrast to the maximum. If we set Y = X, the program still works, but the brightest white level is darker than it should be (Figure 3-29).

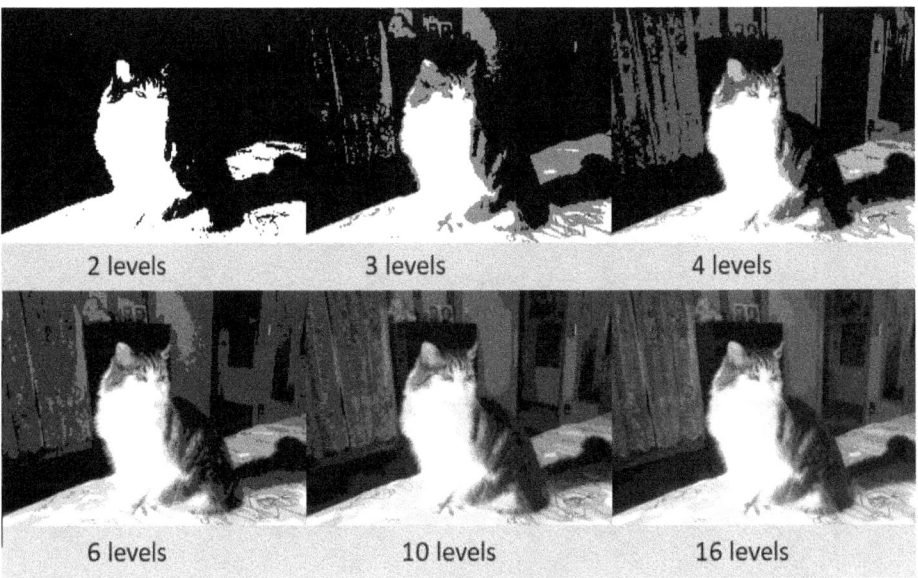

Figure 3-29. *Thresholding of an image using multiple levels. Equally distributed values*

Instead of dividing the range equally, we could try to assign equal numbers of pixels to each threshold. The previous method will effectively use a threshold of 128 when N=2, for example, which divides the range into two parts. We could instead have the same number of pixels as black and white, which would be like using the mean as the threshold.

For **M** thresholds, we first calculate the histogram **H** for the image **X**. The number of pixels is **N**, the product of the width and height of **X**. Now create an array **T** of **M** thresholds, initially all 0, and let **k** = **N/M** so that each threshold will select **k** pixels. Now to find the thresholds, start at histogram element i=0 (=value 0) and add the values in the histogram bins i+1, i+2, and so on until the sum exceeds k, and use the value of **i-1** as the first threshold, **T[0]**. Start again and sum histogram values until the sum again exceeds **k**, and again **i-1** is the next threshold, **T[1]**. Continue until all histogram bins have been used (i>255). Now the array T holds all of the thresholds in ascending order.

CHAPTER 3   VALUE

Figure 3-30. *Multiple level thresholding using an equal number of pixels*

Now we threshold the image. For each pixel value V, find the element T[j] that is the first one to be greater than V – step through T until we find it. Replace the pixel value with T[j-1], which, in other words, uses T[j] as the threshold. Continue until all pixels have been changed.

Depending on your sense of aesthetics and the nature of the image, this method usually produces better images (Figure 3-30).

Marilyn

We now have a lot of tools using value and line that we can use to create art. We're probably not accustomed to thinking in terms of these kinds of operations when making an artwork, so some examples of generative art creation from images might be appropriate.

We have found a nice photo of Marilyn Monroe and wonder what we might do with it. Quite a few projects start this way: with an interesting image. This particular image has a white background, making some manipulations simpler (it was probably edited). Here is one process, but of course there are many others.

126

CHAPTER 3 VALUE

Figure 3-31. *Original image.* `https://en.wikipedia.org/wiki/File:Marilyn_Monroe,_Epoca.jpg`

Figure 3-32. *Thresholded image*

127

First, let's try thresholding it. We should be able to get a nice outline. The histogram does not tell us much. All values occur in the image, and there is no obvious place to threshold it. Looking at all possible thresholds (remember – there are 256 of them), we see there are some that preserve the essential character of this portrait. These are in the range of 150-170.

Any threshold results in a lot of "fuzzy" boundaries that are not typical of human artworks. The image of Figure 3-32 uses a threshold of 155. Note the random black pixels appearing on the neck and along the arm. The usual thing to do in these situations is some kind of *averaging* – a mean or median filter. These come in different sizes that reflect the size of the areas being averaged. The larger the size of the region, the more blur we will introduce. This means that we'll have to try multiple sizes to see which one works best.

Median filters are generally better since they always use values that really occur in the image, and the region is usually circular and not rectangular. Looking at the results of median filters of sizes 2, 3, and 4 (Figure 3-33), we can observe a blurring of boundaries as the size increases. For the purposes here, let's choose the size 4 result.

Figure 3-33. *Median filter of size 2, 3, and 4 applied to the Marilyn image*

CHAPTER 3   VALUE

Figure 3-34. *Thresholding after smoothing*

Thresholding this image yields a result that perhaps we can use. But for what, exactly? Sometimes we're not sure at the outset. In this case, something in the style of the 1960s pop artist *Roy Lichtenstein* comes to mind, perhaps because the subject is Marilyn. Lichtenstein made frequent use of halftoning, although in color, and his work had a comic book quality.

We've already processed Marilyn's image so that it has been smoothed with a median filter of size 4 (Figure 3-35B) and threshold (Figure 3-35C). This image is a bit unsatisfying, as there are gaps in the outline. This may be what you want, but we'll make an overall outline by thresholding the original image (yielding Figure 3-35D) and finding the boundary pixels (Figure 3-35E). Combining these two images yields the image for

129

the next step – halftones. Using the thresholded image, change the black to a medium gray and then make halftones (Figure 3-35F). The white background is unchanged, but the formerly black part is now an array of dots. Combine this with the previous image to make Figure 3-35g.

Finally, let's build a background. It would be boring if the background was a constant value, so an image of some kind behind her would be better. The use of complex visual patterns and optical illusions was in vogue in the 1960s, and the internet is a vast resource for such things. The pattern shown in Figure 3-35I was chosen from hundreds of possibilities. Placing this underneath what we have is not trivial, but we can take a technique from movies and TV – *green screen*. Set the background pixels of Figure 3-35G to green, or some unused value U. It's easy to do in Paint, and we could do it by setting all white pixels in Figure 3-35D to green. Now replace all green pixels in Figure 3-35H by the corresponding pixel in Figure 3-35I, and we get the final result.

CHAPTER 3 VALUE

***Figure* 3-35.** *(A) Original image. (B) Median filter size 4. (C) Threshold B. (D) Threshold B. (E) Extracting boundaries from D gives an outline. (F) Halftones from the gray version of D. (G) Combining C, E, and F. (H) Set the background to an identifiable value. (I) Op-art background. (J) Final result using the green screen technique to place I under H*

The tools we used are as follows:

Median filter to smooth the original image, giving B. (median.pde)

Threshall to look at the result of all possible thresholds in B. (threshall.pde)

Thresh to threshold the image B into C. (thresh.pde)

Thresh to threshold the median-filtered image, giving D.

Bound to find the outline of D giving E. (bound.pde)

CHAPTER 3   VALUE

Make a temporary image Da, which sets the black pixels to gray 128. *Paint*?

Halftone to tone Da and produce F. (halftone.pde)

Overlay to combine C, E, and F into G. (overlay.pde)

Paint can be used to change the background of G to be green.

Overlay is used to green screen G over the background I to give the final result. (overlay.pde)

Filled Contours

The idea here is to create multiple contours based on value and then fill them (color them) with a value that distinguishes them from their neighbors. People familiar with contour maps will have seen this. It is similar to multiple-level thresholding, but we get to define the values being used. This means that we (the artist) specifically choose the difference between the values used for each region.

This sounds a bit abstract, so look at Figure 3-36. The original color picture can be thresholded using any method, but neither allows us to select the levels of thresholding. Thresholded using the equal distance or equal number of pixels methods, but neither allows us to select the levels of thresholding. The idea here is to pick the threshold values so that the best result happens. This is, of course, subjective. It takes some time and trial and error.

The process was to, first, smooth the image (Figure 3-36B). This will become standard practice. Now use various thresholds on that image in an attempt to find a good distance between adjacent levels – good in a visual sense. Each thresholded image is then modified so that the black values are changed to the threshold value, and then the images are drawn on top of each other, replacing the white pixels in the previous layer with dark pixels in the current one (Figure 3-36E). The result is Figure 3-36F.

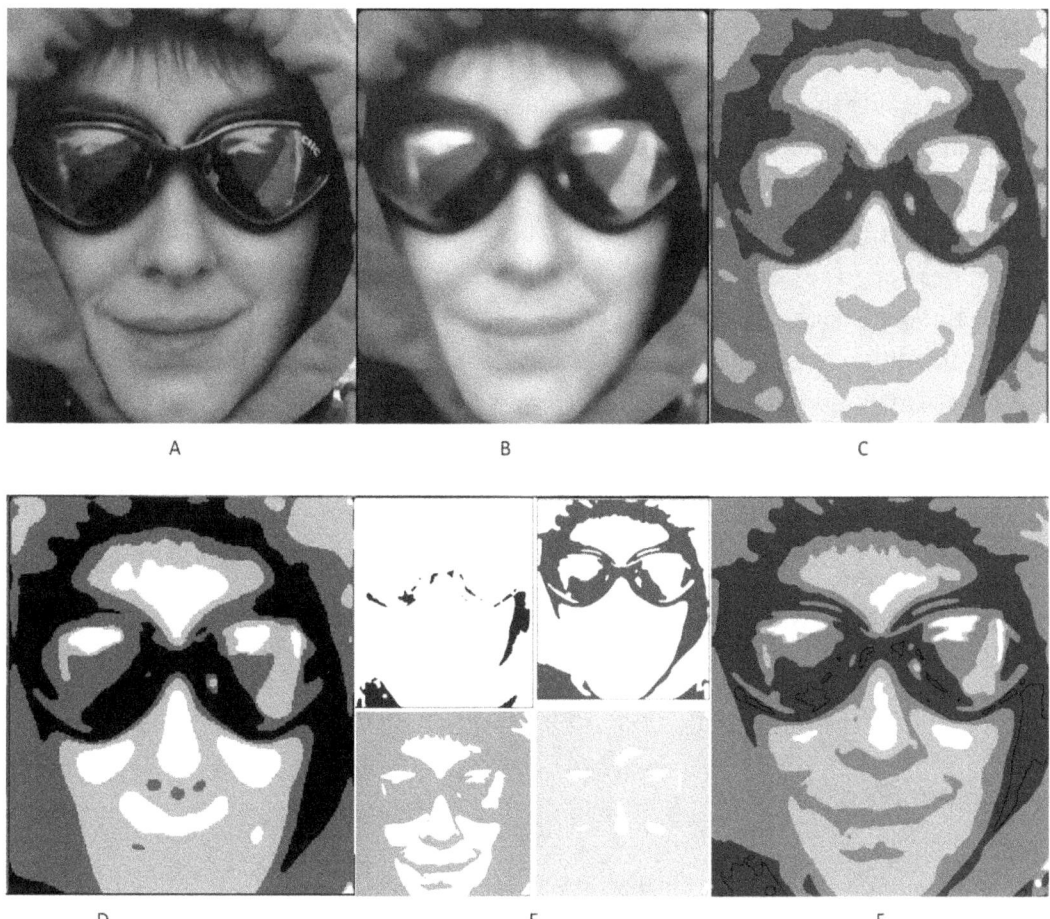

Figure 3-36. *(A) Original image. (B) Median filtered, size=8. (C) Multi-level thresholding using fixed differences between levels. (D) Multi-level thresholding using fixed number of pixels in each level. (E) Four manually selected thresholds. (F) Final result*

The tools we used are as follows:

Median filter to smooth the original image, giving Figure 3-36B. (median.pde)

Threshold multiple times to threshold Figure 3-36B into Figure 3-36E. (thresh.pde)

Overlay to combine the four images in Figure 3-36E to make Figure 3-36F. (overlay.pde)

CHAPTER 3   VALUE

Summary

Value refers to the brightness of a point in the scene, which is a pixel. Brightness is represented as a number between 0 and 255, with 255 being white and 0 being black. Images can be converted from color to gray by averaging the color values of each pixel. The gray-level histogram tells us how many pixels there are of each value in an image and can be used to adjust the brightness and contrast of the image.

A *boundary* is located at pixels where two regions in the image meet, and an *edge* is where the difference between values of adjacent pixels is large. Noise and distortions can cause artifacts, and we can smooth these by averaging over a small neighborhood of pixels using the mean or the median. Values can be represented by spatially distributed black and white pixels, which is what we call *half-toning* or *dithering* depending on how we do it.

Tools and Examples

ColorHist	- Draw r, g, b histograms
Gamma	- Gamma adjustment
Histogram	- Draw a histogram
HistogramEQ	- Equalize contrast using histogram
HistogtramFit	- Make an image fit a given histogram

Library Code

colorToGrey	- Convert to gray levels using the average of RGB
compareValue	- Compare two images for equality
contour	- Reduces gray levels to N
histogram	- Generate a histogram from an image
histogramMax	- Find the maximum value in a histogram
histogramMin	- Find the minimum value in a histogram
histogramMean	- Find the mean value in a histogram
histogramSD	- Find the standard deviation of a histogram
histogramDraw	- Draw a histogram
histogramNormalize	- Cause the histogram to contain values between 0 and 1
toGrey	- Convert an RGB value r color to a gray level specifying mode
bound	- Boundaries based on a threshold of gray/color. Output is "res.png"
canny	- Canny edge detector. Output is "cannyedges.png"
greenscreen -	
halftone	
histogram	- Build a display histogram of a gray image. Result in "histo.png"
grad	- Impose a linear left-to-right gray gradient on an image
median -	
overlay -	
stats	- Compute mean and standard deviation of image values
thresh	
threshall	- Provide thumbnails of all thresholds applied to an image. Result in "thumbs.png"

CHAPTER 3 VALUE

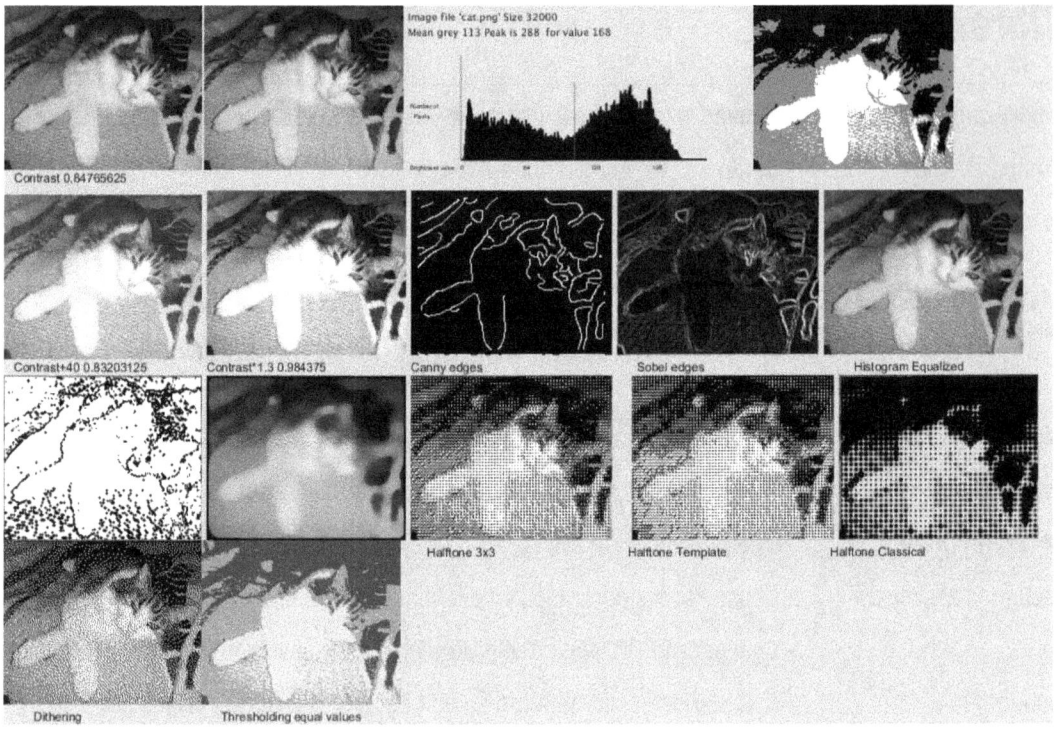

*The result of executing the program **library03**, which tests the library for this chapter.*

CHAPTER 4

Color

Color in *reality* is about the way that we humans perceive various frequencies of light and how we perceive combinations of frequencies. Color in *art* is about how we use those perceived frequencies and combine them to define shapes, create spaces, and – a fundamental aspect of art – to communicate emotions and create atmosphere. When using a computer to create art, an artist uses color in much the same manner as does an artist using paint, at least in terms of design. The differences lie in how each artist manages colors. When thinking in terms of computer vision and analysis, where we want a computer to do some interpretation of an image or scene, color is a feature of each region and pixel that might be related to other pixels.

As we have seen, a computer can only manipulate data that is in the form of numbers, and so we must have a way to represent a color as a number or collection of numbers. Of course we did that with value in the previous chapter by encoding a level of gray as a number. We've looked briefly at color on a computer, but now is the time for a deep dive.

Color Representations

When we were very young, we learned to identify colors by the names that people called them. Blue was, well, *blue*. We were *told* it was blue. Because of human perception, even young children can determine that various kinds of blue are still blue. But not all – blue has a transition into green, and at some point it's hard to say whether it's *blue* or *not-blue* (maybe green, in this case). Imagine that you have two different people looking at Figure 4-1 starting at the top. Tell them to point out where the image stops being blue and starts being green. People will nearly always indicate different locations.

CHAPTER 4 COLOR

Figure 4-1. *A color gradient moving from green to blue*

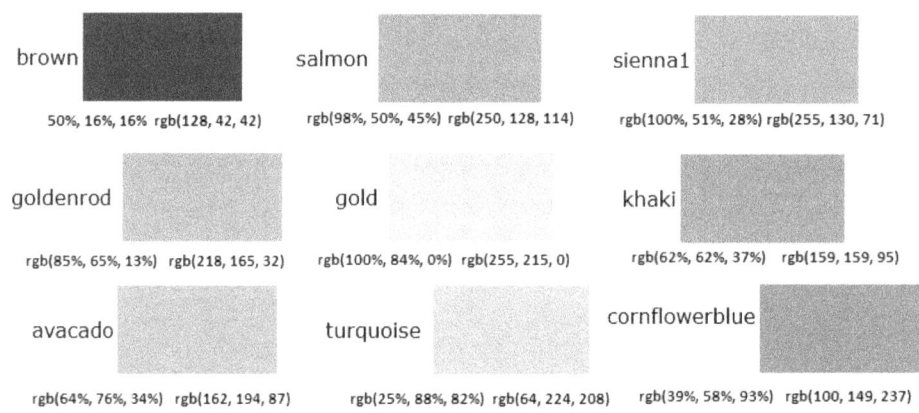

Figure 4-2. *Named colors and their percentage and RGB representations*

Human color perception is, as discussed in Chapter 1, "Art, Vision, and Computers," based on the three color sensors in our eyes: sensors for red, green, and blue. These will be called the *primary* colors. We will represent every color we perceive as a combination of these amounts of red; we can see none (0%), and the most is 100%, and the same is true for green and blue, then we can represent every color we can perceive as three numbers, the percentage of red, green, and blue at every point in our eye (on the retina). Most of the colors we see are in fact combinations of the three basic ones, and many of them have names. In Figure 4-2, there are a variety of named colors and their percentage values of red, green, and blue (in that order) and the conventional RGB value used on computers. If **C** is the color value of a pixel, then the component colors are **red(C)**, **green(C)**, and **blue(C)**. This is sometimes referred to as *additive color*. This is not how artists normally think of color.

In many programming environments each component will have a numerical value between 0 and 255, just like gray levels. A red component of 10% or 0.1 would be, in this environment, a red value of .1*255 = 25 (or 26). If we think of the three color components as three geometric axes, like x, y, and z, then all of the colors that are possible form a cube 255 units on each side (Figure 4-3). The color black is at the origin, being (0,0,0). The other extreme is white, which is (255,255,255). Along each axis, one of the colors changes from 0 to 255 (Figure 4-4).

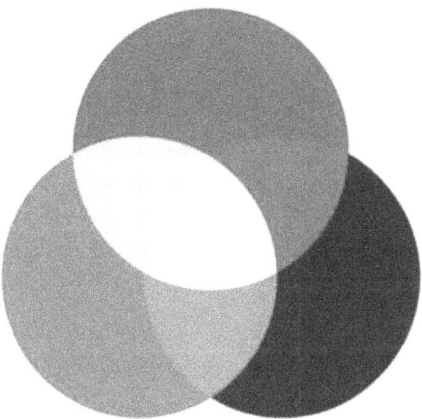

Figure 4-3. *How RGB colors combine*

CHAPTER 4   COLOR

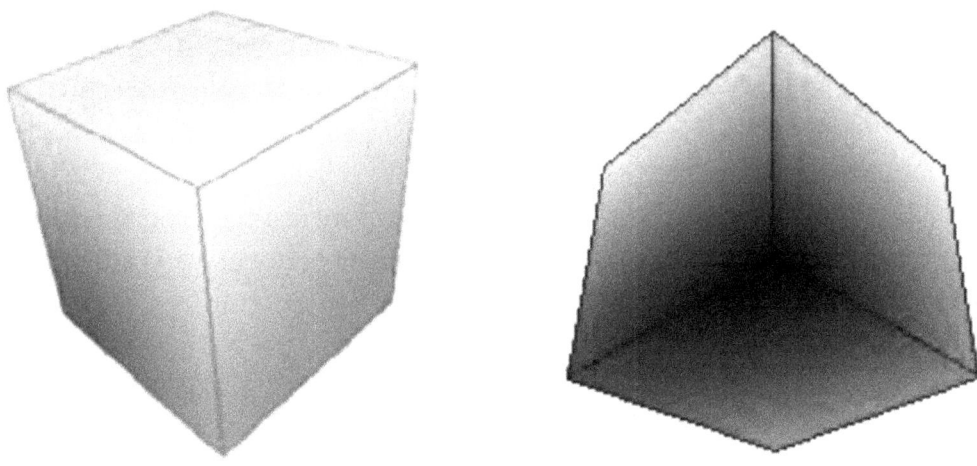

Figure 4-4. *The complete range of possible RGB colors can be shown as a cube, with each color – red, green, and blue – being one axis and increasing from 0 to 255*

The way that these colors appear to any person could vary, and by quite a lot, from how they seem to any other person or any other creature. An obvious example is that of red-green color blindness, where the sensors for red or green are missing, weak, or non-functional. If someone has no sensors for red, then they see the color completely in shades of green and blue.

So we see that color perception is relative. Some people (and animals) see color differently from others. This could be important when creating some artworks. It's also important to remember that humans all have similar cultural biases about colors based on what they have learned, and that's probably more relevant.

Let's return to childhood for a moment. Colors have names. If a child is given crayons, then the colors in that set will define to a great degree what colors they can use in an artwork. A six-crayon box might have yellow, purple, red, green, blue, and black, and that would therefore be our spectrum, our *palette*. Mom's face might well be yellow and my dog purple, because they have to use what they have. A box of colors allows them to define colors more precisely, because the colors are specified by using a *name*.

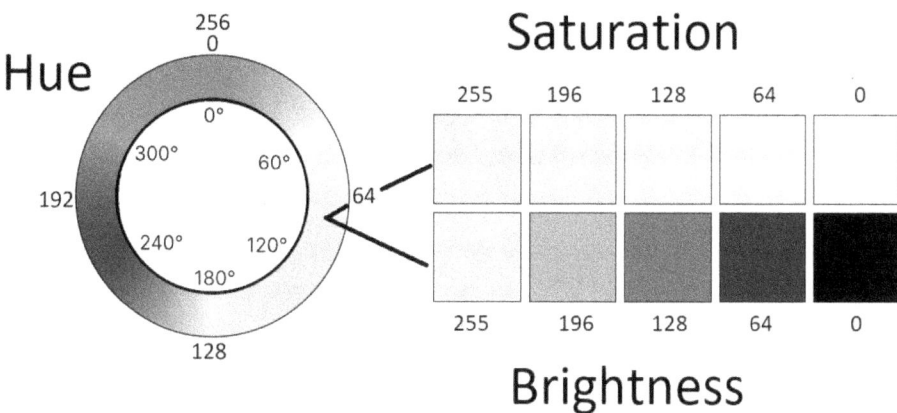

Figure 4-5. *(Left) The visual display of numeric values for hue. (Right) The effect of decreasing the saturation and brightness*

Hue, Saturation, and Brightness

Imagine we have a photograph, and we want to select all the *red* pixels for some reason. Maybe we're looking for apples. The problem is which pixels are those, exactly? Can we look for pixels that have a red component of, say, 250 and above? No. The color white has a red component of 255. The difficulty arises because we have a three-dimensional problem. The color red occupies a *volume* of the color cube; that is, a range in each of the red, green, and blue dimension. This makes it tricky to identify colors in pictures.

The hue, saturation, and brightness system, or HSB, simplifies this by separating out the color portion from the rest of the pixel components. The H in HSB stands for hue, and this refers to the color. It's still a number, but each hue value is one identifiable color, beginning with **h=0** as red. As **h** increases, the red changes in nature so that it becomes the next color, orange, and then the next, yellow, and so on. This means that the color *red* is now a simple range of hue values, as defined by the individual artist. The value of the hue increases to its maximum, which is 255, and then back to 0. That means that if the color changes are to be smooth, a hue of 255 is right next to red, but from the other direction. Confusing? Check out Figure 4-5. We can see that hue forms a circle of colors that change smoothly toward another color as **h** changes. Because this is a circle, it makes sense to think of hue values as angles, from 0 to 360 degrees. We can do this without modifying the basic idea. So a color of 180 degrees is *cyan*, and *green* is about 120 degrees. All we've done is multiply the hue values by a number that changes the range. The value 128/255 is the same as 180/380, and both represent the same color.

141

CHAPTER 4   COLOR

What is *saturation*, the second component? It is the *amount* of color, the intensity, from a minimum of 0 to a maximum of 255, which means as much of that color as we can display. As saturation gets smaller, the color fades through pastels and to white. Saturation can create the illusion of spatial depth. It can also draw attention to a specific point of focus.

Figure 4-6. *Monet's Impression, Sunrise*

An example of art that uses a high level of color saturation is Claude Monet's *Impression, Sunrise* (1872) (Figure 4-6). There is a generally low color saturation, but higher intensity is evident in the sun, which becomes the focus of the painting.

Brightness is what it sounds like: how much light is in the color. It is the *value* as discussed in the previous chapter. As the brightness value gets smaller, the color gets darker until it becomes black. This is how artists achieve *low-key* and *high-key* works. Brightness changes add emphasis.

The HSB color model, sometimes called HSV (V for value) or HIS (I for intensity), can be converted into RGB. Actually, this must be true because the same devices display both. However, the conversion is a rather opaque mathematical formula that does not really affect us because we can always get the HSB values from a pixel **P** using the functions **hue(P)**, **saturation(P)**, and **brightness(P)** in *Processing*. Other graphics systems have an equivalent.

CHAPTER 4   COLOR

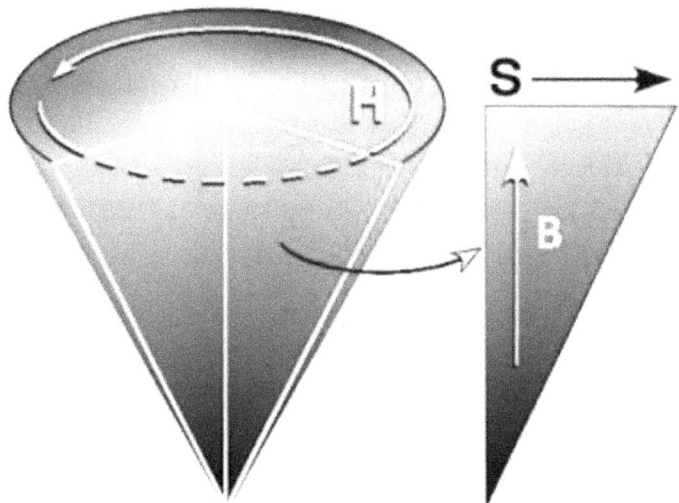

Figure 4-7. *The HSB color cone*

The set of all RGB values forms a color cube, as we mentioned. HSB values form a *cone* (Figure 4-7). The hue values form a circle; brightness is the vertical axis, and as saturation gets smaller, the radius of the hue circle decreases. That's because saturation refers to the vividness of a color, and chroma is purity. As we add white to a color, it becomes less saturated, and saturation changes with value. Saturation depends on the range of values (brightness); when the range is 0, the color is gray, and saturation=0. As the range of values gets smaller, the range of saturation does too, hence the cone shape. This makes for a nice picture, but what it really means is that the hue value has less meaning as brightness and/or saturation gets smaller. Using our original example of finding red pixels, we now know that we can define *red* as a pixel between 0 and 10 and between 245 and 255. But if the saturation of that pixel was, say, 10, then the hue would be meaningless because the pixel would look white. If the same pixel had a brightness of 10, then it would appear to be black. Yes, it would still technically be red, but not to the eye.

Of course, artists generally use *subtractive* color mixing, because that is the process used when mixing paints, pastels, and so on. RGB and HSB are foreign concepts to most artists. Hue is understood, and saturation is connected to something artists call *chroma*. Brightness is the same as *value*. The three as a combination that defines color is not a usual idea. Is it possible to make color mixing more intuitive to a typical artist? Yes, but it is not natural for a computer and the usual displays it uses.

143

Paint and Subtractive Mixing

When using paints, we can mix the colors together to make different ones. Mixing blue and yellow gives a green color, yellow and red give orange, and so on. We learned this process in school after we used crayons, and it lets us make any color we want, in principle. It is interesting that it does not work the same way that mixing colors using a computer does. Mixing pigments is different from mixing light in pixels, because paint works by *absorbing* light.

Can we do this on a computer? Sure. But it can be conceptually difficult and differs from the usual RGB mixing. Visually, mixing paints is quite clear. The math is unusual, though, and computers use math *all* the time.

The RYB Color Model

In this model the primaries are red, yellow, and blue, which is probably what you learned in art school. Mixing yellow and blue yields green, a characteristic of subtractive color systems, and is something that does *not* happen when using RGB. Computer scientists and engineers, and not artists, devised the fundamentals of computer graphics in the 1960s and 1970s. RGB is logical based on how we detect color in our eyes, but it's not intuitive for an artist.

There are not many computer implementations of RYB available that we can use as examples, and it's difficult to find a correct algorithm for converting between RGB and RYB. There are a few articles published, but too many of them have errors. Here's something that appears to work.

Converting RGB to RYB

This process will be described without a detailed *why* explanation. Unlike RGB, the RYB color space is not based on any psychological perception model but is instead based on experiences of idealized paint mixing. The variables **r**, **g**, and **b** are the color channels to be converted into RYB space. First, scale these to values between 0.0 and 1.0 by dividing by 255.0. Then remove the white from the color. White is **min(r,g,b)**:

```
r=r/255; g=g/255; b=b/255;   // Scale
w = min(r, g, b); // Remove the whiteness from the color.
r -= w;
g -= w;
```

```
b -= w;
```

We now remove the yellow from the red/green channels. Red/green creates yellow in RGB, and white has equal values of r, g, and b. We"ll add it back after converting.

```
y = min(r, g);
r -= y;
g -= y;
```

If this color combines blue and green, then we will reduce these components by ½ so that we preserve the maximum range.

```
if (b>0 && g>0)
{
    b /= 2.0;
    g /= 2.0;
}
```

The remaining green is now distributed between the new yellow component **y** and the blue channel (yellow+blue= green):

```
y += g;
b += g;
```

We now normalize again to keep the range 0.0 .. 1.0:

```
mg = max(r, g, b);
my = max(r, y, b);
if (my!=0)
{
    n = mg / my;
    r *= n;
    y *= n;
    b *= n;
}
```

Now we add the white back in and return the color, rescaled to 0..255::

```
r += w;
y += w;
```

```
    b += w;
    return color(r*255, y*255, b*255);
```

We are using the built-in type **color** from *Processing* to return one value instead of three color channels. We must remember that in this case we are using the green channel as *yellow*, and we can't display this value directly. Similarly, the function **green** actually returns the yellow component.

This code comprises the function **toRYB(r, g, b)**. To convert back, we provide the function **toRGB(r, y, b)**.

Mixing

Mixing RYB colors is not a matter of adding the components, as it is when using RGB; it is supposed to be a subtractive mixture (Figure 4-8). If we simply add the components, the brightness will increase, which is incorrect. We need an algorithm for the subtractive mixing process.

Let's say that we want to mix two RYB colors, **a** and **b**, and have a blending value **f** specified, where if **f=0**, then the result is all from **a**; if **f=1**, it is all from **b**; and if **f=0.5**, it is a 50-50 mix of the two. The first step is to invert each color component by component: r = 255.0-r, y = 255-y, b = 255-b. Color **c** is the inverse of **a**, and **d** is the inverse of **b**. Then subtract **c** and **d** from pure white, giving new color **e**, making sure to keep the range between 0 and 255. Like this:

```
red(e)    = max (0.0, 255-red(c)-red(d))
yellow(e) = max (0.0, 255-yellow(c)-yellow(d))
blue(e)   = max (0.0, 255-blue(c)-blue(d))
```

The color **e** is a purely subtractive result. Next compute the distance (Euclidean) between **a** and **d**:

```
cd = dist(red(a), yellow(a),
         blue(a), red(b), yellow(b), blue(b))
```

Now convert this into a value that regulates how much additive/subtractive mixing gets done:

```
cd=4.0*f*(1.0-f)*cd;
```

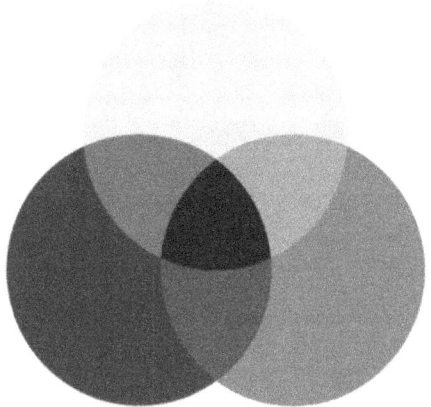

Figure 4-8. *How RYB colors combine*

This ensures that small values of **f** give colors very close to **a** or **b**. Finally, we additively mix colors **a** and **b** in the proportions given by **f** and then use the value of **cd** to blend this with the purely subtractive result **e**:

```
// Additive mix of a and b
    mixr =
      (1.0f)*red(a)+f*red(b)
// A linear interpolation
    mixy = (1.0-f)*yellow(a)+f*yellow(b)
    mixb = (1.0-f)*blue(a)+f*blue(b)
    mixr = (1.0-cd)*red(mixr)+cd*red(e)      // Subtractive mix
                                             // of this with e
    mixy = (1.0-cd)*yellow(mixr)+cd*yellow(e)
    mixr = (1.0-cd)*blue(mixr)+cd*blue(e)
```

The color **(mixr, mixy, mixb)** is the final result. (From https://github.com/ProfJski/ArtColors) Figure 4-9 shows some results of this way of mixing colors. Note particularly that mixing two reds that are exactly the same gives the same color as the result, which is what we would expect, and that the results are darker than the originals. NOTE that we must convert RYB to RGB before displaying the color, because a monitor can't display RYB.

CHAPTER 4 COLOR

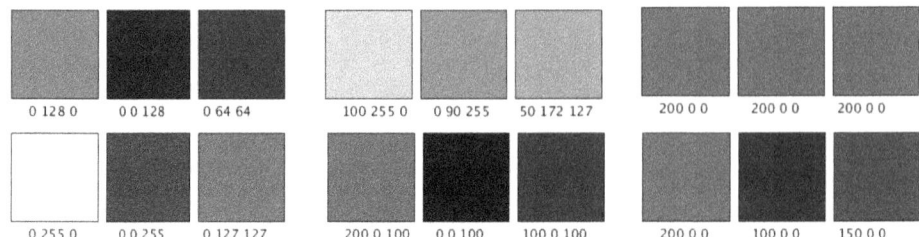

Figure 4-9. *Mixing RYB colors using the subtractive process described*

The CMYK Color Model

The **CMYK** color coordinate space is also subtractive. It's used in computer printers to print color on paper, and it also has similarities to mixing paints, although it is restricted by the limited color range of a printer. The primary colors in this model are **C**yan, **M**agenta, and **Y**ellow, and there is a black coordinate **K**.

Any color coordinate system should allow all of the colors possible in other systems, and so it should be possible to convert from one to the other, as we could between HSB and RGB. Without doing any unnecessary math, the conversion from RGB is:

$$C = \frac{1 - \frac{R}{255} - K}{(1-K)} * 255 \quad M = \frac{\left(1 - \frac{G}{255} - K\right)}{(1-K)} * 255$$

$$Y = \frac{\left(1 - \frac{B}{255} - K\right)}{(1-k)} * 255 \quad K = \left(1 - \left(\frac{\max(R,G,B)}{255}\right)\right) * 255$$

This gives CMYK values in the usual range. Now let's see how combining them works. If we combine red and green in RGB, we get yellow: red is (255, 0, 0), green is (0, 255, 0), and the result of adding them is (255, 255, 0).

Now convert into CMYK. In those coordinates, R=(255, 0, 0) is (0, 255, 255, 0); G=(0, 255, 0) is (255, 0, 255, 0). **By the way, in CMYK there is no such color as "white."** White in CMYK is *visually* white if the background has no color, which assumes that the background is white paper.

148

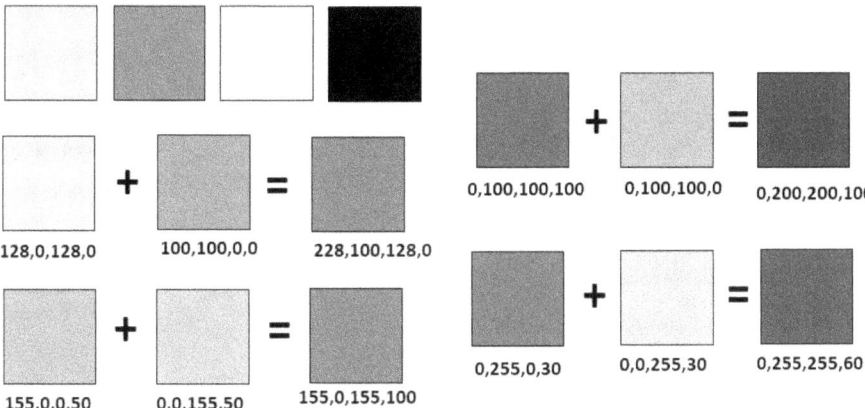

Figure 4-10. *CMYK colors and their mixtures*

As usual, the concept of color mixing is not simple, and there are many ways to do it. Our method of mixing RYB differs from how we mix RGB, for example. If we add two CMYK colors together, coordinate by coordinate, the result is darker unless we add nothing (0 value) (Figure 4-10). We can't display a CMYK color on the screen directly, though, so we must convert it into RGB as we did before. With CMYK colors, subtractive mixing occurs when the components are summed; we treat them as paint, and in a real sense they are if they are being sprayed onto paper.

Munsell

A man named Albert Munsell devised a system that tried to accurately describe the psychological experience of color, or in other words, its *perception*. Other systems describe the *physics*, more or less. They describe *light* of a specific frequency that has bounced off an object and passed through a mathematical function that is a simple model of a human eye. They deal with the technical aspects of the light. Munsell was trained as an artist, so he had a different insight into color.

Munsell notation describes what color some *object actually is.* Which is to say, it is an effort to describe what people perceive when they look at the object. It also describes the colors of objects as we see them under a wide variety of illuminants. Mr. Munsell conducted extensive experiments with human subjects using clever devices of his own design. As a result, all the Munsell scales represent actual human data, and he calibrated the value so that equal differences at all levels represent equal perceived changes seen by a typical human with normal vision. Thus, the Munsell codes are quite difficult to convert into other representations we use on a computer.

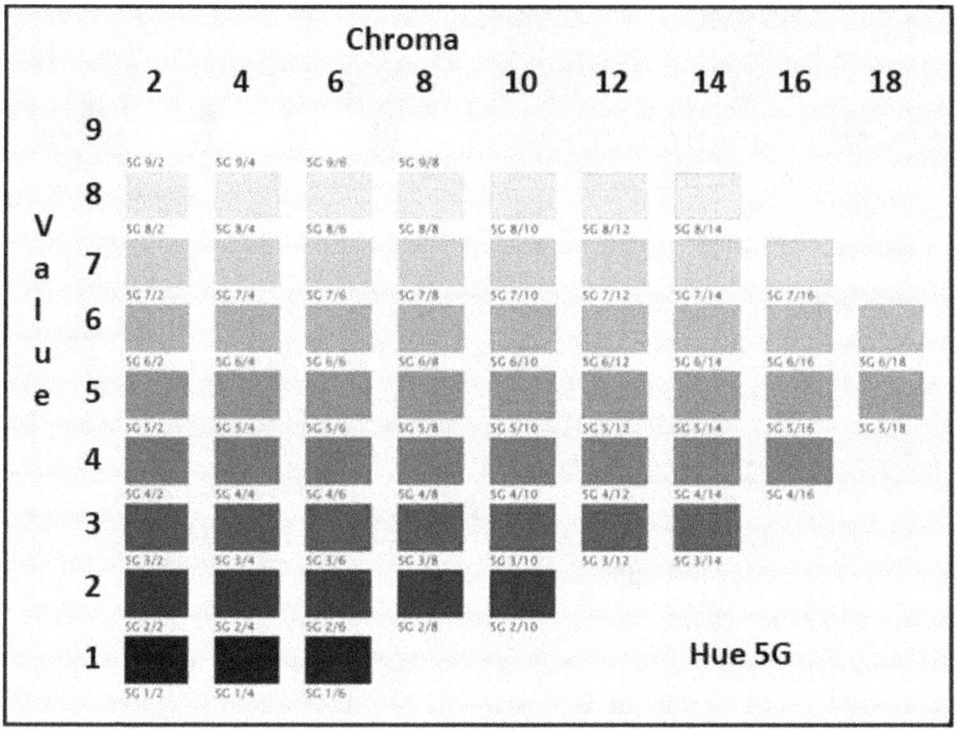

CHAPTER 4   COLOR

Figure 4-11. *The Munsell color chart for the hue 5G (green)*

Munsell defined three attributes that sound very much like the HSB system; however, his work predates HSB and in many ways differs from it. The three values he named were *hue*, *value*, and *chroma*.

The *hue* represents the color itself: green, blue, and so on. These are not numbers; they are letter codes like **R** (red) and **Y**ellow-**R**ed (**YR**). There are five principal hues: **R**ed, **Y**ellow, **G**reen, **B**lue, and **P**urple. There are five intermediate hues, each being halfway between two principal ones (e.g., **YR** is halfway in between **Y**ellow and **R**ed). This gives 10 colors, and each is broken into 10 sub-steps for a total of 100.

Value is, as always, the lightness or darkness of the color. Lighter colors have higher numbers. The range is 0–10.

Chroma represents how strong the color is, similar to saturation. It is also a number, typically between 2 and 14, with higher numbers representing stronger colors. Interestingly, *there is no upper limit to the chroma value.* Some colors, fluorescent ones for instance, have chroma values in the 30s. We can use this system to represent colors that cannot be displayed on a computer screen, and in fact some that would be difficult to actually use in reality. Think of them as theoretical in the higher range.

Figure 4-11 shows an example of a Munsell color chart. The name of the hue is given as text, in this case in the upper right. Value increases from the bottom to the top of the chart. Not all values have to appear. Chroma increases from left to right. Each row shows colors with the same value, and each column has the same chroma.

There are many of these charts, and because the numbers are perceptual, a mathematical conversion is not really possible. What we do is try to match RGB values to a Munsell color and then use *interpolation* to find the value in between. Interpolation is a mathematical estimate of what value should be between two others given that we can find some pattern in those numbers. There is no formula to convert Munsell to RGB and back.

It is difficult to use this system in generative art because the media, which is to say screens and printers, do not reproduce accurate colors, and there are many Munsell colors that do not have a digital (RGB) representation and vice versa.

Munsell Digital Tool

We have data files of Munsell *renotations,* or conversions to RGB, obtained from Paul Centore, 2011. A sample rgb to Munsell entry is:

```
136     68      204     2.17P   4.30    16.90
```

which says that RGB=(136,68,204) is the "same" color as Munsell 2.17P 4.30 16.90
A reverse example is:

```
5.0R    1       6       64      2       29
```

CHAPTER 4 COLOR

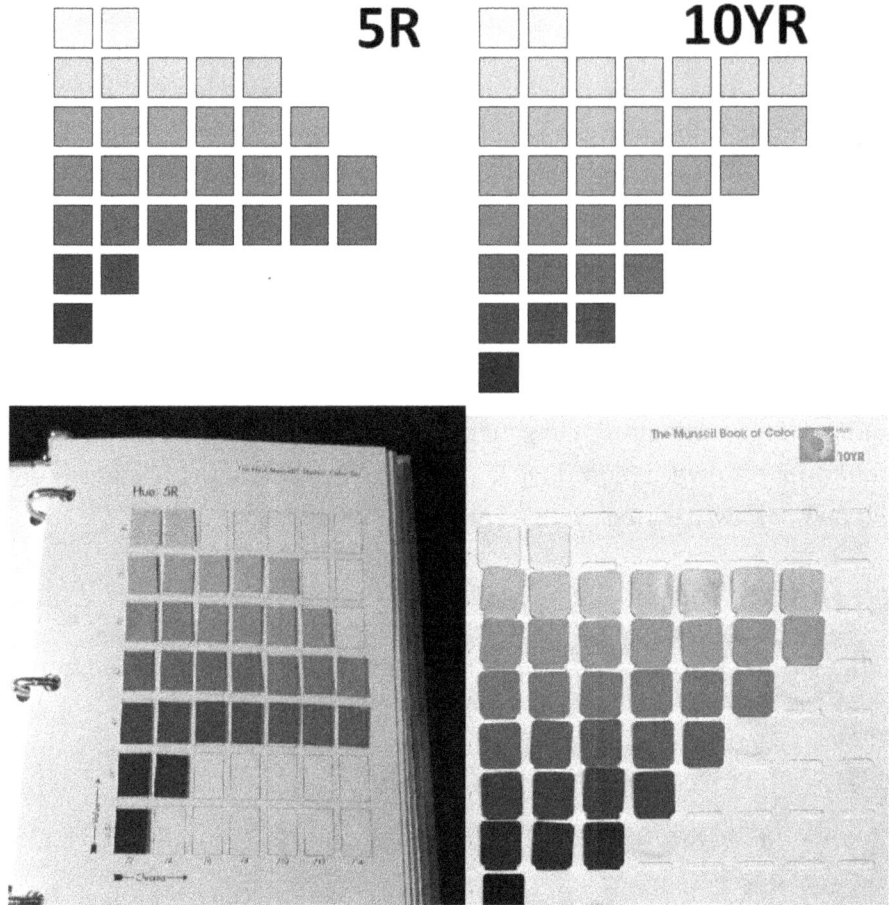

Figure 4-12. *(Top) The results from the conversion system are presented here. (Bottom) The same colors from the Munsell Book of Color*

which says that 5R/1/6 is RGB (64,2,29).

Because these are tables, an entry for some RGB or Munsell value may not exist. In that case an interpolated value is the best we can do, or we could use the nearest value. It won't likely be exactly right, but it should be close.

Our scheme uses a file of 6624 entries, each being a Munsell code and an equivalent RGB code. Given a Munsell code (H, V, C), the method first finds a hue in the data file that is nearest to the hue H requested. This gives the hue a priority in the search. We then look for hue values near to H that are the best match for (V, C). Finally, we use the RGB values for that Munsell color as obtained from the file.

Munsell would be spinning in his grave, because he went to such trouble to get just noticeable differences in his colors, and here we are playing fast and loose. The results of our conversion will be based only on the data files that we have, and even those are not perfect. RGB coordinates did not exist when Munsell did his work. This conversion is an approximate one only.

The program takes a Munsell color (e.g., 5R/5/12) and gives an RGB triplet that will be near to that color. The accuracy is limited, but we can see from Figure 4-12 how this program compares to the actual Munsell *Book of Color*. Of course, the samples from the book are photographs and are not at all perfect either.

Color from Value

We know how to convert a color image into gray: use the HSB brightness value, or average three r, g, and b channels. This conversion discards that color (hue) component completely. There can be many quite distinct colors that have the same gray value by these methods. We'd expect that, because we're throwing away 16 bits of data (the hue and saturation) for each pixel. That's a lot of information.

Can we recover that information? No. So the problem of adding color to a monochrome image is, in principle, an impossible one. We have, on the other hand, seen old movies that have been *colorized*. How does that work? Using a lot of manual intervention.

Pseudocolor (False Color)

Figure 4-13. *Monochrome images converted into color using a lookup table (LUT)*

CHAPTER 4   COLOR

Some images are intrinsically gray. When taking photos in the infrared, as an example, the camera only captures the value of all frequencies as gray, and so it's pretty easy to convert this into color – simply map grays onto colors using a table, where we assign brighter grays to "hotter" seeming colors. The same is true of X-rays, CAT scans, range images, and many others. Smaller values (darker) might represent cooler temperatures on account of how the images are produced by the device in this case, so the visual appearance might be fairly accurate to a human.

These simulated color images are often created using a *look-up table*, or *LUT*. A computer program or a human creates a mapping of the gray values to colors and places these in a table. Indexing the table at index v for gray value v gives a color that has been assigned to that gray level. The color that is used for gray level v is lut[v].

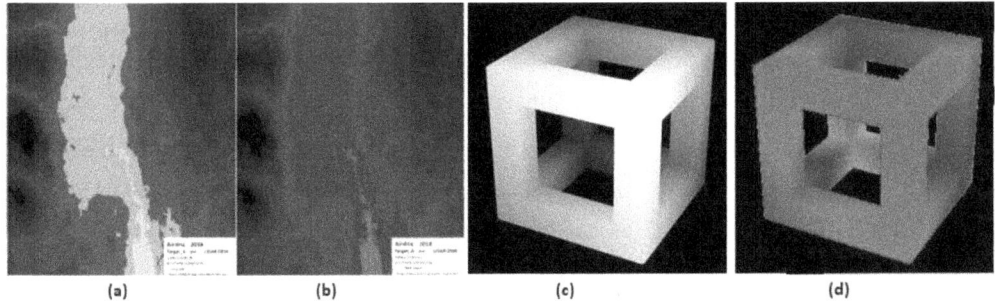

Figure 4-14. *(a) Digital elevation model data frequently yields low-contrast images. The model after condensing levels and contrast enhancement. (Right) False color. Lower elevations are in the blue range and indicate possible flooding areas. (c) A range map, where near distances to the object are light values and distant ones are dark. (d) Mapping colors onto value so that near pixels (white) become red and far colors (dark) become blue.* `https://www.flickr.com/photos/dominicspics/5393875375/`

We've created a LUT that's designed for infrared images. It has 256 colors, with the lower indices being cold (blue) and large ones being hot (yellow-red) (Figure 4-13).

Figure 4-14 shows a type of range image, where distances are given different levels of gray or color. This is a *digital elevation model (DEM)*, where height above sea level rather than distance from the camera is recorded. Coloring the image can clearly show low-lying areas, where floods are most likely to occur. They are blues in this image and were created by using the histogram to find where the images changed value and then assigning hues to distinct levels.

There are inexpensive devices that will use sound to digitize an object in three dimensions. They too create an image in which values correspond to distances. Figure 4-14c and d shows the distance map generated by such a device and a color rendering.

Space Images

In some cases, usually older ones, cameras were monochrome for technical reasons, and there was special technology used to add color. The Voyager space probes, in fact, had monochrome cameras and had a series of color filters they could place in front of the lens to capture frequency-dependent images. Combining these can create a full-color image. Voyager would take a sequence of images of, for example, Jupiter through multiple filters. Of course, Voyager would move between images, and so we had to align them, and then the three colors are collected together into each pixel.

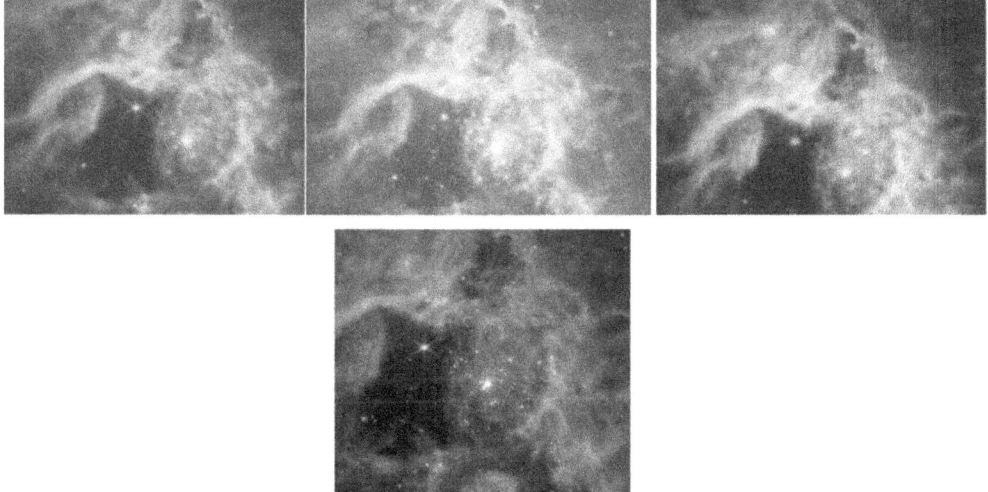

Figure 4-15. *The three monochrome images taken through color filters in a Hubble telescope image, and the color combination that results. NASA*

Oh, and the filters are not red, green, and blue but are orange, violet, and blue. We can't just stick the values into a color channel and hope they work out. It takes a great deal of fiddling about and mathematics to get the great images that we see on the Internet. We can see the input data and simple result for an image from the Hubble telescope looking at a nebula in Figure 4-15. The red, green, and blue images are shown first, and they are clearly different in detail. When we assign pixels in each image to color channels and put them together in one image, one possible result is shown on the right.

Colorization

In the early days of colorization, the frames of the film were colored by hand, one at a time. There are 24 frames per second, 1440 per minute, and 86,400 per hour. That's a lot of human work. When computers could process images, they were used to colorize films, again using human input, but the programs could identify the regions that had certain colors and modify the brightness and saturation as the regions changed from frame to frame.

A human would color one of the frames by hand. The trick is to color the *next* frame automatically, based on the given colors and motion that occurred between the two frames. We could call this *tracking*. The pixels in a small region will be in a similarly placed region in the next frame; positions don't change too much in 1/24 (film) or 1/30 (television) of a second.

These days we do colorization using *deep learning* and *neural networks*, so the older methods have become obsolete.

Color Temperature

Color temperature references color as *warm* or *cool* hues. That term refers to how we feel about the colors, but there are many reasons to understand something about color temperature. For example, we can make paintings more interesting and dynamic if we understand that cool colors will appear to move to the back of a painting, whereas warm ones seem to be in front. Thus, we use warm colors for things we want in the foreground. Objects like mountains far away in real life have a cool blue color due to atmospheric effects.

People who specialize in lighting, as in lighting for homes and galleries and theaters, also use a color temperature, but it differs from what we are speaking of here. When considering lights, there are issues such as how that light affects what we see (a gallery), what kind of impression we want to make, and what real-world scene we are making. For example, sometimes daylight in the morning and evening has a "warmer" color temperature. When speaking of lighting, the cooler colors have a higher temperature, strangely. This differs from the idea of color temperature in art generally.

CHAPTER 4 COLOR

Color temperature is somewhat subjective and not well quantified, so little effort has gone into digital implementations. We *do* know that we can make an image or color warmer by increasing the red component, and we can make it cooler by increasing the blue component. Thus, an implementation that changes the temperature of an image by amount *delta* is:

Code: file `temperature.pde`

Algorithm: *temperature* – adjust the color temperature of an image

```
void temperature (PImage res,
            float delta)
  color p;
  float r, g, b;
  for(int i=0; i<res.width; i++)

    for (int j=0; j<res.height; j++)
    {
      p = res.get(i,j);
      r = red(p); g = green(p);
      b = blue(p);
      r = r + delta;
      if (r>255) r=255;
        else if (r<0) r = 0;
      b = b-delta;
      if (b>255) b=255;
        else if (b<0) b = 0;
      res.set(i,j, color(r, g, b));
    }
}
```

Given a temperature adjustment on the range delta = -100 to 100,

apply the following adjustment to each pixel in the image:

Get the pixel color

Increase red by delta
Check the range 0–255

Decrease blue by delta
Check the range 0–255
Write the new color to the image

157

CHAPTER 4 COLOR

Figure 4-16 shows this applied to a landscape image. The left shows the original; the center shows the image warmed by 20 degrees (delta = 20); the right shows the image cooled by 20 degrees. The effect on the image is obvious. Using this tool, we can adjust colors to achieve various composition goals.

Color temperature has various visual effects that we can play with:

- It can create a sense of perspective.

- It can make the same object appear dull or bright.

- It creates and enhances contrast.

- Desaturated colors seem cool (e.g., pastel colors).

- Warm colors can make a space seem bigger, while cool colors make it seem smaller.

- Color temperature is relative – the same color will look different depending on what it's next to.

Variations on a Color

We have all been in a hardware store or paint store and seen the variety of colored chips that we can use to select the perfect paint for the kitchen. Very often each card has variations on a single color, sometimes very slight ones. There can be twenty or more cards, each with ten color variations (usually named) on one basic color, hundreds of different greens or blues. People love color and love these variations.

Figure 4-16. *(a) Original image. (b) Image warmed by 20 degrees. (c) Image cooled by 20 degrees*

Commercial paints, inks, monitors, and printers use the standard names Pantone® for maintaining the standard. That is, these colors are matched against a paint to ensure that the colors are always the same. (We can find it there at https://www.pantone-colours.com/). Computer monitors used by artists, for example, need to be calibrated

CHAPTER 4 COLOR

from time to time to ensure that the colors displayed are faithful and can be duplicated precisely on another calibrated monitor. In any room with multiple computer screens, it's easy to see how widely the colors can vary. It turns out that there are standard ways to modify colors to get specific variations.

Tints

A tint is specifically the adding of pure white to some color. When using RGB coordinates, it is a matter of adding values to each of R, G, and B. It's not the *same* value, though. 255 is the maximum value of a coordinate. Let's call 255-R the *headroom* in the red color, which is to say it is the number of values remaining until it reaches the maximum. Each color has a different headroom in most cases, and the value we add to each is dependent on that. For each coordinate, the tint is determined, for some factor f between 0 and 1, as:

```
r = headroom(r)*f + r = (255 - r)*f + r
g = headroom(g)*g + g = (255 - g)*f + g
b = headroom(b)*b + b = (255 - b)*f + b
```

So each color coordinate has a different value added to it that depends on the color being modified. The factor f is the degree or amount of the tint; the greater the factor, the lighter the tint.

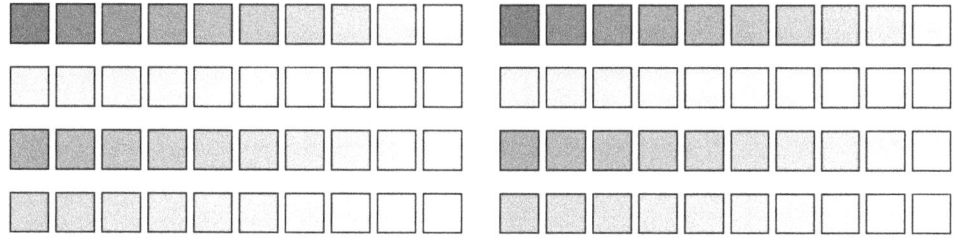

Figure 4-17. *Tints of the colors teal, lawn green, orchid, and tan. (Left) Using RGB. (Right) Using HSB*

When using HSB coordinates, things are a little different. We have to modify both saturation and brightness. The brightness is increased, but the saturation is decreased. We know that as saturation gets smaller, the color changes toward white. The headroom

159

CHAPTER 4   COLOR

for brightness is the same as for RGB, but for saturation, it is the difference between the current value and 0, or simply the saturation itself. So we have:

```
h = h
s = s - s*f
b = (255-b)*f + b
```

Figure 4-17 shows some examples.

Why would we care? Because color is often used to characterize objects in a picture. Objects can vary in color with the illumination and due to their shape. A red sphere will not have the same value of red everywhere in a photograph, but we can hope that they will be tints of each other.

Shades

We get a *shade* from a color by adding black. This is easy to do, because the headroom for each color value is the value itself: the distance to 0. We can simply multiply each value by the specified factor **f**, where **f** is between 0 and 1. Smaller values of **f** make the shade darker.

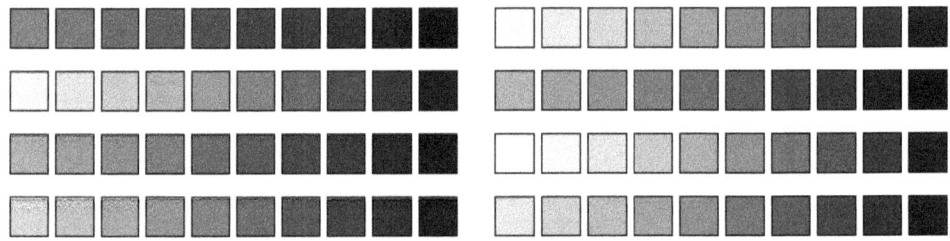

Figure 4-18. *Shades. Beginning colors, counterclockwise from upper left: teal, lawn green, orchid, tan, lavender, tomato, yellow, and thistle*

```
r1 = r*f
g1 = g*f
b1 = b*f
```

If we used the formulas developed for tint, then we'd have:

```
r1 = r-r*f
g1 = g-g*f
b1 = b-b*f
```

These have the same results *except* that the role of **f** changes: now *larger* values of **f** make the shade darker. Figure 4-18 shows examples of shades.

Tones

Tones are more complex visually because they involve adding gray to a color. Gray, of course, consists of white and black, both being components of both tints and shades. The result can be colors that are either lighter or darker than the original hue, depending on the type of gray you're mixing it with.

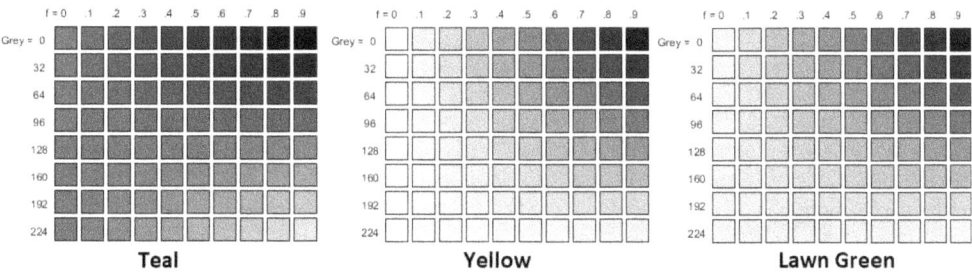

Figure 4-19. *The tones are created using specific colors, factors, and gray values*

The implementation uses something called a *weighted average*. We specify a color, a gray value, and a factor between 0.0 and 1.0. The result is the color value weighted by **f** added to the gray value weighted by **1-f**. A gray value is a color in which the three components are equal, so we only need one number here, between 0 and 255, indicating the brightness of the gray. The calculation of the new color given **f** and **grey** is:

```
r1 = r * f + (1-f)*grey
g1 = g * f + (1-f)*grey
b1 = b * f + (1-f)*grey
```

This number can never exceed 255, so the range will be fine. There are two parameters here, and that makes interpreting things more complicated than it was for shades and tints. Using a very light gray can lighten the color; a dark gray will darken it. In either case the color is muted, essentially becoming less intense or less saturated. Figure 4-19 shows examples of tones.

Most colors we actually encounter in real life are not pure, intense colors. Muted colors such as tones create a feel of quiet and calm. On the other hand, large areas of such colors are boring and fail to attract the viewer's attention. It is common to see bright, saturated colors in cartoons because they *do* attract attention, and so using them too much often causes the resulting work to seem "cartoony" or unsophisticated. We should use a variety of tones and more saturated colors to create contrast and draw attention to critical parts of the composition.

Figure 4-20. *The Night Café (1888) by Vincent van Gogh. This painting used red and green (complementary) to express what van Gogh called "the terrible human passions." Public domain, via Wikimedia Commons*

Color Pairings

Artworks use multiple colors, as a rule. Artists have themes that involve specific palettes, or groupings of colors. Sometimes colors go very well together, and sometimes they clash. How do we select colors that we know will be compatible with a given main color? We call this color harmony, and it usually means using a limited set of colors. We also want to balance saturated and muted tones and match warm and cool colors. Artists usually have a good sense for colors that go well together, but it can be calculated.

Complementary Colors

Complementary colors are on opposite sides of the hue color wheel. This is independent of tone or shade and is a high-contrast pairing of colors (Figure 4-20). We find them on opposite sides of the color wheel (Figure 4-21).

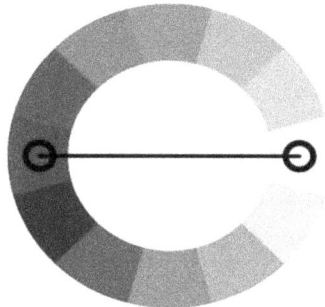

Figure 4-21. *Complementary colors*

Every pair of complementary colors has one warm and one cool color. If you want a lively sunset or simply strong, vivid colors, this is what you want. We can think of one of the colors as dominant, which we use in the larger areas of the work, and the second color will be more of an accent.

We can also mix complementary colors together to make a less vibrant hue.

Split Complementary Colors

There are three colors in this selection: a dominant color and two accents. Again, using the color wheel, we select these by using an isosceles triangle (Figure 4-22). The angle between the dominant color and the two others is important but not critical up to a point – the relationship remains.

CHAPTER 4   COLOR

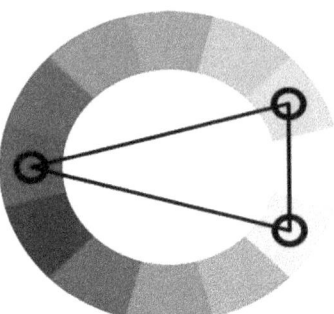

Figure 4-22. *Split Complementary Colors*

These colors are easy to use and hard to get wrong, but it is possible to create some combination that is too loud for a specific purpose.

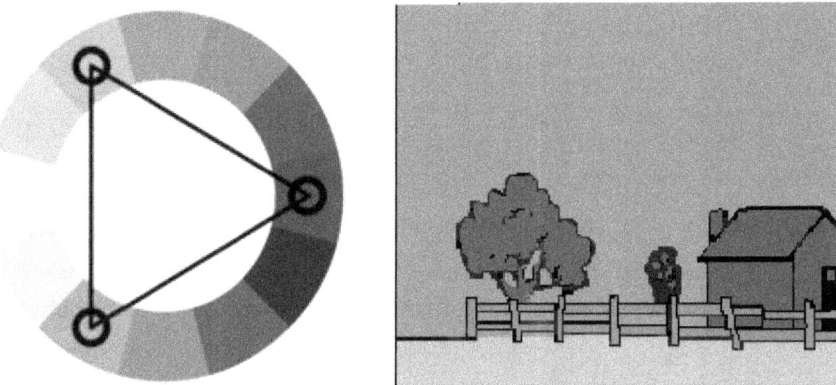

Figure 4-23. *The triadic color scheme and an example*

Split complementary color schemes draw attention to the work; the colors are generally in balance, having a mix of warm and cool shades. The combination can inspire complex emotions, since they combine well, and each color inspires a different kind of emotion. Again, tints and shades inspire the same effects.

Triadic Colors

Triadic colors form a triangle too, but an *equilateral* triangle, which has equal angles. Thus, for any one color, there is only one way to form a triadic pattern. They tend to create an exciting rant and playful feel. When used properly, they can be fun and pleasing to the eye.

Examples would be purple, green, and orange, or red, yellow, and blue. Figure 4-23 shows the color wheel and a sample of the use of triadic colors. There is a childlike appeal, especially when the colors are toned down.

Analogous

Analogous colors are near each other on one part of the color wheel (Figure 4-24a). The result of using this scheme is a calm, peaceful look. Limit your palette to three or four colors, or the result could be too busy and confusing. In addition, make sure that the colors are far enough apart, even though they are in the same region of the color wheel; otherwise, there will not be enough contrast, and again the image will be flat. An analogous scheme can be used along with a color on the opposite side of the wheel to create a startling contrast, drawing attention to a specific object. It is clearly possible to have all colors in this scheme be either warm or cool.

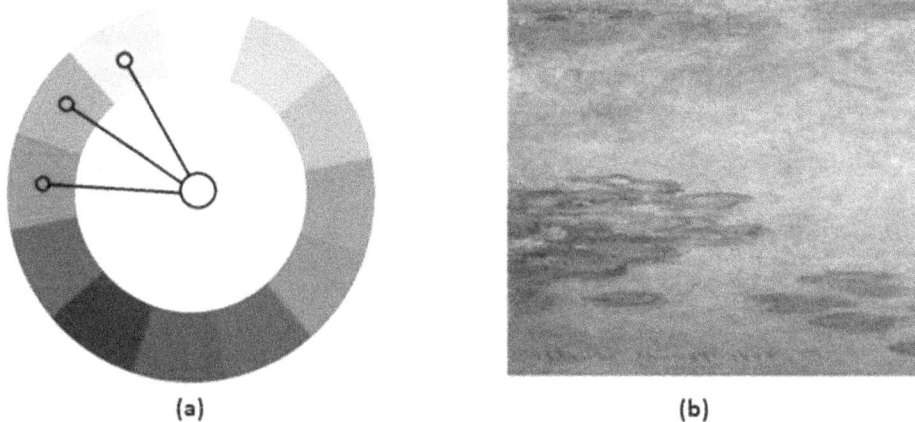

Figure 4-24. *(a) Analogous colors are near each other on the color wheel. (b) The calm, peaceful appearance when used in a painting, in this case, Water lilies by Monet*

Monet's Water Lilies is a famous painting that uses an analogous scheme. (Figure 4-24b) Monet's *Water Lilies* is a famous painting that uses an analogous scheme (Figure 4-24b).

CHAPTER 4   COLOR

Transparency

There is actually a fourth color channel that we haven't talked about, partly because it's not really a color. It's called *transparency*, or sometimes *alpha*. It represents the degree to which the color hides what is behind it. Behind, of course, means "drawn before." If we draw a rectangle at (100,100), and then draw one at (150, 150), the second one is drawn over top of the first. Unless otherwise defined, a color is opaque, and parts of the first square will be covered by the second.

If the second color is transparent to some degree, then the first square will be at least partly visible behind (through?) the second. In most implementations transparency is a number between 0 and 255, just like colors are. A transparency of 0 means that the color is completely transparent and will not be visible at all. A value of 255 means it is completely opaque and will cover and color what was drawn before. In between we have differing degrees of transparency.

This is done by most graphics systems automatically when transparency is specified. The actual calculation that is being done is a weighted average between the background color **bg** and the transparent foreground color **fg** at each pixel, with the weight being the transparency **op** value between 0 and 1. We've been specifying the transparency value as a number between 0 and 255, so **op** = **transparancy** /255. Then for each pixel (Figure 4-25):

```
r = op*red(fg)   + (1-op)*red(bg);
g = op*green(fg) + (1-op)*green(bg);
b = op*blue(fg)  + (1-op)*blue(bg);
```

The transparency value really indicates how the color will be combined with another color that already exists at the same location. It appears transparent to us because we are used to seeing transparent objects behave like that in real life. Objects made of glass and plastic are often transparent, so being able to specify this is important. It's also very useful in computer games, where sprites usually have a transparent background color so that they can be drawn over a complex scene.

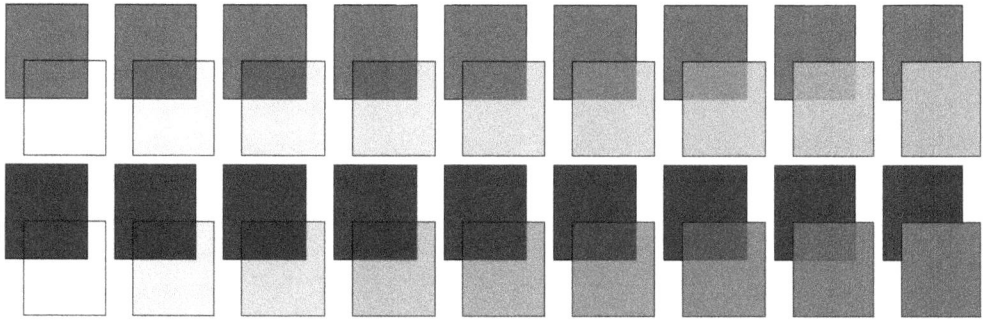

Figure 4-25. *Transparency. The overlap area between rectangles has a combination of the colors of the two basic rectangles, simulating the visual effect of the top rectangle being transparent to a degree*

Restricting the Number of Colors (Quantization Again)

We have discussed reducing the number of values in the previous chapter. When dealing with color, we have hugely more to choose from: 256*256*256 = 16,777,216 as opposed to 256 grays. The effect of random changes in a color image is much more significant than in gray images, therefore. There are many more ways for the pixels to be affected by noise and other artifacts. Probably the most significant problem comes from using JPG images as a starting point. The compression methods used introduce a significant variation in color values, especially at edges.

A *quantization* step is important if we are going to identify regions in the image, or if we want to change colors over an area. Given that there are so many colors to deal with and that the problem is three dimensional – red, green, and blue – the solution to the problem "reduce the number of colors in this image to 8" is not obvious (Figure 4-26). It's clear that the color mapping should be from a set of colors to one *similar* color, whatever that means. Whatever method we use should also keep the overall color balance the same. So, if the image consists largely of blue colors, then when mapping to N colors, the result should largely consist of blue colors.

CHAPTER 4 COLOR

Equal Distance Between Colors

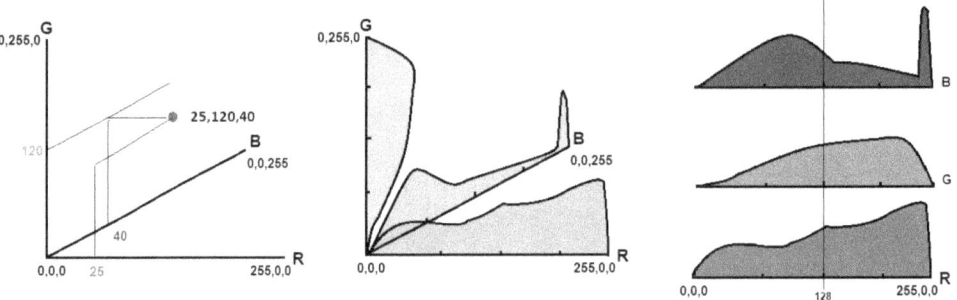

Figure 4-26. *Three color channels drawn as a 3D axis. Each color has a histogram. When we split on the axis into two parts, we double the number of colors*

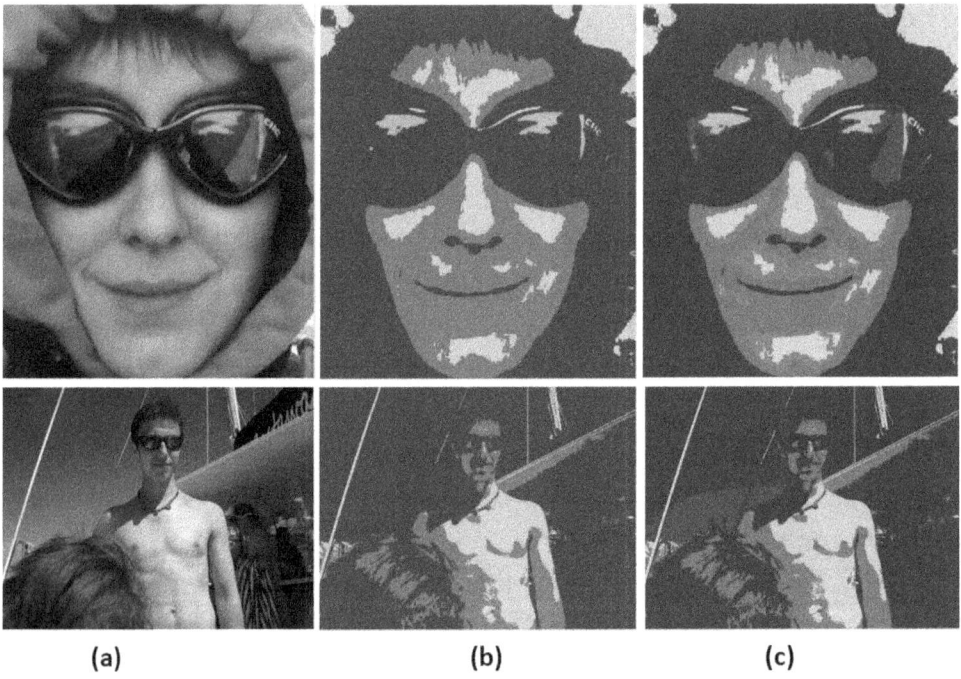

Figure 4-27. *(a) Original images. Bailey (Top) Max (Bottom) (b) Linear method, four colors. (c) Linear method, eight colors*

We know that the RGB coordinates give us a three-dimensional system that we can look at as a color space. Any color that we can represent has a unique coordinate in that space (Figure 4-27a). Each color has its own histogram of frequencies. We can divide those axes into equal parts, for example, at the value 128 (Figure 4-27c), and this will give 8 colors:

```
  0 <= r < 128,    0  <=g < 128,     0 <= b < 128    =>  (64,64,64)
  0 <= r < 128,    0 <= g < 128,   128 <= b < 192    =>  (64,64,192)
  0 <= r < 128,  128 <= g < 256,     0 <= b < 128    =>  (64,192,64)
  0 <= r < 128,  128 <= g < 256,   128 <= b < 256    =>  (64,192,192)
128 <=  r < 256,    0 <= g < 128,     0 <= b < 128    =>  (192, 64 64)
128 <=  r < 256,    0 <= g < 128,   128 <= b < 192    =>  (192,64,192)
128 <=  r < 256,  128 <= g < 256,     0 <= b < 128    =>  (192,192,64)
128 <=  r < 256,  128 <= g < 256,   128 <= b < 256    =>  (192,192,192)
```

Here we chose the color in the middle of the range as the final one, but we can select the smallest, largest, average, or any value that we choose. We don't have to split each color axis either; we could split only one (resulting in 2 colors) or any two (resulting in 4 colors). We can also split any axis into as many parts as we like, but this algorithm does so using equal values along the axis. We split into two at the value 128, into four at 64, into 7 at 256/6=51, and so on. The number of colors created by the splits will be the product of the number of splits on each axis. Dividing each into 5 parts gives 5x5x5 = 125 colors. Dividing red into 2, green into 3, and leaving blue as 1 gives 2x3x1 = 6 colors.

Median Cut

The equal distance algorithm ignores the distribution of the color values. If, for example, there are a lot of red values in the range 250–255 and a few in the range 0–3, then dividing that set of values in the middle still results in most of the red values being in the high ranges. The median cut filter adds two important aspects:

1. It divides the range of any color value at the median of the range, not in the middle. This splits the ranges in halves that are equal in size, whatever the value is where it is split.

2. It splits the axis with the largest range each time a split is desired. This means that the color that is being exploited to the greatest degree will be split and might be split multiple times before any other color.

CHAPTER 4   COLOR

As an example, consider the following RGB values in an image:

	1	2	3	4	5	6	7	8	9	10	11	12	13	14	15	16	17	18	19	20	21	22	23
R	0	9	32	44	57	65	76	86	95	100	111	124	167	173	188	193	195	201	221	245	251	252	255
G	9	12	21	24	33	49	55	67	71	83	92	93	121	134	135	178	189	193	212	213	228	231	233
B	55	62	63	67	73	78	80	86	91	931	96	99	110	115	116	122	131	133	134	140	143	144	151

	1	2	3	4	5	6	7	8	9	10	11	12	13	14	15	16	17	18	19	20	21	22	23
Red:	0	9	32	44	57	65	76	86	95	100	111	124	167	173	188	193	195	201	221	245	251	252	255
Green:	9	12	21	24	33	49	55	67	71	83	92	93	121	134	135	178	189	193	212	213	228	231	233
Blue:	55	62	63	67	73	78	80	86	91	93	96	99	110	115	116	122	131	133	134	140	143	144	151

The red range is 255-0 = 255, the green range is 233-9 = 224, and the blue range is 151-55 = 96. The largest range, red, is split at the median, which is 124. We now have two red ranges, a green, and a blue:

	1	2	3	4	5	6	7	8	9	10	11	12	13	14	15	16	17	18	19	20	21	22	23
R1	0	9	32	44	57	65	76	86	95	100	111												
R2												124	167	173	188	193	195	201	221	245	251	252	255
G	9	12	21	24	33	49	55	67	71	83	92	93	121	134	135	178	189	193	212	213	228	231	233
B	55	62	63	67	73	78	80	86	91	931	96	99	110	115	116	122	131	133	134	140	143	144	151

Now the green range is the largest, so we split the green range at the median, which is 93.

	1	2	3	4	5	6	7	8	9	10	11	12	13	14	15	16	17	18	19	20	21	22	23
R1	0	9	32	44	57	65	76	86	95	100	111												

	1	2	3	4	5	6	7	8	9	10	11	12	13	14	15	16	17	18	19	20	21	22	23
R2	124	167	173	188	193	195	201	221	245	251	252	255											
G1	9	12	21	24	33	49	55	67	71	83	92												
G2	93	121	134	135	178	189	193	212	213	228	231	233											
B	55	62	63	67	73	78	80	86	91	93	96	99	110	115	116	122	131	133	134	140	143	144	151

At this point, the blue range is 96, the largest green range is green1 at 140, and the largest red range is red1 at 111. Thus, we split green again and leave blue alone. The median of green 2 is 189, so the pixel colors are now:

	1	2	3	4	5	6	7	8	9	10	11	12	13	14	15	16	17	18	19	20	21	22	23
R1	0	9	32	44	57	65	76	86	95	100	111												
R2	124	167	173	188	193	195	201	221	245	251	252	255											
G1	9	12	21	24	33	49	55	67	71	83	92												
G2	93	121	134	135	178	189																	
G3	193	212	213	228	231	233																	
B	55	62	63	67	73	78	80	86	91	93	96	99	110	115	116	122	131	133	134	140	143	144	151

CHAPTER 4 COLOR

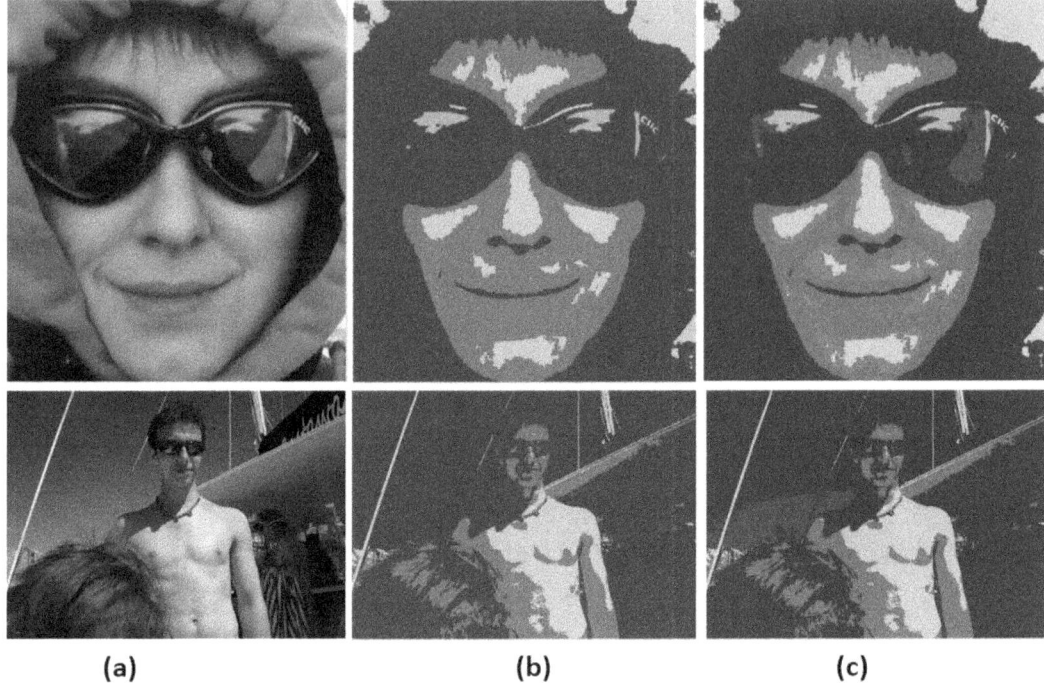

(a) (b) (c)

Figure 4-28. *(a) Original Images. (b) Median cut, red/green (4 colors). (c) Median cut 8 levels*

If we split again, we'd split red1. If not, this is the final set of colors. Using the median of each set to represent the color, we get red1 becomes 65, red2 becomes 201, green1 becomes 33, green2 becomes 135, green3 becomes 228, and blue becomes 99.

Figure 4-28 shows the result of using the median cut method on the Bailey and Max images.

Smoothing

Color images potentially have millions of numerical values that are possible, and as we found when looking at values, there are many ways that these become changed and randomized during the image capture and storage process. Colors can vary in 3 or 4 dimensions, so it is critical when doing things like re-quantization that the variations be smoothed out. We can use the median filter that we developed in the previous chapter and apply it to each color channel individually. The transparency levels we should probably leave alone. The effect of variations on transparency can be strange and unpredictable.

172

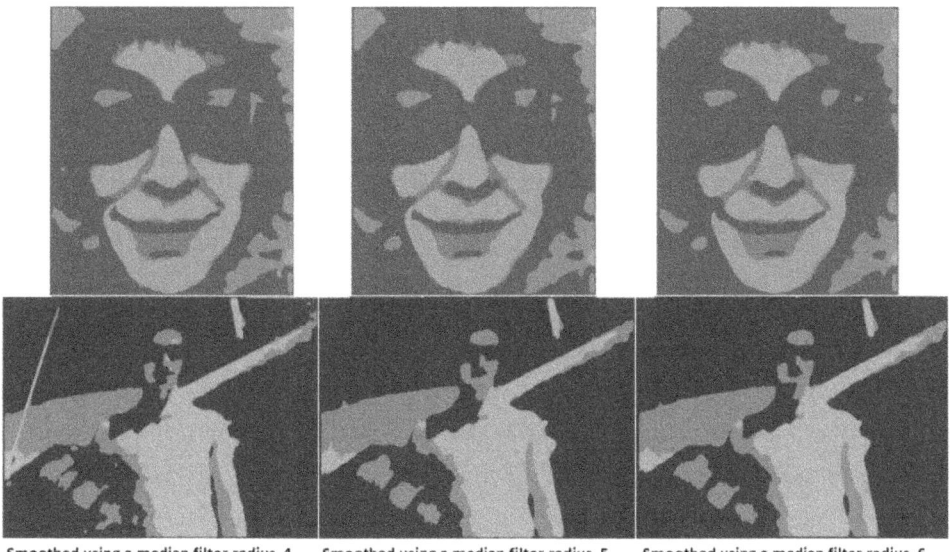

Figure 4-29. *A median filter (smoothing) is applied before reducing the number of colors*

We know how to do a median filter on a gray image, and doing the same on a color image just means treating each color channel as gray. The overall visual effect is sometimes quite different from what we might expect.

As an example, let's redo Bailey and Max *after* a median filter. Obviously, the size of the filter will matter and will be visually relative; some will like one size more than another. Figure 4-29 gives three versions of the output from the median cut filter after smoothing using sizes of 4, 5, and 6 on the Bailey and Max images. Anyone can select the one they like best; it's a matter of opinion.

Color and Edges

In Chapter 3, "Value," we discussed finding edges and boundaries based on gray level or intensity. It is a natural extension to use color. If using RGB, we could use existing methods to find edges in the red, green, or blue channels. Just treat them as values. Using red, green, and blue as values and using a Sobel edge detector is shown as an example (Figure 4-30).

CHAPTER 4   COLOR

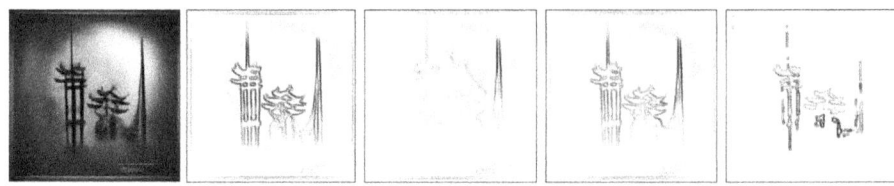

Figure 4-30. *(a) Original painting (b) Red edges. (c) Green edges. (d) Green edges (e) Hue-based edges*

For the red channel, the edges correspond to places where red pixels are next to non-red pixels, which is to say any other color. Remember, some colors like white and yellow contain a lot of red but don't look very red. This means that a red region next to a white or yellow region will not show much of an edge, if any. We could use *hue* as the basis for detecting edges (Figure 4-30d), and when we do that, is seems that the distinction between color regions is more clear. Remember that as saturation and value decrease, the significance of the hue declines. At low saturation values, for example, the colors are indistinguishable.

We can compute edges based on a specific color by defining the difference of a pixel from its neighbors as a 3D Euclidean distance from the target color, rather than a simple difference in values. The values are normalized (changed to between 0 and 1) and then converted to values between 0 and 256. Figure 4-31 shows an example of this using the target color yellow=(250,250,0).

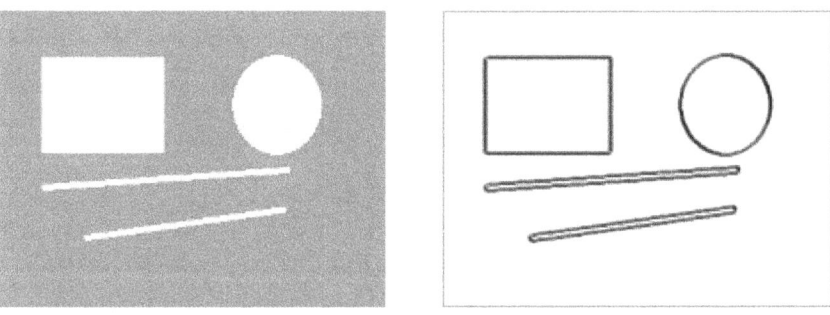

Figure 4-31. *An example of detecting edges of a specific color (yellow)*

Color Psychology

When looking at color images, it seems reasonable that the color of the light that we used when we captured the image would have an impact on the colors that appear in the image. It also seems reasonable that we would perceive an orange, for example, as still being an orange under a variety of illuminations. This would help us recognize objects in the real world. This only works for a limited range of color illuminant, probably because extremes of illuminant color don't commonly occur in the real world.

We call this effect *color constancy*, and it's easy to demonstrate. Simply look at an object under various kinds of illumination and see if you can identify its color.

The *Land effect* is interesting, because it suggests that all colors can be perceived if only two are present (Figure 4-32). One model of color perception (the *Retinex* theory) suggests that the color we perceive is the product of the color that the object reflects and the color and intensity of the illumination:

```
Resulting Image = Reflectance(r)*Illumination(S)
```

Where **r** is the reflectance of the surface, and **S** is the illumination on the surface. This rather makes sense, that the color we see is a combination of the object and illumination color. How can we use this? In computer graphics we use it to render colors more realistically. In art we may want to find other things to do with this idea, which might inspire artworks based on the principle.

Figure 4-32. *The Land effect. A source image is converted to a red+white image as follows. The red component is the same as the original red channel, while the white component is the average of the three RGB channels. The resulting image is simply the sum of the red and white components. We perceive colors in this image – there are only reds and grays*

CHAPTER 4   COLOR

Figure 4-33. *A startling demonstration of color perception. All of the eyes in these images are the same color, which is (127,131). They look very different because of the surrounding (illumination) color*
www.psy.ritsumei.ac.jp/~akitaoka/colorconstancye.html

The thing is that color in many ways is very strongly based on perception, which is how our eyes (sensors), optic nerve (transmission line), and brain (interpreter) collectively process the inputs. Figure 4-33 shows how the surrounding color can affect the details we see. This can be used to advantage in artworks if we know how.

Psychologist Carl Jung divided human experience into four parts and assigned each a specific color. These are culturally specific.

Yellow: Intuition   Symbolizes: shining and radiating outwards. Cheerful, uplifting, spirited, and enthusiastic.

Blue: Thinking – Symbolizes: cold like snow. Unbiased, objective, detached, analytical.

Green: Sensation - Symbolizes: earth, perceiving reality. Still, tranquil, calming, soothing.

Red: Feeling - Symbolizes blood, fire, passion, and love. Positive, decisive, bold, and assertive. Often used to represent danger or warning. Red stimulates the appetite.

Non-Jungian color effects are:

Orange: Warm and stimulating, energetic. It attracts the eye and is used for important content.

Indigo: Associated with spirituality and intuition.

Violet: Wisdom, creativity, and magic. It also denotes royalty and luxury, so it is used when we want a product to seem exclusive.

One's use of color in an artwork could depend partly on what kind of emotion is intended or what kind of message is being sent.

Finding Color Regions

As we learned when using values, pixels that have similar colors often belong to the same object, especially when they are close to each other physically. The same is true of color. That's how we find objects in an image; we collect pixels into regions using both connectivity and properties of the pixels. We start at a pixel that is known to belong to a group of pixels that we wish to find. Since all pixels belong to *some* group, we could start anywhere, but we usually use color to determine where to begin.

Imagine that we have an image I and wish to find dandelions in that image. They are yellow, so we could begin by finding a yellow pixel, using a range of hues. Now we look at all geometric neighbors of that yellow pixel that are also yellow, using the color of the start pixel as a basis and allowing a range of hues near that color to be accepted. Place any such pixels identified into a set, and then do the same with those, and keep repeating until we can find no more pixels that satisfy the color constraint. The pixels in the set form a region of similar pixels and likely belong to an object or to connected (touching) objects.

Another possibility is to base regions on any pixel we find. We'd select a pixel, build a region around it, then another pixel, and so on until all pixels belonged to a region.

In either instance we have to process the entire image, so we must not assign the same pixels to different regions. This means somehow removing them from consideration when looking for the next and successive regions. There are many ways to do this, and a simple one involves creating a second image, a *memo* image, the same size as the original and setting all pixels to white. And pixels that we examine in the original image will be set to gray in the memo image. Pixels that belong to a region we are seeking are set to black. When all pixels in the original have been examined, the memo will contain black where the regions were found, and the original image will be unchanged. In addition, when considering images for a new region, any that are not white in the memo need not be considered.

The memo need not be an actual image. It could be a two-dimensional array or set of numbers initially set to 0. When we examine a pixel, the corresponding memo element is set to -1. When we find a pixel belonging to a region, we set the corresponding element

CHAPTER 4   COLOR

in the memo to an integer that increases with each region found, meaning that at the end of the process we know how many regions there are and which pixels belong to which region. Let's look at an example.

The algorithm in detail is:

Let **T** be a threshold value used to define what *similar* means. Pixels are *similar* if the color or value is within **T** of each other or of the mean value of the region. The source image is **I**; the **memo** image is the same size but all black pixels.

1. Select a starting pixel **P(i,j)**. It could be *any* pixel, the *next* pixel, or one of a specific color.

2. Set the starting color/value **H** to that of **P(i,j)**. Set **mean** to **H**, **N** (number of pixels in the region) to 1, and **sum** to **H**.

3. Add **P(i,j)** to a list of pixels **L**. **L** will be the collection of pixels that have been selected for the region but have not yet been added to it. Mark the pixel **(i,j)** as having been used in the image **I**, and set the pixel **memo(i,j)** to the color **H**.

4. While **L** is not empty:

5. Remove one pixel from **L**, and assign it to **z**.

6. For each neighbor **q** of **z**:

7. If **q** is marked as used, go to step 4.

8. If the color/value of **q** is within **T** of the **mean**:

9. Add **q** to **L**.

10. Add the value of **q** to **sum**, add 1 to **N**, and recompute the **mean** as **sum/N**.

11. Mark **q** as used and set the corresponding pixel in **memo** to **H**.

12. **L** is empty, and the region has been identified.

Example: Orange Tree

Figure 4-34. *A subject for an artwork, a branch of a fruiting orange tree*

Consider the image in Figure 4-34, which is a branch from an orange tree. In order to paint this subject, we need to distinguish the regions. There are oranges, leaves, branches, and everything else (background). A normal human eye can separate these regions and apply various colors of paint to a canvas to create a representation. Using what we know about pixel color and about regions, we can create a first draft of such a painting.

There are many ways to identify regions here. We could define three regions by type and color: oranges, foliage, and background (everything else). Or we could simply assume that each pixel belongs to some region and grow regions from each one.

We know that orange as a color has a hue in a range around the value of 32 degrees (23/255). Foliage is green and has a pretty wide range of hues; we use 65-122 here. Selecting colors in this simple way leads to the result in Figure 4-35. The oranges are a distinct set of regions from the foliage, and all pixels not selected for any region are set to a dark blue. We get the result in Figure 4-35c.

CHAPTER 4   COLOR

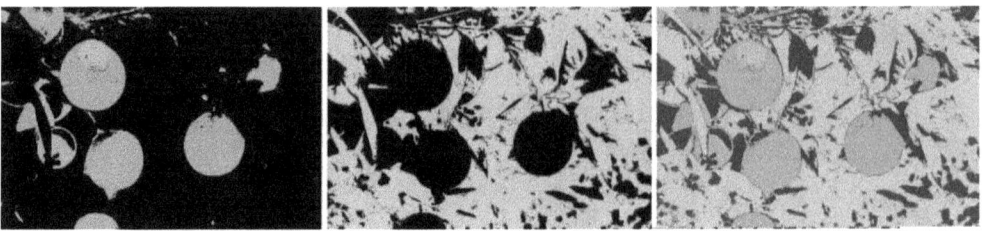

Figure 4-35. *Selecting oranges (hues near 32), foliage (hues 65–122) and everything else*

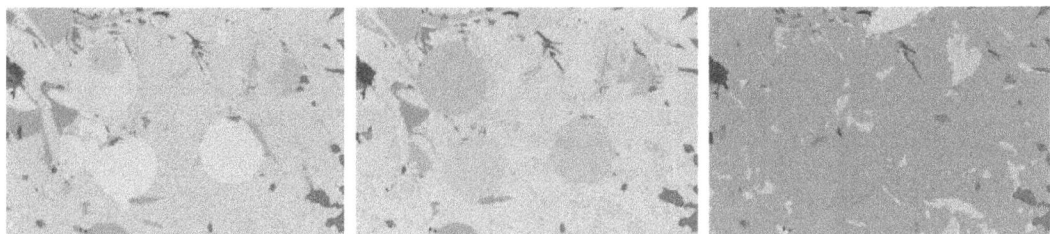

Figure 4-36. *The threshold for "close enough" changes the appearance quite radically. 10-20-40*

This has many variations. The way we decide *close enough* can be changed, for example (Figure 4-36). There is noise in all images, so we could do a median filter before finding regions. We can experiment with the threshold; small thresholds create more regions with more colors. We can use either RGB or hue as the main color indicator.

Region growing is very useful in computer vision, where it can be used to identify objects that could have a color gradient. Here the parameters can be used for that purpose or to create more abstract views of a scene that could be used to build an interesting work.

Example: Sepia Toning

Sepia is a brownish color that many people associate with old photos. They did not turn that color as they aged, though. The brown tint is the result of a chemical process used in the darkroom to prevent the photo from fading over time. It used silver sulfide, which is more stable than metallic silver, and this provides the color. The color was possibly a surprise and was certainly not planned.

We can use thresholding to transform a normal image into a simulated sepia-tone image. The discussion so far has been used to find a threshold that splits the image into two-pixel classes, but we could use the same technique to create any number of classes. In the case of the Brandenburg Gate image in Figure 4-37, we chose four levels. We have four brightness values, so we need three thresholds, and we could just pick them. Values of 64, 128, and 196 seem reasonable because they split the 0-256 range into four parts. However, what we probably really want is to have an equal number of pixels in each class, and we do that using the histogram.

If **H** is the brightness histogram of the image I being transformed, and there **are N = I.width * I.height** pixels in the image, then the first threshold value t1 will be selected so that there will be N/4 pixels with a brightness smaller than **H[t1]**. We wish to select t2 so that N/2 pixels have a brightness smaller than H[t2] and t3 so that ¾N pixels are smaller than H[t3].

The color sepia has RGB coordinates (112, 66, 20). The program we will create will set pixels having a brightness value smaller than **t1** to this color. This is the darkest color in the photo, because it corresponds to the pixels with the smallest brightness. For pixels between **t1** and **t2**, we use the same hue but decrease saturation (by 20) and increase brightness (by 30). For pixels between **t2** and **t3**, we do that again, using the same hue, decreasing saturation (by 20), and increasing brightness (by 30). Do that again for pixels with a brightness greater than t3, and the image is now complete.

Figure 4-37. (a) An actual sepia image, a photo of Albuquerque, New Mexico, in 1880 (By New York Public Library - NYPL Digital Library, Public Domain) (b) The Brandenburg Gate, Berlin, 2015). (c) Sepia-toned version of the Brandenburg Gate image. https://commons.wikimedia.org/w/index.php?curid=14751003)

CHAPTER 4   COLOR

Summary

Color is a complex perceptual concept, as well as being a physical property of objects. When using a computer, there are many ways to represent a color, all using numbers. RGB uses a red, green, and blue component of the incoming light, and each value (channel) is a number between 0 (least) and 255 (most). This system is based on how humans see color. The HSB system uses a *hue* value that tells us what color we are seeing (red=0 through orange, yellow, green, blue, violet, and red again at 255); *saturation* indicates how much of that color is present, or how intense the color is; and *brightness* is the value associated with that color. These systems are *additive*, in that colors are created by combining different colors of light. The RYB system uses numerical values for red, yellow, and blue components and is *subtractive*, which is how we refer to a model that mimics how we mix paint. The CMYK model is also subtractive and is used commonly in computer printers. *Munsell* color predates computers and is superficially similar to HSB. Artists have been using it for a century. It is based on measurements of just noticeable differences in color as measured on human subjects.

Colors can be manipulated by a computer by treating each color channel as a value. Thus, we can apply methods previously learned for values, such as smoothing and median filtering. We can select colors that a human eye will find pleasant using simple algorithms. We can also vary a color (tone, shade, tint) algorithmically.

Some colors are warmer than others, and certain colors carry emotional information. Objects tend to have similar colors throughout, and a region-finding method can be used to find these in an image.

Tools and Examples

adogs	- Display an image as a dog would see it. Save as "canine.out."
cmyk	- Color picker CMYK and RGB.
land	- Illustration of the Land effect. Save as "land.out."
munsell	- Create the Munsell 5R table
ryb	- RYB color picker

Library Code

analogousa	- One analogous pairing for a color
analogousb	- The second analogous pairing for a color
hueDiagfade	- Create a hue gradient, fading diagonally
hueHfade	- Create a hue gradient, fading horizontally
hueVfade	- Create a hue gradient, fading vertically
hueVgrad	- Vertical hue gradient between two hue values
medianFilterColor	- Median filter fill color, size R
quanteq	- Requantization, equal distances
quantMed	- Requantization, median value
regions	- Region growing, threshold specified.
satHfade	- Vertical saturation gradient given a hue
satVfade	- Vertical saturation gradient given a hue
shadergb	- Find the shade of an RGB color given a factor of 0–1.
sobelAngle	- Angles of the Sobel edges displayed as colors
sobelBlue	- Blue edges from the Sobel detector
sobelGreen	- Green edges from the Sobel detector
sobelHue	- Hue-based the Sobel edges
sobelRed	- Red edges from the Sobel detector
splitComplmentarya	- One split complementary pairing for a color
splitComplmentaryb	- The second split complementary pairing for a color
temperature	- Adjust color temperature by a factor
tIntrgb	- Find a tint of a given RGB color
toneRGB	- Find a tone of an RGB color given f and a gray value
toRGB	- RYB to RGB conversion
toRYB	- RGB to RYB conversion
triadica	- One triadic pairing for a color
triadicb	- The second triadic pairing for a color

CHAPTER 4   COLOR

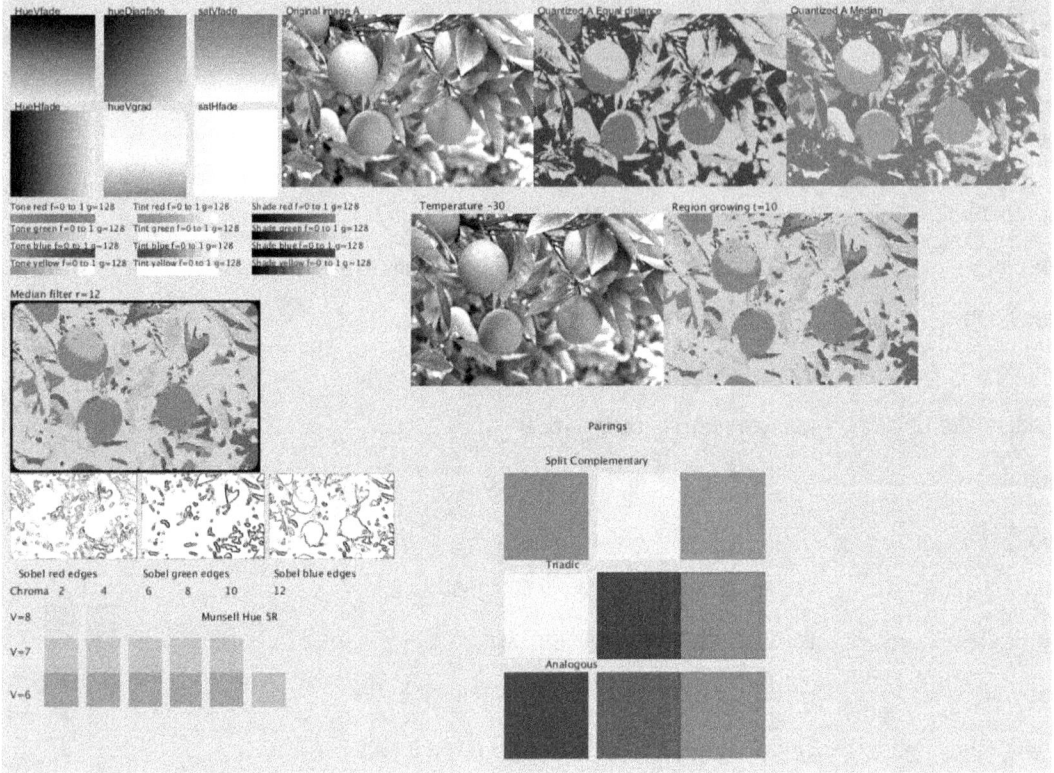

*The result of the test program **library04**, demonstrating the library code for this chapter.*

CHAPTER 5

Shape

Shape is possibly the most important element in art. Certainly, the previous three – line, value, and color – are all integral in defining shape in an artwork. Without them there is no shape. One could suggest that it is their purpose. That's because all *objects* have a shape, and much of visual art is involved in the representation of objects. Even when we think of an artwork as *abstract*, the basic components are frequently objects.

A human artist will view a scene as an arrangement of objects, but a computer first "sees" them as pixels, simple spots of color arranged in a pattern. A human can apply an interpretation to an object because they know what it is. They have seen things like it before. We can paint a horse as angry or sad, busy or idle, engaged or bored, whatever the subject's actual demeanor. It is, first and foremost, a *horse*. To do this using a computer, one must develop complex algorithms for labeling regions in a scene, which is the same thing as *recognizing* the objects. A program must be able to identify a horse (meaning: connect the object with a label), connect the label "horse" with other characteristics (meaning: gait, its parts, possible colors), know what parts of the horse are not visible in the scene (and how to represent them), have some context of where horses belong (meaning: barn, field; not at the sea bottom or piloting an aircraft), and consider many other possible aspects of the label *horse*.

Recognizing objects is a very difficult task in both programming and algorithm development. It is what the field of computer vision is all about, which is one of the most difficult areas of computing to master. The subject uses a lot of rather advanced math, too, which often scares people away. The goal of this chapter is to do the impossible, which is to explain the basics of object recognition without getting into too much mathematics, to explain the geometry of shapes, to discuss machine learning without exposing too many complex algorithms, and to apply what we have learned to creating generative artworks.

An object in an image is a collection (set) of pixels that are related by a logical connection rather than a physical one. The pixels may not form a single connected region; the pixels may not be the same color or may even be wildly different colors.

CHAPTER 5   SHAPE

Multiple examples of the same object in the same scene can be various sizes. The object may be three-dimensional, and thus, we can view it from multiple orientation that make it appear very different. Object recognition seems like an impossible task. In general, it is, and even humans fail at it sometimes.

There is a large collection of research on the subject of object recognition in images, and it can't be presented in one small book. The idea here is to give the outline of how it can be done and to show some tools that an artist can use if they feel that they cannot create the code themselves. What we need is the ability to identify a relatively small set of things - basic shapes – and then possibly combine them into more complex objects, such as animals or vehicles. We won't develop recognizers for many things, but we will have a few by the end of the chapter, and that number can be increased with time and experience.

One way to define a shape is to say it is a collection of features that define some object arranged in a specific manner. A feature is some aspect of something that we can measure or calculate from measurements. It can be as simple as length, for example, or color. In the real world, which consists of things we can observe, shapes can be quite complicated; in mathematics, they can be very simple. So that's where we will start.

A shape is a region (area) enclosed by lines: a line forms the boundary of the shape, the shape is the area enclosed by that boundary. A shape is nearly always characterized by lines in some geometric combination. Three lines are used to create a triangle, while four lines can make a square, but not always. We can also define shapes using value, color, or texture, but there is always an implicit boundary and a line that could be used as a demarcation of the shape as opposed to background to differentiate them. Methods we have already seen could be used to create a line (boundary) where colors are being used to distinguish shapes. In those cases, it is the contrast between the objects that makes the shape visible.

Geometric Shapes

A geometric shape can always be characterized in a word or two. There are details in parameters like size, but the shape itself is always obvious: *circle*, *square*, *triangle*, and so on. Moreover, geometric shapes have precise mathematical characterizations that can be used to draw them or recognize them.

Polygons

A polygon is a shape enclosed by straight lines. We refer to a polygon that is composed of **N** lines as an *N-gon*, but the common ones have special names like *triangle* and *rectangle*. If all of the sides are the same length, then it's called a *regular* polygon. We also call a regular triangle an *equilateral* triangle, and a regular rectangle is a *square*. The angles between the sides are important too. A 4-sided polygon where the angles are all 90 degrees is a rectangle, but there are other 4-sided shapes that aren't: rhombus and parallelogram (Figure 5-1). We need to know about a shape in order to classify it.

Many human-made objects contain polygons, especially rectangles. Buildings, windows, tables, signs, license plates, and so on tend to be rectangles. Indeed, sharp edges and straight lines characterize human-built objects.

Processing has functions to draw some polygons:

triangle (x0,y0, x1,y1, x2,y2) = The three points (x_i, y_i) define a triangle.

rect (x, y, w, h) – Draw a rectangle with width **w** and height **h** with the upper left corner **(x, y)**.

Some new ones that don't exist but that might be useful are:

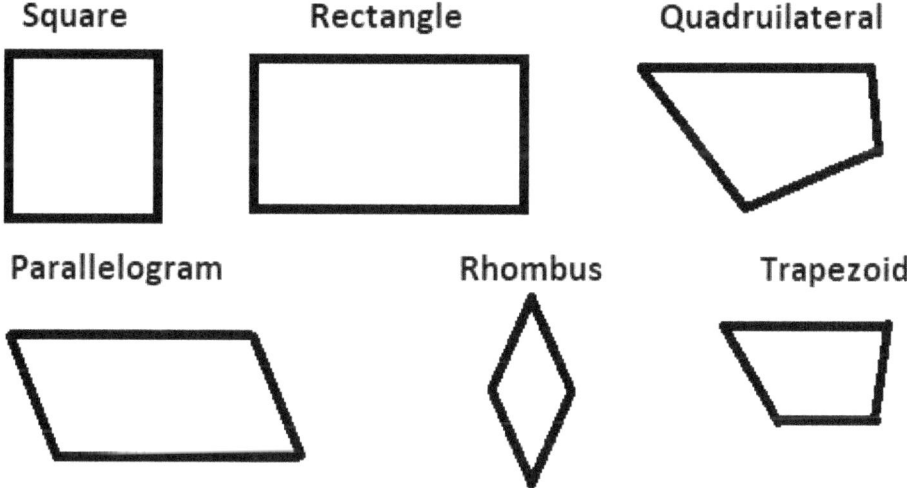

Figure 5-1. Polygons with four sides

polygon (x, y, s, N) – Draw a regular polygon with upper left **(x,y)**, edge length **s**, with **N** sides.

quadrilateral (x0,y0, x1, y1, x2,y2, x3,y3) – polygon with four edges and four vertices, or corners.

CHAPTER 5   SHAPE

parallelogram (x0, y1, x1, y1) – a quadrilateral with two pairs of parallel sides and opposite or facing sides of a parallelogram are of equal length.

rhombus (x, y, l1, l2) – a rhombus is a quadrilateral whose four sides all have the same length.

trapezoid (x0, y0, l0, x1, y1, l1) – Convex quadrilateral with at least one pair of parallel sides

poly (x[], y[], N) – Arbitrary polygon with N sides.

Circles

We can define a circle as a *curve everywhere equidistant from a given fixed point*, which is the center. The distance is the radius. We could draw a circle, therefore, by setting all pixels that are a distance **r** from the center pixel (**cx, cy**):

```
void draw1(int cx, int cy, int r)      Draw a circle centered at (cx,cy)
                                       having radius r
{
  for (int i=0; i<width; i++)
    for (int j=0; j<height; j++)       for all x coordinates
                                       for all y coordinates

      if ((int)dist(cx, cy, i,j) ==        if the distance between
              radius)                      the center and the point
                                           (i,j) is equal to the
                                           radius
        ellipse (i,j,1,1);                   set pixel at (x,y)
}
```

This is an awful algorithm because it looks at *all* pixels in an image to draw any circle, which makes it very slow. Still, it allows us to draw more interesting and variable circles. The standard *Processing* function circle draws a circle quickly but has limitations: fixed color and fixed line size.

CHAPTER 5   SHAPE

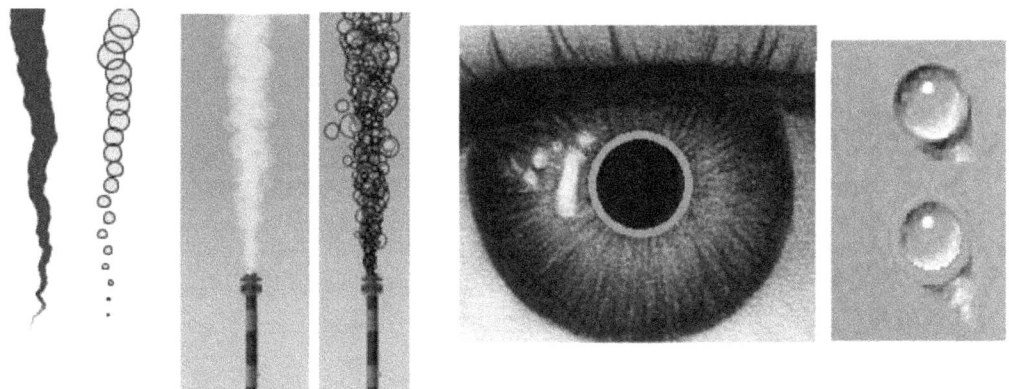

Figure 5-2. *Examples of the use of circles in art. (a) A liquid running down a surface. (b) Smoke. (c) The pupil of an eye. (d) Water droplet*

Circles are a very important part of artworks. Many real objects are circular, and other objects consist of *parts* or variations of circles, so we need to know how to draw them. Consider Figure 5-2, where we have a few examples of using circles to build more complex objects. First is a drip, such as paint or water running down a surface (Figure 5-2a). It is made by drawing multiple circles of decreasing size as the **y** coordinate increases and positioning the center randomly from its previous **x** position, making a smoothly jagged path. The effect is more impressive if animated.

Next is what looks like smoke emanating from a chimney. The chimney is an image; we make the smoke using many small circles placed randomly and filled with a smoke color. The circles get larger as **y** *decreases* this time and begin at the location of the chimney mouth. The pupil of a human eye is a circle. A water droplet is a circle. We need circles, even though they seem so simple.

By the way, a circle has a mathematical equation that we can use for drawing it. That equation is:

$$(x-cx)^2 + (y-cy)^2 = r^2$$

Using our own algorithm for circle drawing, we could change the color and sizes and even shapes of each pixel we draw (Figure 5-3). We can change the size of the pixel and/or its color at any point. A faster drawing method uses a bit of trigonometry: we divide the circumference into 360 parts (end points are 1 degree apart) and draw lines between those parts. It works like this:

CHAPTER 5 SHAPE

```
void circleTrig (int x, int y, int rad)
{
  float x0, y0, x1, y1;

  x0 = cos(0) * rad; y0=sin(0)*rad;
  for (int i=1; i<360; i++)
  {
    x1 = cos(radians(i*1.0)) * rad;
    y1 = sin(radians(i*1.0)) * rad;
    line (x0+x, y0+y, x1+x,y1+y);
    x0 = x1; y0 = y1;
  }
}
```

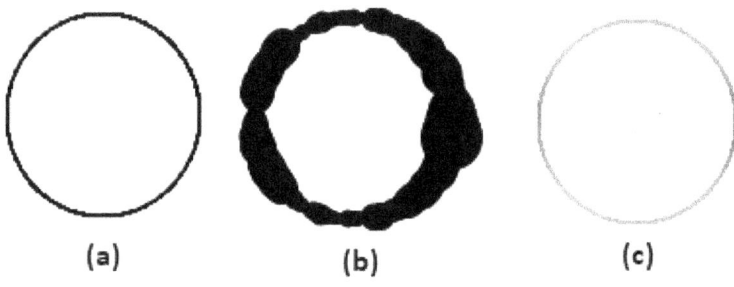

Figure 5-3. *(a) Circle drawn using the algorithm given. (b) Circle with varying-sized line. (c) Circle with changing colors*

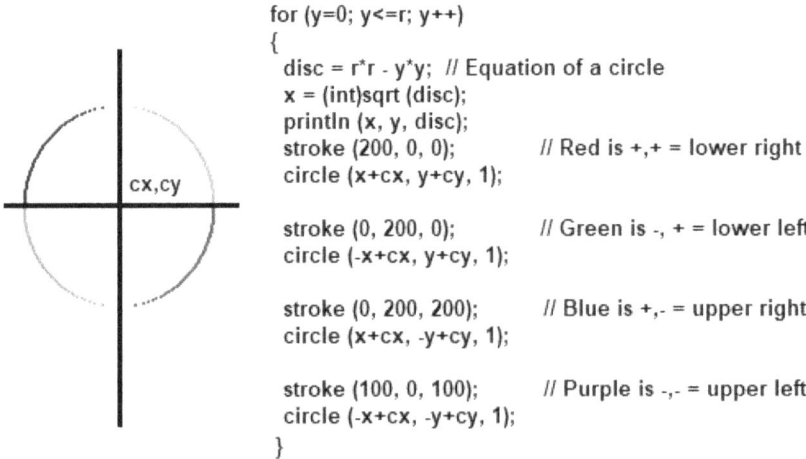

Figure 5-4. *Drawing a circle using symmetrical pixels*

190

where (**cx,cy**) is the center and **r** is the radius. Any pixel (**x,y**) that makes this equation true is a pixel that lies on the circle. Or, for any coordinate **y**, the corresponding x coordinate is:

$$(x-cx)^2 = r^2 \cdot (y-cy)^2$$

$$(x-cx) = \text{sqrt}(r^2 \cdot (y-cy)^2)$$

$$x = \text{sqrt}(r^2 \cdot (y-cy)^2) + cx$$

The square root has a positive and negative value, so there are two **x** values for any **y**, one on the left of the center and one on the right. Because the grid is discrete (integer), this does not draw very good circles. It leaves gaps between pixels near the top and bottom.

A circle is symmetrical, and so we only need to look at points in one quadrant (Figure 5-4). If y takes values between 0 and r, then we can calculate x for each of these as x = **sqrt(r*r - y*y)**, and then we can set the pixels (**cx+x,cy+y**), (**cx+x,cy-y**), (**cx-x, cy+y**), and (**cx-x,cy-y**).

Ellipses and Ovals

To many people, an *ellipse* and an *oval* are the same thing. Not true, although they have a similar appearance. An ellipse has a mathematical definition, as a circle does. It is symmetrical about two axes, looking like a circle that we have stretched in a specific direction. Figure 5-6 provides the definitions of some of the essential parameters of an ellipse. The eccentricity **e** is a measure of how extended the ellipse is. If **e=0**, we have a circle. If **e** is very large, the ellipse is much larger in one direction than it is in the other.

The mathematical formula for an ellipse that is aligned with (major axis is parallel to) the x-axis is:

$$\frac{(x-cx)^2}{a^2} + \frac{(y-cy)^2}{b^2} = 1$$

where (**cx, cy**) is the center, the semi-major axis length is **a**, and the semi-minor axis length is **b**. A function that draws an ellipse by setting pixels within a region that satisfies the equation is:

CHAPTER 5   SHAPE

`void drawEllipse( float x, y,`	X , Y coordinates of the center
`           float w, float h)`	
`{`	Width,Height of the ellipse
`  int a, b;`	
`  float yy;`	
`  a = (int)(w/2*w/2);`	a is half width squared
`  b = (int)(h/2*h/2);`	b is half the height squared
`  for (float i=(x-w/2-1);`	
`           i<(x+w/2+1);`	
`           i+=0.01)`	Scan x from the leftmost X point to the rightmost x point.
`  {`	
`     yy = b*(1.0-(i-x)*`	
`              (i-x)/a);`	
`     yy = sqrt (yy);`	
`     set (round(i),`	Calculate the y value that corresponds to the x=i
`          round(y+yy),`	value using the equation of the ellipse.
`          color(255,0,00));`	
`     set (round(i),`	
`          round(y-yy),`	
`          color(255,0,0));`	Set (i,yy) and (i,-yy), offset by the center, to *red*
`  }`	
`}`	

CHAPTER 5 SHAPE

An *oval* has no specific definition. Some say that an oval is *egg-shaped*, but for the purposes here, it will be two circles joined by straight lines *tangent* at the top and bottom of the circles, making a smooth shape. The two circles can be the same size (as in an Olympic speed-skating oval or NASCAR race track) or not (as in an egg). Figure 5-5 illustrates an ellipse and an oval.

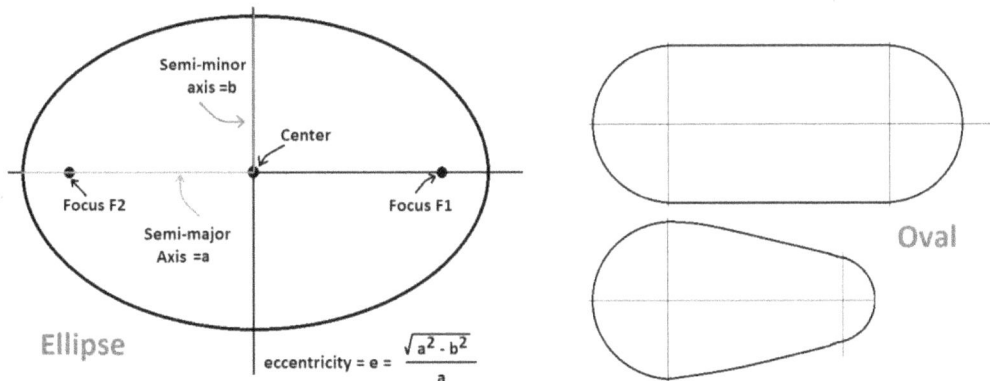

Figure 5-5. An ellipse shape is not the same as an oval

We can draw an ellipse as we drew a circle, using the equation and symmetry. *Processing* has a function to draw ellipses as well: **ellipse (x, y, a, b)**. If we want an ellipse that has an axis not aligned with **x** and **y**, we can draw it, then rotate it. We have to draw an oval using a program that we write, and so we have to figure out a way to specify it.

An oval has two circles, one at each end, so we could specify it that way: using the two centers and the two radii. So we could code the function:

oval (cx1, xy1, r1, cx2, xy2, r2)

This function is more difficult to write than you might think. There are two circles, and the lines that join them must produce a smooth meeting – we called it a tangent – where they intersect the circle. Also, we should only draw the part of the circle that is *outside* of the oval. This is a bit nasty, mathematically, but we have solved it, and this function is provided. It involves a function that provides the line that is tangent to two circles simultaneously and one that finds a point where a line (this tangent) intersects a (each) circle. We then draw a line tangent to the circles above and below and a circle between each pair of line endpoints. A solution that works for situations where the two circle sizes are similar and the distance between the circles is greater than twice the largest diameter is:

CHAPTER 5   SHAPE

```
void oval (float cx1,float cy1,float d1,          Circle centers are cx1,cy1 and cx2,cy2,
           float cx2,float cy2,float d2)          diameters d1 and d2.
{
  float r1, r2, a, b, c, d;                       Make sure that (cx1,cy1) is to the left
  if (cx1 > cx2)
  {
    r1=cx1; cx2=cx2; cx1= r1;                     r1,r2 are radii.
    r1=cy1; cy2=cy2; cy1= r1;
    r1 = d1; d1 = d2; d2 = r1;                    Angles for drawing the arcs (See: Chapter 2
    r1 = d2/2; r2 = d1/2;                         arc function)
    a = radians(90.0);
    b = radians(270.0);
    c = radians(270.0);
    d = radians(450.0);
  } else                                          Arc start/end angles differ for left and right
  {                                               circles.
    a = radians(270.0);
    b = radians(450.0);
    c = radians(90.0);
    d = radians(270.0);                           Left circle
  }
  r1 = d1/2; r2 = d2/2;                           Right circle

  noFill ();                                      Top line
  arc (cx1, cy1, d1, d1, c, d);
```

(continued)

```
    arc (cx2, cy2, d2, d2, a, b);            Bottom line
    line (cx1, cy1-r1, cx2, cy2-r2);
    line (cx1, cy1+r1, cx2, cy2+r2);
}
```

Results are in Figure 5-6. Note that when the centers are too close together, the lines do not meet the arcs smoothly.

A general oval drawing method requires knowing some more geometry and programming it correctly. Figure 5-7 shows the general and correct method, which requires:

- Equation of a line between two points (we have this, Chapter 2, "Line")
- Equation of a line perpendicular to another line at a specific point.
- Points of intersection between a line and a circle.

The discrete geometry library provided with this volume contains the needed functions.

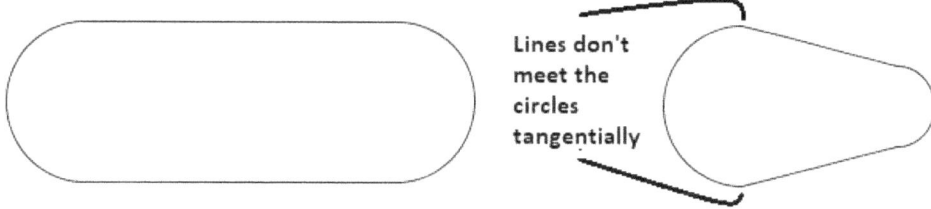

Figure 5-6. *Drawings using the oval function. (Left) A good example. (Right) The centers are too close together*

Shapes – Closed Curves

In *Chapter 2*, "Line," we drew curved lines using splines and the Processing functions **beginShape()**, **curveVertex()**, and **endShape()**. If the start and end points of such a curve are the same, then we have a *closed* curve, which qualifies as a shape: *a region enclosed by lines*. We can make almost arbitrary shapes in this way, remembering that we have to define the set of coordinates for points along the shape outline. The coordinates can be data points, such as those we could read from a file, or coordinates computed by an algorithm.

CHAPTER 5 SHAPE

We could create an oval-like shape by drawing the half-circles using calculated points and joining the two halves with curved lines. We can draw it all as one sequence of vertices. We can create a square with rounded corners. Indeed, we can draw any closed curve using the *begin-end shape* and *curveVertex* spline implementation. These are especially useful for random and *organic* shapes.

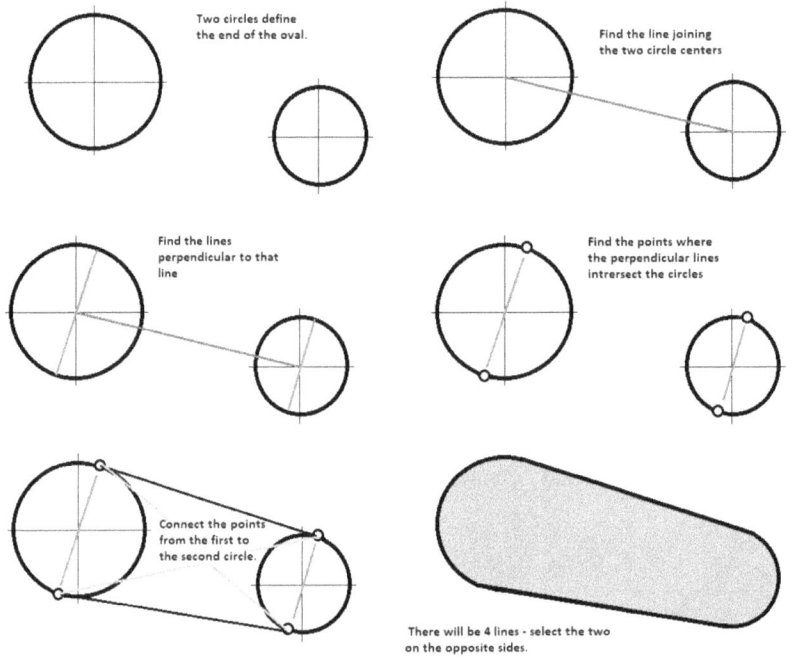

Figure 5-7. *The correct and general way to draw an oval*

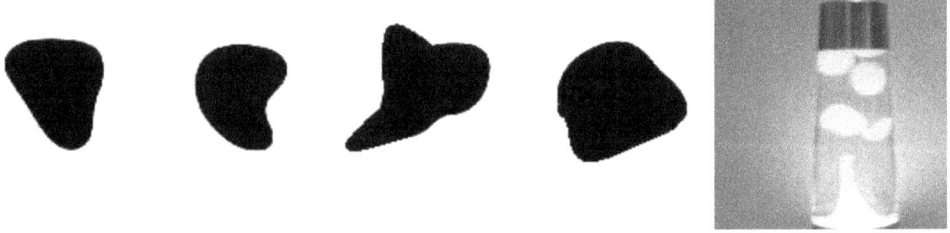

Figure 5-8. *Blob shapes are organic, irregular smooth curves*

Organic Shapes

Geometric shapes are mathematically well-defined; organic shapes are not. A precise definition of an organic shape is elusive, but they are irregular, sometimes random, often asymmetrical, and resemble forms found in nature, like leaves, amoebas, and river stones. They often have soft, curving contours and do not have the precise angles and symmetry associated with human-created objects and geometric shapes.

A shape is *smooth* if one pixel on the outline is *relatively near* the previous and next pixel. *Nearness* refers to a small distance compared to the size of the object. This is relative, but ½ the distance is not smooth, whereas 1/100 would be smooth. In between we'll have to make up a criterion for deciding.

Example – Blobs

A blob is a closed curve having random-appearing shape parameters and a smooth outline. A good example might be an amoeba or the melted wax shapes inside of a *lava lamp* (Figure 5-8). These shapes appear often in artworks as fruit or vegetables, seeds, flower petals, and a host of real organic objects. Rendering one is not difficult, but the parameters of the shape depend on what sort of actual object is being drawn.

There are two straightforward ways to draw a blob. The first way is to draw filled overlapping ellipses in the same location with different eccentricities. The shape of the ellipses and the offset from a central position are random numbers based on the object's size. A function for this is given in Figure 5-9. The value **delta** in the figure is used to define the offset of ellipses from the (x,y) center and to define the shape and size of the ellipses.

```
void blob (int x, int y, float siz)
{
  float delta = siz/8;

  noStroke ();
  fill (90, 200, 110);

  for (int i=0; i<5; i++)
    ellipse (x+random(delta)-delta/2,
             y+random(delta)-delta/2,
             random(delta)*2+delta,
             random(delta)*2+delta);
}
```

CHAPTER 5   SHAPE

Figure 5-9. *Overlapping ellipses create a blob effect. Random positions and sizes modify the shape*

Another way to draw a blob uses splines and a selection of points at random within the area of the blob. This way is more complicated, in that it requires more code and a cleverer design but can yield better results. Additionally, we can define the number of *lobes* (rounded projections or bumps) in the shape.

If we want a maximum of four lobes, we first determine four random points in the four quadrants around the center point, using the specified size to find the distances. Possible code is given in Figure 5-10.

The corner points are easily found because they are +x,-1, +y, and =y. For more than four lobes, we would use trigonometry to find points that were spaced at equal angles around the center and use random radii to find the x,y coordinates for each.

```
void blob2 (int x, int y, float size)
{
 float x0, y0, x1, y1, x2,y2, x3, y3;

  fill (200, 0, 200);
  x0 = x + random(size);
  y0 = y + random (size);
  x1 = x - random(size);
  y1 = y + random (size);
  x2 = x - random(size);
  y2 = y - random (size);
  x3 = x + random(size);
  y3 = y - random (size);
```

```
  beginShape();
    curveVertex(x0, y0);
    curveVertex(x1, y1);
    curveVertex(x2,y2);
    curveVertex(x3, y3);
    curveVertex(x0, y0);
    curveVertex(x1, y1);
    curveVertex(x2,y2);
  endShape();
}
```

Figure 5-10. Using splines to draw blobs. The result is smoother

Example: Spatter or Splat

This is like a blob, but one that has fallen from some height. Like paint splatters. The outline is more irregular than a blob and often has spatulate extensions. These are trickier to implement because of the number of parameters present and how they interrelate. Consider that the function we are building is:

splat (x, y, size)

We can begin with a blob at (x,y) having the given size. We want some number of extensions **N** from the blob that are curves, creating a thinning line, then increasing again to form the spatulate end. One way to implement this is shown in Figure 5-11. We can add small randomly placed circles as extra spatter marks if we like.

CHAPTER 5 SHAPE

Example – Natural Organic Shapes

Shapes that occur in nature are frequently of the organic type and have random components. They are recognizable because the random aspects are small relative to the overall shape. A good example might be a plant leaf (Figure 5-12). Each leaf on a particular plant differs from the others in detail but is the same in overall shape, color, and general nature. In fact, we can usually identify a plant from one leaf.

```
void splat (int xx, int yy, float aa, float siz)
{
  float dx, dy, sz, x, y, a;
  int n;

  noStroke();
  sz = siz/2; x=xx; y = yy;
  a = random(-5, 5) + aa;
  n = (int)random (10, 20);
  dx = (random(sz)*cos(radians(a)))/n;
  dy = (random(sz)*sin(radians(a)))/n;
  blob((int)x, (int)y, sz/2);
  r = sz;
  for (int i=0; i<n; i++)
  {
    circle (x, y, r);
    x += dx; y += dy;
    r = r*random(0.89, 0.92);
  }
  for (int i=0; i<n; i++)
  {
    circle (x, y, r);
    x += dx; y += dy;
    r = r*random(1.0, 1.09);
  }
}
```

CHAPTER 5 SHAPE

Figure 5-11. *One way to draw a splat*

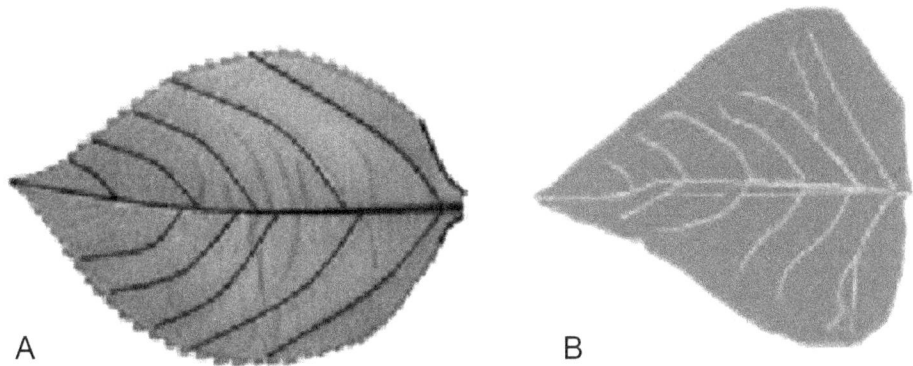

Figure 5-12. *A lilac leaf, scanned for measuring*

When trying to draw a leaf, we should look at the ways that real leaves can be random and the ways they vary in shape between plants. Botanists use features like the overall leaf shape (oblong, elliptical, linear, etc.), the shape of the margin (ciliate, dentate, serrate, etc.), the pattern of the veins (arcuate, parallel, reticulate, etc.), and others. Being an artist means having to be willing to learn a wide variety of things. The example leaf in Figure 5-12a would have a rhomboid shape, serrated edge, and cross-venulate veins. The number of possibilities is enormous in reality.

201

CHAPTER 5   SHAPE

We'll design the overall shape first (called *top-down* design). This is a *rhomboid* leaf, and we need to vary the shape slightly each time we draw one. Because there are so many types of leaf, and each defines the plant they belong to (or vice versa), we should start with some real leaves. The example here is a lilac leaf; a number of them were collected and scanned as digital images, of which Figure 5-12 is an example. The proportions of each leaf were measured, along with the starting, middle, and endpoints of the major veins. This was done using a software tool **capture.pde** written for that purpose, which allows the user to click at points along any curve, whereupon the **x,y** value of that point is printed out. When a space is typed, the program begins a new curve. The coordinates can be scaled to the size of any desired leaf (divide by length), and averages can be calculated.

The plan is to find measurements typical of a lilac leaf and use them as the basis of leaves that we will generate based on statistics we find – averages of the measurements. The lengths and widths of the sampled leaves were averaged and normalized to a length of 1.0. The widths at various X locations were also measured, averaged, and normalized. Now we can draw the "average" leaf, but not only that we can create variations on that leaf at random. Figure 5-12b shows a sampled leaf being drawn using the measured data.

The main vein running from the step to the tip can also be drawn as a spline, as can the upper and lower outlines. If the outline is serrate, we can simulate the serrations graphically using outline points some N pixels apart. The coordinates of the veins were also sampled, and we can also draw them with random variations based on random values we choose.

Example – Invented Shapes (Midcentury Modern)

The design style that we call *Midcentury Modern* (1945-1965) makes extensive use of organic shapes. The iconography of the time is easily identifiable, reminding us of the visuals in the Sean Connery *James Bond* films, which were filmed in that period. The question of *why* these specific shapes were reflective of that period in Western culture is best left for sociologists, but characterizing their shape and color is certainly within an artist's scope. Designing new icons in that style is a creative, human task (*design*), but reproducing existing ones and producing variants is a task that an algorithm can accomplish, especially since the first step is an analysis of the shape by a human.

CHAPTER 5   SHAPE

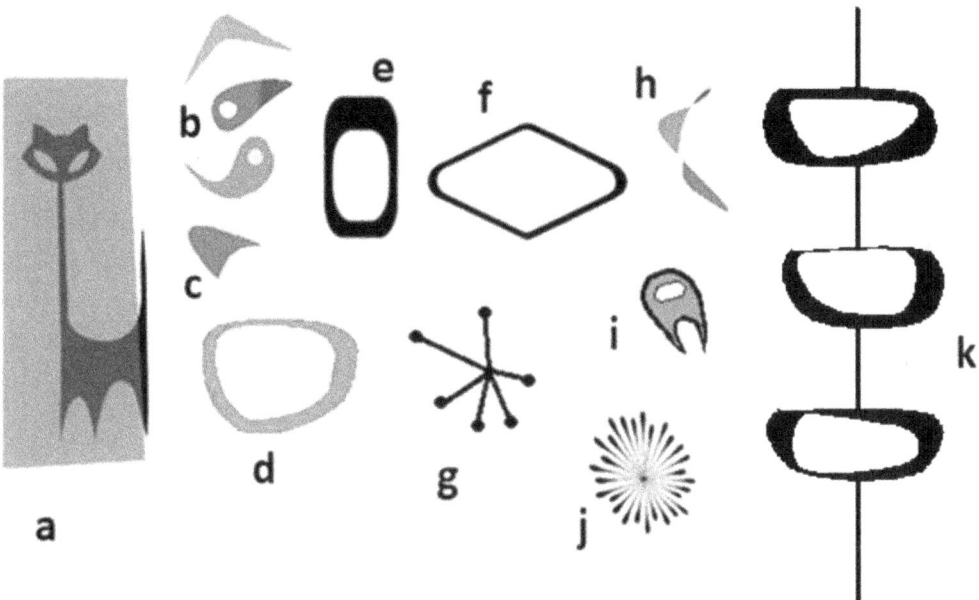

Figure 5-13. *Midcentury modern iconography often used organic, if abstract, shapes*

With that in mind, let's look at a couple of those shapes with the goal of generalizing them. We'll begin with the shape in Figure 5-13g. Let's call it the ***n-flower***.

Drawing the *N-Flower*

It will be drawn using a function:

void icong (int px, int py, int w, int h, int n)

where (**px, py**) is the position of the upper left corner, (**w,h**) is the width and height of the enclosing rectangle, and **n** is the number of circles to be drawn on the outline. The design proceeds as follows:

1. Find the center of the object as **cx=(x+w)/2** and **cy = (y+h)/2**. Set a size **r** to the minimum of the width **w** and height **h** divided by 2. Draw a circle of diameter **r** at (**cx, cy**).

2. Let **d** be 360 degrees divided by **n** and let **a** = 0.

203

CHAPTER 5 SHAPE

3. For each of **n** angles **a**: draw a circle around the center

   a. Let a = a + random (-d/3, d/3)+d, or +- 1/3 of d from a

   b. Let z = random (min(w,h)/5, min(w,h)), the length of the line from the center to the next circle. Should never be 0.

   c. Find x, y as the center of the next circle using trig.

   $$x = \cos(\text{radians}(a))*z + \mathbf{cx}$$
   $$y = \sin(\text{radians}(a))*z + \mathbf{cy}$$

   d. Draw a line from (**cx,cy**) to (x,y)

   e. Draw a circle of size **r** at (x, y)

Figure 5-14 shows variations drawn by this method.

The Zoop Pole

This is the shape shown in Figure 5-13k. It consists of three elliptical blobs (*zoops*) connected on a vertical line. It vaguely resembles a pole lamp from the same era.

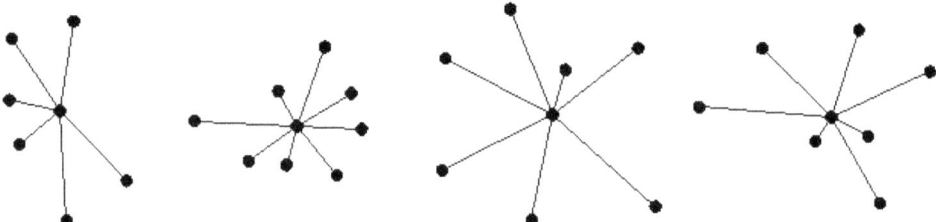

Figure 5-14. *The N-Flower in some of its random permutations*

Drawing A *Zoop*

The hard part of this icon is the *zoop* (the name is not universal). It consists of the outer shape and the inner one, both being four-sided shapes with curved corners. The inner one must be completely within the outer one, and the area in between the two is filled with a color.

Figure 5-15 shows an example and the steps in the design. Given an upper left corner (x,y) and a size (w,h), four points on a closed curve are determined that are within that rectangle by a small, random amount:

Upper left: x0 = random(w*.15)+x, and y0 = random(h*.2)+y

Upper right: x1 = x+w-random (.2*w) and, y1 = y+random(.1*h)

Lower rightx2 = x+w-random(.2*w), and y2 = y+h-random(.13*h)

Lower left: x3 = x+random(.25*w) and y3 = y+h-random(.2*h)

These points are joined by a spline curve using a set of **curveVertex** calls and are filled with black.

The next closed curve is inside of this curve, and so the upper left vertex is moved right and down, the upper right vertex is moved left and down, and so on.

Upper left: x4 = random(w*.2)+x0 and y4 = random(h*.13)+y0;

Upper right: x5 = x1-random (.2*w) and y5 = y1+random(.2*h);

Lower right: x6 = x2-random(.2*w) and y6 = y2-random(.2*h);

Lower left:x7 = x3+random(.23*w) and y7 = y3-random(.22*h);

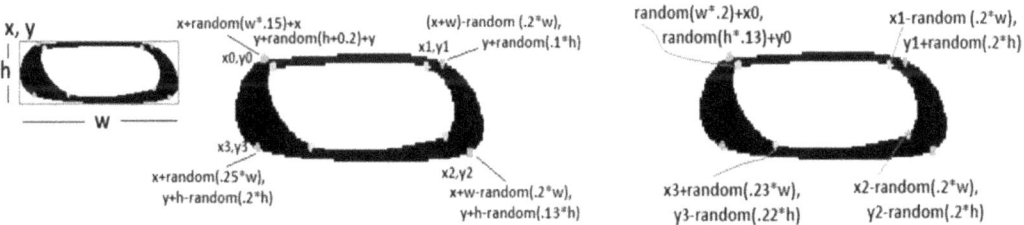

Figure 5-15. *The design of a zoop. The shape is enclosed in a rectangle at (x,y) that is (w,h) in size. A closed curve is drawn inside of that rectangle, filled with a color. A second closed curve is drawn inside of the first, filled with white*

These vertices are also linked using **curveVertex** but filled with black. The numeric constants can be changed but were selected to place the curve completely within the rectangle in the case of the outer curve and completely within the outer curve in the case of the inner curve.

CHAPTER 5   SHAPE

The Pole

This part's easy. The pole is a vertical line that passes through the center of each zoop, which are spaced vertically at equal distances from each other. But how do we make sure that this line just barely touched the top and bottom of each zoop shape? We simply draw it first so that the zoops are drawn over top of the line. The program is:

```
strokeWeight(3);
line (x+w/2, y, x+w/2, y+h);
strokeWeight(1);
zoop(x+10, y+h/12, w-20, (int)(w*0.3));
zoop(x+10, y+3*h/12, w-20, (int)(w*0.3));
zoop(x+10, y+5*h/12, w-20, (int)(w*0.3));
```

Identifying Patterns

The human mind has an amazing capacity to recognize and describe patterns. In fact, it might be what we do best. In the context of art, one theory is that what we consider interesting artworks are those that have complex and non-obvious patterns in them. Art that is too organized (regular, geometric) or too random (obviously no pattern to find) tends to be boring. Of course, color and other elements always play a part.

Why do we want to recognize shapes in an existing image? Because any artistic representation of a scene involves a representation of the components. This can be done more rationally is we have an idea about what those components might be. In many cases, the viewer of an artwork has a better chance of appreciating the work and of understanding the artist's intentions if the objects in the piece are at least recognizable as variations of real objects.

Figure 5-16. *(Left) Mondrian's Geometrische Komposition. (Center) Sketches by Hopper showing a lot of geometry in his preparation. (Right) Hopper's famous Nightawks.* https://www.openculture.com/2014/09/how-edward-hopper-storyboarded-his-iconic-painting-nighthawks.html

Finding shapes can be a valuable activity for a generative artist. For one thing, it is an important step in abstracting an image. Precise, geometric shapes are not common in nature, or even in photos generally, but finding approximate shapes allows us to determine relationships, find regions that are not obvious, and ultimately to combine them in new and interesting ways. Consider the Mondrian painting in Figure 5-16. There are clearly geometric – rectangular, in fact – elements, arranged with a distribution of sizes and filled with bold primary colors. It speaks of stability, organization, and also somewhat random placement of sizes and colors.

Extracting Shapes from Images

For the most part, a shape will represent an object. Finding objects in an image can be done in a couple of ways, most commonly using regions of similar color or value, or regions enclosed by a connected boundary. Computer vision experts often use neural networks to find objects, but the details of this will be beyond what this discussion should deal with – it's just too technical. On the other hand, AI tools based on neural nets exist, and we can use them without having to implement them ourselves.

When using regions of a similar color, smoothing should be a first step; perhaps a median filter. We then use a color region growing algorithm (as we created in Chapter 4, "Color"), followed by the selection of the region that is wanted. Figure 5-17 shows some images of a hand, both on a plain background and on a complex one. Using color region growing, a hand shape can be found in each. The process is:

1. Grow color regions in the image. The similarity threshold may vary from image to image, but should be similar in a class of images. Smoothing with a median filter first can help.

2. Pull out the color regions one at a time. The one we want is often one having a known color in the original image or the largest one.

3. Copy the object/shape into a second image, changing foreground pixels to black and background pixels to white.

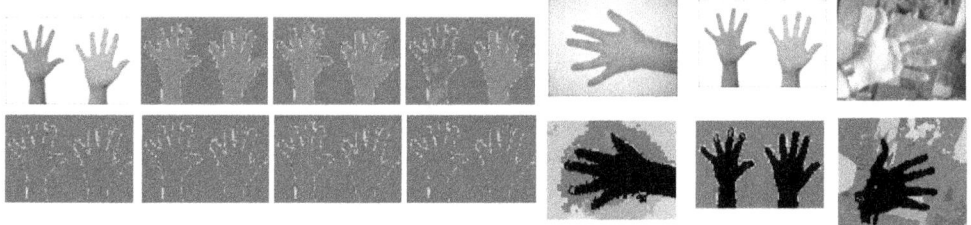

Figure 5-17. *Using region growing to locate shapes and objects*

Now the object can be measured for its shape using any of a number of relevant methods.

Using edges or boundaries is trickier, because it's hard to figure out which edges of many possible belong to one object as opposed to another. One way to improve the situation is to reduce the number of colors so that the object stands out from the background (Figure 5-18).

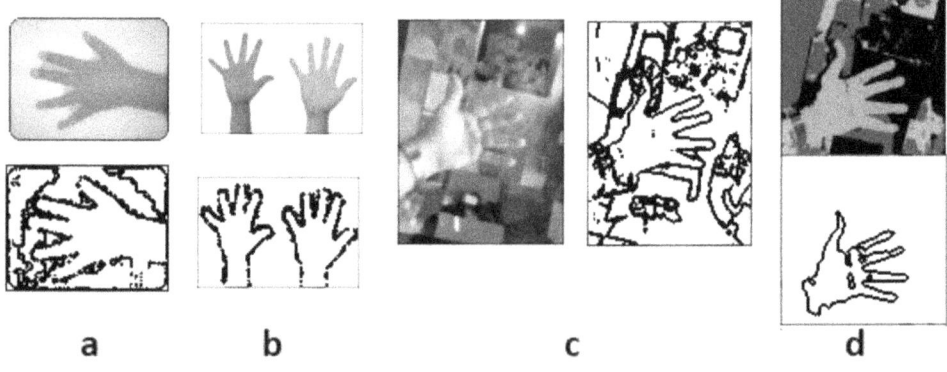

Figure 5-18. *Using boundaries to extract objects. (a,b) Plain background. (c) Noisy background. (d) Reducing colors before boundary extraction*

Using *Features* of Shapes

A *feature* is some information about the content of an object, a property that we can measure. Sometimes we can identify a shape by the values of a specific set of features (e.g., a specific face or a brand of vehicle); other times an object can be placed into a class of objects (a horse or an aircraft). Features are used in computer *pattern recognition* and *computer vision* applications to characterize objects in images, and so can be used by artists to label objects and then use the properties of the objects in the artwork. An artist can recognize a human figure in an image and use that knowledge to produce a work based on what humans can do or how they move, for example. A generative artist should have that ability as well.

We use features to recognize objects by selecting multiple features that we can see do a good job of characterizing the shape. We might use one set for searching for cars and a very different set for recognizing cats. We then measure the features of many objects in an image and see which ones have values that are most similar to the shape we're looking for.

The first step is deciding *what* features to use to recognize a shape, which is experimental; we might try many different features before choosing one or two. As we experiment, we are collecting a set of objects of a certain class (*cats*, for example) to be used as *models* of those shapes. Then we measure those features on shapes in an image to see how well they match the set of features we got from the models. This process is far from perfect, but then humans can't do it perfectly either.

Features That Are Scale Dependent

An orange is an orange no matter what its size in an image. Thus, it would seem that a scale-dependent feature would not be useful in recognizing an object. This is true, but these features can be used for normalizing an object, which is to say to make it or other features independent of scale.

Area

We generally measure the area of an object in terms of the number of pixels that it occupies in an image; a pixel is, after all, an area. In previous chapters we have used region growing as a way to identify areas of similar pixels; the pixels that belong to an object are likely to be similar to each other in value or color. Once we identify a region, we can simply count the pixels that belong to it.

The *Convex area* is the area of the smallest convex region that encloses the shape. The more irregular the outline of the shape is, the more this will differ from the basic area.

Perimeter

Perimeter is a linear measure, not area, so measuring it in terms of the number of pixels in the outline would not be technically correct. It is true that pixels are usually the same size in the horizontal and vertical dimensions, so perhaps it would not be impossible to use pixels as a measure of linear distance. It is pretty common to do so in practice.

In Chapter 2, "Line," we defined something called a *chain code* that we used to describe the outline of a monochrome object. The chain code includes codes for 8 directions, and these are of two kinds: *axis aligned* (i.e., horizontal and vertical) and *diagonal*. If we find the chain code for an object, we have a good measure of perimeter, because the diagonal codes, which represent the direction to a pixel, are longer than the others. If a pixel is 1x1 unit in size, a diagonal corresponds to the length of the diagonal of a 1x1 square, which is $\sqrt{2}$ units in length.

Thus, the perimeter of an object is the number of horizontal and vertical pixels in the chain code added to the number of diagonal pixels multiplied by $\sqrt{2}$

Length and Width

The *length* of a shape can be defined as the length of the longest line (*major axis*) that can be drawn through it. We could try every pair of pixels belonging to the shape to see which has the greatest distance between them. The angle that this line makes with the X axis can also be used as a feature if we like. This angle is **arctan((y_2-y_1)/(x_2-x_1))** for endpoints (x_1,y_1) and (x_2,y_2).

The *width* could be defined as the maximum length of a line that is perpendicular to the width axis while staying within the shape.

Features That Are Scale Independent

Circularity

This feature refers to how close to a circle a particular shape is. It's just a number, defined as **c = perimeter^2/(4π*area)**. For a circle, c=1. This is sometimes called *compactness*.

Rectangularity

This refers to how much a shape differs from a rectangle. Rectangularity is the ratio of the object to the area of the *minimum bounding rectangle.* or the *bounding box*.

We can find the bounding box by finding the smallest x and smallest y coordinates in the object and the largest x and y coordinates in the object and then use those to define a rectangle. All pixels in the object will be inside the box. The area of this box is its height **h=ymax-ymix** plus its width **w=xmax-xmin** multiplied by 2, or **2*(w+l)**. Its area is **w*l**. Rectangularity is then **area/(w*l)**.

Signatures

A general meaning of the term *signature* is some characteristic that identifies an object or individual, as in a person's handwritten signature. In the context of digital images and identifying objects, a signature is the set of distances from the center of an object to its outline as we look in angles from 0 to 359 degrees. This is explained in Figure 5-19. The signature is an array of numbers indexed by 0 .. 359.+

The center of an object is the mean of the x and the y coordinates. We'll call this point (**cx,cy**). Now draw a line at 0 degrees to the boundary of the object from this point. The length of that line is the value of the signature at 0. The length of a line from (cx, cy) to the boundary at angle 1 degree is the value of the signature at index 1. And so on. We should scale this to a known range so that the object's size does not affect the signature. Figure 5-19 shows the signature for the image of a pear.

CHAPTER 5 SHAPE

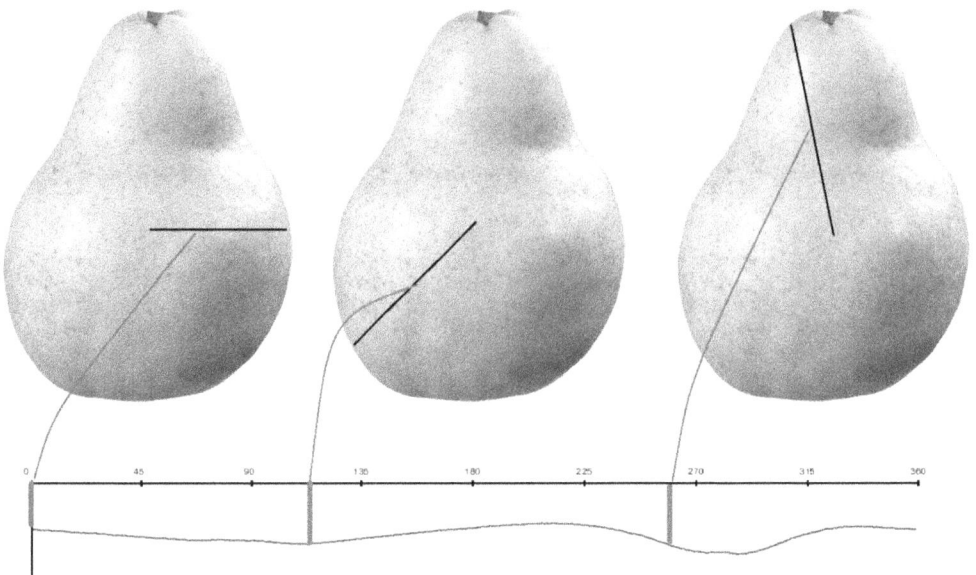

Figure 5-19. *The signature is a curve of the distance to the object boundary and every angle*

The signature is a curve, basically, but it does represent the object's shape. It has a valuable property: rotating the object merely shifts the signature in the x direction. This simplifies using the signature in real images, which are rarely oriented horizontally or vertically.

We can use the signature for identifying a shape by comparing an incoming shape against the signatures for known shapes. Each signature has 360 elements, so we compare two signatures point-by-point, accumulating a total error over the entire signature.

After finding and isolating an object, the process of using a signature to identify it involves matching it against a collection of known objects.

Assume there is a set of signatures **S** already computed for objects we know about and want to identify. Let T be the signature of an object we are trying to identify (the *target*). Then:

1. Let **i=0** and let S_i = signature **i** in the set **S**. Let **M=36000**, **besti=-1**
2. Calculate m_i = the ***match*** between S_i and **T.**
3. If m_i is smaller than **M** then set **M=M_i** and **besti =i**.
4. Let i=i+1

212

CHAPTER 5 SHAPE

5. If **i** is a legal index into **S**, go to 2.
6. The best match is object **besti**.

The **match** between two signatures s_1 and s_2 is calculated as follows:

1. Let a=0. Let d_a = 36000.
2. For each angle a between 0 and 359 inclusive
3. Let d=0
4. For each value of **i** between 0 and 359 inclusive:
5. Let **d = d +abs((s1[i+a]%360] - s2[i])**
6. If **d < d_a** then set **d_a = d**
7. The match value is **d_a**.

The match is calculated as the smallest match between s_1 and s_2 over all rotations of s_1.

Figure 5-20 shows matches between various objects and shows that a hand-drawn figure matches the template of that object, although not perfectly.

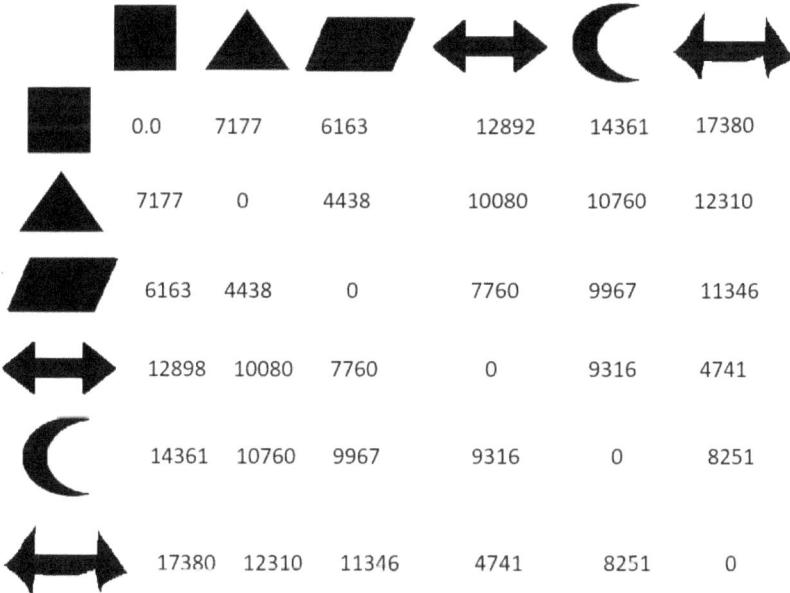

Figure 5-20. Signatures match between shapes. Computer-drawn objects match perfectly with themselves, but note that the hand-drawn double arrow matches the computer-drawn one (smallest match value)

213

CHAPTER 5 SHAPE

Convexity

If a polygon has the property that a line between any two points on the outline lies completely inside the polygon, then it is said to be *convex*. A circle and square are convex, but the hand shapes in Figure 5-18 are not.

Convex Hull

The convex hull is the convex polygon having the smallest area that can contain a set of points. Specifically in the context here, if we have a non-convex polygon, then the convex hull is the smallest (in area) polygon that can contain it. So, it can provide a convex polygon given a non-convex one, or for *any set of points*. It can be easily determined using multiple algorithms; we'll discuss one called *Jarvis' March*.

We begin with a collection of points. They could be data points or simply the vertices of a polygon of some sort: call this set **P**. A second set of points will be the convex hull, and we'll call this **H**. We will identify points in **P** that belong to the hull and copy these into **H**. As an example, let's use the points shown in Figure 5-21.

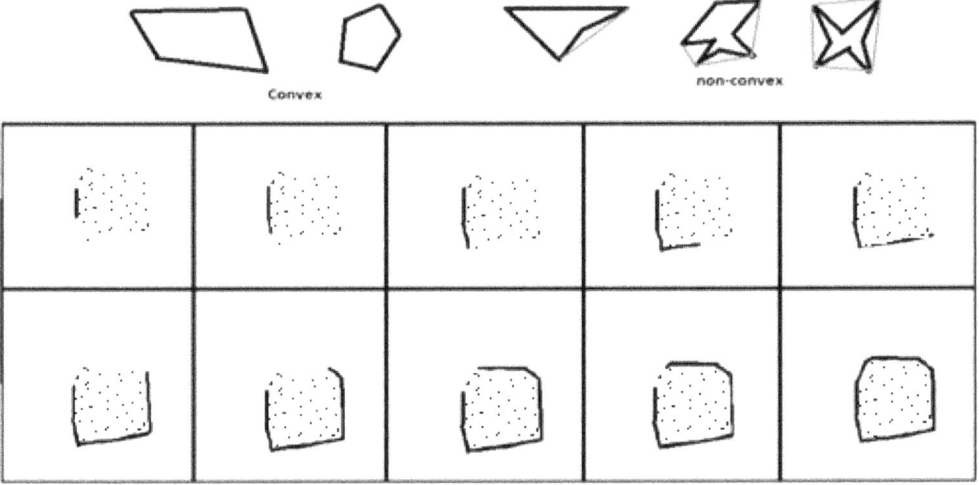

Figure 5-21. Convex and non-convex polygons, and steps in finding the convex hull

The point in **P** that has the smallest x coordinate has to be in the convex hull, so let's begin with that point: call it **start**. If there's more than one such point, use one of those with the smallest y coordinate. Finding **start** is the first step.

Now we need to find the *next* point on the convex hull. Left point **a** to **start**, initially. We look at all of the points **b** in the set **P** such that all points are to the left of the line ***a-b***. By left of we mean that when at point **a** facing point **b**, the point being considered is on our left. A function that does this is (math explained in Appendix I):

```
boolean leftof (float cx, float cy,
                float ax, float ay,
                float bx, float by)
{
  return (bx - ax)*(cy - ay) > (by - ay)*(cx - ax);
}
```

The code that creates the convex hull, which is just a set of points that are vertices on a convex polygon, does the following:

1. Find the **start** point. Set **a** = **start**, remove **a** from **P**, add **a** to the hull.
2. Select the next point **b** from the set of all points **P**.
   If **b=start** go to step 6
3. Select a (next) point **c** from the set **P.**
4. Is **c** to the left of **a-b**? If not, go to 2
5. All points are left of **a-b**, so add **b** to the hull. Goto step 2.
6. Hull is complete.

Figure 5-21 shows steps in finding the hull for one set of points. The convex hull has a lot of uses in computing, but when thinking about shape, it can be quite useful indeed.

Convex Area and Convex Perimeter

The convex area is simply the area of the convex hull, as opposed to the area of the polygon based on its vertices. Similarly, the convex perimeter is the perimeter of the convex hull of the polygon. These will be the same or larger than the normal area and perimeter values. The interesting aspect of these measures is how they differ from the normal ones:

```
Ca = area/(convex_area - area);
Cp = perimeter/(convex_perimeter - perimeter);
```

215

CHAPTER 5 SHAPE

Finding the *area* simply means counting the pixels that comprise the object, and finding the *perimeter* means counting the pixels in the object's outline or boundary.

Finding the *convex area* means determining the convex hull of the object and then finding the area of the hull. To do this:

1. Find the convex hull of the object.
2. Fill the background of **X** with white.
3. Draw the hull as a polygon into image **X** using color **C**.
4. Fill the background of **X** with color **C**.

Convex Area = the number of white pixels

Finding the convex perimeter is similar except we can stop after step 3:

1. Find the convex hull of the object.
2. Fill the background of **X** with white.
3. Draw the hull as a polygon into image **X** using color **C**.

Convex perimeter = the number of **C** pixels

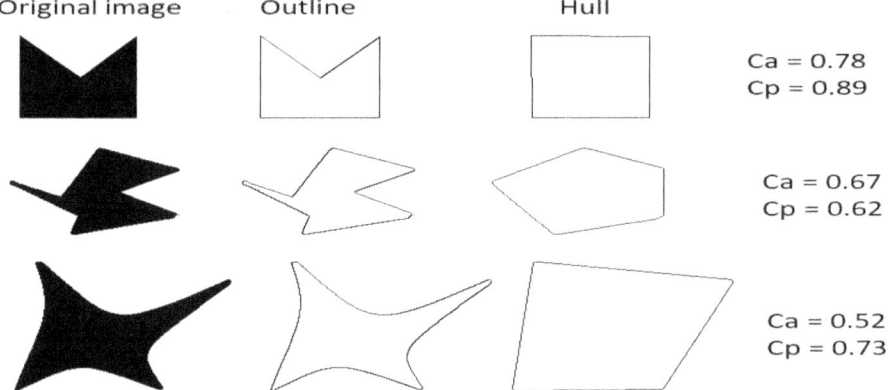

Figure 5-22. *Finding the convex area and convex perimeter, and the convexity measures*

CHAPTER 5 SHAPE

Figure 5-23. *Convex deficiencies. This shape has three of various positions and sizes*

The measure of convexity can now be described as based on either area **Ca** or perimeter **Cp**. Figure 5-22 shows how these are computed and what the values are for a couple of shapes.

Convex Deficiencies

A convex deficiency is a place on the outline of a polygon *where* the outline differs from being convex and by how much (Figure 5-23). The shapes in Figure 5-22 each have between one and four locations where the actual shape differs from the convex hull. These are places where the pixels in the original differ from the pixels in the hull when rendered as a polygon.

When such pixels are set to a known color, they form a pattern of smaller shapes having various sizes and locations around the center of the original object. This pattern can be descriptive of a particular shape.

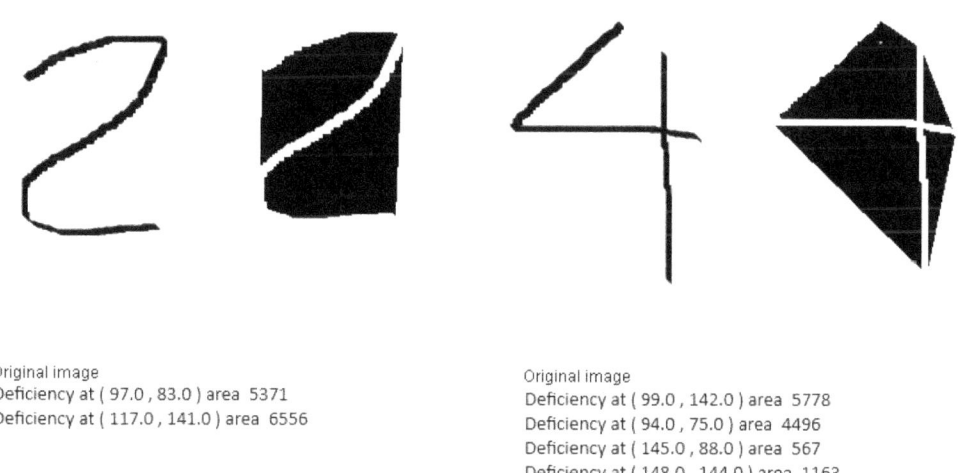

Figure 5-24. *Convex deficiencies can be used to characterize and identify specific shapes*

217

CHAPTER 5 SHAPE

Template Matching

We can locate specific shapes in an image by trying to match the shape, pixel by pixel, to pixels in the image. Let's make a small image containing only the shape we wish to identify. This image will be called the *template* and will have the shape drawn in pixels of one value and the background in another. In its simplest form, template matching involves placing the template image over top of the image being examined and identifying places where the pixels agree with each other. The template is placed over all possible locations, and the degree of agreement is recorded at each location. Locations where there is a high degree of agreement correspond to places where the template object exists within the image.

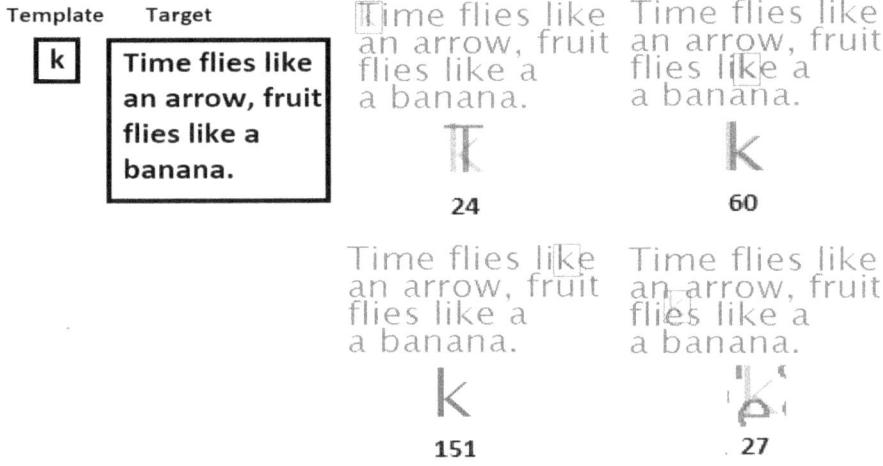

Figure 5-25. *The template of the letter "k" is placed in all locations in the target image, and the number of matching pixels is found*

Figure 5-25 shows how this works. The template is a monochrome image of the letter "k," and the image being searched for this template is an image of some text. We place the template in every location in the image to see how well the pixels in the two images agree. In this case, agreement will be defined as the pixels being identical in value. So we look at all pixels in the template to see which pixels in the image are the same, in this case black or white. If the template is NxM pixels in size, then the best possible match is N*M, when all pixels agree, and the worst possible match is 0, when none agree. It should be mentioned that if none of the pixels agree, then the pattern can actually be said to match except in reverse, with the back in the template being white in the image, and vice versa, so the method can ignore the background pixels (as in the figure).

218

Example: Ghosts

This artwork begins with the image of a building. There are windows and an entrance, although not much can be seen inside of the building (Figure 5-26). In this stage of the work we're going to locate some of the windows so that we can replace them with a new window that has a different image, one that can either represent a shadow of a person or a "ghost," or a green screen that we can use to map another image on later.

We could use a template to find some of the windows. A window copied from the image is shown as Figure 5-26a, and when used in this way, we find that it matches many of the windows pretty well. It does not match all of them because the pixels visible through each window is different, and the illumination and perspective vary a little. The replacement images are created from others, which are scaled to fit the window opening.

The replacement windows could be stored as coordinates or could be "green screen" images that would later be replaced by images or animation frames. Chapter 9, "Dynamism," will reprise this example using animations for each window.

The process is:

```
Read and display the building image.
Repeat N times
   -Perform template matching to find where the image template  can
    be found in the image.
   -Read a substitution image, scale it to fit, and draw it at the
    location where the match occurred.
   -Set the pixels in the original building image to white where the
    window was found.
end
```

Summary

Shape can be defined as the form of an object or its outline, outer boundary, or outer surface. It is how humans recognize and classify objects. Shapes can be polygonal/geometric, meaning that they can be defined using mathematics, or organic, which are more irregular, curved, and smooth. We can draw polygons using lines joining the vertices, or corners, of the polygon. Processing has a function for drawing the most basic polygons, lines, and points. Circles and ellipses can be defined by polynomial equations, which can also be used to draw them. An oval is two separate circles joined by two tangent lines.

CHAPTER 5 SHAPE

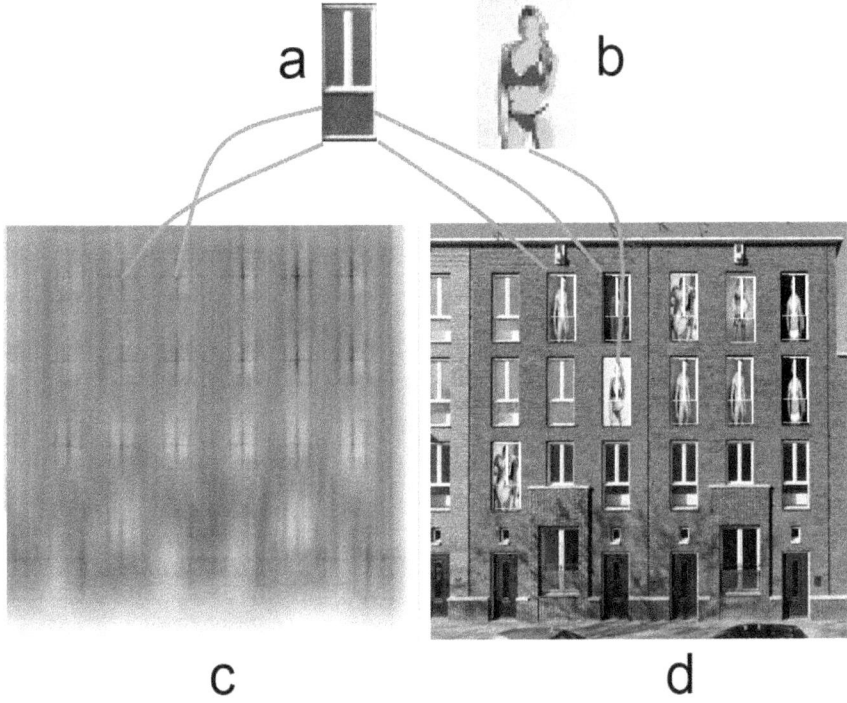

Figure 5-26. *(a) A template, a window image. (b) An image to replace the template. (c) Values where the template matches the image. (d) The result of finding the windows and replacing them with other images*

Blobs and organic shapes can be drawn using overlapping ellipses or by using a spline connecting randomly generated points on the outline. A spatter looks like a paint droplet and adds some small spatter marks on the outline. A natural organic shape like a leaf can be created using a digitized example and then creating random variations. Humans have invented a great many shapes for advertising, art, and amusement. Each needs to be analyzed carefully to create an algorithm for drawing it.

Shapes can be found in existing images by isolating them and measuring various features, then comparing those features to those from objects we know. Such features include circularity, rectangularity, and its signature (shape of the outline). Convexity can also be used, and a convex area and perimeter can characterize a shape. We can also try template matching, where we use an example of a shape to match to shapes in the image, pixel by pixel.

Library Code

blob0	- A blob using elipses
blob2	- Blob using curveVertex/splines
circlevc	- Draw a circle with varying color circumference
circlevs	- Draw a circle with varying size outline
closedoval	-
deficiency	- Convex deficiencies.
doHull	- Convex hull
drawEllipse	- Complete code for drawing an ellipse
extr	- Extract a region
icon2	- MCM icon, rectangle 2 colors
icon6	- Circle with a window.
Icon7	- Outlined trapezoid
iconk	- A zoop pole
icong	- An "n-flower"
oval	- Draw an oval
parallelogram	- Draw a parallelogram
polygon	- Draw an N-sided polygon.
poly	- Draw a polygon using an array of vertices
quadrilateral	- Draw a quadrilateral.
regions	- Identify a region using color
rhombus	- Draw a rhombus
sigImage	- Compute a signature from an image
spatter	- Draw a spatter pattern
templateMatch	- Basic template match

(continued)

CHAPTER 5 SHAPE

templateM2	- Second matching method
trapezoid	- Draw a trapezoid
example .	- the artwork in Figure 5-26.
smoke	- particle smoke

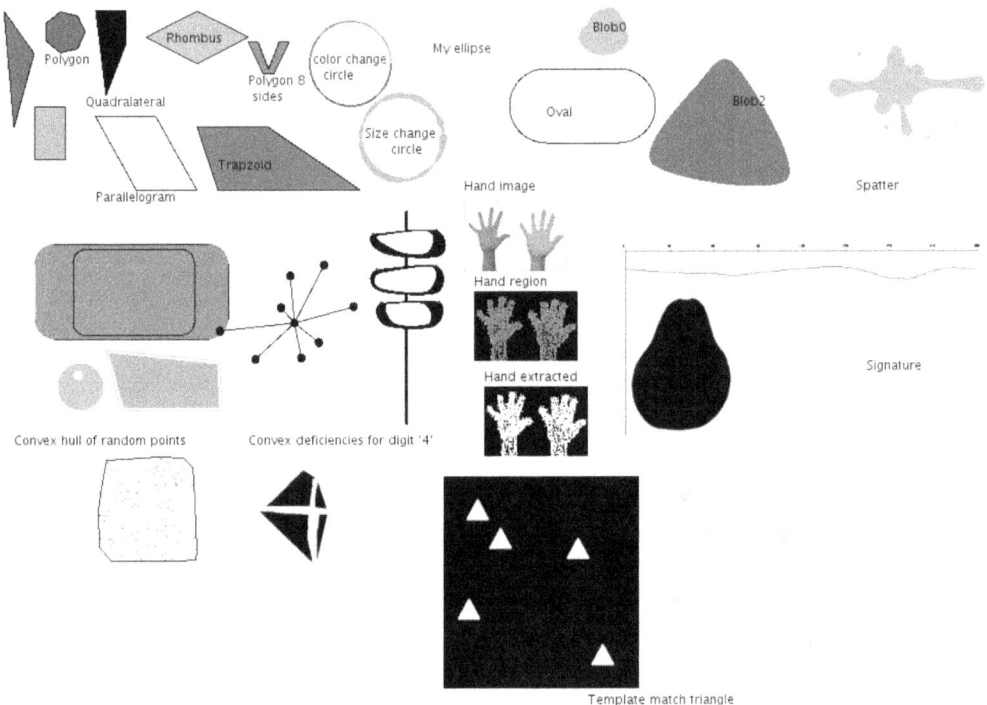

*The result of the test program **library05**, demonstrating the library code for this chapter.*

CHAPTER 6

Texture

Shading and texture are used by the human visual system as ways to determine the shape of three-dimensional objects, so their use in accurately rendering objects like trees is critical. *Shading* is the use of color or intensity variations across an area being drawn to illustrate shape. In particular, it is used to simulate the effect of illumination on the object. *Texture* amounts to the surface detail of a real object. It is a difficult concept to convey simply, and yet most people understand texture implicitly. Texture is a pattern that appears on the surface of an object. It's probably tactile but is also visual and identifies the nature of the material. Wood, cloth, metal, and stone have tactile (touch) and visual texture, and they help humans identify objects and their shapes and orientations. As a result, when we draw objects, we need to apply what we know about textures to the rendering process.

Although there is no agreement on a formal definition of texture, a major characteristic is the *repetition of a pattern or patterns over a region.* The pattern may be repeated exactly or as a *set of small variations* on the theme, possibly a function of position. There is also a random aspect to texture that must not be ignored – the size, shape, color, and orientation of the elements of the pattern (sometimes called *textons*) can vary over the region. Sometimes the difference between two textures is contained in the degree of variation alone or in the statistical distribution found relating the textons.

The degree of random variation in a texture can vary widely. A checkerboard pattern is a texture that is quite regular, whereas a wood grain or stone texture has unpredictable variations in the pattern. It is the irregularities that make textures seem natural, because the forces that cause a tree to grow in a specific way and create the wood grain pattern can't be determined and vary day to day and year to year. Apparent randomness is a typical characteristic of nature.

To impart a natural character to images, we often use textures. Painters create their own, of course, but in generative art, we have a couple of choices: we can try to create our own, or we can use images of real textures. These textures can be drawn over top of the polygons of an object to produce a realistic rendering to whatever degree we like. Traditional artists use textures all the time and "map" them onto their paper or canvas using basic *textons*. These can be strokes, circles, or other patterns. When using a computer, we map textures pixel by pixel from a texture onto a polygon or surface.

Texture is a property possessed by a region that is sufficiently large to demonstrate its recurring nature. A region cannot display texture if it is small compared with the size of a *texton*. This leaves us with a problem of *scale*, in addition to the other problems that texture presents. Indeed, the same texture at two different scales will be perceived as two different textures, provided that the scales are different enough. As the scales become closer together, the textures are harder to distinguish, and at some point they become the same.

Applying Textures

Most commonly, a texture is an *image*: a photograph or drawing of a texture pattern. In normal use, the texture is placed within a specified area, which is usually a polygon, by copying the image pixel-by-pixel into that area. This is referred to as *texture mapping*. As an example, the image in Figure 6-1a represents a beginning or a rendering of a house. The colored areas represent different parts – doors, windows, and so on. Without more detail, it does not look much like a house.

Figure 6-1b shows a few textures that could be used to decorate this so-far mundane piece. There are a couple of stucco textures, some concrete, and some images of doors and windows. A first step will be to copy the background textures, like the stucco, onto the areas where they belong. In this case we'll do that using color for simplicity, but that's not usual practice. Here, the white pixels in the house image will be replaced by pixels from the stucco image, and the gray pixels from the lower portion of the image will be replaced by pixels from a concrete texture image. The result can be seen in Figure 6-1c.

When texture mapping using color, we simply replace pixels of a known color in the target with corresponding pixels from a texture image. In *Processing*:

```
// dest is the target image, c is the color of pixels to be replaced,
// and tex is a texture image
void map1 (PImage tex, color c, PImage dest)
{
  color pix;
```

CHAPTER 6　TEXTURE

```
for (int i=0; i<dest.width; i++)     // For every pixel
  for (int j=0; j<dest.height; j++)  // in the target
  {
    pix = im.get(i,j);      // If that pixel has the
    if (pix == c)           // color c, replace it.
      im.set (i, j,         // by one from the texture
        tex.get(i%tex.width, j%tex.height));
  }
```

When mapping a door or window, we have to be mindful of the boundaries in the target where they are to be placed. The texture images must fit into the rectangle provided. If the texture is larger than the rectangle, then only part of it will be copied; if the texture is smaller than the rectangle, then it will be repeated so as to fill it. In this example, we find pixels having a specific color, determine the rectangular area that they occupy, scale the texture image to fit that area, and then copy the pixels into the target from the texture. Again, in *Processing*:

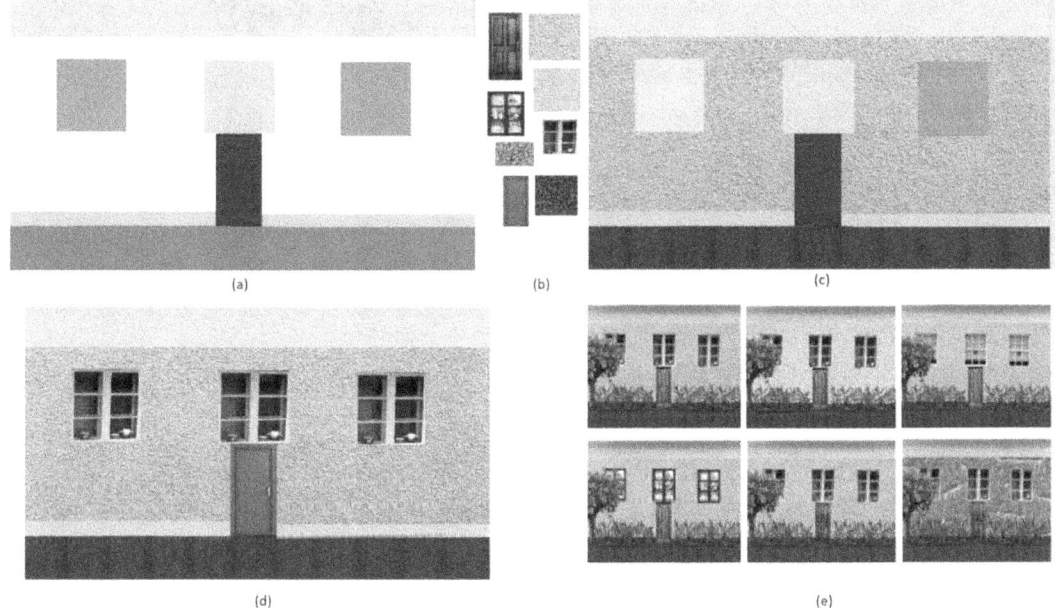

Figure 6-1. *(a) A simple template for a house. (b) Sample textures to make the house look better. (c) The house after applying the background textures. (d) The house after applying windows and doors. (e) These textures can be changed, creating a wide variety of houses from one template*

CHAPTER 6 TEXTURE

```
void mapFit (PImage tex, color c,      // Scale the texture to fit the region
             PImage dest)              t = tex.copy();
{                                      t.resize (lrx-ulx, lry-uly);
  color pix;
  int ulx,uly, lrx,lry;                // Copy pixels from the texture
  // selected area
  PImage t;                            //  to the target
                                       for (int i=ulx; i<ulx+t.width; i++)
// Find the size of the area             for (int j=uly; j<uly+t.height; j++)
  ulx = dest.width*2;                    {
  uly = dest.height*2;                     pix = im.get(i,j);
  lrx = -1; lry = -1;                      if (pix == c)
  for (int i=0; i<dest.width; i++)            im.set (i,j, t.get
                                              (i-ulx, j-uly));
    for (int j=0; j<dest.height;       }
    j++)
    {                                  }
      pix = im.get(i,j);
      if (pix == c)  // The right
      color?
      {
        if (i<ulx) ulx = i;
        if (j<uly) uly = j;
        if (i>lrx) lrx = i;
        if (j>lry) lry = j;
      }
    }
}
```

The bounding box, or minimum enclosing rectangle, for the colored region is found and used as the new size for the texture image, which is then mapped as before.

Traditional Texture Mapping

Using a texture in a computer graphic (*texture mapping*) is usually done onto polygons, often in three dimensions, and not using additional color. The polygon might not be a rectangle; the edges may not be parallel, and mapping onto triangles is also common. These things complicate the process, making it geometric and mathematical.

The basic idea is simple, though. For each pixel in the polygon to be texture mapped (the *target*), we identify the pixel or pixels from the texture image that correspond to that pixel and replace the target value with the value(s) from the texture. The mapping is defined using the coordinates of the vertices. Each vertex corresponds to a specified pixel in the texture as defined by the artist/programmer. We have already seen how the *vertex* statement is used to define shapes. Now we extend it to also specify textures.

Drawing a quadrilateral in *Processing* using the vertex operation is done as:

```
beginShape(QUADS);
  vertex (100, 100);
  vertex (340, 270);
  vertex (390, 450);
  vertex (120, 330);
endShape();
```

Now let's add a texture image **tex** and map it onto this polygon. The texture is a rectangular image, but the polygon is not rectangular, so the pixel mapping is complicated. Fortunately, *Processing* does it for us, as does most graphics software. All we need to do is specify which pixels in the target correspond to which ones in the texture. First, we say:

```
textureMode (NORMAL);
```

which means that the texture image will have X coordinate values that run from 0.0 to 1.0, whatever the actual size of the image, and the same for Y coordinates. Next:

```
beginShape(QUADS);
  texture (tex);
```

This starts the drawing of the polygon and specifies what the texture image will be. The first point will be, in this example:

```
vertex (100, 100, 0, 0);    // Coordinate 100,100 corresponds
                            // to texture 0,0 = upper left
```

CHAPTER 6 TEXTURE

This says that the first vertex in the polygon being drawn is (100,100), and that it corresponds to (0,0) in the texture image, which is the upper left corner. Using normalized coordinates means that we don't have to care what the actual size of the texture image is. The other three vertices are:

```
vertex (340, 270,  1, 0);  // Image coordinate (340,270)
                           // corresponds to texture (1,0)
vertex (390, 450,  1, 1);  // Image coordinate (1,1)

vertex (120, 330,  0, 1);  // Image coordinate (120,330)
                           // corresponds to texture (0,1)
endShape();
```

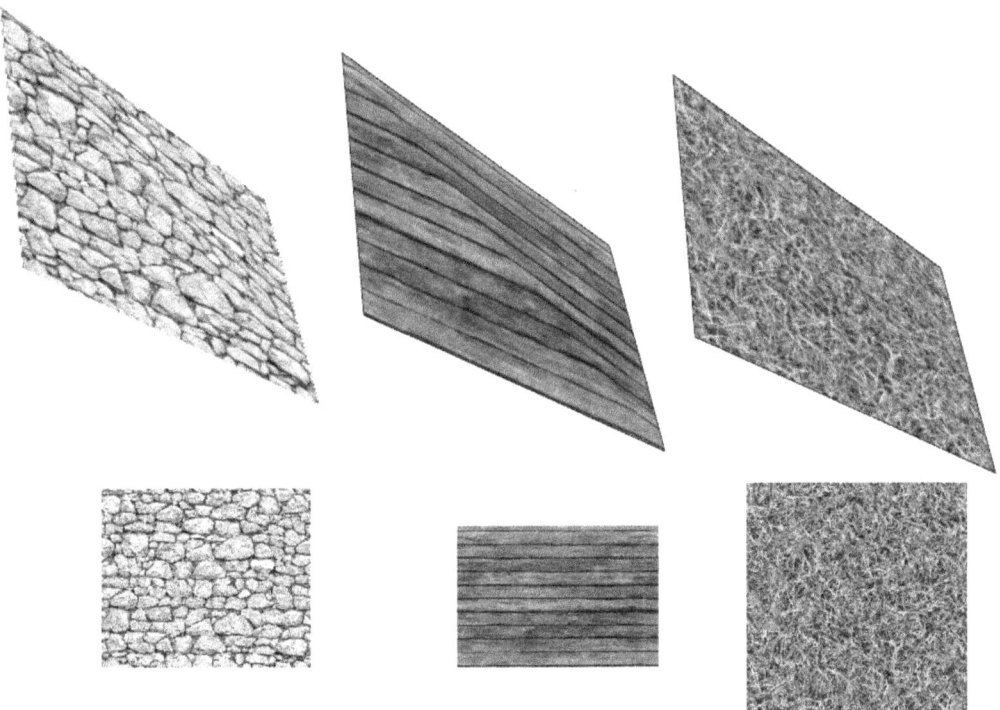

Figure 6-2. *Texture mapping onto parallelograms. The target image is examined pixel by pixel, and values are copied to it, rather than scanning the texture image*

We're mapping the texture vertices clockwise, from upper left to upper right, to lower right, to lower left. The result of this code is shown in Figure 6-2 for three different textures. The texture in each case has been bent so that it follows the shape of the polygon that was drawn.

CHAPTER 6 TEXTURE

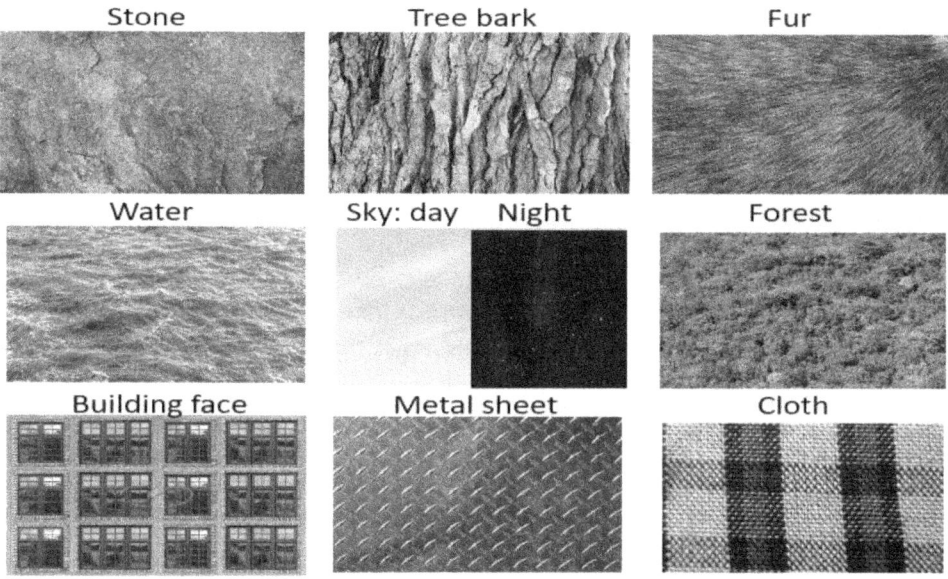

***Figure* 6-3.** *Photos of natural textures that can be used in artworks*

Natural Textures

Natural textures are those that we encounter in daily life and that lend reality to scenes and images. They don't have to be textures that occur in nature but can be urban or based on human activity. We can classify textures crudely as those based on plants or animals, those based on nature and its activities, and those based on human structures and actions. Figure 6-3 gives some examples.

Textures from nature tend to have a higher degree of randomness than other kinds, containing few consistent structural elements and few geometric shapes. Human-based textures tend to have linear features and sharp boundaries, with repeating patterns. Human textures can also *contain* natural ones: a stone wall has a human texture pattern consisting of smaller stone (natural) textures.

We can make textures for use in art simply by photographing the ones we see in scenes. These may need to be modified before being used. If the texture image is large enough, then it may need to be modified for brightness or contrast. If the texture is too small, it might have to be repeated or tiled over the target polygon. In this case, the left and right edges of the texture need to align with each other, or the join where the two texture images meet will be visible. The same applies to the upper and lower edges.

229

CHAPTER 6 TEXTURE

Tiled Textures

When a texture is applied to a polygon, the polygon and the texture image could be of very different sizes. In the case where the texture image is smaller than the polygon, it should not seem to obviously repeat its pattern across the image in any direction. The texture image should match pixel by pixel at the left and right edges and the top and bottom edges so that the repetition would not be obvious.

The well-known artist M. C. Escher was famous for creating tiled images using complex shapes. Filling a region like this is called tessellation. It's possible to find tileable textures online, at websites. It's also possible to create them using graphics tools like Photoshop.

Reflection

The simplest way to create a texture that can be repeated (tiled) without an obvious seam is to *reflect* it across the right side and the bottom. The image **a** is left-to-right reversed into a second image **b**, and then the two images are placed next to each other in a third image. The pixel at **a(width-1,0)** will match the pixel at **b(0, 0)**, and **a(width-1,0)** will match **b(0 1)**, and so on. This can be seen as an obvious symmetry in the resulting texture image, but the pixels *will* meet seamlessly (Figure 6-4). Even simple drawing programs like Paint can do this.

CHAPTER 6　TEXTURE

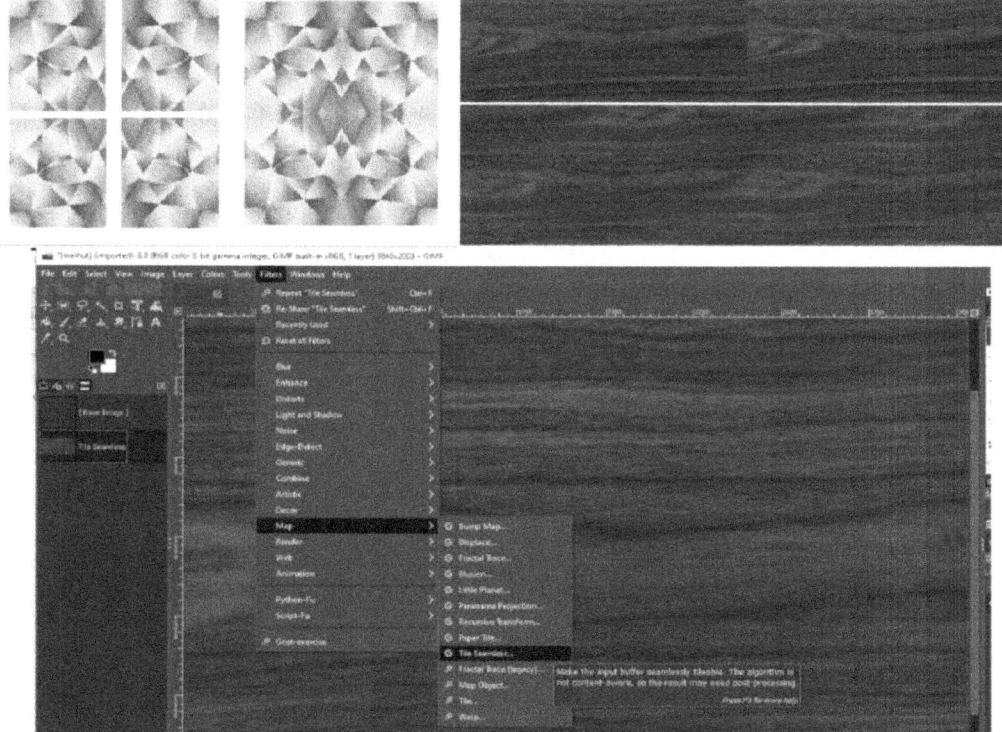

Figure 6-4. *A folded texture to make it symmetric, and a wood texture made seamless using GIMP*

GIMP

The Gnu Image Manipulation Program, or *GIMP*, can do many interesting operations, including the creation of seamless textures. What it actually does is a complex analysis, matching, and smoothing of portions of an image. The effect is to modify the images so that they can be tiled seamlessly. The program is easily downloaded, and it is free and safe. Run the program and load the texture image. Then select Filters ➤ Map ➤ Tile Seamless. This is the easiest way to create a seamless texture.

Doing a web search using a phrase like "create a tileable texture" or "make a seamless texture" can yield multiple websites that allow tileable textures to be created from simple images. Some use basic image processing methods, some use AI, but most are quite acceptable. It is a bit difficult to get an AI tool to make a seamless texture, but they can be made to make some very large and realistic ones.

231

CHAPTER 6   TEXTURE

Synthetic Textures

A *synthetic* texture is one that is created by a computer program. If we're trying to produce something that is something that could be found in the real world, then we have to try and simulate the textures that naturally occur. Each instance will be different. We did this when we made a pencil texture in a previous chapter. In some sense, all textures created and used by traditional artists are synthetic, because they are made from the artist's perception of the texture but don't exactly duplicate it.

A computer program that creates a grass texture will be quite different from one that creates wood grain or rock, because we need to model the visual properties of each texture. This is often based on statistics. All that we can do is describe the techniques that apply in general and suggest ways to use them in specific cases. Each texture will have a specific color range, a variation on that range, and a selection of properties that can have random parameters.

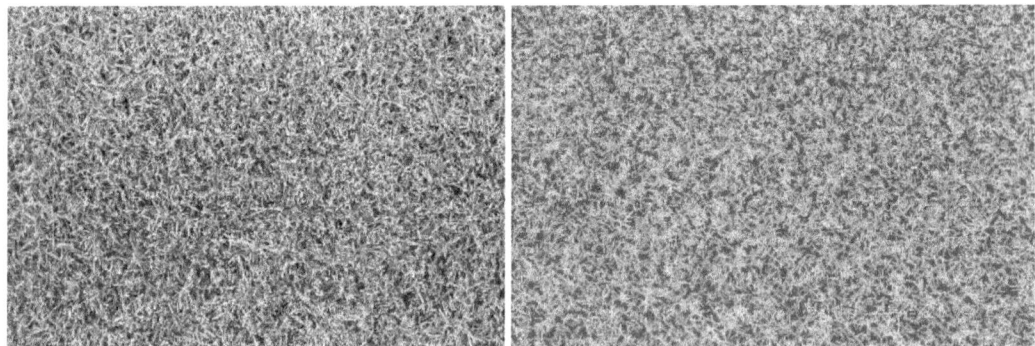

Figure 6-5. *Real grass and synthetically created grass texture*

A good example of a synthetic texture is grass. Real grass is a large collection of simple plants, linear in shape and pretty uniform in color. Slight variations in color, orientation, position, and length can be used to generate a pretty realistic texture. Figure 6-5 shows an example. The image on the left is a photograph of some actual grass, whereas the image on the right is generated by a program. Differences can be seen, but that would be true of any pair of photos of grass, and the effect is convincing. The code that does this is surprisingly brief. First a random position within the drawing area is generated and stored as variables **x** and **y**. Then a change in x and y, called **dx** and **dy**, is created with random directional parameters. Then a line is drawn between (**x,y**) and (**x+dx, y+dy**) using a random shade of green between (100,155, 100) and (100,255, 100). This is done 140000 times.

```
void draw ()
{
  int x, y, dx, dy;
  for (int i=0; i< 140000; i++)
  {
    x = (int)random (width);                // X position
    y = (int)(randomGaussian ()*400);       // Y position
    dx = (int)((random (25)-13)*y/800);     // Change in X
    dy = (int)(random (12) * y/800);        // Change in Y
    stroke (100, random (100) + 155, 100);  // Random green
    line (x, y-100, x+dx, y-100-dy);        // Line segment
  }
}
```

This is an easy example to program because grass has simple texture elements (line segments), simple color variation (shades of green), and a large number of overlapping elements. Textures having very small degrees of randomness or very high degrees can be easier to render convincingly. Grass has a high degree of random variation.

Controlled Randomness – Value Noise

Imagine generating pixel values that are completely random. The result will look terrible from a visual perspective. That's because in real life, as well as in art, pixels don't change much in value if they are near each other unless there is an edge, and even then edges form contiguous patterns. This is not seen in a purely random image. We'd like two adjacent pixels to change value with some random characteristic but to still have values that are *near* to each other in some way. For example, as we move from x=1 to x=10, it is likely that the value will increase or decrease continuously between the values at x=1 and x=10.

This is something we can do, and the method described here is called *value* noise. The idea is that, instead of neighboring pixels being given random values, we give random values to pixels N locations apart and then interpolate the values between them. The interpolation causes adjacent values to be near each other over a relatively small distance, while allowing the overall number sequence to change randomly. As an example, let's generate ten random values:

```
X:     0     1      2     3     4     5     6     7     8     9
V: 165.4 ,189.8 ,121.6 ,109.7,139.2, 137.7 ,178.9,131.3 ,115.9 ,153.5
```

CHAPTER 6   TEXTURE

When drawn, these points are completely random and give a poor degree of continuity between adjacent points. Real-world boundaries are never this jagged. To control the randomness here using value noise, we first move the points apart. Instead of being 1 pixel or x coordinate apart, make them, as an example, 10 apart:

```
X:     0    10    20    30    40    50    60    70    80    90
V: 165.4 ,189.8 ,121.6 ,109.7,139.2, 137.7 ,178.9,131.3 ,115.9 ,153.5
```

Now compute the values that are at each of the 10 *X* coordinates between each pair of *V* values. If we use *linear interpolation* as we've done elsewhere, this corresponds to joining the points with straight lines. Let's look only at the data between X=10 and X=20. We start at location x=10, which is 189.8, and add the difference between V at X=10 and V at X=20 divided into 10 parts, which is -(121.6-189.8)/10, at each step.

```
X:     10    11    12    13    14    15    16    17    18    19
V:  189.8 182.2 176.2 169.3 162.5 155.7 148.9 142.1 135.2 128.4
```

This gives us a nice ramp from X=10 to X=20. It is still not very realistic, because there are drastic changes in direction (*discontinuities*) at X=10, X=20, X=30, and so on. That's due to the linear interpolation.

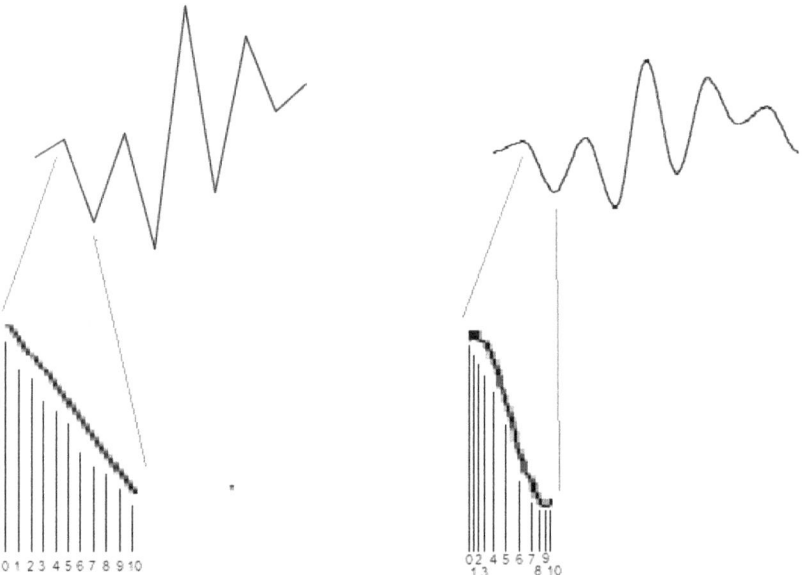

***Figure* 6-6.** *One-dimensional interpolation to create value noise. (a) The random noise values and interpolating between them. (b) Cubic interpolation makes the curve smoother at join points*

Figure 6-6 shows the completely random data, the linearly interpolated result, and the result of the cubic interpolation. The cubic interpolation gives a smoother result and is a more reasonable version of an actual natural random data set, where the neighboring values have an influence over each other. Real measurements rarely differ radically in a small area. Edges and boundaries are exceptions to this, but the value on each side of the edges will be similar to each other.

This is, of course, one dimensional. Images are two dimensional. We can do two-dimensional interpolation to solve the 2D problem for images, and that can be implemented as a variation on 1D interpolation. Again, we generate random values to begin with, but now these are the pixel values at the corners of a rectangle. We need to fill the rectangle with pixels that represent a continuous change from each of the four corners.

The first step is to do a 1D interpolation to find the value at the top and bottom of the rectangle. The pixel value Q11 is the upper left value, and Q21 is the upper right, and interpolating between these at each intervening pixel will give the continuous sequence we need. We do the same for pixel Q12 and pixel Q22 at the bottom. Now we interpolate between each of the pixels at the top and bottom of the rectangle to fill in the columns. We're interpolating between two values that are in fact interpolations themselves. That's the essence of how 2D interpolation works.

The code provided for this chapter gives a function **vnoiseLinear** that will take two random values and interpolate linearly between them:

```
// f(x1)=Q1 and f(x2) = Q2. What is f(x)?
float vnoiseLinear(float Q1, float Q2, float x1, float x2, float x)
{
  float r, xx;
  r = (x-x1)/(x2-x1);           // Scaled position of x in the range
  return r*(Q2-Q1)+Q1;
}
```

When using this code, **x1** is a starting x location and **x2** is the end. The values of the function being interpolated are **Q1** = F(**x1**) and **Q2** = F(**x2**), and the value of **x** is the location where the interpolation is to be calculated; **x** must be between **x1** and **x2**.

CHAPTER 6 TEXTURE

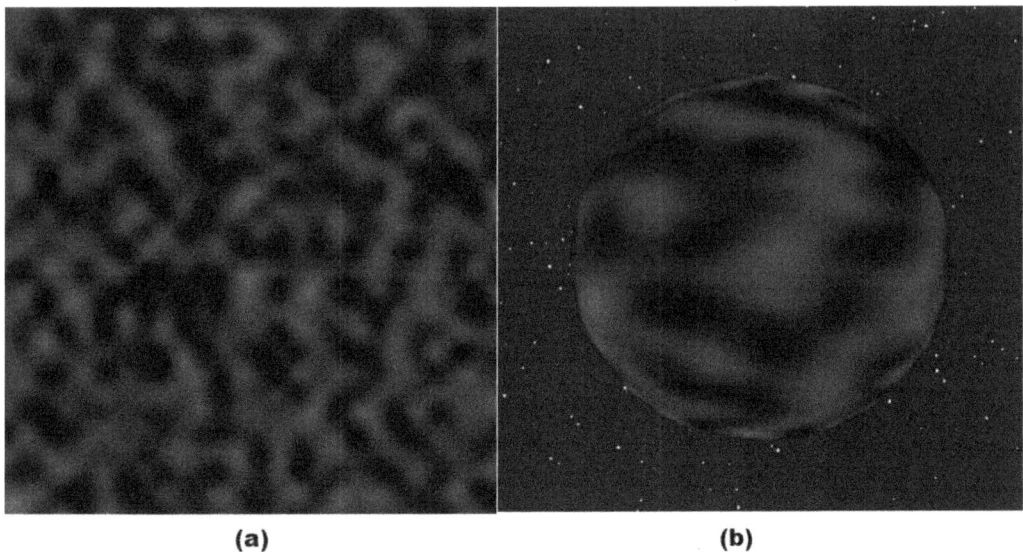

(a) **(b)**

Figure 6-7. *Two-dimensional cubic interpolation makes random noise useful for many situations, like planets, water, and fire textures*

Cubic Noise

Cubic noise is really just upscaled random noise that uses cubic interpolation in two dimensions. There is a cubic interpolation function in the code library:

float vnoiseCubic (float p0, float p1, float p2, float p3,
             float x1, float x2, float x)

where **p0, p1, p2,** and **p3** are known (random?) values, **x1** and **x2** are the extents of a range in the X direction being considered, and **x** is the actual location between **x1** and **x2** where we wish the interpolation to be calculated. Figure 6-7 shows this two-dimensional case and shows this texture used to simulate a planet.

We could use a more complicated polynomial instead of a line to find values between the points. A *cubic* interpolation uses a polynomial **a**x^3 + **b**x^2 + **c**x + **d** to find the values between the end points. The problem has been solved by others: we must know the values of **a, b, c,** and **d** for the calculation to succeed, and these values are:

$$a = -p0/2.0 + 3.0*p1/2.0 - 3.0*p2/2.0 + p3/2$$
$$b = p0 - 5.0*p1/2.0 + 2*p2 - p3/2.0$$
$$c = -p1/2.0 + p2/2.0$$
$$d = p1$$

236

where **p1** is the value at the starting point, **p2** is the value at endpoint, **p0** is the value at the point *before* the starting point, and **p3** is the value at the point *after* the endpoint. For a linear interpolation, we need 2 data points. For a quadric interpolation, we'd need 3, and for a cubic we need 4. In the case we described, **p1** is the value at **X=10**, **p2** is the value at **X=20**, **p0** would be the value at **X=0**, and **p3** would be the value at **X=30**. In our example we're breaking the interval into 10 parts, so the starting value of **x** is 0 (corresponding to **p1**), and we increment **x** by 0.1, which is 1/10, at each step. If we had divided the interval into 100 parts, then we'd increment **x** by 1/100, and so on. Now each increment, which is to say the value at each step x, would be calculated as $ax^3 + bx^2 + cx + d$, which is a collection of cubic curves and not lines.

If the points **p0 … p3** form a straight line, then the cubic interpolation gives a straight line too. If they are random, then the interpolated points form a smooth curve between those points, like we had with a spline curve. As an example, if the points are:

$$p0 = 190.0; \; p1 = 100; \; p2 = 50.0; \; p3 = 90.0;$$

and p1 is the data at x=10 and p2 is the data at x=20, then we get:

X:	10	11	12	13	14	15	16	17	18	19
V:	100	92.8	86.0	79.2	72.8	66.9	61.6	57.1	53.3	51.2

This is only one section of the data; remember that we took random values and split the interval between them into many points, in this instance 10 of them. Let's say that we have 100 random samples. How do we connect them after interpolating? There are four samples needed per interval, after all.

The solution is to overlap them. If we name our random samples **P0, P1, …, P99,** then we can make the first interpolated interval the one between **P1, P2, P3**, and **P4**. The next one would be **P2, P3, P4, P5**, and so on. The interval from **P0** is a problem because we need a previous sample. One solution is to generate more samples than we need, such as an extra one at the beginning. Another is to use the last sample as the one before the first; that is, the first interpolated sequence would be using **P99, P0, P1,** and **P2**.

CHAPTER 6 TEXTURE

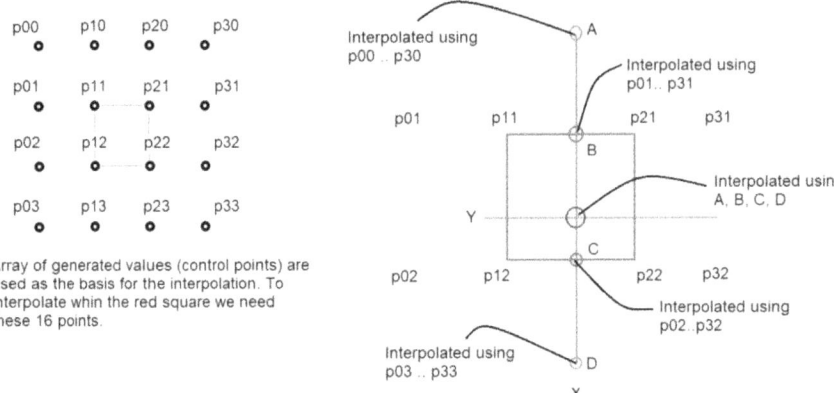

Figure 6-8. *Two-dimensional interpolation for noise begins with generating random noise in a 2D array. Each portion of the grid needs 16 values for interpolation calculations. First, using the x coordinate for the point being computed, we interpolate the 4 values A, B, C, and D using 1D cubic interpolation. We then us A, B, C, and D to interpolate the Y coordinate. The result will be inside the rectangle (p11, p12)(p22, p32)*

Making this two dimensional needs more code than in the bilinear case. We first need to generate the random 2D array of grid points:

```
float n2d[][] = new float[100][100];

  for (int i=0; i<100; i++)
    for (int j=0; j<100; j++)
      n2d[i][j] = random (0.0, 1.0);
```

Now we scan this array and interpolate between X values, then Y. However, there are four values needed in each direction, so we require 4x4=16 values to interpolate between four points. That is, to interpolate between (p11, p21) and (p12, p22), we need all of the values that surround it (Figure 6-8).

The code that creates a 2D interpolation based on the figure is:

```
  for (int i=1; i<98; i++)
  {
    for (int j=1; j<98; j++)
    {
      for (int ii=0; ii<50; ii++)
      {
```

```
    for (int jj=0; jj<50; jj++)
    {
      x0 = getValue (p00(i,j), p10(i,j), p20(i,j), p30(i,j),
          (float)ii/50.0);
      x1 = getValue (p01(i,j), p11(i,j), p21(i,j), p31(i,j),
          (float)ii/50.0);
      x2 = getValue (p02(i,j), p12(i,j), p22(i,j), p32(i,j),
          (float)ii/50.0);
      x3 = getValue (p03(i,j), p13(i,j), p23(i,j), p33(i,j),
          (float)ii/50.0);
      v = getValue (x0, x1, x2, x3, (float)jj/50.0);
      set (i*50 + ii, j*50+jj, color(v*255,v*255,v*255));
    }
  }
 }
}
```

Cubic interpolation values provided by **vnoiseCubic** can be organized into a hierarchy and used like *Photoshop* layers, where the final image is the sum of the individual layers. Each layer has a different level of detail and provides a different value component. These layers are called *octaves* [Talle 2017]. We can have as many octaves (layers) as we like, and each is drawn over the previous layers using a greater degree of transparency, beginning at the coarsest scale.

Controlled Randomness – Perlin Noise

Ken Perlin, lately of NYU, devised a procedural method for creating noise that can be used for textures in many types of visual objects, including video games and movies. In fact, this was used in the 1982 Disney file *Tron* and received an Academy Award for special effects. This kind of noise is built into *Processing*. The mathematics of it can be found on the Internet, but the basic idea is that the noise has a more controlled structure and is the sum of noise generated over several intervals. Details of the noise can be controlled using a parameter. Consider the following code:

```
background(255);
xn = 0; yn = noise(xn);
```

CHAPTER 6 TEXTURE

```
step = 0.05;
while (x < width)
{
  x = xn + step;
  y = noise(x);
  line(xn*(1.0/step), yn*100, x*(1.0/step), y*100);
  xn = x; yn = y;
}
```

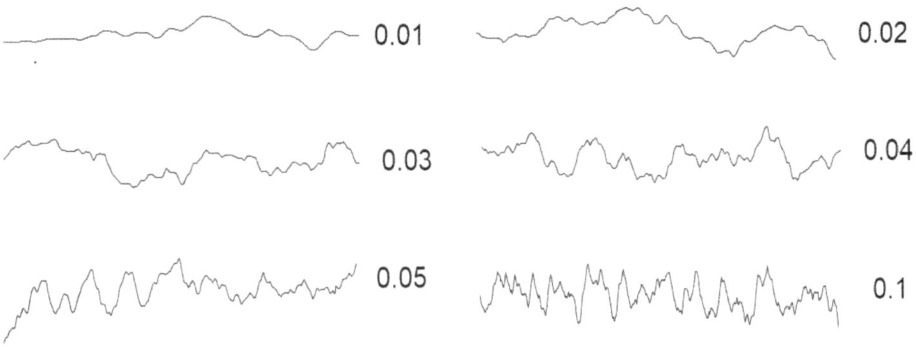

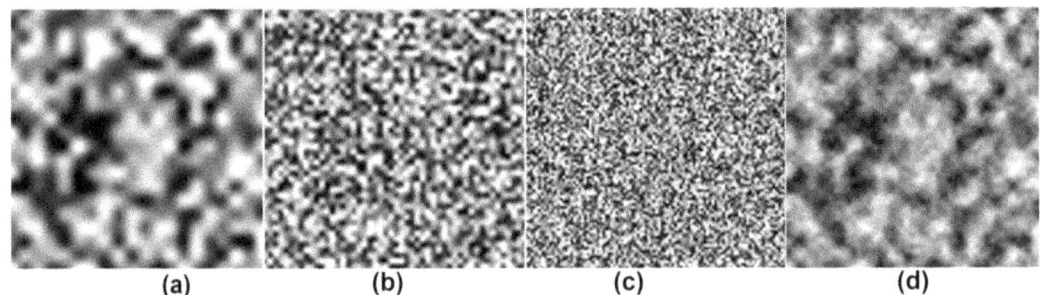

Figure 6-9. *Perlin noise using the Processing noise function for different step sizes*

Figure 6-10. *Using octave or layers. (a) Cubic noise at scale 50. (b) Cubic noise at scale 20. (c) Cubic noise at scale 10. (d) Layering all three images with the base level as* **a**, *the next level* **b** *at 25% transparent, and the final detail level* **c** *at 12.5% transparent*

This code draws lines between consecutive noise values. The step size, or the distance between consecutive **x** values, is 0.05 in this case. Figure 6-9 shows the variations in the noise patterns when using various step sizes. Clearly sizes in the 0.01 to 0.05 range seem to yield smooth patterns that might be useful to us.

240

CHAPTER 6　TEXTURE

A great thing about this **noise** function is that it can generate 2D and even 3D noise that can be used to make textures. The function **noise (x, y)** will create a noise value that is a function of two parameters, which can be thought of as *position* values in each dimension; changes to these are by a small amount, which can be thought of as a *scale* or *step* value. To generate random textures, use the position added to the step value to get a new noise value Figure 6-10. **Noise (0.1, 0.1)** will always return the same number. We'll use **noise (x+deltax, y+deltay)** for changing values of **deltax** and **deltay**. Given that, let's generate a 2D texture for a planet, as before but with different colors:

```
earth = loadImage("perlin2d.png");
globe = createShape(SPHERE, 200);
globe.setTexture(earth);
globe.setStroke(false);

for (int i=0; i<width; i++)
  for (int j=0; j<height; j++)
    set (i,j, color (noise (0.01*i, 0.01*j)*150+50,
            noise (0.01*i, 0.01*j)*100+20, 20));
```

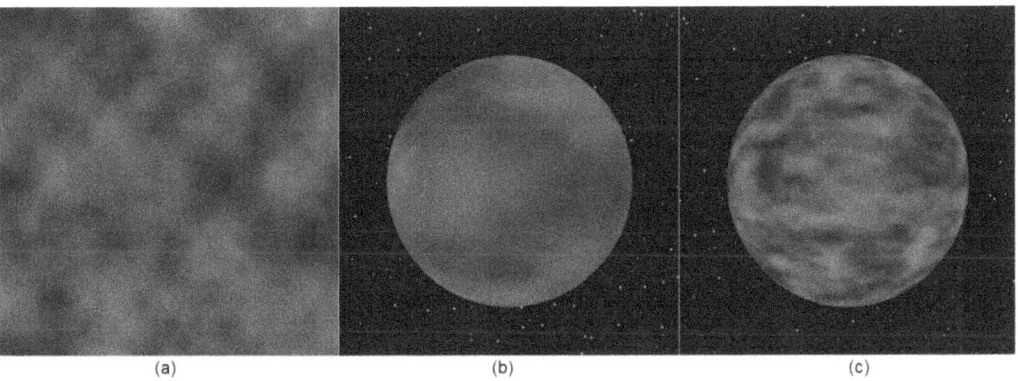

Figure 6-11. (a) Perlin noise using the code presented. Scale is 0.001. (b) A sphere mapped with this texture. (c) Perlin noise using a scale value of 0.05 instead of 0.001

CHAPTER 6 TEXTURE

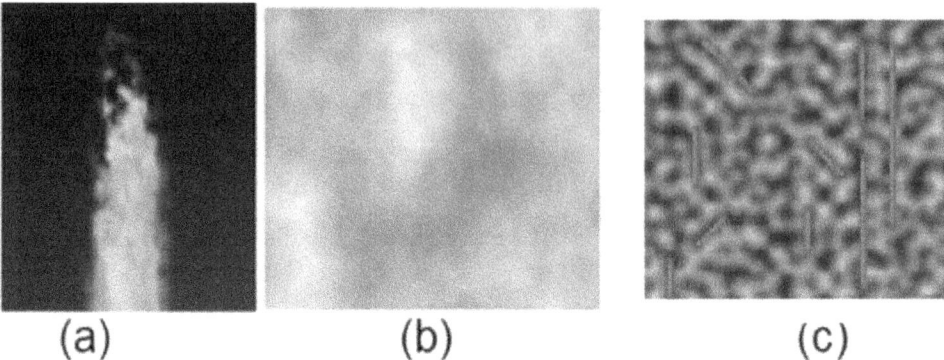

Figure 6-12. *Uses of noise textures, and Perlin noise specifically. (a) Fire. (b) Clouds. (c) Linear artifacts in 2D Perlin noise*

The important part of this code is where we set the color, which is to say the texture value at some point:

set (i,j, color (noise (0.01*i, 0.01*j)*150+50,
             noise (0.01*i, 0.01*j)*100+20, 20));

The red component uses Perlin noise with a scale of 0.01 based on the (x,y) location of the pixel and gives a value between 50 and 200. Similarly, the green component uses Perlin noise with a scale of 0.01 based on the (x,y) location of the pixel and gives a value between 20 and 120. Blue is always 20 (Figure 6-11).

Value noise and Perlin noise can be used to create water, cloud, and fire effects and useful textures of all kinds (Figure 6-12). It is used in video games to create random terrain surfaces, mountains, and planets. Perlin noise can result in linear artifacts not seen in bicubic interpolation, although most people do not notice them.

Shading

Shading is the use of lines or other geometric marks to represent gradations of color or darkness in a rendering. We could use an actual variation in intensity, of course, and when using a pencil this is accomplished by varying the pressure on the drawing instrument - the harder one presses, the darker is the resulting mark. An option is to use space-filling methods like cross-hatching. This is a use of texture for representing value.

We understand about color values and gray-level intensities from Chapter 3, "Value," and have some experience with converting color into gray values and with remapping a set of colors onto a smaller set. What we mean by shading in this context is to use a colored texture or a dithering process, such as scumbling or shading lines, to impart grays. A first step may well be to reduce the number of possible color values.

Using Characters

On a text screen, characters have fixed locations where they can appear, but on a graphics screen, they can be positioned anywhere to one-pixel accuracy. When using characters or other symbols to represent values, there are multiple things to consider: what is the size of the symbol, what is the size of the region to be drawn, what character will be used, what color the symbol will be drawn with, and perhaps others. Figure 6-13 shows an example of how a character rendering of gray and color would appear for a specific example image.

Figure 6-13. *Using characters to provide shading. (a) Original image. (b) Using characters in bi-level. (c) Matching the color of the character to the pixel color*

The usual process is to consider small rectangular regions of the scene, as projected onto a surface. The entire region, which consists of **N** pixels, will have a value determined by the average value over all of the pixels that comprise it: call this **V**. V should be measured as a percentage of pixels that should be set to black.

Each symbol or character used will have, for a specific size, a number of pixels that will be set for it to be drawn. This means, of course, that the number of characters that we draw to represent a specific value will not be the same as V; it will be, in fact, V/k, where **k** is the number of pixels set for that character.

CHAPTER 6   TEXTURE

One process for character/value rendering is to examine all pixels within each rectangular area. First determine the mean value for that area, **V**. Now we wish to draw characters within that area so that the correct number of black pixels will be set, at least approximately, and the characters should be randomly placed in that area.

The first algorithm that we'll use will draw a character at any location within a region with a probability that depends on the gray level. High probabilities produce a dark region as compared to low probabilities. The probability is determined from the level, and in this case, we used a manual selection: character density values were based on a range between 0 and 255 using seven gray levels. After some experimentation, the following situation was arrived at:

```
if (v <= 50) p = 70;
else if (v <= 80) p = 40;
else if (v <= 100) p = 20;
else if (v <= 128) p = 10;
else if (v <= 180) p = 2;
else if (v < 220) p = 1;
else  p = 0;
```

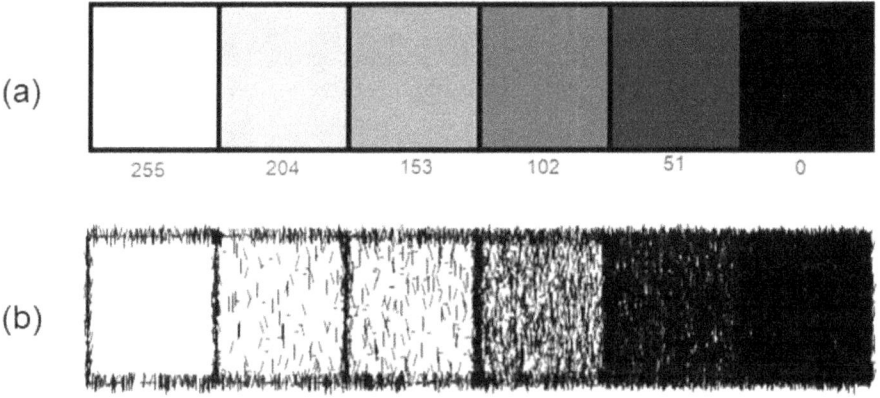

Figure 6-14. *(a) The six gray levels we will simulate using characters. (b) These levels are created using different densities of black-only characters "|", "/", "-" or "\"*

Figure 6-14 shows a calibration of this method, where known values are shown against the result from the algorithm. The characters used vary and are one of "|", "/", "-", or "\".

The code for this technique is:

```
// Processing
void plus (int i, int j)
{
  int di, dj;
  di = (int)random (4);
  if (di < 1) text ("|", i, j);
  else if (di<2) text ("-", i, j);
  else if (di<3) text ("/", i, j);
  else text ("\\", i, j);
}


void shade (int ii, int jj, int rr)
{
  color c;
  int v=0, n=0;
  float sd = 0, p=0;

  for (int i=ii-rr/2;i<ii+rr/2; i+=3)
  {
    if (i<0||i>=width) continue;
    for (int j=jj-rr/2;j<jj+rr/2;
           j+=3)
    {
      if (n<=0) return;
      v = v/n;  // Average region
                //   value
      if (v <= 50) p = 70;
        else if (v <= 80) p = 40;
        else if (v <= 100) p = 20;
        else if (v <= 128) p = 10;
        else if (v <= 180) p = 2;
        else if (v < 220) p = 1;
        else  p = 0;

      if (random(100) < p)
          plus(ii, jj);
      else p = 1;
    }
}

void allshade ()
{
  for (int i=0; i<width; i++)
    for (int j=0; j<height; j++)
       shade (i,j, 5);
}
```

(continued)

CHAPTER 6 TEXTURE

```
    if (j>=height || j<0)
        continue;
    c = img.get(i,j);
    v = v + (int)red(c);
    n = n + 1;
  }
}
```

There are many ways to use characters to display an image. In fact, we can convert an image for display on a pure text screen by assigning gray levels to specific characters and then printing the character that represents the value for each small area in the image. This is one way to create *ASCII art*, which is not technically related to textures but which is interesting and useful.

One set of characters to use is " "@XeOnu7j>. ", in order from darkest to lightest value. There are 11 characters, so each one represents about 23 levels: 0–23 will be represented by "@", 24-47 by "X", and so on. When using pure character images, the font used must be fixed width (such as Courier), or the "pixels," represented by characters, will differ in size. There will likely be some variation in the overall aspect ratio as well. Figure 6-15 shows one example of this method applied to a portrait. It adds the characters to strings, which are then saved to a file using the Processing **saveStrings**() function.

```
PImage root;
String greys = "@XeOnu7j>. ";
int g,k, indx=0;
color c;
String s[] = new String [110];

root = loadImage ("jim1.jpg");
size (900, 900);

fill (0);
background(255);
for (int i=0; i<root.height; i++)
{
  s[indx] = "";
  for (int j=0; j<root.width; j++)
  {
    c = root.get(j,i);
    k = (int)((red(c)+green(c)+blue(c))/3);
    g = (k/24);
    if (g<0) g = 0;
      s[i] = s[i] + greys.charAt(g);
  }
  indx = indx + 1;
}
saveStrings ("out.txt", s);
```

Figure 6-15. *Using ASCII characters to represent gray values in a raster image*

Grunge Textures

A computer graphic can sometimes be identified because it is clean and smooth. It is not difficult to draw a brick wall, but brick walls in real life tend to be stained and dirty. This is where *grunge textures* or *grunge maps* come in. A grunge map is basically an image of scratches, dirt, oil, and grime – whatever sort of wear and tear that might appear in the object being drawn. This image is used as a texture to place over the other textures. It is partly transparent, so the object can be clearly seen through the grime, but it lends a sense of reality to the object.

Consider the map in Figure 6-16. As paper ages, it tends to turn yellow and acquire wrinkles and stains. The original map on the left has very bright cartoon-like colors in uniform hues over each country. It was obviously drawn on a computer or was painted recently. The center image is that of pure grunge. It is a distressed paper texture having no content. When the grunge texture is overlaid on the map in a partly transparent way, we can still see the map, but now it appears as if the map is older and used.

CHAPTER 6 TEXTURE

Figure 6-16. *A simple map has an image of distressed and dirty paper drawn over it using transparency, making it look older*

There are a few ways to do this in *Processing*. First, we could read both images and draw the map first. Then we pass over the screen pixel by pixel and extract the color value from the grunge image, add a transparency (alpha) value to the color, and apply that color over a small area of the screen, drawing over the map. We draw a tiny ellipse using the grunge map pixel as the fill color.

```
// Apply a grunge map method 1
PImage x, g;

void setup()
{
  color c;
  float alph=50;

  x = loadImage ("brazil.png");
  g = loadImage ("gmap3.jpg");
  image (x, 0, 0);
  size (372, 408);
  noStroke();
  for (int i=0; i<width; i++)
  {
    for (int j=0; j<height; j++)
    {
      c = g.get(i,j);
      c = color (red(c), green(c), blue(c), alph);
```

```
    fill(c);
    ellipse (i,j,2,2);
   }
  }
}
```

Another possible implementation acknowledges that the resulting pixel in the screen will be some average of the map pixel and the grunge pixel. We can read the corresponding pixels on each image, average them, and draw them on the screen. In the code presented here we simply take the mean of the two, but in general some other weighting of the two pixels will probably have to be done for the best result.

```
for i in range (0, width):
  for j in range (0, width):
    c = g.get(i,j)
    d = x.get(i,j)
    c = color ((red(c)+red(d))/2,
              (green(c)+green(d))/2, (blue(c)+blue(d))/2);
    set(i,j,c)
```

Finally we have the *Processing tint()* function. This function takes R, G, B, and Alpha as parameters and applies these to each pixel that is displayed. For example, the code:

```
tint(0, 153, 204);  // Tint blue
image(x, 0, 0);
```

will apply a blue overall tint when the image **x** is displayed. To apply transparency to the grunge image without affecting its color, we would use white as the tint color and specify an alpha value. In the code below we used **tint (255,255,255, alph)**.

```
float alph=120;

x = loadImage ("brazil.png");
g = loadImage ("gmap3.jpg");
image (x, 0, 0);
size (372, 408);
noStroke();
tint (255,255,255, alph);
image (g, 0, 0);
```

Each of these programs will produce slightly different results, and we have to adjust the parameters to get the desired result.

Where do we get the *grunge* from? It's not usually possible to extract it from a real-world image, so we must manufacture them or borrow them. There are a great many grunge images on the internet that are free to use and easy to find. On the other hand, we could use *Photoshop* or *Gimp* to create the grunge image that we want, but they tend not to be very realistic. There are online tutorials about how to do this.

Identifying Textures

In a digital image it can be important to identify areas that have the same texture. A *lawn* is a distinct region and different from *ploughed soil*, *rocks*, or *pavement*. A region having a particular texture, while having a wide variety in its gray levels or colors, must have some properties that allow animal visual systems to identify them, but we don't generally know what those are. It is unlikely that a large collection of texture elements is specifically recognized by any seeing creature; it is more likely that similarities and differences can be seen and that a biological vision system can measure these and use them to characterize different textural regions and find the borders between them (e.g., Rosedahl, 2018).

Areas that have the same texture probably belong to the same object. When identifying areas having the same texture, we have to use a *region* within the image, because texture is a property of a region, not a pixel. However, each pixel belongs to a single region, so we look at the pixels surrounding a pixel to decide what the properties of that are and assign to that pixel a value that indicates what region it belongs to. As an algorithm, this is:

Create image **K** the same size as I.

```
Let Ws be the size of a window in pixels, and w = Ws/2.
For each pixel p(i,j) in image I:
  Measure a texture property V of the region in I from (i-w,j-w) to
    (i+w,j+w)
  Let K(i,j) = V
```

The resulting image **K** has pixel values that depend on the texture value measured in the area of size **Ws** centered at each pixel in the original image. In the perfect situation,

CHAPTER 6 TEXTURE

K would have a different value for each textured area in **I**. This almost never happens in practice, unfortunately.

To be very clear, identifying regions in an image that correspond to a particular texture is very difficult, and no general technique is known that will work in the general case. Using color is simply segmentation on color, not texture. That works only when textures differ mainly in color. Textures also have a spatial distribution and orientation of texture objects, and that's hard to identify. These days using neural networks for this sort of thing is typical, and even then it rarely works in the 90% range of success. This is support for the idea that animal visual systems use exemplars in texture recognition. Neural networks are really beyond the scope of our discussion, but just as an example, let's talk about one method that gets used: *local binary patterns* (LBP).

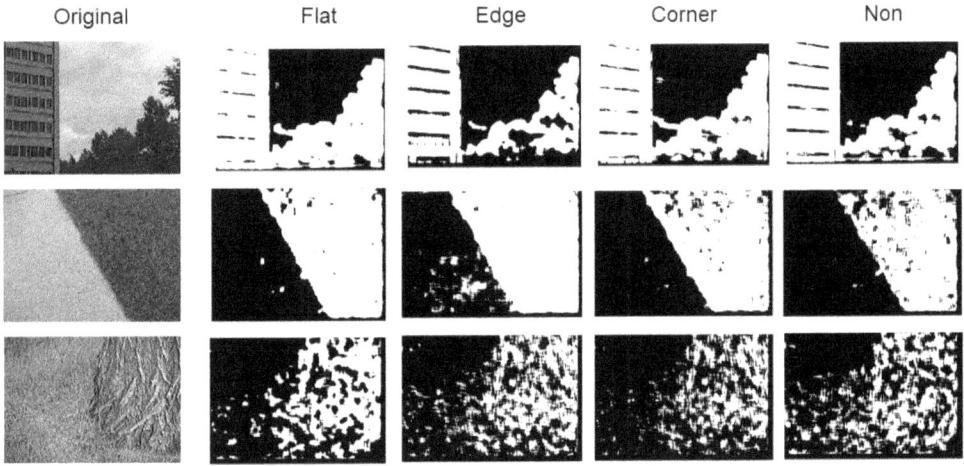

Figure 6-17. *Using local binary patterns to identify textures. The LBP images have been smoothed (mean) and thresholded to show which areas belong to which textures*

Local Binary Patterns

When using this technique, 3x3 regions are used to calculate a feature value at each location. We can use larger regions if we like. The value in the center of the region is compared to selected pixels around the outline. In the 3x3 case, these could be:

```
    Flat         Edge        Corner     Non-Uniform
  * * *        o o o        o * *        o * *
  * X *        * X o        o X *        o X o
  * * *        * * *        o o o        o * *
```

The center pixel **X** is compared against the pixels marked *. We can make a histogram of the pixels that are greater or smaller, giving a vector of values showing a spatial pattern. Or we can, as in the library for this chapter, simply compute a value showing how many of the * pixels are greater and how many smaller than **X**. The resulting values, when placed within an image, show a similarity to each other within textured regions. This will vary a bit from pixel to pixel, so a mean can be used to smooth the result, and then the texture in one area will be (we hope) a distinct gray value as compared to a neighboring area. Figure 6-17 shows a result for three images and each of the texture templates shown here. In the top images the sky region is black; in the middle image sequence the grass is white, and the concrete is black. In the bottom image the grass is black and the tree bark is white. There are varying degrees of success in localizing the textures, of course, and this leads to pixels and small regions that exist in one texture region and are classified as a different texture. Smoothing can help correct this in artworks.

Summary

Texture is the *repetition of a pattern or patterns over a region* to form a recognizable yet partly random arrangement. The elements of the pattern are called *textons*. Textures usually take the form of images and can be mapped pixel by pixel onto a polygonal shape, usually a triangle or quadrilateral. When the texture image is smaller than the polygon, it should not appear to repeat its pattern across the image in any direction but should match at the left and right edges and the top and bottom edges so that the repetition would not be obvious.

Natural textures are those that we encounter in daily life and that lend reality to scenes and images and are usually photographs. A *synthetic* texture is one that is created by a computer program. Noise, which is a random set of pixel values, should not be completely random but should instead show a relationship between nearby values so that the result is visually smooth. Two ways to do this are *cubic noise* and *Perlin noise*, the latter being implemented in the standard *Processing* library.

We can use textures to shade an image, which is to say, to provide values to be used to indicate shape and shadows. We can use arbitrary textures that have been classified to represent specific values over a small region, and one example of this is the use of characters. A *grunge map* is basically an image of scratches, dirt, oil, and grime used as a texture to lend a sense of reality to an object.

CHAPTER 6   TEXTURE

A texture can be identified in an image using color or statistical measures over small areas, such as *local binary patterns* (LBP). When texture regions are found, they can be seen to identify specific shapes or contiguous regions on the image.

Library code

allshade	- Shade an image using characters
cubic2d	- Cubic value noise
gmap	- Grunge map
grass	- Synthetic grass texture
house	- Draw a house from a template and textures
lbp	- Local binary patterns, for 4 patterns
map	- Map a texture onto a rectangular image
map2	- Map a texture onto an irregular 4-sized polygon
octaves	- Multiple layers of noise (3)
planet	- Value noise on a sphere
perlinnoise	- Shade a planet with Perlin noise
tile1	- Using symmetry for tiles

CHAPTER 6   TEXTURE

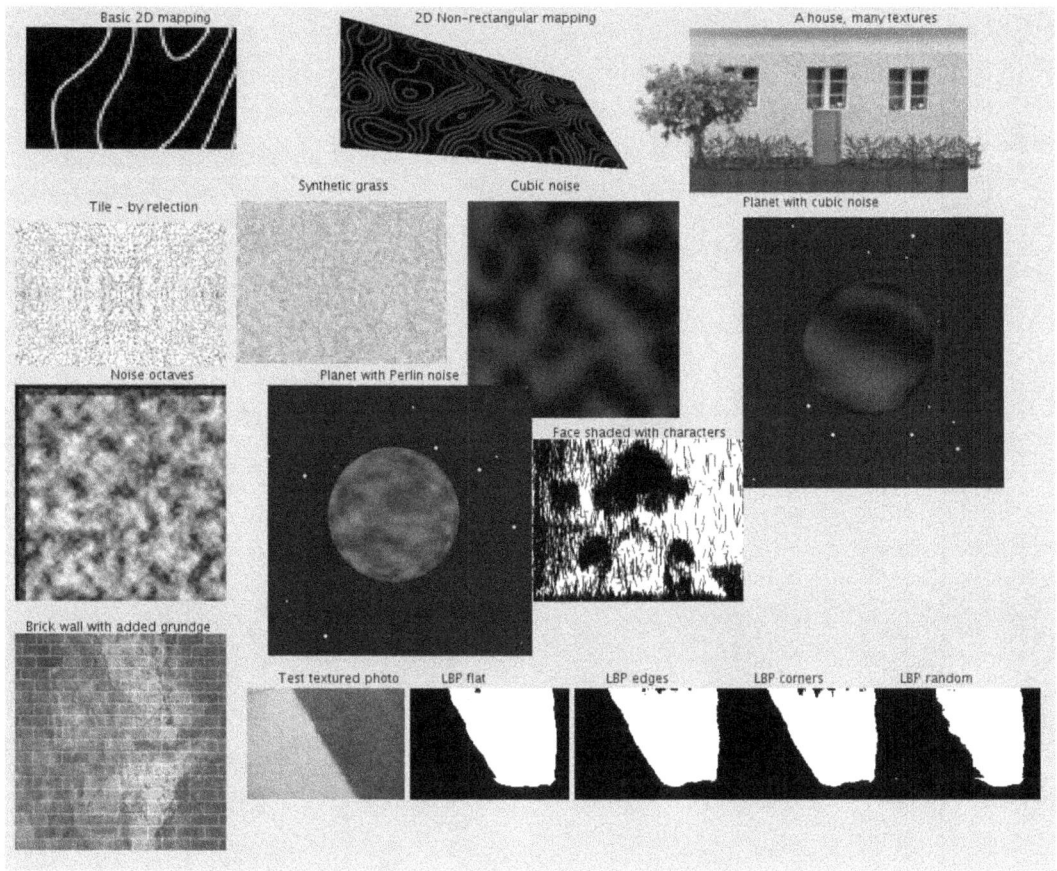

*The result of the test program **library06**, demonstrating the library code for this chapter.*

CHAPTER 7

Form

Form is about the third dimension. It is the element of art that has volume. We see three dimensions all the time, but visualizing things in three dimensions is more difficult. Artists see in 3D and render in 2D as a matter of nature and training, but a generative artist must be able to imagine objects in 3D and manipulate them in abstract ways before rendering.

Once we have composed or conceptualized the scene or object in 3D, we must then convert it into 2D. The big problem here is that of representing a third dimension on a two-dimensional surface so we can represent it on a screen or canvas.

All students of art learn about *projections*, specifically about *perspective*, which is the transformation of a three-dimensional scene onto a two-dimensional flat surface. Anyone with two functional eyes (and we understand that this does not include *everybody*) has some experience with the ideas of perspective. Objects that are farther away appear smaller than those that are near, for example. When we render a scene, it is usual to apply this rule, at least partly because that's how we see it.

Historically older artworks show a lack of knowledge of how to render a 3D scene. Flat renderings were common in Egyptian, Greek, and Roman art, although some Roman paintings from the 1st century BC show a knowledge of convergent projection, which is not quite one-point perspective (Figure 7-1). This skill was lost until the 15th century by artists like *Giovanni di Paolo* and Duccio di Buoninsegna during the Italian Renaissance and Albrecht Dürer in the North.

CHAPTER 7 FORM

Figure 7-1. (Left) Egyptian wall painting. (Right) Cubiculum M of the Villa of Publius Fannius Synistor

When drawing in two dimensions, as we almost always do these days, we consider the horizontal (X) and vertical (Y) directions as being principal. When drawing or painting a real scene, we instinctively draw what we see, which has perspective built in – that's how we always *see* things. We don't think much about the process until we must, such as in art school or when presented with a difficult scene.

When we draw a scene, the objects within it are usually three dimensional, but we can only see part of it, the part that faces us. This is a critical difference between 2D and 3D. There are parts of the 3D image that we don't know about. If we, the artists, change position, then we can see more of the object, but parts we could see before are hidden now. The place from which we are looking at the scene is the *viewpoint* and is a critical part of 3D rendering. Not only is the location important, but also critical is the direction we are facing. We can't see things behind us at all.

The viewpoint is a part of the geometry of perspective, as shown in Figure 7-2. There are three principal axes, X, Y, and Z. Objects being seen and drawn are projected to the artist's eyes through a 2D plane, which is drawn onto the paper or canvas. If the plane or the artist moves, then the painting changes.

Much of the discussion of form, 3D, and perspective concerns how we take three coordinates (x, y, z) and convert them into the 2D canvas coordinates.

CHAPTER 7   FORM

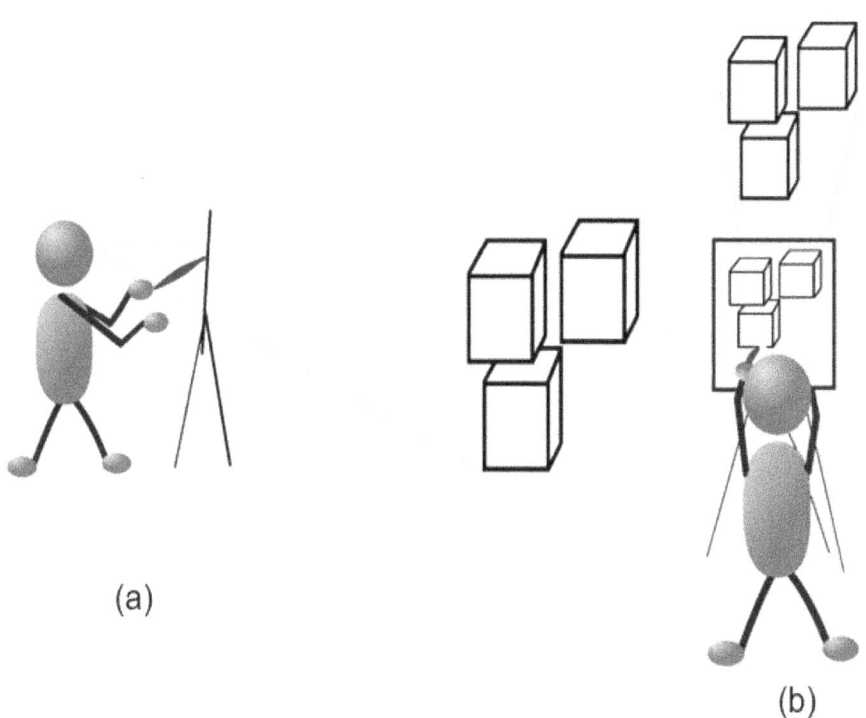

Figure 7-2. *(a) Projecting a 2D scene onto a 3D canvas. (b) Changing the position and orientation of the artist changes the projection*

Coordinates in 3D

When we specify a point in two dimensions, we use two numbers: the X and the Y coordinates. A line, for example, is drawn from (x_0, y_0) to (x_1, y_1). In three dimensions, we use *three* coordinates: X, Y, and Z. We can think of these as width, height, and depth. We might draw a line in a program as:

`line (x0, y0, z0, x1, y1, z1)`

We obviously can't draw all three coordinates on a computer screen directly, but as we suggested before, we can imagine the third coordinate, Z, to be projecting *into* the screen, and the program would first have to transform **(x0, y0, z0)** into two coordinates **(a0, b0)** on a plane, which is to say the canvas or screen. It would also have to transform (x1,y1) into (a1,b1) and then draw the line between (a0,b0) and (a1,b1). The magic is in the transform, which is a mathematical projection of the three-dimensional coordinates onto a plane. This projection, called the *perspective projection* or *perspective*

259

CHAPTER 7   FORM

transformation, has been known for a long time. It's not necessary to understand the math, but one should appreciate specific parameters of its operation. Once we define a perspective transformation (there are many possible), it remains in effect until changed, and that transformation is applied to all coordinates specified for everything we draw. It's not easily possible to move between 2D and 3D coordinates, although that would sometimes be useful.

Coordinate Systems

The origin of a system of coordinates and the encompassing scale and orientation can vary. When using a computer, there are four-coordinate systems of interest (Figure 7-3):

> **Object coordinates**: in this case a single object has its own system of coordinates. We define vertices on the object relative to its origin, which is usually either the upper left corner of the object or its center.
>
> **World Coordinates**: these are coordinates we defined in the scene used as the basis for the image. The origin (0, 0, 0) can be anywhere in the 3D volume being viewed, and objects are located according to their positional relation to that location.
>
> **Camera Coordinates**: The camera is the place from which we are viewing the scene, and so these are also called *viewpoint* coordinates. Here the location from which we are seeing the scene is being the origin (0, 0, 0), and we identify all other positions relative to that position.

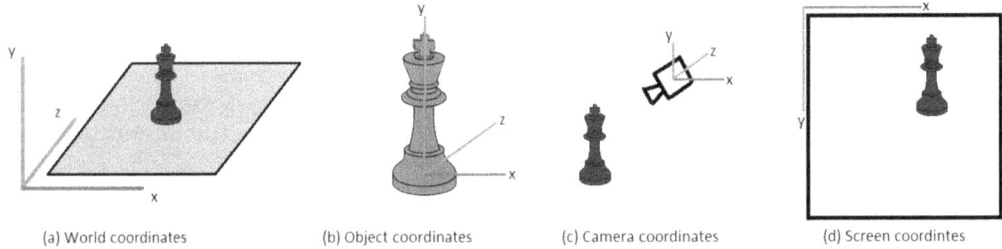

(a) World coordinates   (b) Object coordinates   (c) Camera coordinates   (d) Screen coordintes

Figure 7-3. Coordinate systems in a 3D computer graphics system

Screen Coordinates: These are always two-dimensional coordinates and refer to a location (pixel) on the display where the image is being displayed. It is almost always the upper left corner of the 2D projection of the scene. When the y value in this system increases, the pixel referenced is farther *down* the screen, rather than increasing y referring to the *up* direction.

Ultimately everything that we draw has to be converted into screen coordinates. Because computers deal only with numbers, this involves some tricky arithmetic sometimes.

Shapes in Object Coordinates

When drawing in 3D coordinates, we know we have to specify three values, (x,y,z), for each vertex (Figure 7-4). We also must tell *Processing*, if that's the system we are using, that we are drawing in three dimensions. We do that in the size command:

```
size (1000, 900, P3D);
```

The name **P3D** refers to what we call a renderer, which is the part of *Processing* that actually draws things on the screen. In this case it says that we'll be drawing.

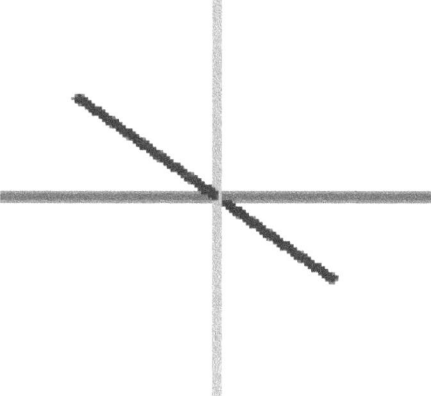

Figure 7-4. *The XYZ coordinate axes*

ng in three dimensions. The default is **P2D**, and it need not be specified. Now when we draw a line, we do so with the code:

```
line (x0, y0, z0, x1, y1, z1);
```

CHAPTER 7 FORM

Drawing the XYZ coordinate axis can be done by drawing three lines, where each one changes only one coordinate. Like this:

```
stroke (200, 0, 0);              // X axis, red
line (cx-d,cy,cz,cx+d,cy,cz);
stroke (0, 200, 0);              // Y axis, green
line (cx,cy-d,cz,cx,cy+d, cz);
stroke (0, 0, 200);              // Z axis, blue
line (cx,cy,cz-d,cx,cy,cz+d);
```

where (cx, cy, cz) is the origin. The Z axis, in blue, seems like it is at an angle to the others, but in fact it is an artifact of seeing it projected into 2D. The Z axis increases in value as the Z value gets larger (into the plane of the screen) and decreases as the Z value gets smaller (toward the viewer).

To understand this better, we need to look at how 3D objects are projected onto a 2D screen or paper.

The Digital Perspective Transform: What Do We Need?

To correctly specify a perspective transformation, we need to specify multiple parameters. These are illustrated in Figure 7-5. This will allow objects to be drawn on a plane in a way that is familiar to us.

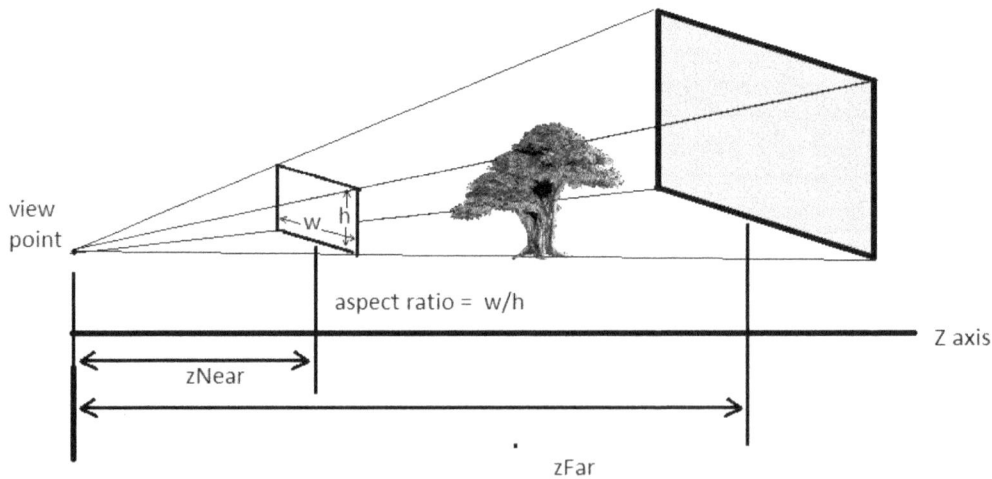

Figure 7-5. *Geometry of the perspective transformation*

The near and far clipping planes (**zNear** and **zFar**) represent the closest and farthest points that we can draw. Something too near our eye can't be viewed properly, and something too far away will seem too small to be resolved. The vertical field of view (**fov**) is an angle in radians, and represents the angle between the extents of what we see without moving. Horizontally, humans have a 120-degree horizontal region where we can see things properly in 3D and a vertical FOV angle of 60 degrees. The width and height of the drawing surface (**w** and **h**) are the number of pixels in the drawing area, and the **aspect ratio** is **w/h**. For example, aspect = 2.0 means the viewer's angle of view is twice as wide in x as it is in y. These really define the change in size (scale) between the scene and the rendering.

When using the *Processing* language, the function that sets up the transformation is **perspective**:

perspective(fovy, aspect, zNear, zFar)

On the other hand, when using *OpenGL*, the function is:

gluPerspective(double fovy, double aspect,
               double zNear, double zFar)

Note that both functions use the same parameters. These values remain in effect until changed, so the basic transformation from 3D to 2D stays the same across multiple drawings, if we want this.

A scene, consisting of many 3D objects, can exist as a set of coordinates independently of any viewer. The question, when trying to determine what the view will be on the screen, is *what can be seen from the viewing position*? This is what we'll call the *viewing transformation*. Imagine that we are using a camera to look at the scene. The camera is located at some set of 3D coordinates that we'll call (**eyex, eyey, eyez**). In addition, we will point the camera in a specific direction, which can be specified as a 3D coordinate somewhere in the scene *(centerx, centery, centerz)*, so named because that coordinate should be in the center of the view. They may better be named (*lookatX, lookatY, lookatZ*) because they really define the point we are looking at.

Finally, we can orient the camera itself around its mounting point. Normally it would be set up so that a horizontal line in the scene would appear to be horizontal in the image, but that need not be so. We will specify the orientation by specifying what direction is ***up***; for this we'll use the three coordinate axes X, Y, and Z. If we say

CHAPTER 7 FORM

that *up* is (**0,1,0**), this means that the positive Y axis will be the up direction. The normal on most computer systems is (**0, -1, 0**), because Y values in a screen increase as we move down the screen. Processing has a way to do this for you, using a function called **camera**:

camera (eyeX, eyeY, eyeZ, lookatX, lookatY, lookatZ,
       upX, upY, upZ)

The point (**eyeX, eyeY, eyeZ**) is the 3D location of the viewer or camera. The point (**lookatX, lookatY, lookatZ**) is the point that the viewer is looking at and defines the viewer's orientation. The value (**upX, upY, upZ**) is a vector that defines the *up* direction, and the values are usually either 1.0, -1.0, or 0.0. This is called a *unit vector*, and the default value is (**0, 1, 0),** which means that up is the positive Y direction, which is typical. The camera function is equivalent to the *OpenGL* function **gluLookAt().**

*Figure 7-6. The **eye** coordinates (viewpoint) and the **lookat** coordinates. **Lookat** defines a direction that we will refer to as the facing angle.*

The values of (**eyeX, eyeY, eyeZ**) and (**lookatX, lookatY, lookatZ**) can change in some applications. For example, in a video game when the player's avatar moves, these values change accordingly so that the game scene is viewed from the new location. In non-animated applications, these values are constant for the entire execution of the program (Figure 7-6).

1. The 3D coordinates of the objects are defined and do not change. What the **camera** function does is:
2. Rotate the camera so that it points to the specified coordinates.

Move (translate) the camera so that it resides at the origin, or the (0,0,0) coordinate.

We will discuss the way we rotate and translate objects in a later section, but **camera** does what we want it to whether we know *how* it works or not. The tricky part is figuring out what the **lookat** and **eye** parameters should be, because moving 3D objects about in one's head is difficult. Too often, if we get it wrong, the program appears to display nothing when in fact it is simply looking in the wrong place.

The default values, which is to say when we do not specify them, for **perspective** are:

```
fov = PI/3.0
aspect ratio width/height
znear = cameraZ/10.0
zfar = cameraZ*10.0
```

where cameraZ is ((height/2.0) / tan(PI*60.0/360.0)). For **camera**, the defaults are:

```
eyeX = width/2.0
eyeY = height/2.0
eyeZ = (height/2.0) / tan(PI*30.0 / 180.0)
centerX = width/2.0
centerY = height/2.0
centerZ = 0
upX = 0
upY = 1
upZ = 0
```

Changing Viewpoint

If the viewpoint (**eyeX, eyeY, eyeZ**) is to be modified, we must call **camera** to make that change. If that is the only change, then the point we are looking at (**centerX, centerY, centerZ**) will stay the same, and we will seem to rotate around that point. This is not always desirable. In a video game, the point of view is the location of the player's avatar, and the player can move forward, backward, or change the direction they are facing, which is α, the *facing angle*. This changes the center point as well and is a more natural way to view things.

CHAPTER 7   FORM

In a video game/VR environment, the location of the avatar is the viewpoint. The facing angle defines what can be seen and what direction motion will be in – moving forward will make a step in the direction of the facing angle α. If a step is a distance **s**, where usually **s=1**, then the change in viewpoint is:

$$ex = ex + s*\cos(\alpha)$$
$$ez = ez + s*\sin(\alpha)$$

So pressing the "**w**" key will move the viewpoint forward by one step using this calculation. We also have to move the center of the view, which also reflects the direction we're looking. The center of the field of view is in the same direction as the facing angle but is just a long distance away from the viewpoint. So let **d=10000** and compute the new center values as:

$$centerX = ex + d * \cos(\alpha)$$
$$centerZ = ez + d * \sin(\alpha)$$

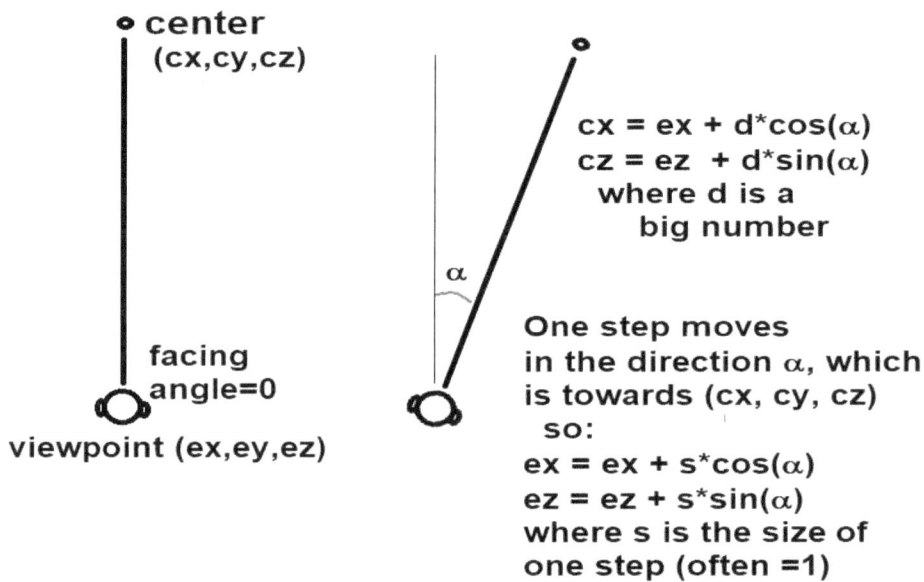

Figure 7-7. *How to change the view based on viewpoint and facing angle*

CHAPTER 7 FORM

This is shown in Figure 7-7, and an implementation is available in the library for this chapter.

Drawing a Cube – Using *Processing*

When using Processing, which is the simplest way to render 3D objects, we begin in the **setup** function when we call **size** to establish the size of the viewing area. The renderer is a default parameter, but to render in 3D, we call size as, for example:

size (640, 480, P3D)

The parameter P3D means to render objects in 3D, not the default 2D. This means that all points, lines, and other objects we draw from now on have 3D coordinates.

Next, we set up a viewing transformation. We can use the default parameters for the perspective function. We'd like the camera function to place the viewer away from the cube and look at it, which means looking at the origin. So:

camera (300, 150, 300, 0, 0, 0, 0, 1, 0);

We're looking at the origin from the point (300,150,300). Now draw the cube. It is two squares with one corner at the origin, and where each face is 100x100 units. Figure 7-8 shows sets of coordinates that can define a cube, first using unit coordinates, and then using those to draw a larger cube by multiplying the unit coordinates by the actual size of the cube (100) and adding an offset (700, 0, 0).

The first square is:

```
line (0,0,0, 100, 0, 0);
line (100, 0, 0, 100, 100, 0);
line (100, 100, 0, 0, 100, 0);
line (0, 100, 0, 0,0,0);
```

CHAPTER 7   FORM

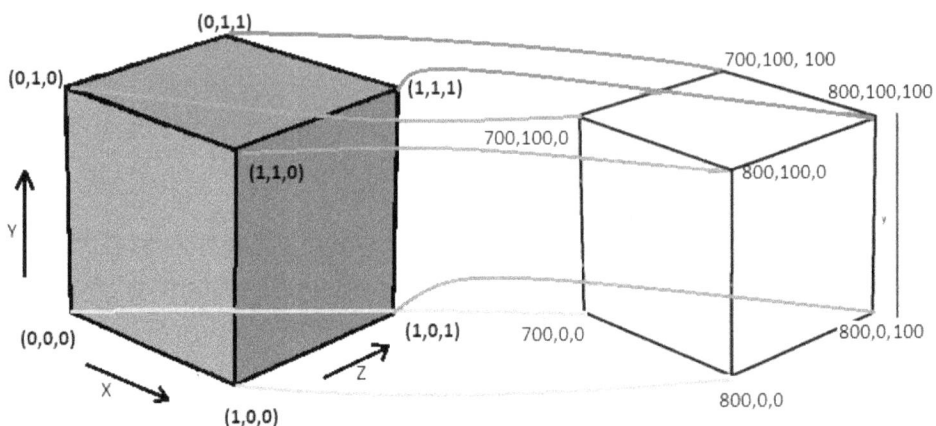

Figure 7-8. *Representation of a cube, showing the coordinates of the vertices in three dimensions. (a) A unit cube is 1 unit in size in each dimension. (b) A more realistic cube has a larger size, in this case 100 units per side. This one has been moved (translated) to (800,0,0) and scaled (size changed, multiplied by 100)*

is in the XY = 0 plane. The next square is 100 units offset in Z:

```
line (0,0,100, 100, 0, 100);
line (100, 0, 100, 100, 100, 100);
line (100, 100, 100, 0, 100, 100);
line (0, 100, 100, 0,0,100);
```

Now connect the two squares:

```
line (0,0,0, 0, 0, 100);
line (100, 0, 0, 100, 0, 100);
line (100, 100, 0, 100, 100, 100);
line (0, 100, 0, 0,100,100);
```

The calls to line use two points, as before, but now each point has *three* coordinates. Figure 7-9 shows the result, using different versions of calls to **camera** (different viewpoints).

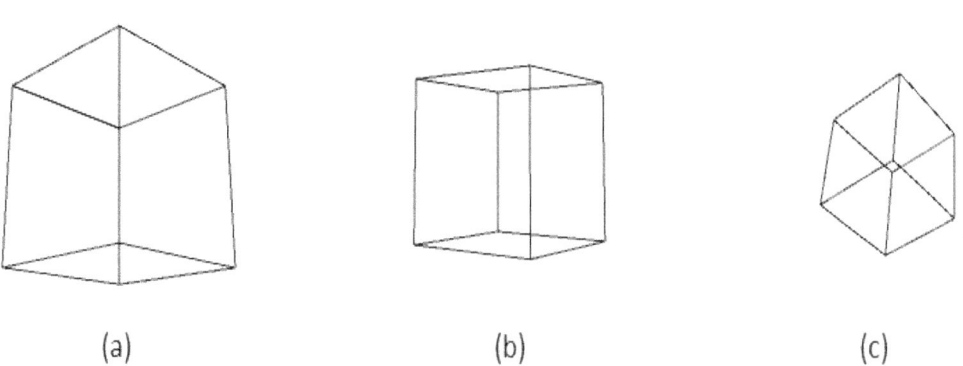

Figure 7-9. *A cube rendered using Processing 3D primitives, seen from three viewpoints: (a) Using camera (300, 150, 300, 0, 0, 0, 0, 1, 0). (b) Using the camera (300, 50, 400, 0, 0, 0, 0, 1, 0). (c) Camera (400, 450, -300, 0, 0, 0, 0, 1, 0)*

Processing has two interesting drawing functions in 3D. One is **box**, which draws a cube at the origin. The call **box(100)** draws a 100x100x100 cube at (0,0,0). The other is **sphere**, which is more interesting. The call **sphere(200)** draws a sphere of radius 200 centered at (0,0,0). It is more interesting because a sphere is drawn as a collection of triangles that are drawn over the sphere's surface. We call this *tessellation*: the tiling of a surface with geometric shapes, in this case, triangles. There is really no other reasonable way to draw a sphere. It is possible to draw something called implicit surfaces, for example, which is simply an equation F(x,y,z) = 0; for a sphere this would be $x^2+y^2+z^2-r^2$ = **0**. on the surface of the sphere, where the color of the points would have to include a degree of transparency, or the sphere would simply look like a circle.

Drawing Basic Objects

We already know how to draw a line in 3D using the 3D version of the **line** function. However, other shapes don't have built-in 3D versions. There is no 3D version of **rect** that will draw a rectangle, for example. We have to create one if we want it. A rectangle in 3D would have a start point (x,y,z) and a width, height, and depth. The function call would look like this:

```
rect (x, t, z, dx, dy, dz);
```

It did not exist, so how would we code it? A rectangle consists of 4 lines, in this case 4-3D lines. The lines begin at the (x,y,z) values provided. Visualizing the rectangle in 3D, we see that the first line can be drawn between (x,y,z) and (x+dx, y, z+dz); we then go down to (x+dx, y, z+dz), back to (x, y+dy, z), and then to the original coordinates (x,y,z). Here is code that will do that:

```
void rect (float x, float y, float z, float dx, float dy, float dz)
{
  line (x, y, z, x+dx, y, z+dz);
  line (x+dx, y, z+dz, x+dx, y+dy, z+dz);
  line (x+dx, y+dy, z+dz, x, y+dy, z);
  line (x, y+dy, z, x, y, z);
}
```

If we want this to be filled with the current fill color, then we have to use **beginShape() - endShape():** (Figure 7-10).

```
void rect (float x, float y, float z, float dx, float dy, float dz)
{
  fill (255,255,0);
  beginShape();
    vertex(x, y, z);
    vertex(x+dx, y, z+dz);
    vertex (x+dx, y+dy, z+dz);
    vertex(x, y+dy, z);
  endShape(CLOSE);
}
```

CHAPTER 7 FORM

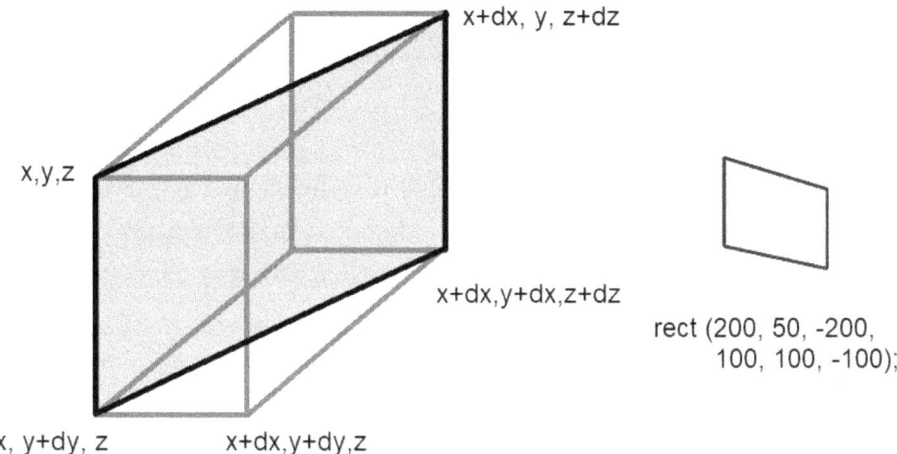

Figure 7-10. *Drawing a rectangle in 3D*

A circle can be drawn in 3D, but it is more complex because if we only specify the center (x,y,z) and the radius, it is not clear what *plane* the circle should be drawn in. We can do that, and then its appearance will also depend on where we are viewing from. We'll look at ways to do that later.

More Complex 3D Objects

Just as with 2D, we can draw objects as primitive operations, usually as lines. However, the process is a bit different. When something is to be drawn, we begin with a function **beginShape(P)**, which tells the graphics system that we are about to render something in 3D. the value of **P** determines what kind of things we'll be drawing, but in all cases we draw by specifying vertices or points in 3D space. P is one of a set of constants; if, for example, we call:

beginShape(LINES)

then the vertices that follow will be line endpoints, and we define a line by using two vertices. Specifying a vertex uses the vertex function:

vertex (x, y, z)

identifies (x,y,z) as the next vertex in 3D. A line needs two vertices, so:

vertex (x0, y0, z0)
vertex (x1, y1, z1)

would result in a line being drawn between (x0, y0, z0) and (x1, y1, z1). Finally, we call **endShape()** to tell the system that we are finished with this object:

endShape()

After the **endShape()** call, the object is drawn on the canvas, and if we don't call it then nothing will appear in the drawing area. In between the **beginShape()** and **endShape()**, we can specify as many vertices as we like. Drawing the cube of Figure 7-8 could be done as:

```
beginShape(LINES);
    vertex (0,0,0);   vertex(100, 0, 0);
    vertex(100, 0, 0); vertex(100, 100, 0);
    vertex(100, 100, 0); vertex(0, 100, 0);
    vertex(0, 100, 0); vertex(0,0,0);

    vertex (0,0,100); vertex(100, 0, 100);
    vertex (100, 0, 100); vertex(100, 100, 100);
    vertex (100, 100, 100); vertex(0, 100, 100);
    vertex (0, 100, 100); vertex(0,0,100);

    vertex(0,0,0); vertex(0, 0, 100);
    vertex (100, 0, 0); vertex(100, 0, 100);
    vertex (100, 100, 0); vertex(100, 100, 100);
    vertex (0, 100, 0); vertex(0,100,100);
endShape();
```

We can't use **curveVertex** to specify 3D spline coordinates (there is no such function for 3D), which would add significant flexibility to what we can draw in 3D. However, *we* can draw complex objects like a helix by drawing a circle as short line segments and increasing the Z coordinate a little bit each time so that instead of closing the circle, the lines continue to draw circular arcs that extend into the Z axis (Figure 8-6a). For the creation of complex lines in 3D, we have implemented a *Catmull-Rom* spline (the one used in *Processing*) for three dimensions, and Figure 8-6b shows a helix drawn using this program (it's part of the **Spline** class).

Here are both versions of the helix function:

```
// Draw a helix using line segments
void helix (float startx, float
starty, float startz, float da,
float r)
{
  float x0,y0, z0, x1,y1, z1, a;

  a = 0.0;
  x0 = r*cos(radians(a))+startx;
  y0 = r*sin(radians(a))+starty;
  z0 = startz; z1 = z0 - 1;
  for (int i=0; i<5000; i++)
  {
    x1 = r*cos(radians(a))+startx;
    y1 = r*sin(radians(a))+starty;
    z1 = z1 - 0.1;
    line (x0, y0, z0, x1, y1, z1);
    x0 = x1; y0 = y1; z0 = z1;
    a = a + da;
  }
}
```

```
// Draw a helix using the Spline
// class
void helixv (float startx, float
starty, float startz, float da,
float r)
{
  float x0,y0,z0, x1,y1,z1, a=0;
  Spline s3d;

  s3d = new Spline();
  x0 = r*cos(radians(a))+startx;
  y0 = r*sin(radians(a))+starty;
  z0 = startz; z1 = z0 - 1;

  stroke(0, 200, 0);
  s3d.beginCurve();
  s3d.add3DVertex(x0, y0, z0);
  s3d.add3DVertex(x0, y0, z0);
  for (int i=0; i<50000; i+=10)
  {
    x1 = r*cos(radians(a))+startx;
    y1 = r*sin(radians(a))+starty;
    z1 = z1 - 0.1;
    s3d.add3DVertex(x1, y1, z1);
    z0 = z1;
    x0 = x1; y0 = y1;
    a = a + da;
  }
```

(continued)

CHAPTER 7 FORM

```
            s3d.end3DCurve();
            s3d.draw3DCurve();
        }
```

When using the *class* (on the right), we add the vertices one at a time as they would be if **curveVertex** was used and have a *start* (**beginCurve**), *end* (**endCurve**), and *draw* (**drawCurve**) stage to the process (Figure 7-11).

The Most Basic Perspective Projection

The use of **perspective()** and **camera()** involves a great deal of mathematics in the background, and the details are not important in most cases. The essential function of the transformation is to take a three-dimensional coordinate and produce a two-dimensional coordinate that can be drawn on the screen and that represents a good approximation to what would be seen from the specified viewpoint. The arbitrary viewpoint is what creates a lot of the mathematical complication.

```
x' = (x*cz)/(cz+z);
y' = (y*cz)/(cz+z);
```

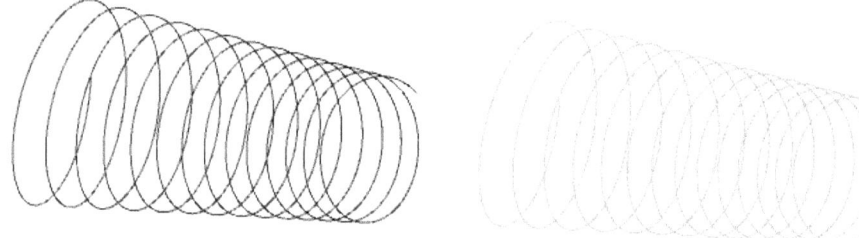

Figure 7-11. A complex 3D object, a helix

The point (x',y') can be drawn directly on the screen or in an image, and functions like **line3d()** are easy to code.

If we use a *fixed* viewpoint, then the equations for the transformation are very simple. Assume that the viewpoint is (0,0,-cz) and we are looking along the Z axis. Then a 3D point (x, y, z) transforms to the 2D point (x', y') as follows:

CHAPTER 7   FORM

One-Point Perspective

We're going to take a diversion from how the *computer* converts 3D to 2D to how *artists* tend to do it. An artist will sometimes use a *vanishing point* to accurately draw perspective. This was the first way that artists drew 3D scenes in the renaissance. When a human looks at a real scene, there is usually a horizon and a vanishing point visible. The vanishing point is often thought of as a location where all of the lines that extend into the distance appear to meet. There's more to it than that, but this is a good starting point.

In Figure 7-12, the scene is a country road. We can see the width of the road shrinking with distance, and the sides of the road, which are parallel in fact, seeming to meet in the distance. We call the point at which they seem to meet the *vanishing point*, and we can identify it in most real scenes. Sometimes an artist will begin by establishing a vanishing point and will use it as the place where parallel lines that extend into the canvas will meet. The result is usually a good perspective view of the scene.

Figure 7-12. *Perspective as seen in reality on a country road. The vanishing point is in the center of the image*

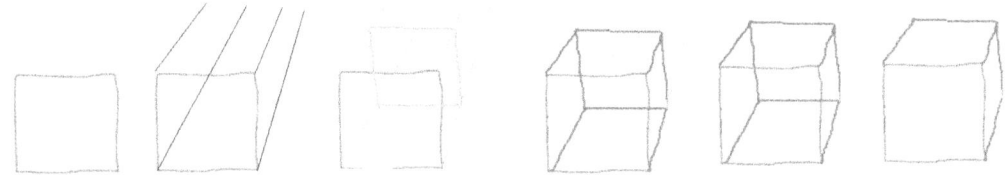

Figure 7-13. *Drawing a perspective cube using a pencil and paper. Steps 1-6 from left to right.*

275

CHAPTER 7   FORM

Let's draw a cube again. If we draw a cube with a pencil, we usually do the following (Figure 7-13):

1. Draw a square.
2. Draw *construction lines* from the corners of the square to the vanishing point.
3. Draw a second square towards the vanishing point, using the construction lines as a guide.
4. Draw lines connecting the corresponding corners of the two squares, following the construction lines.
5. Erase the construction lines.
6. (Optional) erase the *hidden* lines

We can use this process to draw any perspective scene, not just simple ones like the cube. The procedure can be adapted for use with computer graphics as well, although it's not a usual way to do perspective using a computer.

One Point Perspective and Computer Graphics

The tools do not exist for using vanishing points to create 3D renderings using a graphics library, so we'll have to come up with something. This always means doing some thinking and probably involves a little math and some programming. The thinking part involves doing some paper-and-pencil geometry. The diagram in Figure 7-14 is the result of this thinking exercise and may seem obvious and simple, but it is in fact the outcome of some hours of effort and many pages of graph paper. Only the final result is shown, not all of the mistakes made along the way.

CHAPTER 7 FORM

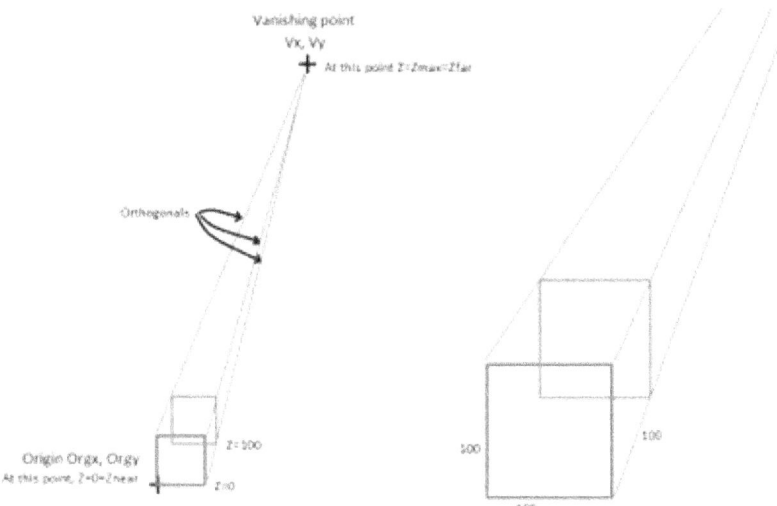

Figure 7-14. *The geometry of perspective using a vanishing point*

In one-point perspective (OPP), one of the coordinate axes is perpendicular to the drawing surface, which means it is being projected onto the paper. For the purposes here, let's assume that is the Z axis. The larger the Z value in the point P=(X, Y, Z) is, the farther away the point P is from the origin. The X axis will be horizontal, as usual, and the Y axis will be vertical, but the coordinate values themselves will be scaled according to their depth as defined by Z. So on the Z=0 plane, which will be the drawing area, the X and Y coordinates will be exactly as specified.

However, as the value of Z increases, the value of X and Y will become smaller (*foreshortened*) and move in the direction of the *orthogonal*, which is the line drawn to the vanishing point. How much the values of X and Y change as a function of Z depends on where the vanishing point is and what the maximum Z value is – we called this *Zfar* previously, the far clipping plane. We'll use Z=0, as the near clipping plane (we called this *Znear*).

In Figure 7-14, we're drawing a cube that is 100x100x100. The red square is the front face, in the XY plane at Z=0. The back face must be at Z=100. What are the width and height at that distance? Another way of asking the same question is "What are the 2D coordinates of the 3D vertices of the square at Z=100"? What are the drawing area coordinates of (0, 0, 100), (100, 0, 100), (0, 100, 100) and (100, 100, 100) given the situation in the figure? The logic of the solution is as follows:

277

CHAPTER 7   FORM

The value of Z from the origin is a distance of 100 units in this case (the Z coordinate). The maximum Z coordinate is **Zfar**. So this Z value is the fraction **dz** = **Z/Zfar** of the total possible distance (to the vanishing point), and **dz** has a value between 0.0 and 1.0. At the vanishing point everything is squished into a single point, X and Y coordinates as well. This means that X and Y values have an effective maximum also. As Z increases towards **Zfar**, the X values all approach V_x and the Y values approach V_y. If we assume that the rate at which they change as a function of Z is the same, then we can produce a formula, and therefore a computer function, that allows us to convert the 3D coordinates to 2D. So we have:

$$X_{new} = (V_x - x) * dz + x$$
$$Y_{new} = (V_y - y) * dz + y$$

Which is to say that the change we should apply to X is related to the fraction of the distance this point is towards its maximum applied to *its* distance to the maximum, and ditto for Y. A function that does this is:

```
float[] xyz (float x, float y, float z)
{
  float t, a, b, c, d1, d2;
  float res[] = new float [2];
// The X coordinate is correct in the Z=0 plane, and moves
// towards the vanishing point with distance.  Linearly.
// Total distance to V
  d1 = dist (x, y, 0, this.Vx, this.Vy, this.Zmax);
  // From x,y,z to V
  d2 = dist (x, y, z, this.Vx, this.Vy, this.Zmax);
  t = z/this.Zmax;            // Fraction of total
  a = (Vx-x)*(t)+x;
  b = (Vy-y)*(t)+y;
  c = (Zmax-z)*(t)+z;
  res[0] = a;
  res[1] = b;
  return res;
}
```

CHAPTER 7 FORM

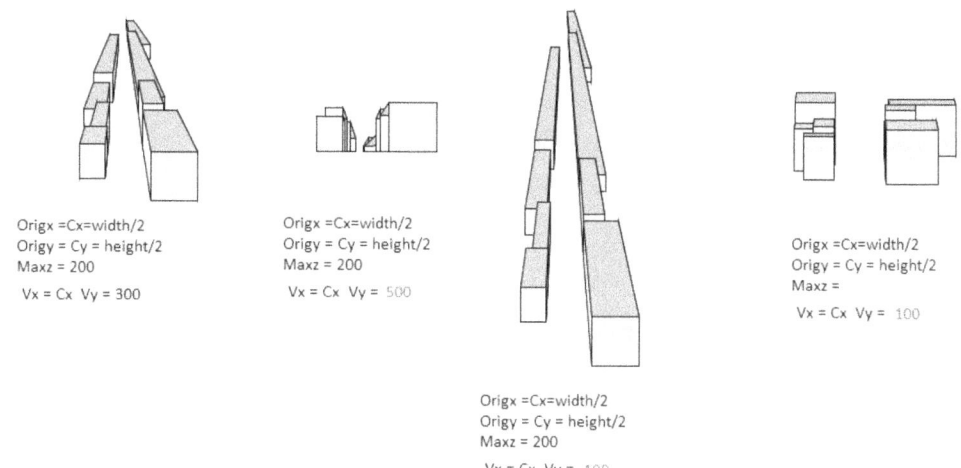

Figure 7-15. *Street scene drawing using various parameters and vanishing points*

In this code, x_{new} is **a** (**res[0]**) and y_{new} is **b** (**res[1]**). These are the screen coordinates for **(x, y, z)**. After all of this *math*, which is really geometry that an artist should be able to handle in some form, we now have a transformation that uses a single vanishing point to draw a 3D image. The parameters to this method are very different from those used by *Processing*.

Here the 2D coordinates of the vanishing point (**Vx,Vy**) are provided explicitly; the origin coordinates (**Orgx,Orgy**) amount to the location of the viewer. **Zfar** and **Zmax** are not really the same, because **Zmax** is the *largest* possible absolute Z value, whereas **Zfar** is the farthest z coordinate that will be *drawn*.

Figure 7-15 shows a basic street scene drawn by computer using a vanishing point. The street has multiple rectangular prism-shaped buildings on the left and right sides of the street (a gap). It shows how the "street" looks when drawn using various parameters. The front face of each prism is colored green, the top face grey. One other essential feature of these renderings is that the hidden lines are not visible – this is a trick, not real hidden line removal, since all that we did was (a) solid color the prism faces and (b) draw the most distant faces and prisms first.

The viewpoint in the first image is the center of the screen. The second is street level, meaning that we gave smaller Y. In the third image the maximum Z value is smaller, and so the same size along the Z axis occupies more pixels. Finally, we increased **Zmax** to 2000, which *shrinks* the apparent Z distance. We drew these images using P2D, so we did not use any of *Processing's* 3D functionality.

279

CHAPTER 7 FORM

Geometric Transforms in 3D

The most frequently used geometric transforms in 3D are the same ones we used in 2D: translation, scale, and rotation. Of these, rotation is much more complicated in 3D because we now have a wide choice of axes around which to rotate. Let's look at these in the order given above.

Translation

Translation in 3D is the same as in 2D but with one extra dimension. We simply add a translation value to each coordinate, and the values can be different in each dimension. A translation by **dx** on the x-axis, **dy** on the y-axis, and **dz** along the z-axis would be:

$$X' = x+dx$$
$$Y' = y+dy$$
$$Z' = z+dz$$

where **(x,y,z)** were the original coordinates and **(X′, Y′, Z′)** are the translated ones.

Scale

Translation in 3D is also the same as in 2D but with one extra dimension. We simply multiply each coordinate by a scale, and again these values can be different in each dimension. A scaling by **sx** on the x-axis, **sy** on the y-axis, and **sz** along the z-axis would be:

$$X' = x*dx$$
$$Y' = y*dy$$
$$Z' = z*dz$$

where **(x,y,z)** were the original coordinates and **(X′, Y′, Z′)** are the scaled ones. If **sx < 0**, then the coordinates get smaller.

Rotation

There are now *three* coordinate axes about which a rotation can be performed: the X, Y, and Z axes. In 2D, rotations are performed about the origin, so there's really *one* axis. Let's consider the X axis; the others will be very similar. A rotation of θ degrees around the X axis is accomplished by modifying the (x,y,z) coordinates of the original point to:

A rotation about the X axis is **rotateX**:

$$x' = x$$
$$y' = y*\cos(q) - z*\sin(q)$$
$$z' = y*\sin(q) + z*\cos(q)$$

A rotation about the Y axis is **rotateY**:

$$x' = x*\cos(q) + z*\sin(q)$$
$$y' = y$$
$$z' =- x*\sin(q) + z*\cos(q)$$

A rotation about the Z axis is **rotateZ**:

$$x' = = x*\cos(q) - y*\sin(q)$$
$$y' = x*\sin(q) + y*\cos(q)$$
$$z' = z$$

This all comes from basic trigonometry.

Rotation About the Object Center

Rotations all take place using the global origin. There are three rotations, one about each axis. To rotate an object about its own center, simply move (translate) that object to the origin:

translate (Ox, Oy, Oz);

where the center of the object is at (Ox, Oy, Oz). Now do the rotations about the three coordinate axes:

rotateX(θ_x);
rotateY(θ_y);
rotateZ(θ_z);

Finally, translate the object back to the original position:

translate (-Ox, -Oy, -Oz);

CHAPTER 7 FORM

Parallel Coordinate Projections

We can define a parallel projection as one in which the center of projection (vanishing point) is at infinity. Parallel lines in the object remain parallel in the resulting 2D image.

Orthographic

In an orthographic projection the *orthogonals* or *projectors* are perpendicular to the surface of the drawing area. It includes the very popular isometric projection, plus dimetric and trimetric projections. In an orthographic projection, all objects with the same dimensions appear to be the same size in the image, regardless of distance (Figure 7-16).

Graphics systems have an orthographic transformation built into the rendering system that works like the perspective transformation: call the function, specifying parameters of the transformation. From then on, that transformation will be applied to all drawn objects. For example, in *Processing* we have the function **ortho**(), where the minimum and maximum values of X and Y are specified. We use this instead of **perspective**:

```
// Same as ortho() with no parameters.
ortho(-width/2, width/2, -height/2, height/2);
```

Drawing an orthographic cube can be done in the following Processing code:

```
  size(400, 400, P3D);
  ortho(-width/2, width/2, -height/2, height/2);
// The following code rotates the cube so that we are
// not seeing it from the front. Otherwise it's just a square.
translate(width/2, height/2, 0);
rotateX(-PI/6);
rotateY(PI/3);
  line (x, y, z, x+dx, y, z);
  line (x+dx,y, z, x+dx, y+dy, z);
  line (x+dx,y+dy, z, x, y+dy, z);
  line (x, y+dy, z, x, y, z);
  line (x, y, z+dz, x+dx, y, z+dz);
  line(x+dx,y,z+dz,x+dx,
        y+dy,z+dz);
  line (x+dx,y+dy,z+dz,x,y+dy,
        z+dz);
```

```
line (x, y+dy, z+dz, x, y, z+dz);
line (x, y, z, x, y, z+dz);
line (x+dx, y, z, x+dx, y, z+dz);
line (x, y+dy, z, x, y+dy, z+dz);line (x+dx, y+dy, z, x+dx, y+dy, z+dz);
```

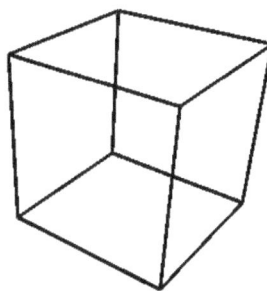

Figure 7-16. *The cube is drawn by the code in the text*

The cube drawn by this code shows an *isometric* form of an orthographic view because the principal planes of the object are inclined at angles with respect to the projection plane. The viewpoint for the view of Figure 7-16 is (500, 400, 400).

An *elevation* projection, or *multiview orthographic*, has the projectors perpendicular to one of the coordinate axes. (Figure 7-17) In that case the viewpoint could be (400, 0, 0) for a view along the X axis. This would show a square, of course, as would all of the elevation views. That's not very educational, so let's consider a more complex object: a simple boat as shown in Figure 7-18. It consists of five simple 3D shapes, as we can clearly see from the two isometric views.

We can also see all six elevations in the figure, one from each of the +x, +y, +z, -x, -y, and -z directions. Given any 3D data, we can view it as elevations simply by changing the viewpoint:

```
camera (400, 0, 0,    0,0,0, 0, -1, 0);    // +x
camera (-400, 0, 0,   0,0,0, 0, -1, 0);    // -x
camera (0, 400, 0,    0,0,0, 0, -1, 0);    // +y
camera (0,-400, 0,    0,0,0, 0, -1, 0);    // -y
camera (0, 0, 400,    0,0,0, 0, -1, 0);    // +z
camera (0, 0, -400,   0,0,0, 0, -1, 0);    // -z
```

CHAPTER 7   FORM

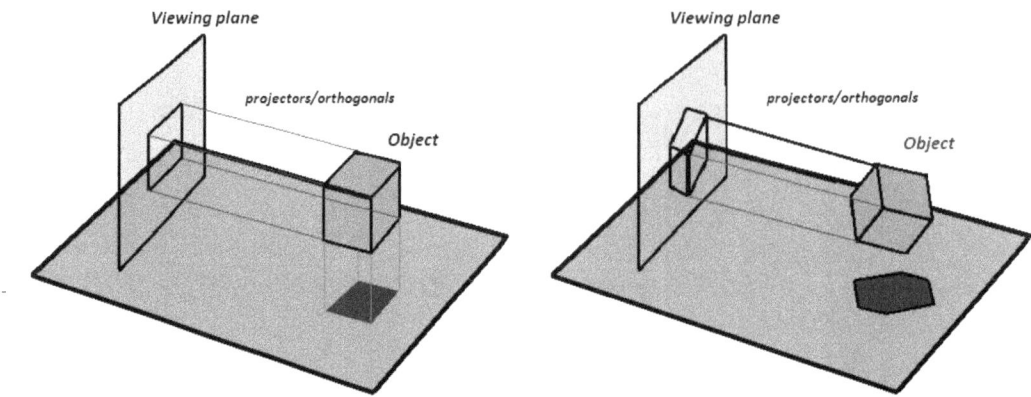

Figure 7-17. (Left) Orthographic view, elevation projection. (Right) Orthographic view, isometric projection

The value 400 in the **camera** call is simply a large enough distance so that we can see the entire object. It will vary depending on what we're drawing.

Finding the Vanishing Point in an Image

How can we find the vanishing point in an image, and why would we wish to?

The *why* part depends on the artist and their goals, but one good reason to find a vanishing point is so that we can add new objects to an existing image and have them appear normal. There are other reasons.

In Chapter 2, "Line," we discussed ways to extract straight lines from images. In a perspective image, most lines will intersect at one of the vanishing points. To find them, all we need to do is find where the majority of the lines in an image meet. Of course, that point may not be inside of the image, but that does not matter. If we know where they are, we can draw new objects using the same vanishing points.

To a human, the vanishing point is usually obvious (Figure 7-18). A computer program would have to go through a set of steps whose parameters are image dependent, but generally the process would be:

1. Edge enhance the image.
2. Threshold so the edges are one color and the background another.
3. Trace the edges into lines, possibly using the method discussed in Chapter 2, "Line."

CHAPTER 7 FORM

4. Find the points of intersection between the lines that are long enough to be significant. so that they intersect.

5. The most common points of intersections are likely to be the vanishing points.

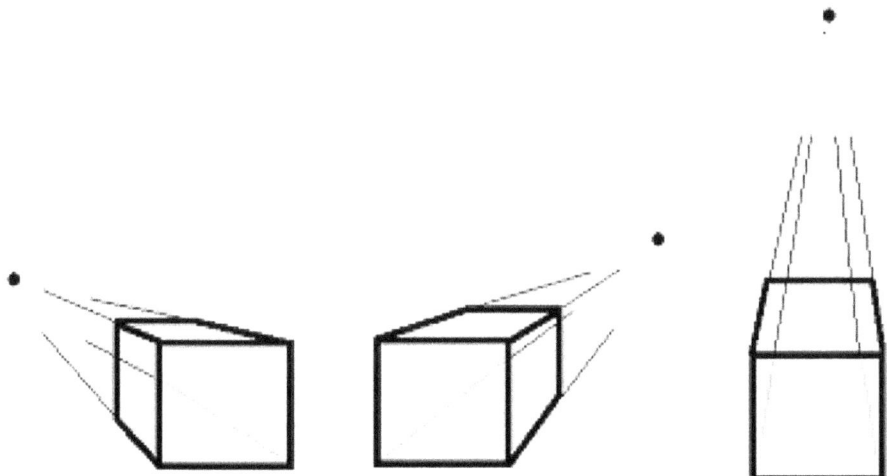

Figure 7-18. *The location of the vanishing point has a significant impact on how the object appear*

A result is shown in Figure 7-19.

Like other computer processes, generative art can have manual steps, and sometimes this is the best way to do something. When finding a vanishing point, it is simple to display the image using *Paint* or *Photoshop*, extend the important lines until they intersect, and then identify the coordinates of the intersection. This can be done faster than doing a proper thresholding, edge enhancement, and line tracing in an arbitrary color image and results in a pretty accurate vanishing point estimate.

CHAPTER 7 FORM

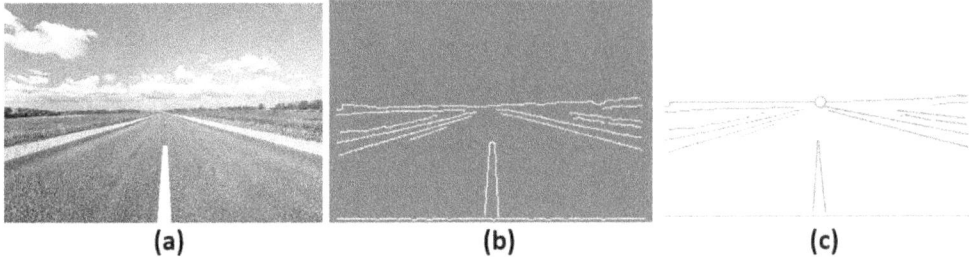

(a) (b) (c)

Figure 7-19. *Finding the vanishing point. (a) Original image. (b) Edges enhanced and thresholded. (c) Edges traced into lines. The intersection of the longer ones is indicated by the circle, which is the vanishing point*

3D Viewing

We can see things in three dimensions, which is to say that we can perceive depth or distance, because we have two eyes separated horizontally. Each eye sees a slightly different scene due to this separation. This is easy to observe by simply looking at some nearby object and closing one eye and then the other. Objects that are nearby will seem to change location more than things that are far apart. We can see the geometry of this in Figure 7-20.

Disparity

Our brain knows how far apart our eyes are and calculates the difference between the left and right images, and hence the distance to the objects, using this difference, which computer vision people call *disparity*. A pixel that is on the edge of an object in the left image will probably not be on that edge in the right image, and the difference between these (number of pixels) is greater for nearer objects. 3D software that involves stereo often calculates the disparity at each pixel and creates a disparity image or disparity map in which the value of a pixel indicates the size of the disparity between that pixel in the left and right images and hence shows the distance between the viewer and the object as a grey value (Figure 7-20).

In order to determine the disparity, one has to solve the *correspondence* problem: given two images, which pixels are the same ones (i.e., *correspond* to each other) in each image. This is impossible for single pixels in general, so what we do is use a small region **R(N,M)** near each pixel **$P_1(i,j)$** and **$P_2(i',j')$** and see if the regions agree, more or less. If so, then those pixels correspond to each other (represent the same location in the two images. This can't be done perfectly for arbitrary images, but many algorithms have been developed that perform well enough in the computer vision domain. What do we need to know about this for artistic purposes?

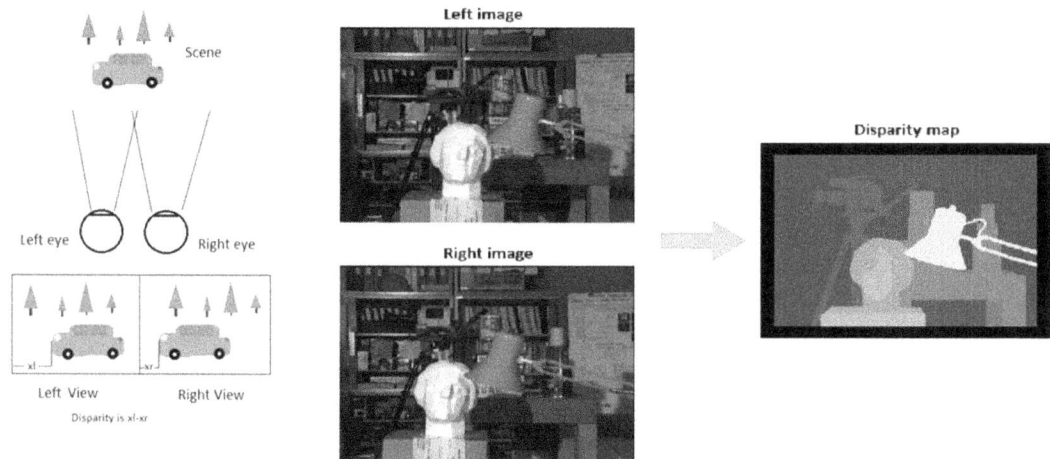

Figure 7-20. Disparity, the distance between objects in two images, for 3D

We should know about how to create 3D (stereo) imagery rather than how to interpret it. We can't take an arbitrary 2D image and make it 3D, but we can create 3D images from scratch, as left and right pairs, for example.

Image Pairs

Drawing a pair of stereoscopic images can be a fun and interesting thing to do and has artistic implications also. We know what the geometry of binocular vision is: two eyes (viewpoints) separated by a fixed distance **d**. If we specify a single viewpoint at **(ex, ey, ez)**, then the two viewpoints we need could be E_L = **(ex-d/2, ey, ez)** and E_R = **(ex+d/2, ey,ez)**. Now create a left image from E_L and a right image from E_R and display them side by side (Figure 7-21) or print them and use a viewer.

One way to do this in practice (using *Processing*) is to use the **camera()** function to create an image for both viewpoints. For the two images, this could involve the following code:

```
perspective();                                      perspective();
camera(-12,200,-200,150, 200,150,200,0,0,1,0);      camera(12,200, -200,0,0,1,0);
```

where d= 24, and the -12/+12 X value in the **camera** gives the difference between the two eyes. Now drawing a 3D line will, depending on which **camera** call was used, produce a left or right stereo image, as in Figure 7-21.

CHAPTER 7   FORM

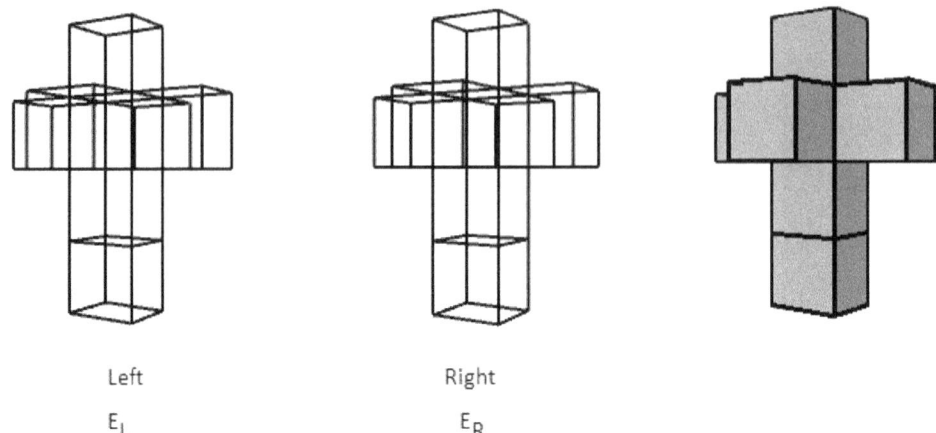

Left
E_L

Right
E_R

Figure 7-21. *Stereo view (3D) of a tesseract. The left and right images, and the shaded image, which is better at showing it without a viewing device*

We can accomplish the same effect by using the simple perspective transformation code we gave previously and specifying a difference of **d** between two views. We could have a function to draw lines in the left and the right images:

```
void line3dL(float x,float y,float z,    void line3dR(float xfloat y, float z,
    float xx, float yy, float zz)            float xx, float yy, float zz)
{                                        {
  int xp, yp, xxp, yyp;                    int xp, yp, xxp, yyp;
  x = x-e/2;                               x = x+e/2;
  xp = (int)((x*d)/(d+z));                 xp = (int)((x*d)/(d+z));
  yp = (int)((y*d)/(d+z));                 yp = (int)((y*d)/(d+z));
  xx = xx-e/2;                             xx = xx+e/2;
  xxp = (int)((xx*d)/(d+zz));              xxp = (int)((xx*d)/(d+zz));
  yyp = (int)((yy*d)/(d+zz));              yyp = (int)((yy*d)/(d+zz));
  line (xp, yp, xxp, yyp);                 line (xp+300, yp, xxp+300, yyp);
}                                        }
```

Again, the horizontal viewpoint position changes by **d** in each image. The lines for the object being drawn are drawn twice in this case, once each for the left and right images.

Anaglyphs

An *anaglyph* uses color to present the left and right images to each eye. The left eye is shown the left image using only one color, for example, red, and the right eye is shown the right image using only green. When using photographs, one needs to have a left-eye and right-eye image, which is to say that we need two images of the same scene captured from locations about an inch apart. When the two images are viewed using special glasses, where the left and right lenses have the correct, matching colors (Figure 7-22e), the image appears to be three dimensional (Figure 7-22a).

If we want to create an anaglyph using computer graphics, we have to create two images of the same object, each in 3D, and display each one using a distinct color and drawing one on top of the other (Figure 7-22b-d).

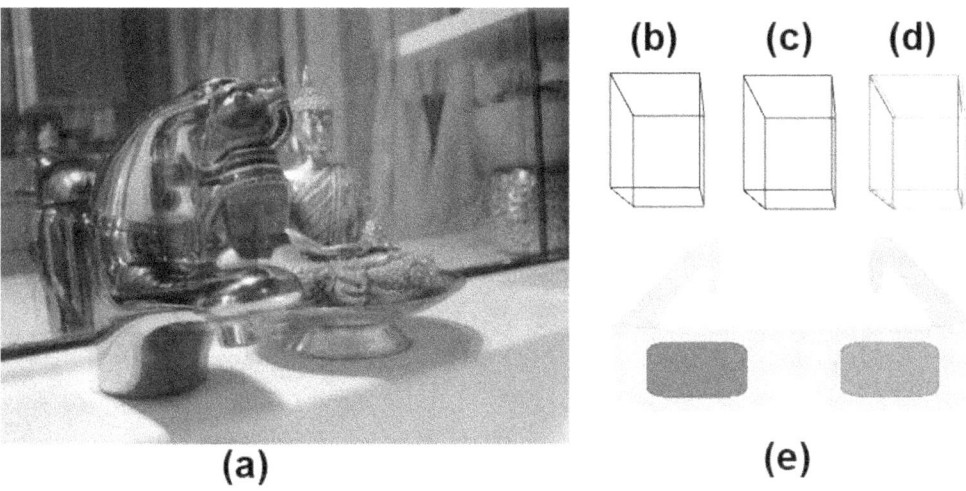

Figure 7-22. *(a) An anaglyph made with a camera from two images. (b) Left image of a cube. (c) Right image of a cube. (d) The left and right images are overdrawn in distinct colors. (e) "Glasses" that can be used to view an anaglyph*

We know how to draw a cube using lines. Making an anaglyph of a cube is a matter of drawing a cube twice using a viewpoint that is a few pixels different in the X direction and using a distinct stroke color for each cube. Here the cubes are seen from locations 2 pixels apart:

CHAPTER 7 FORM

```
stroke (255, 0, 0);
rect (200, 160, 200, 40, 50, 60);
stroke (0, 255, 0);
rect (202, 160, 200, 40, 50, 60);
```

Textures in 3D

Graphics systems make it easy to apply textures to polygons drawn in 3D; the texture mapping is built right in. In *Processing*, it's part of the **vertex** function. As a reminder, here is the way we could draw the face of a prism in *Processing*:

```
beginDraw(QUADS);
 vertex (  0,   0,0);
 vertex (100,   0,0);
 vertex (100, 100,0);
 vertex (  0, 100,0);
endDraw();
```

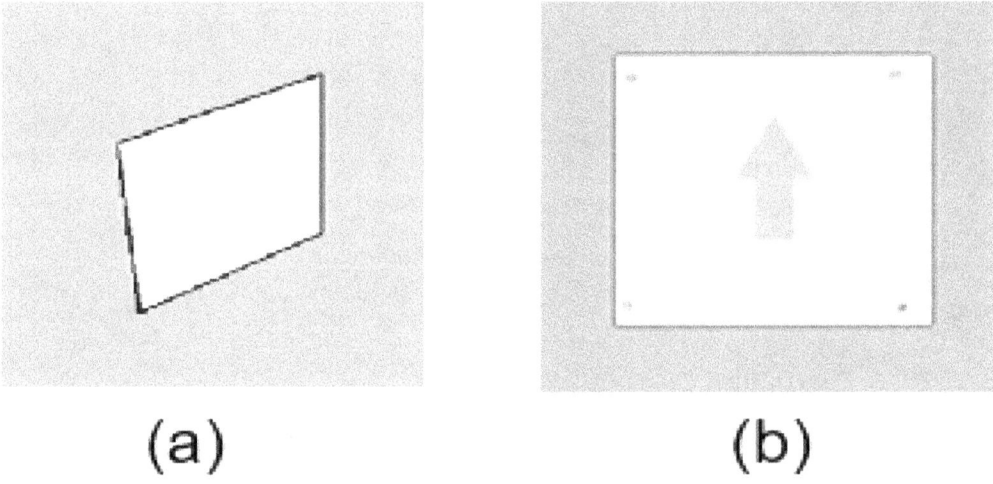

(a) (b)

Figure 7-23. *(a) One face of a prism, no texture. Texture mapping the image of an arrow*

Remember, a texture on a computer is an image. To map it onto a surface, we first need to read it in as a **PImage** variable; let's call it **txt**. An image is a rectangle, and so is a quad, so the mapping will be simple, but we need to define how the system must do it. We map the corners of the image onto the vertices of the quad. The quad is 30x30 pixels,

CHAPTER 7 FORM

and the first texture image we'll map is 500x500. We wish to map the upper left of the quad to the upper left, or (0,0) pixel, of the image. We specify the texture image with:

```
beginDraw(QUADS);
  texture (txt);
```

Now the first vertex, which will be the upper left. Specify it to be at (0,0,0), and also specify what coordinate of the texture will map onto this vertex: in this case it will be the upper left of the texture image, or (0,0):

```
vertex ( 0,    0, 0,    0,   0);
```

The final two coordinates are those of the texture. The next vertex is the upper right, which is (100,0,0); the upper right of the image is (500, 0), so:

```
vertex (100,   0, 0,    500,  0);
```

We're moving clockwise, so the next vertex is the lower right, or (100,100,0), and the lower right of the texture is (500,500):

```
vertex (100, 100, 0,    500, 500);
```

and finally we get to the lower left:

```
vertex (0,   100, 0,    0, 500);
endShape();
```

The result is shown in Figure 7-23. This program didn't use much in the way of 3D viewing. The entire function that draws this is:

```
void face100()
{
  background(0);
  translate(width/2, height/2);
  stroke(255);
  fill(127);
  beginShape(QUADS);
   texture (txt);
   vertex ( 0,    0, 0,    0,   0);
   vertex (100,   0, 0,    500,  0);
   vertex (100, 100, 0,    500, 500);
```

291

CHAPTER 7 FORM

```
    vertex (0,    100, 0,     0, 500);
  endShape();
}
```

A couple of things need to be added: *normalized* texture coordinates and the 3D viewing transformation.

Figure 7-24. *Texture-mapped image with **up** being negative*

The program above requires that you know how large the texture image is. That's not a huge problem, but it can be eliminated by specifying *normalized* – that is, between 0 and 1 – coordinates. In normalized coordinates the upper left is still (0,0), but the upper right is (1,0), the lower right is (1,1), and the lower left is (1,0). It is as if the texture image is 1x1 in size. Of course it's 1.0 x 1.0, so the center would be (0.5, 0.5). The code that draws the same texture quad as before would now, using normalized coordinates, be:

```
  textureMode(NORMAL)
  beginShape(QUADS);
   texture (txt);
   vertex ( 0,     0, 0,   0, 0);
   vertex (100,    0, 0,   1, 0);
   vertex (100,  100, 0,   1, 1);
   vertex (0,    100, 0,   0, 1);
  endShape();
```

Now all texture images can be treated in the same way, as long as the quad and texture image have the same shape.

When we use coordinate projections and a viewing transformation, there's another issue. Let's specify the default perspective projects and an eye position at 0,0,300:

```
perspective();
camera (0, 0, 300, 0,0,0, 0, -1, 0);
```

Now when we draw the quad, it appears upside down, as in Figure 8-d. Why? Because in the **camera** call we said that *up* was -1. Normally that's right, but it makes the textures look upside down. To make the textures work properly with the rest of the graphics, we must either draw them upside-down or make the texture images upside-down and left-to-right as files. Changing the files is simpler. There is a lot of code in some programs, and it's easy to make a mistake.

Making a Building

A building is almost always some variation on a rectangular prism, and we know how to draw one of those. To make it more realistic, we can map a texture onto each face, and now we know how to do that too. The first step is to acquire some texture images for the building. Photos can be used, or sometimes one can find suitable ones on an Internet site. These can cost money but are often worth it.

We can edit these images to make them suitable and then save them as front, back, left, right, and top texture images. Now we simply map each one onto a side of the prism. There are six faces on a prism, and some can use the same texture. We don't always need a texture for the bottom of a building or other object. There are also some basic rules for texture mapping a prism:

1. The texture function should be within its own beginShape - endShape and will apply to that sequence.

2. Each face should be within its own beginShape - endShape code sequence, rather than one beginShape for all texture mappings. This allows us to specify a different texture for each face.

3. You can use only one textureMode call, just before beginShape.

Here is a function that draws a textured prism using globally defined images. It is included here in its entirety because it can be a model for other code that is very useful and shows how to use the built-in facilities in *Processing* properly.

```
void prismv(float x, float y,float z,        beginShape(QUADS);   // left
            float dx, float dy, float dz)      texture (left);
{                                              vertex (x, y, z,         0, 0);
  textureMode (NORMAL);                        vertex(x, y, z+dz,       0, 1);
  beginShape(QUADS); // Back                   vertex (x, y+dy, z+dz,   1, 1);
    texture (back);                            vertex(x, y+dy, z,       1, 0);
    vertex(x, y, z+dz,       0, 0);          endShape();
    vertex(x+dx, y, z+dz,    1, 0);          beginShape(QUADS); // top
                                               texture(top);
    vertex(x+dx, y+dy, z+dz, 1, 1);            vertex (x, y+dy, z,      0, 0);
    vertex(x, y+dy, z+dz,    0, 1);            vertex(x+dx, y+dy, z, 0, 1);
  endShape();                                  vertex(x+dx, y+dy, z+dz, 1, 1);
  beginShape(QUADS); // Bottom                 vertex (x, y+dy, z+dz,   1, 0);
    vertex (x, y, z);                        endShape();
    vertex(x+dx, y, z);
    vertex(x+dx, y, z+dz);
    vertex(x, y, z+dz);                      beginShape(QUAD); // front
  endShape();                                  texture (front);
  beginShape(QUADS); // right                  vertex(x, y, z,          0, 0);
    texture (right);                           vertex(x, y+dy, z,       0, 1);
    vertex (x+dx, y, z,      0, 0);            vertex(x+dx, y+dy, z, 1, 1);
    vertex (x+dx, y+dy, z,   0, 1);            vertex(x+dx, y, z,       1, 0);
    vertex (x+dx, y+dy, z+dz, 1, 1);         endShape();
    vertex (x+dx, y, z+dz,   1, 0);        }
  endShape();
```

The five parameters to vertex() are x, y, z (3D position), followed by u and v (texture coordinates where 0,0 is upper-left and 1,1 is lower-right of the texture image).

Figure 7-25a shows the three textures that were used, and the result of one call of this function is 7-25c. Of course, we can call this function as often as we like with differing parameters and create an entire city of the same building (Figure 7-25d) just as easily as drawing just one building. This is a part of the power of generative art.

For most artistic purposes we will need distinct textures for each size of the prism so that the object looks real (if that's wanted). Buildings look different on each side as a rule, as do many 3D objects – cars, bottles, boxes, and so on have distinct faces.

Texture Mapping Triangles

Images are rectangular, and triangles are not. How can we map a rectangular texture image onto a triangle? That's what the texture coordinates are for – we don't have to use all of the texture image.

A pyramid can have four triangular faces and a rectangular base. Here's an example of some code to draw one face:

```
textureMode (NORMAL);
beginShape(TRIANGLES);
  texture (steps);
  vertex(x,y,z,          0.5, 0)
  vertex(x-dx,y-dy,z-dz, 0, 1);
  vertex(x+dx, y-dy, z-dz,1, 1);
endShape();
```

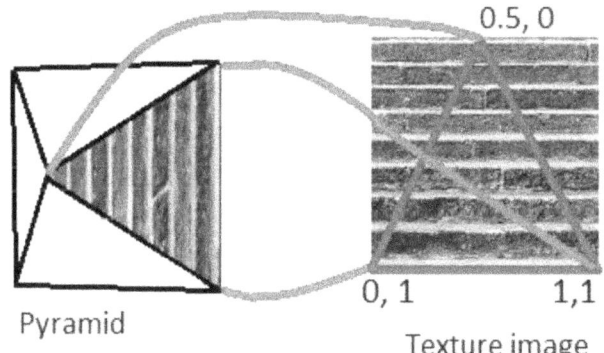

Figure 7-25. *Texture mapping triangles. The texture image is rectangular, so it has to be made into a triangle using normalized coordinates. 0.5, 0 is halfway between 0,0 and 1,0 and is a good coordinate for the tap of a triangle here.*

CHAPTER 7   FORM

The peak of the pyramid is (0, 0, 0) and dx, dy, dz are 100. The texture coordinates use the pixel in the center of the top row of the image as the pixel at the peak of the pyramid. We draw the triangular face from that point to the lower left and lower right corners of the image (0,1) and (1,1) (Figure 7-26).

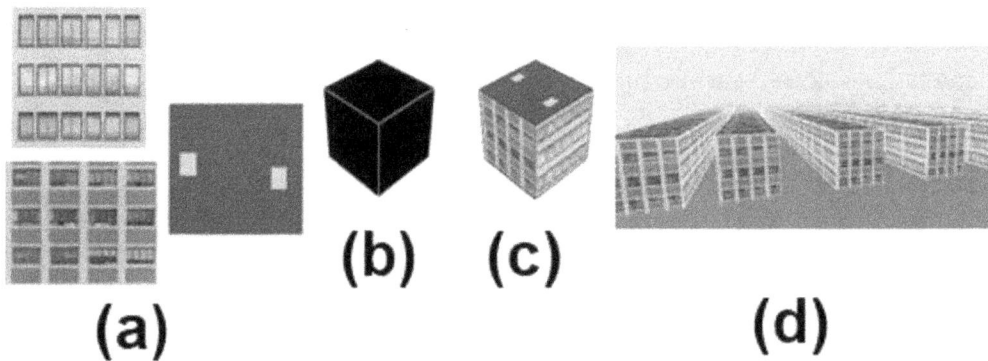

Figure 7-26. *Making a building by texturing a prism. (a) Front, side, and top textures. (b) The prism. (c) Textured prism. (d) This can be repeated as often as needed*

3D Models

Video games and related 3D graphics systems rely on artists to create three-dimensional objects. This is accomplished using either a 3D scanner, which collects (x,y,z) data points of real objects, or by drawing the object using a modeling program like *Maya* or *3D Studio Max*. These programs allow the artist to create a 3D shape using the mouse and clever software tricks. Then the program converts the shape into quads or triangles (*polygonalization* or *triangulation*) and saves it in a file. A game can read these files and reconstruct the object and render it at its proper location within the game space.

There are multiple modeling packages, and often each one has its own format for storing the polygons, although they all have to do basically the same thing. The most common formats are the following:

> **STL** – One of the oldest formats (1987). File names end in "**.stl**"; only stores the geometry.

> **OBJ** - Developed by *Wavefront Technologies,* this 3D file format has the extension **.obj**. Can encode color and texture information. One of the most popular formats.

296

FBX - proprietary file format that's widely used in the film industry and in video games. It is owned now by *Autodesk*. Popular for animation.

3DS – A proprietary file format also owned by Autodesk and associated with the modeling program *3D Studio Max*. Has the extension **.3ds**.

There are many others. Let's take a look at **.obj** files as one example of these files.

.OBJ Files

There is text and a binary version of these files, with the binary version being proprietary. To begin with, here is a hand-generated .obj file for a cube:

```
# Hand generated .obj file - a cube
v    0   0   0
v  100   0   0
v  100 100   0
v    0 100   0
v    0   0 100
v  100   0 100
v  100 100 100
v    0 100 100
# front
f 0 1 2 3
#back
f 4 5 6 7
#left
f 3 7 4 0
# bottom
f 0 1 5 4
# top
f 3 7 6 2
# right
f 1 2 6 5
```

CHAPTER 7 FORM

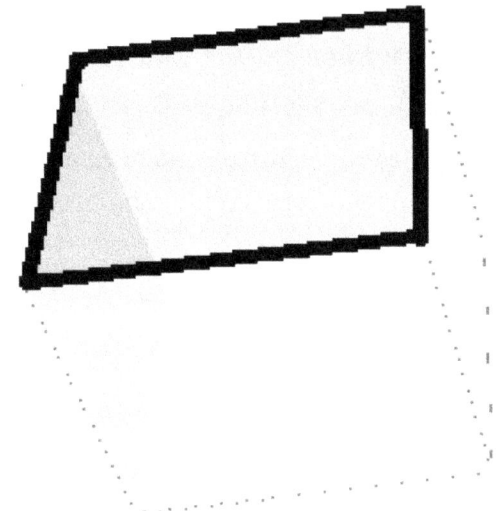

Figure 7-27. *The cube drawn from a .obj file*

Lines beginning with a "#" are comments and are to be ignored. The first section of the file contains 3D coordinates of vertices. Each line begins with "v" and is followed by the x, y, and z coordinates. A cube has eight vertices, and so there are eight lines; a vertex is known by a number, which is the number of the line where it is defined. So vertex 0 here is (0,0,0), and vertex 4 is (0,0,100). Looking at these data, it's obvious that the cube is 100x100x100 pixels.

The next section in *this* file consists of faces, which are polygons. The line in the file defining a face begins with "f" and is followed by numbers that indicate vertices. There is more than one way to specify a polygon, but in this file they are all quads. Since a quad has four vertices, a face is defined as "f" followed by four numbers, and each number is the vertex number to be used. The first face has vertices 0,1,2,3, which corresponds to (0,0,0), (100,0,0), (100,100,0), and (0,100,0). There are six faces in a cube and six face definitions in this file.

The cube that is represented in this file looks like the one in Figure 7-27. Colors were added by this program. This has been drawn by the simple OBJ file reader accompanying this book, named *readObj*. This program is very limited, reading only the basic geometry data. An OBJ file can also contain:

- *Normals*, which are directions that are perpendicular to a face. These are used for illumination calculations.
- Texture coordinates.

298

- Names of texture files (.mtl).
- Groups (collected vertices/faces that are related).

and a few other things.

Most 3D models are created at a pretty high resolution and consist of many thousand polygons. The *readObj* program only renders the faces (polygons) and not textures or colors, although it can add flat colors to polygons.

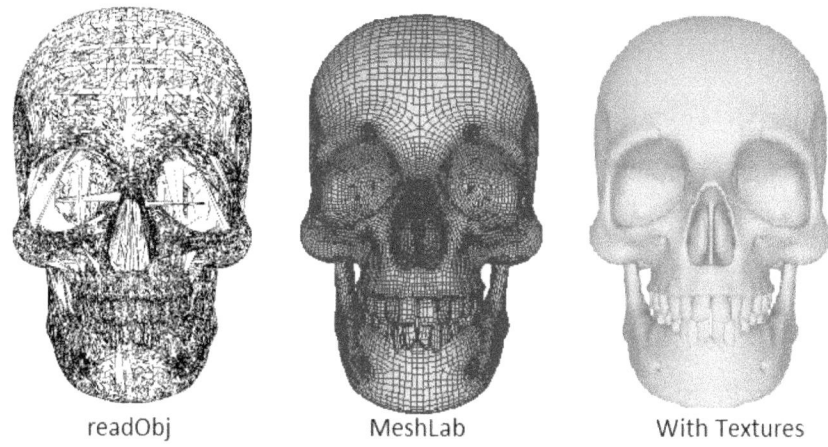

Figure 7-28. An obj file with 80000 triangles displayed in various ways

As an example, a model of a human skull was found on the Internet and is shown in Figure 7-28. This model has 40,062 vertices and 80,016 triangles. That seems like quite a lot but is typical of a medium-resolution model. The *readObj* program tries to display *all* of the polygons as a mesh, which is pretty ugly, but the *MeshLab* program seems to reduce the number to make them more easily visible.

Illumination Models

Simply having a polygonal mesh does not provide a visual 3D appearance to the object. Texture helps quite a lot because it offers many visual cues, but a sphere viewed from a distance with a solid color looks like a circle – *unless* we provide some simulated illumination. We see things by reflected light, and light bounces off of objects in a geometrically predictable way: the angle that the light source makes to the surface (*incidence* angle) equals the angle of reflection that the light reflects (*reflection* angle) from the surface. The effect, in 3D given a viewpoint, is that there is a resulting

CHAPTER 7   FORM

distribution of light intensity across the sphere (or any) surface that we interpret as shape information. We now know that objects in 3D graphics are not continuously curved but are comprised of polygons. This makes computing the reflections relatively simple. The polygon is a plane, and light arriving at every point will reflect at the same angle.

We need to figure out how much light is reflected back to us by each polygonal facet of the object. The amount of light we see will be **I** and will depend on the kind of light, the position of the light, the viewpoint, and the material the polygons are supposed to represent.

Ambient Light

Light that is *ambient* simply seems to surround you, the source not being in any specific place. Some call it *indirect* light, although that's not a good description. Since the light has no specific source, the angle that the source makes with the surface is not relevant. All we need is the intensity of the light and the amount that the surface reflects light. The light we see from the object is **I = K I$_a$**, where K is the amount of light reflected by the surface (between 0 and 1) and **I$_a$** is the brightness or intensity of the ambient light. The result is a flat, uniform surface brightness.

Diffuse Reflection

In this lighting model the surface is rough or grainy. This is a 3D texture, and so each pixel could have a distinct angle at which light bounces off of it. The surface appears equally bright from all viewing directions, and the brightness at each point is proportional to the cosine of the angle between the line to the light source and the line perpendicular to the surface at that pixel. That's because we observe that a surface perpendicular to the light source (where the cosine = 1) is brighter than one at a more oblique angle. The formula for the brightness of a point on the surface is **N$_d$ L$_p$ cos(θ)**, where **θ** is the angle between the light source and the polygon's perpendicular.

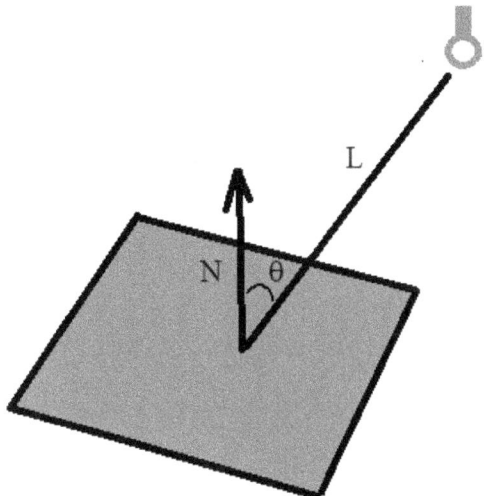

Figure 7-29. *Geometry of reflection, flat shading*

Flat Shading

In flat shading, a polygon is colored entirely with the same intensity, and that is a function of where the light is, where the observation point is, and the location and orientation of the polygon. The sphere in Figure 7-26a is flat shaded. The geometry is shown in Figure 7-29. All points on the polygon have the same surface normal **N**, and if the light source is far enough away, the angle θ is the same everywhere too, so the brightness is the same everyplace.

Gouraud Shading

If we represent a curved surface as polygons, it makes sense to assume that the reflection from the surface will change across the polygon surface. We can no longer assume that the polygon normal is the same in all locations, so the reflection from the polygon will vary. How? Well, we could assume that where the polygons meet, the normal is the mean (average) of all of the polygons that meet at that point. From this normal we can calculate a reflectance value. At all vertices of any polygon, therefore, we have a calculated reflectance value (Figure 7-30).

CHAPTER 7　FORM

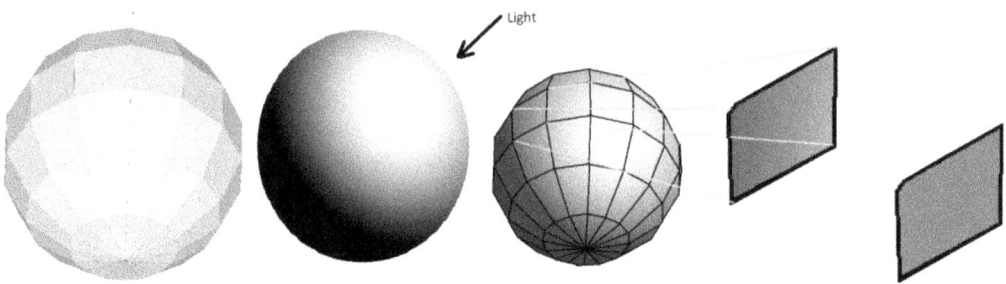

Figure 7-30. *Gouraud shading interpolates the levels to provide a smooth shading*

The Gouraud shading algorithm interpolates these between vertices (along edges) and then again interpolates along scan lines. This gives a unique value for each polygon that approximates what we would see in a curved surface. The method is described as (Figure 7-31):

1. Find the normal vector at each vertex of each polygon by averaging the neighbors.

2. Interpolate the value at each pixel along each edge using the two vertex endpoints as extreme values and setting the values between them according to the distance from each vertex.

3. Scan horizontally from top to bottom, selecting the starting and ending pixel on the polygon, and using the values at those points to interpolate each pixel along that line in the polygon.

This process is quite computationally intense, especially when one considers the number of polygons that we usually use to represent an object. As a result, this calculation is nearly always performed on the graphics processor and not the CPU. Indeed, graphics processors have been specifically designed for this kind of computation.

Shading is done in *Processing* when 3D objects are drawn with illumination specified. We don't have to do it using our own code.

CHAPTER 7   FORM

Example: Cubism

A part of the cubist process is to represent 3D in novel ways: to use color to represent distance, for example, or to show multiple portions of the 3D scene simultaneously. What will be described here is only one way to interpret that idea.

We'll begin with an image, as usual, in this case Cezanne's *Still Life with Apples*, painted in 1890 (Figure 7-32). Almost any image should work well. This was selected because Cézanne is widely suggested as a precursor to cubism, and a still life works well here.

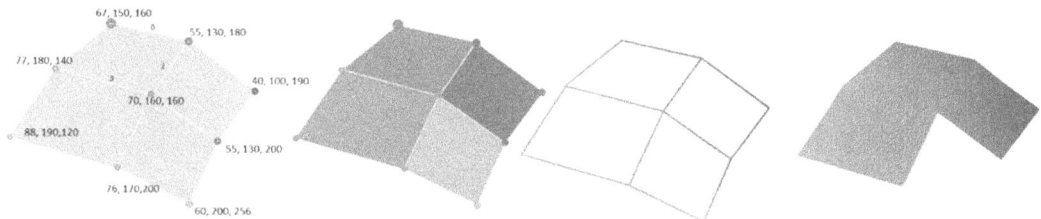

Figure 7-31. Gouraud shading of four polygons

Figure 7-32. Still life with apples (Paul Cézanne, 1890) The final cubist version of still life with apples

303

CHAPTER 7   FORM

The idea behind the cubist transformation of this painting is to triangulate it in the third dimension. We don't have any actual 3D data, so random values will be used, but we could have used color as a cue, or we could have manually added depth values. The triangulation, the slicing of the image into triangles, should not be regular, although that is the easiest thing to do. A regular triangulation makes the result look a bit like a quilt or a sweater, which is not the look we're after.

The triangles will have a basic size as specified by parameters **w, h, dx, dy,** and **dz**. The fixed width and height are given by **w** and h. The **dx**, **dy**, and **dz** parameters are the amount of random variation allowed in each direction. The actual vertices of the triangles will be stored as 2D arrays **tx**, **ty**, and **tz** where:

```
tx[i][j] = (int)(i +random (-dx, dx));
ty[i][j] += (int)(j + random (-dy, dy));
tz[i][j] = random (-dz, 0);
```

The **z** coordinate is completely random in a given range. Any vertex (i,j) is modified by a random variation of the offsets **dx** and **dy**. This creates a set of irregular triangles in 3D (Figure 7-33a). The triangles are actually created as quadrilaterals cut along the diagonal. The quad from (i,j) to (i+1,j+1) is cut along the line from (i+1,j) to (i, j+1), as in Figure 7-33b. A 3D triangle can be drawn as:

```
// Triangle 3D:

vertex (ax, ay, az , (float)ax, (float)ay);
vertex (bx, by, bz ,  (float)bx, (float)by);
vertex (cx, cy, cz ,  (float)cx, (float)cy);
```

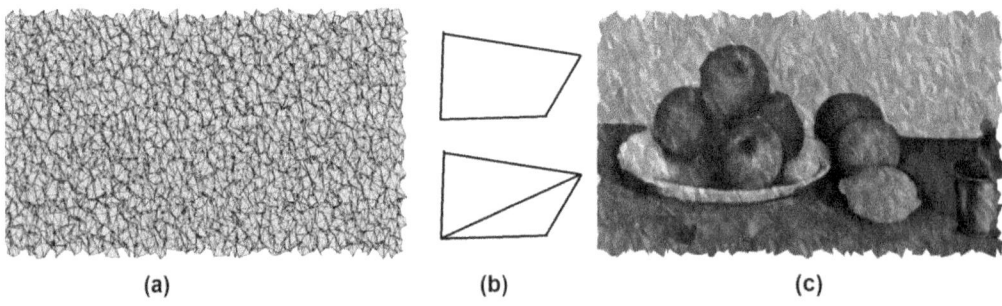

(a)   (b)   (c)

Figure 7-33. *(a) Triangles created using a randomization process. (b) Triangles are actually quads divided into two triangles along a diagonal. (c) The result when the original painting is textured over the 3D triangles*

where we are using **beginShape(TRIANGLES)** and normalized texture coordinates. The triangles are then drawn as:

```
triangle3D (tx[i/w][j/h], ty[i/w][j/h],
 tz[(int)(i/w)][(int)(j/h)], tx[i/w+1][j/h], ty[i/w+1][j/h],
 tz[(int)(i/w)+1][(int)(j/h)],tx[i/w][j/h+1],  ty[i/w][j/h+1],
 tz[(int)(i/w)][(int)(j/h)+1]);
triangle3D (tx[i/w+1][j/h], ty[i/w+1][j/h],
  tz[(int)(i/w)+1][(int)(j/h)], tx[i/w+1][j/h+1],
  ty[i/w+1][j/h+1], tz[(int)(i/w)+1][(int)(j/h)+1],
  tx[i/w][j/h+1], ty[i/w][j/h+1],
  tz[(int)(i/w)][(int)(j/h)+1]);
```

where **i** and **j** run over all pixels in the Cezanne image. The result will texture the original image over the 3D triangles, as seen in Figure 7-33c. This does not give the effect we're looking for. Instead of texturing the image over the triangles, a distinct texture could be used for each, or we could simply fill a triangle with the color of one of the vertices in the original image, which is what was done in Figure 7-34.

Figure 7-34. The final cubist version of still life with apples

The final result was enhanced by adding illumination. *Processing* provides ways to illuminate an object. This image was illuminated using directional light:

```
directionalLight (100, 100, 0, 255, 255, 0);
directionalLight (-700, 100, 0, 255, 0, 255);
directionalLight (0, -300, -100, 255, 0, 0);
```

The first three parameters here represent the location where the light is coming from, and the last three parameters are the color (RGB) of the light. Other forms of illumination are:

> **spotlight** – allows much greater control of the light, including direction, size of the illumination cone, color, and how the light varies from the center to the boundary of the cone.
>
> **ambientLight** – specifies a generalized light with no specific source, but it does have a color.
>
> **pointLight** – A spotlight with a 180-degree cone, a color, and a position. Like a lamp.

If you use any of the illumination functions, you must first call **lights()** to initialize things.

Summary

The art element *form* refers to the third dimension. Scenes that we draw and paint have three dimensions, but the canvas has only two, so we have to project the scene onto the paper. This means converting three-dimensional coordinates (x,y,z) into two-dimensional ones (x,y). Doing this means knowing where the artist is located and what direction they are looking.

The *perspective transformation* depicts a scene as a person would see it. Faraway objects appear smaller than near ones, and parallel lines appear to meet at a distant vanishing point. It requires that we know the field of view and the aspect ratio, and it defines a range of z values within which we can view the scene. The viewer is defined by a camera transformation that specifies the position of the viewer and the point they are looking at and defines the *up* direction.

In *Processing* we can specify the rendering to be in 3D using size(w, h, P3D). Then the perspective transform and camera transformation need to be defined, and we can draw in 3D using beginShape() ... vertex() ... endShape() operations.

Artists usually use perspective and vanishing points in their works, and we can do that using a computer but usually don't. It involves making parallel lines meet at a point. Vanishing points can be found in an image by extracting lines and then tracing them to a common point of intersection. The *orthographic* projection is a *parallel* projection where the lines representing the line of sight are parallel. We can also draw *elevations* that each show one side of an object. Translation and scale are the same in 3D as in 2D, but rotation differs because in situations of multiple rotation, it depends on which rotation is done first.

Images that can be viewed in 3D are created by using a different image for each eye, where the point of view is shifted by the space between human eyes. Complex objects like buildings can be made more real by texture mapping actual building images onto a prism. Artists can make models of 3D objects and save them as files, then software can read those files and display the object. Computer games do this frequently. Illumination can be critical to seeing the third dimension, and so software has to model this too: *flat* shading and *Gouraud* shading are examples.

Library Code

anaglyph	- Draw an anaglyph of a prism
extractVP	- Find the vanishing point
helix	- Draw a helix using lines
helixxv	- Use the Spline class
isometric	- Isometric view of the "town."
prism	- Draw a rectangular prism, using lines
prismb	- Draw a rectangular prism, using faces (each a different color)
pyramidRect	- Rectangular pyramid
pyramidTri	- Triangular pyramid
rect	- Draw a 3D rectangle
Spline	- 3D spline class

CHAPTER 7   FORM

Stand-Alone Demo Programs

pdemo – use keys to change viewpoint.

      w = Increase viewpoint X by 100

      s = Decrease viewpoint X by 100

      a = Decrease viewpoint Y by 100

      d = Increase viewpoint Y by 100

      z = Increase viewpoint Z by 10

      x = Decrease viewpoint Z by 10

gdemo – Use keys to change viewpoint as in a video game

      w = Take a step forward

      s = Take a step backward

      a = Turn counter clockwise (left)

      s = Turn clockwise (right)

texture – Texture mapping to create "buildings." Use keys to change viewpoint as in a video game

      w = Take a step forward

      s = Take a step backward

      a = Turn counter clockwise (left)

      s = Turn clockwise (right)

my3d – Make a stereo line pair of a tesseract.
Cubista – Create a cubist version of an image.

CHAPTER 8

Space

Space, as an element, depends on all of the other elements that the artist uses in a piece. The arrangements of those elements *creates* the space in the work, and the process is called *composition*. We can characterize this only after we define what space means.

> "Composition is the art of arranging in a decorative manner the diverse elements at the painter's command to express his feelings."- Henri Matisse in "Notes of a Painter."

Space can be described as an area in a two-dimensional canvas. It includes the space between objects in a painting, space around the main scene, and certain *kinds* of space. It is about spatial relationships between things, the distance between objects, and their relative positions on the 2D canvas. There are rules used by artists concerning how to use space, and these rules seem to be very *flexible*, shall we say, and are violated as often as they are followed.

The composer Claude Debussy once said, "Music is the space between the notes." All music has space between notes; otherwise, all of the notes would be played at once, and noise would result. Perhaps the same concept applies in visual art. A good artist *plays* with space so as to communicate the ideas they wish to present.

How can we use an algorithm to manipulate space, to *play* with it? We must first have some comprehension of what space is in the context of a digital image and then develop some tools for manipulating it.

An image is a two-dimensional pattern created by the way light arrives at a sensor. It is a *spatial* relationship of light at a detailed level. Artists are taught of *space* early in their training as one of the seven basic elements of art, referring to the areas or volumes (distances) relating the basic objects or elements of a piece. So, we can handle space in many ways.

Space, in the art sense, can be *positive* or *negative*, *open* or *closed*, *shallow* or *deep*, and *two dimensional* or *three dimensional*. It can be *explicitly* rendered or *implicit*, but it is found in every work of visual art. So where can we begin? Perhaps with an empty

CHAPTER 8   SPACE

canvas, what an artist once referred to as the *white terror*, because many new artists are afraid to put marks on an empty canvas. We're going to use an empty canvas and a process for creating a specific painting as a way to begin our discussion of space and as an introduction to some of the terms, concepts, and heuristics. Nothing is written in stone, and rules are meant to be broken.

Empty Canvas

The canvas does not have to be white, but it starts out without artist-made marks. An artist has some idea about what they wish to do with this empty space. Let's begin there. This discussion concerns a real artwork, and some of you will recognize it at some point in the narrative. Imagine that you look out of a farmhouse window and see a person, a girl who cannot walk due to polio, crawling towards the house. She hates wheelchairs and crawls everywhere.

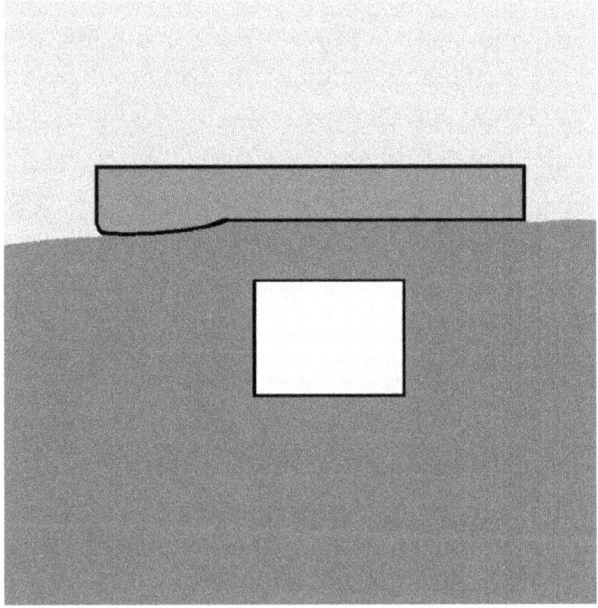

Figure 8-1. *The first subdivisions of space on a blank canvas. The four regions represent critical parts of the painting, the focus being the girl in the center pink area*

CHAPTER 8   SPACE

This inspires a painting, but instead of the view from the window, you decide to paint it from behind the girl as she makes her way to the house. This means that the farm will be farther away from the viewer than the girl is, and perhaps it would even be in the *background*. This would place it in the upper part of the image. Why? That's a general rule of composition using space, and the artist knows this – although it can be changed. The girl will be in the *forground* and is, in fact, the *focus* or *emphasis* of the painting, the most important thing from the artist's point of view. If a painting has no focus, then the viewer's eye feels lost, wandering across the canvas looking for a place to rest. The remainder of the painting is relatively unimportant except that if it were absent, then the painting would make no sense. Figure 8-1 is an example of this initial outline of the painting, in which the blue area is probably sky, brown is where the farm will be located, roughly, the girl will be in the pink box, and the green is the rest. A painter usually will do this in their head, possibly making crude, quick marks on the canvas as an outline.

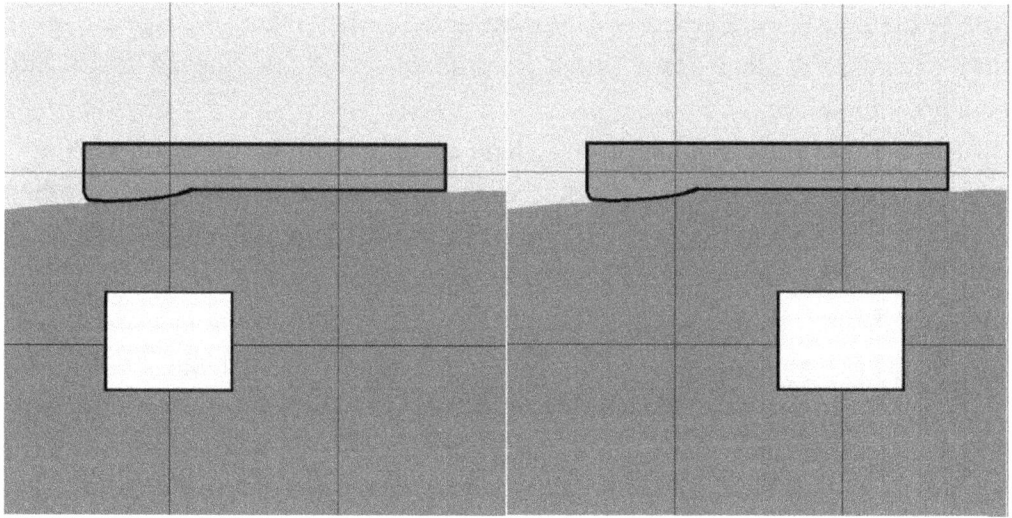

Figure 8-2. *We could place the center of focus at any of the intersections of any of the dividing lines*

311

CHAPTER 8   SPACE

Figure 8-3. *Roughing in versions of the objects*

Next, we can place some of the objects, starting with the focus. Any photographer knows better than to place the principal object in the exact center, so the position of the girl should be moved. But tow where? Artists and photographers have been using something called the *rule of thirds* for helping with this. We divide the canvas into three equal parts horizontally and vertically and place the focus at or near the intersection of two of the dividing lines. The sensible locations are shown in Figure 8-2. The girl must be in the lower part of the image; she's in the *foreground*. Let's choose the left image; it does not matter at this point.

The farmhouse will be in the brown area on the opposite side of center from the girl. She's crawling towards it, moving diagonally across the scene. We can place other buildings at the same level in different locations depending on our imagining of the scene or the buildings in the actual scene. The green region is hay or grass; the blue will be sky. We can now fill in some of those areas and sketch in the building and girl.

The sketches are intentionally rough, because artists generally *rough in* objects and do details later. The overall composition has been roughed in here, and the other parts would be the girl, the house, and the barn (Figure 8-3).

Let's fill in the background and then place the rough objects. Figure 8-4a shows the background painted in detail, and 8-4b shows the rough objects placed there according to the plan shown in Figure 8-2. You can now see clearly what the painting will be or *is* because this is an actual well-known painting by Andrew Wyeth entitled *Christina's World*, and is probably not exactly what Wyeth was thinking. The final painting is shown in Figure 8-5.

312

CHAPTER 8   SPACE

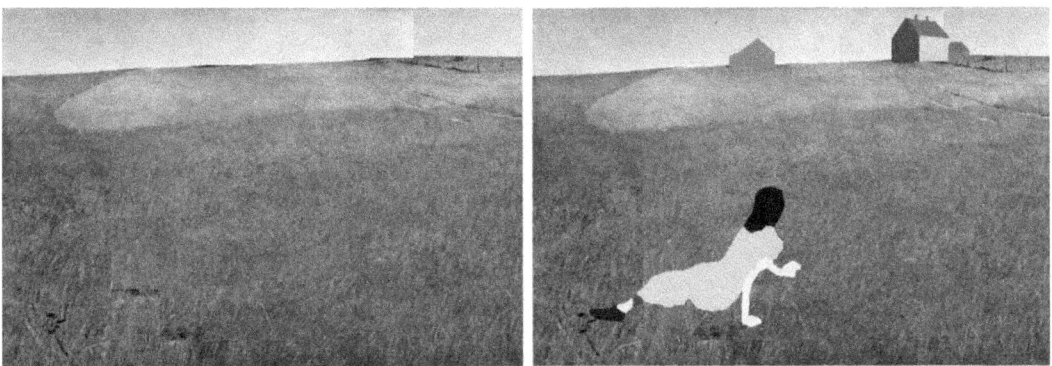

Figure 8-4. *The background and the roughed-in objects placed where we think they should go*

The process that has been described concerns the *composition* of the artwork and the order in which the painting is executed. The location on the canvas of the principal objects is critical in the design and construction of the work, and that's what the *space* element is all about. If the subject of the work is an existing scene, or a person, or a still life, then composition is largely defined by the existing elements. An artist can sometimes set those up in the scene or modify the elements a bit while drawing or painting, of course.

The scene depicted in this painting exists only in the artist's mind. The *what* of the objects has been decided upon; the *where* is a matter of composition. Many artworks are in this category, even though they are not abstract. Abstract paintings also have compositional principles related to object or shape positioning. These rules are difficult or impossible to automate but should be understood by generative artists in any case.

CHAPTER 8   SPACE

Figure 8-5. *The final painting, Christina's World by Andrew Wyeth*

The other aspect of this discussion involves the roughing-in of shapes and objects, or in other words, the level of detail involved at each level of composition. At first the objects are quite crude, involving only side and general shape. Color is added, and then details of the objects, like, for instance, windows and clothing. Finally, the textures and shading of the objects are done to give the final impression of reality.

Let's deal with the basic overall elements of composition first. We have seen some of these elements in previous chapters, since we'll be dealing with 3D space, shape, and color.

Positive and Negative Space

In art, positive space consists of the shapes or objects of interest, and negative space is the space between them. In Wyeth's painting Christina, the barn, and the house comprise the positive space, and the field and sky are the negative space. An artwork should make the positive space the most obvious and interesting part of the work. It is in some sense the *point* of it. Negative space is what you leave out.

CHAPTER 8 SPACE

Figure 8-6. *Michelangelo's The Creation of Adam (c. 1512)*

Consider the painting *The Creation of Adam* by Michelangelo (Figure 8-6). The figures of God and Adam take up half or less of the overall work but fill the positive space and are the important things to be seen. The negative space (background) is relatively empty. It contains no objects of importance. The gap between the finger of God and that of Adam creates a sense of anticipation of an event about to occur. The open space in the painting actually draws our attention to the focal points. Negative space can be critical to the composition, in that it often draws the eye to the areas the artist wants you to focus on.

What parts of an artwork are positive space, and what are negative? The negative space should be relatively featureless or contain textures or objects of little importance. No one color can be said to be representative of positive or negative space; it depends on the colors of the focus of the image. In the example of *Christina's World*, we built the background first, and it consisted of textures mainly: the sky and the pasture. The details within were not important.

Three-Dimensional Space

3D space was discussed at length in the previous chapter, but there we were talking about ways to take actual 3D spaces and convert them into 2D spaces. Here we are talking about providing an illusion of the third dimension using 3D coordinates. A

CHAPTER 8   SPACE

simple example of this is to use overlapping objects. In Figure 8-7a, we see a green square and a black circle. The entire green square is seen, while part of the circle is covered, implying that the square is in front of the circle.

Objects that are larger are often perceived as being nearer than objects that are small, especially when they are the same shape. This can change if the object is recognizable by the viewer, because they will have an idea of the actual size of the object (Figure 8-7b).

Objects that are placed higher on the canvas will seem further away than lower objects. This is likely related to our perception of vanishing points and the horizon (Figure 8-7c).

Distant objects tend to be cooler in color temperature and/or have a lighter value. Our normal perception of the distortion caused by the atmosphere is responsible for this (Figure 8-7d).

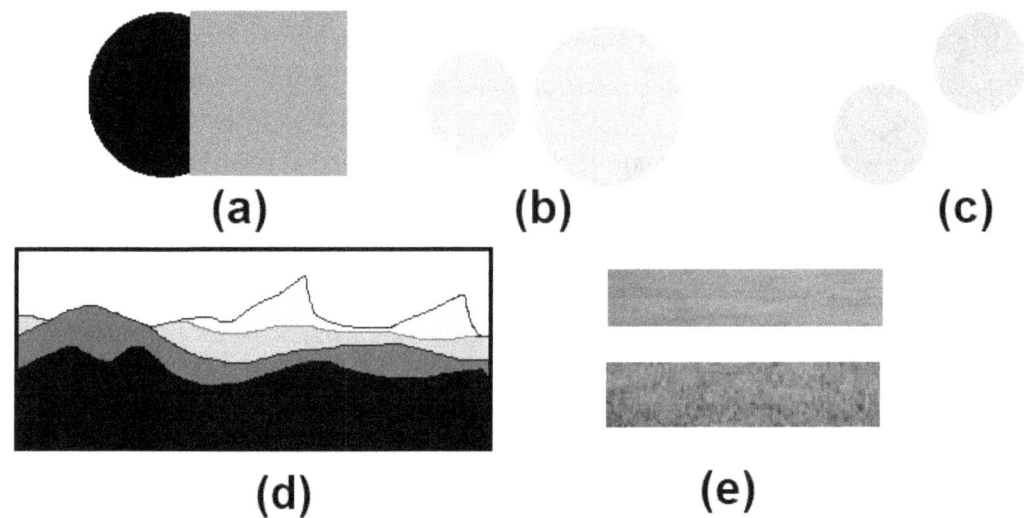

Figure 8-7. (a) The square is nearer because it occludes part of the circle. (b) The large object seems nearer. (c) The lower object seems nearer. (d) The darker area seems nearer. (c) Greater detail implies that the object is nearer

Our ability to see fine detail decreases with distance, so far away objects should be given less detail than near ones. This effect increases when used with one of the others, such as size, in many circumstances. Being able to see the fuzz on a peach or the dimples on an orange improves as the object becomes nearer, but obviously the size will also increase in those situations (Figure 8-7e).

We add these to the standard form elements of perspective and vanishing points to give a compelling illusion of 3D space.

Deep and Shallow Space

Figure 8-8. *(Left) Deep space example, Delivery of the Keys (Pietro Perugino). (Right) Shallow space example, Self Portrait at 34 (Rembrandt)*

Deep and shallow space refers to the *degree* of a third dimension (depth) a picture plane has. *Deep space* can be a full three-dimensional representation, with a foreground, middle ground, and background. Viewers can see the subject matter that is further away as well as closer to us.

An example is the Renaissance *Delivery of the Keys* (Figure 8-8). Here we see the illusion of depth created using size, position, color, overlapping objects, various techniques, atmospheric perspective, and vanishing point. As a contrast, the portrait in that same figure is an example of *shallow space*, which has a very limited third dimension.

Early human artworks were all examples of shallow space, either because ancient artists didn't know how to render the third dimension or because they didn't *want* to. Gradually deep vs. shallow space became a choice and became a characteristic of certain types of art.

Portraits and still life paintings are typical examples of shallow space, but in the past few decades a dominant example would be the *video game*. In some games like *Pac-Man* or *Tetris*, the gameplay takes place in two dimensions, so the artwork reflects this.

CHAPTER 8   SPACE

 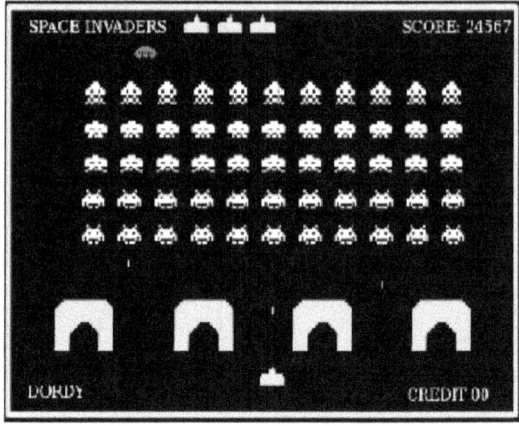

Figure 8-9. *Many video games use shallow space art because the action of the game takes place in two dimensions*

Digital Image Space

We could discuss general aspects of space in art for a long time, but as generative artists we are most interested in digital images specifically and how the space element is reflected there and used in design. What are the characteristics of digital images that affect our use of space?

What we'll call *digital image space* is really hypothetical, or imaginary. A canvas has fixed dimensions; a digital image can be as large as we can imagine and can contain as many colors as our computer memory allows. These colors don't even have to be *real*, which is to say we could have colors in a digital image that cannot be seen by humans.

In digital terms, a space is mathematical. It contains all possible relationships and values. This is hard to understand, but let's consider a 2 × 2 pixel image that can have either black or white values only. There are a total of 4 pixels here, each having two possible values. The total number of possible images of this kind is 16, which is 4^2 – the number of pixels to the power of the number of pixel values. So for a 256 by 256 image with 8 possible grey levels there would be $(256*256)^8$, or 3.4×10^{38} different images. Some number of those would be images of your face and the face of everyone you ever met.

Is that mind-boggling? If so, then ask how many faces could be painted on an empty canvas. That would be the *real* image space, and it is a lot larger.

CHAPTER 8 SPACE

Digital Image Space is Inaccurate

We know from the previous chapters that digital images are *samples* of reality, having limits in resolution and value and color range. We cannot magnify the image very much to reveal new information. It is a common trick in movies of the *police procedural* genre to magnify a poor image to reveal a license plate or text on a document. This is rarely possible and always has serious limits. The problem is that the pixels are an average value over a fixed area at any moment, and when magnified, all we can do reliably is to make that pixel larger, not see within it. A pixel is a single number.

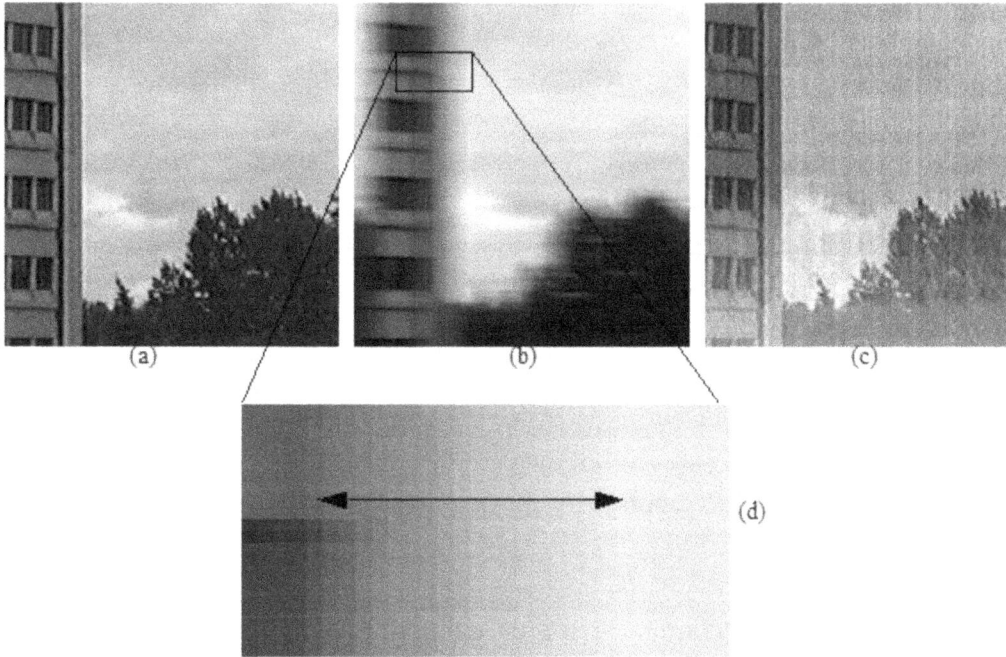

Figure 8-10. (a) *The actual scene.* (b) *Blurring caused by horizontal motion* (c) *We can repair the blur to some extent knowing what caused it*

Having said that, computer scientists have devised ways to reorganize pixels so as to enhance specific objects of interest. We have seen edge detection, for one example, but it does go further than that. Images can be improved, if only approximately. Imagine that you are in a moving vehicle and take a photograph of a building (Figure 8-10). While the shutter is open the scene changes, and the result is a photograph that is blurred in (at least) the horizontal direction. What this really means is that each pixel in the image is the sum of some number of pixels in the correct (unblurred) image in the horizontal

319

direction, and the number of pixels involved depends on the speed of the vehicle and the amount of time the camera shutter was open. We can reduce the degree of blur seen in the photo by attempting to *undo* the motion and its effect on each pixel. This can be done, not perfectly, but pretty well, using mathematical operations on the image given an estimate of what kind of blur there is. This process still only uses quantized pixel values, though, and does not create new information. It simply reorganizes what is already there.

Digital Images Are Distorted for Convenience

The *JPEG* and *GIF* formats for storing images in files both represent an image only approximately. In neither case can a pixel be extracted from the file directly – the image in the file must be decoded first, because the original pixels have been passed through a *compression* algorithm that permits the overall file size to be reduced. In the case of *JPEG*, this introduces visible artifacts, especially where the image has rapid changes in the values as a function of distance (e.g., edges). In the case of *GIF*, the distortion happens in the colors of the pixels, since there are only 256 colors available in this format. Colors in many images are thus only *near* to the actual color.

These distortions can't be fixed and have been introduced as a compromise between fidelity and image size. In the current era, size is much less of a problem on account of the low price of computer memory, but many digital cameras still store the captured images in *JPEG* form on the camera, meaning that the distortions are present from the very beginning.

Finally, there is the matter of *resolution*, or the area sampled by each pixel, and *quantization*, or the overall number of bits used to represent color. These can be increased as much as we like, but they will never represent the actual scene exactly. This is not convenience as much as it is a physical limitation. By distortion in this case we mean *approximation*. Digital images are always approximate representations of the real scene.

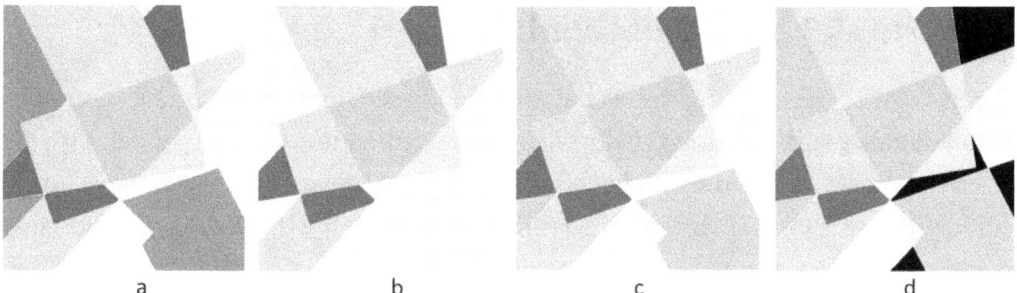

Figure 8-11. *(a) The first try of a painting (b) Lightening the dark blue. (c) Too much – make it a bit lighter. (d) Replace the white background with black (Parker, 2024).*

We could make a philosophical argument that this only applies to images captured from real scenes and the artworks derived from them, and that more abstract or hypothetical digital images could be thought to be perfect, an ideal representation of what is fundamentally a digital object. Perhaps, at some level, that is true, but digital lines, curves, and shapes always have a fundamentally discrete quality that makes them differ from those we normally think about. We also need to consider the human being's visual perspective on this, which includes the idea that a line is not really a collection of little squares connected to each other but is something more.

Digital Image Space Is Malleable

The word *malleable* means "easily controlled or influenced" or "adaptable." This is a key feature of digital image spaces for generative art. Artworks can be easily and quickly changed if the artist decides to do so. Figure 8-11a shows a simple artwork. The artist decides that the dark blue is the wrong color – it's too dark. So, she lightens it (Figure 8-11b). Oops. Too much. Try a sky blue (Figure 8-11c). Better. Now, the white regions near the left edge bother her. She turns them black (Figure 8-11d). Better yet. This would be a very difficult process using oil paint or acrylics.

In the digital space, all pixels are temporary, which is to say they can be modified. Indeed, one can think of them as they might in quantum mechanics, where they could be in all states (colors) at the same time until we "collapse" it into one image, which happens when we print it.

CHAPTER 8   SPACE

Digital Image Space Is Relative

In the real world, we see things as we have learned to see them, and we have learned how to evaluate the size of things using visual cues. Humans are pretty good at this, even if we can be fooled. Something ten feet from us can be evaluated very accurately for size and proportion, but as distance increases, the precision with which we can do this decreases. We assess distance by parallax, as we discussed in the previous chapter, and then use the distance to assess size. Sometimes we use perspective or size compared to other objects.

None of these things are necessarily the same in digital image spaces. We can play games with size, proportion, perspective, shapes, and anything else we choose. If the digital image has been captured, we still only have the one image, which can have been designed or modified to portray a desired, not real, scene. Digital images do not tell the truth unless all of the parameters of them are known.

Digital Image Space Can Be Imaginary

A generative artwork always begins in the mind of the artist. To some degree that's true of all art, but in the case of generative art the artist is forced to consider not just the visual they are designing, but also how it can be created and represented starting with nothing at all. From nothing, the artist conjures electrons to do her bidding, eventually creating photons for the final representation.

This all seems very mystical, but in fact a computer program does consist of electrons in its useful form (executing), and an artist does in fact create a system that builds the final image from nothing. Yes, the computer exists, but the algorithm and program start out as nothing at all. What does this really mean in practice? It means that there are few limitations on what our creation can be.

The Example of a Tesseract

A *tesseract* is a 4-dimensional cube (also called a *hypercube*) and is an object that can't exist in reality and is a good example of what we mean when we say that digital image space is imaginary. We can, using digital methods, render such an object as if it existed. We have seen how to project a 3D object onto a 2D plane so that we can display it on a screen or paper. Displaying 4D objects means reducing the dimensions from 4 to 3, then to 2. And, of course, 4D objects are very difficult to visualize in one's head. That's why we use a cube – it's a very simple shape.

To imagine a tesseract, let's begin with a line, which is a one-dimensional shape. A square is two dimensional, and to make a square from a line, we add another line at each end of the existing one so that it is at 90 degrees from it – into the 2nd dimension. We then connect the ends of the two new lines with a fourth line (Figure 8-12b).

To get a cube from the square, we do a similar thing. Begin with a square. On each end (edge) of the square, draw another square at 90 degrees to the existing one (into the 3rd dimension), and finally, draw a final square that joins all of the top edges (Figure 8-12c).

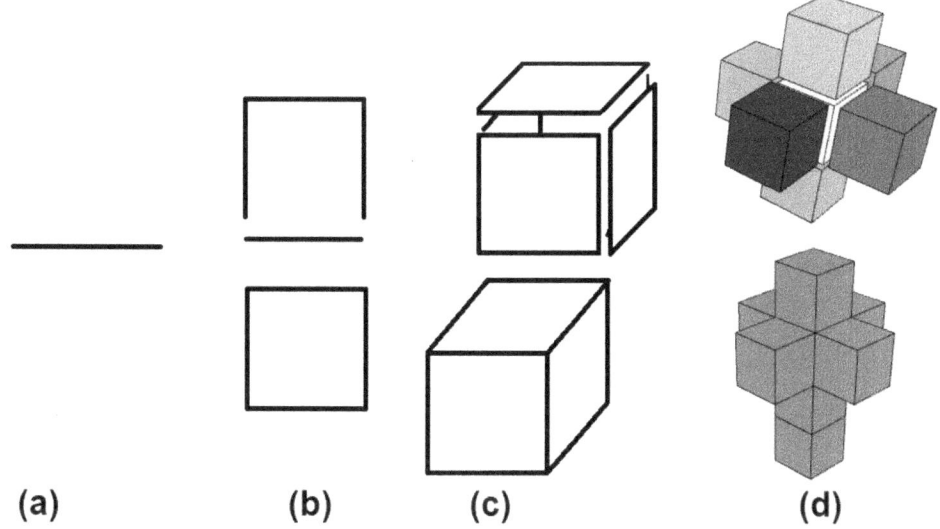

(a)   **(b)**   **(c)**   **(d)**

Figure 8-12. *(a) A one-dimensional cube is a line. (b) A two-dimensional cube is a square made by adding one-dimensional cubes to the ends of a one dimensional cube extending into the second dimension. (c) A three-dimensional cube is a two-dimensional cube with two dimensional cubes added to its ends (edges) extending into the third dimension. (d) A four-dimensional cube is a three-dimensional cube with three-dimensional cubes on each face that extend into the fourth dimension*

To get a tesseract from a cube, we begin with a cube. On each face we draw another cube at 90 degrees to the existing face (into the fourth dimension) and complete that with a final cube that joins all the others (Figure 8-12d). That last step is a doozy. We can't draw that on paper; we have to resort to a 2D projection of a 3D projection of the original. It's quite unsatisfactory, but it's the best we can do.

CHAPTER 8   SPACE

It is important to realize that the angles in the 4D cube are all 90 degrees, and some are into the fourth spatial dimension. In Figure 8-12d, the right face of the red cube is the same as the left face of the pink cube. They have been bent in the imaginary fourth dimension at 90 degrees so that they meet.

The fourth dimension is difficult for us to grasp because it is completely foreign to our perception, and yet it is possible to implement and manipulate as a digital space. We could create four-dimensional displays or games, for instance. These would behave in strange new ways from our point of view. Objects will be sliced in strange ways and can even vanish. The only thing we can do is to use 3D-to-2D analogies to explain this behavior.

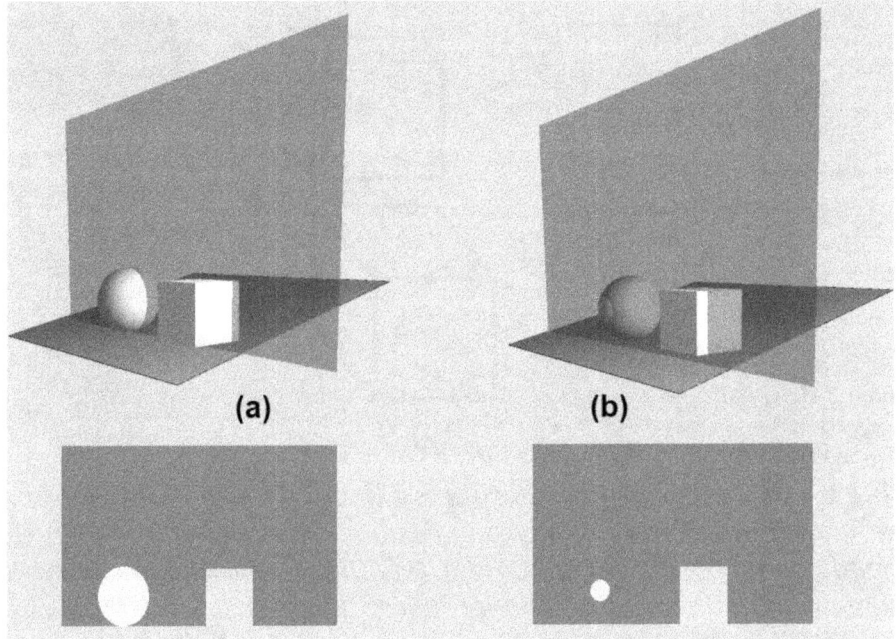

Figure 8-13. *(a) A sphere and cube sliced by the viewing plane. (b) As the viewing plane moves, the view from the point of view of the 2D observer changes inexplicably*

CHAPTER 8   SPACE

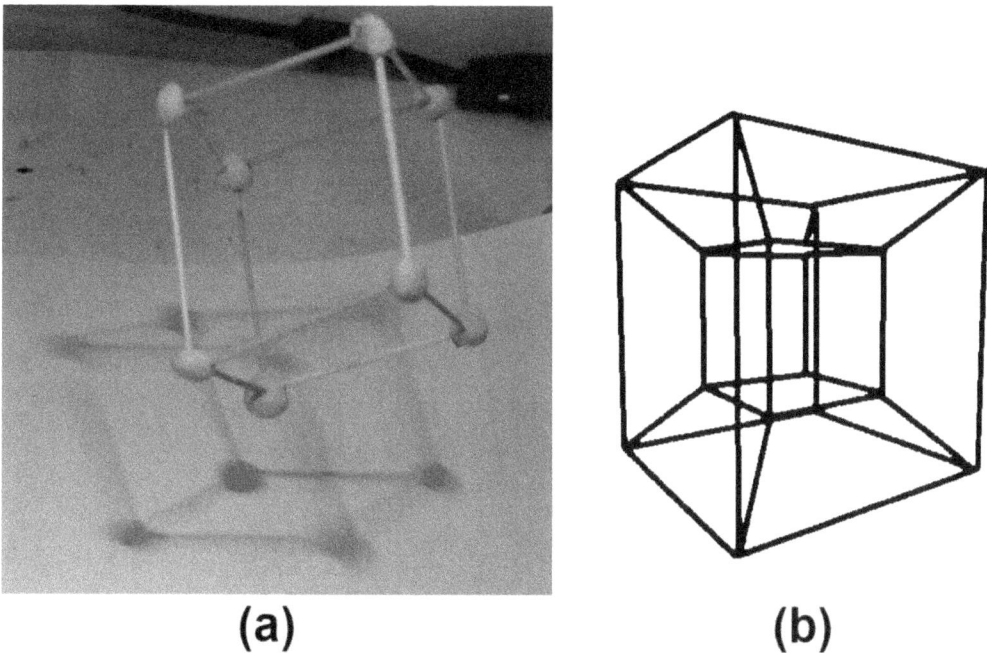

(a)   **(b)**

Figure 8-14. *Another way to visualize a hypercube in 3D. (a) The way we draw a cube on paper is really a shadow of the cube. (b) This rendering of a hypercube is a 3D **shadow** of a 4D object*

Figure 8-13a shows a sphere and cube in a 3D space, showing the viewing plane and how it is placed relative to the objects. From the point of view of a 2D observer, the sphere and the cube look like a circle and a square resting on the bottom of the image. When the viewing plane moves forward, the sphere is cut at a different place, and the circle now appears to be floating above the lower plane (Figure 8-13b). If the viewing plane moves too much, the objects will disappear completely into the third dimension, now being invisible to the 2D viewer. Similarly, from the point of view of a 3D observer, 4D objects behave strangely, changing shape and seeming to vanish as they move in and out of the viewing volume.

A different, and possibly better, way to draw a tesseract is as its 3D shadow, as in Figure 8-14b (projected to 2D, of course, so it can be rendered on paper). In the same way that the cube drawn in Figure 8-12d is the 2D shadow of a 3D cube, Figure 8-14a also shows the 2D shadow of the 3D cube.

CHAPTER 8   SPACE

What we now have is an entirely new dimension to play in. We can make imaginary 4D objects and textures and create artworks in this new dimension. People have done this already, of course. The 4th dimension is simply one example of how digital image spaces are imaginary.

Digital Image Space Is Outside of Time

A photograph or painting is captured at a point in space and time, and that cannot be changed. When we look at a painting, it is unmoving and silent. As was pointed out in the book *Ways of Seeing*, historically paintings were relevant in the context in which they were displayed – churches and homes, for example. Now paintings are treated as images and can be stored, transmitted, and displayed anywhere. They are still static, though.

A digital image is not necessarily representative of any specific time and can, in fact, change as a function of time as the artist chooses (Chapter 9, "Dynamism").

Space and Vision – The Rendering Process

When an artist paints a scene, there is a typical process of analysis and rendering that is used. It is based on our experience, education, and visual interpretation and acuity. We should examine that process from a digital perspective.

Visual Response

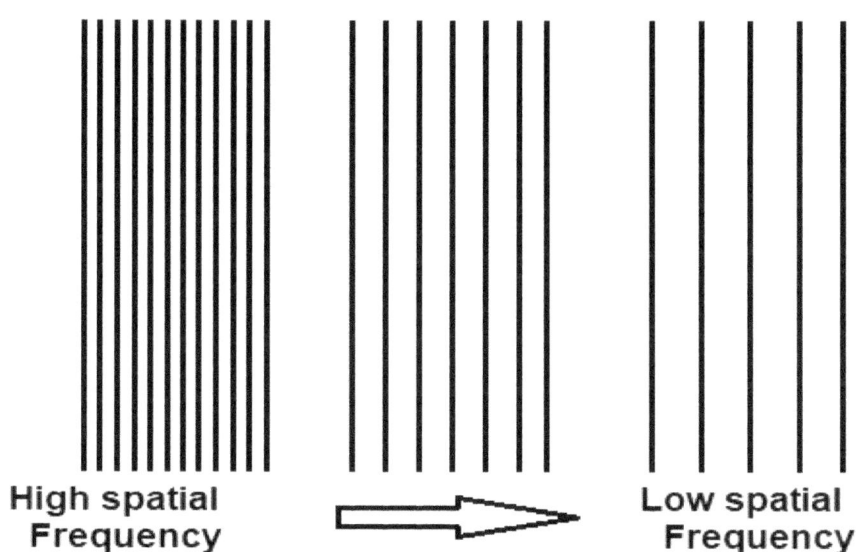

Figure 8-15. *Spatial frequency can be defined as the number of visible features per millimeter*

There are some terms that we need to understand here even if we avoid the mathematics. These concepts turn out to be important in understanding vision and perception. One such term is spatial frequency. This is a measure of how often a repeating component occurs, or could occur, per unit distance. In computer vision and physics, these repeating components are often viewed as sine waves, but they can be any repeating element. The elements need not actually repeat; in fact, this is a *measure of what level of detail can be perceived*. High spatial frequencies refer to a high level of detail, and low spatial frequencies reflect overall shape.

This is important because any real physical system, like the human visual system, can only respond to a limited range of spatial frequencies, just as the human ear can respond only to a limited range of audio frequencies. When confronted with data that is outside of the defined range, the system can respond inappropriately or incorrectly. Sometimes the result is what we call an *optical illusion*. In addition, the spatial frequency response could vary with light intensity or color.

CHAPTER 8   SPACE

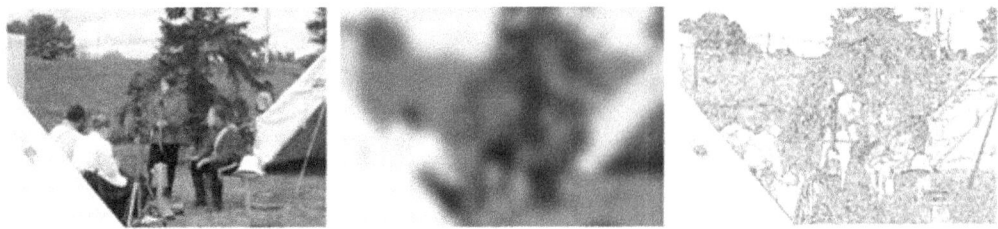

Figure 8-16. *(a) Original image. (b) Low-frequency information (c) High-frequency information*

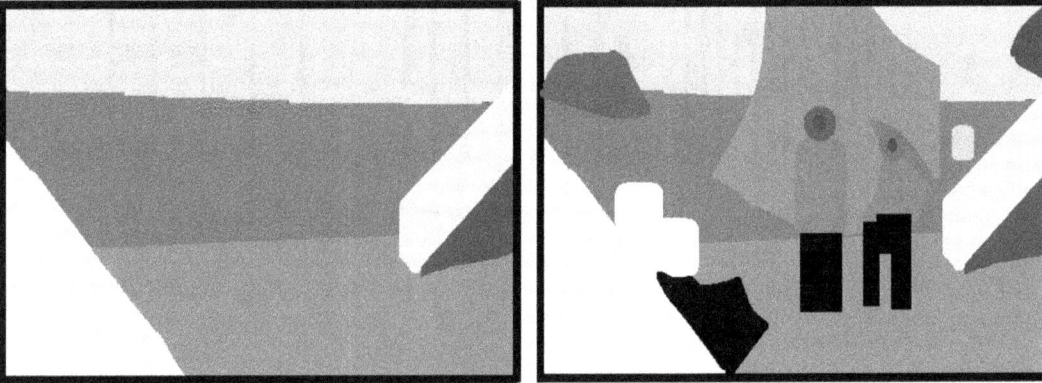

Figure 8-17. *Painting the scene of Figure 8-16 would begin with the lowest spatial frequencies. Then higher frequency regions would be added successively until all needed details were present*

Units of spatial frequency are cycles (or units) per millimeter, with high values representing fine details and low values representing larger areas or regions (Figure 8-15). We can devise computer programs that can remove or enhance specific spatial frequencies or frequency ranges. An example is shown in Figure 8-16, where it seems obvious that the background of a scene (a painting) would consist of very low frequency information. Large regions, such as the uniforms, grass, and tents of this scene, are somewhat higher frequencies, and the details of objects and faces would be the highest of all (Figure 8-17). The overall representation of the scene is the sum of all of the information in all frequencies; the visual system computes the spatial frequencies as a part of the perception process. When we watch how artists often develop a painting, we can see that the lower spatial frequencies are painted first, followed by increasing higher frequencies (Figure 8-18).

CHAPTER 8   SPACE

Humans don't see each frequency equally. There is a *response curve* that shows how well we see each range of spatial frequencies (Figure 8-19), and of course there are individual variations as well. To see what that curve looks like, we can plot a sequence of vertical lines that are progressively nearer to each other. These lines start as black and become lighter and lighter as they reach the top, fading to a light grey. This makes them harder to see. What we observe is that some of the lines seem to vanish before others. This is the effect of the spatial frequency response of our visual system. We can draw a curve along the tops of the lines as they disappear, and we see what amounts to a graph of visual acuity vs. spatial frequency, which is the response curve. There is a peak in the middle frequencies, which means that these are the ones we see best. The system has a limited bandwidth (the range it can process), and this can cause some perceptual issues. What we see as humans seems perfectly fine, but artifacts can creep into our interpretation of things.

Figure 8-18. *The process that one artist uses when painting a portrait*

Figure 8-19. *Illustration of the spatial frequency response of a human visual system*

An example is the common optical illusion seen in Figure 8-20. Here an array of black squares separated by white lines appears to have a grey region at the intersection of each line pair. When we subject this image to the human visual system as implemented by a filter that accounts for the limited spatial bandwidth, we see that these grey regions are actually present as far as our perception goes. We cannot help but see them because they are artifacts of the nature of the retina and optic nerve.

Running an image through a simulation like this can be very enlightening about what we can actually see and how an artist might perceive a subject. Indeed, we might be able to manipulate what the virtual artist sees, perhaps simulating some sort of perceptual difference between that artist and other people. It has been suggested, for example, that Vincent Van Gogh may have suffered from lead poisoning, which swells the retina and causes a halo around lights, as seen in the painting *Starry Night*. Claude Monet had cataracts later in life, blurring the images that he saw (*Water lillies*) and Degas (1834-1917) probably had a retinal disease that caused macular damage, also creating a visual blur.

Figure 8-20. *The Hermann Grid Optical Illusion. A viewer sees dark areas where the white lines intersect. As spatial frequencies are filtered out, we can see that the dark areas are actually present in the final filtered image. We can't help but see this, because it is an artifact of our vision system*

Having said that, we know that images can sometimes be processed to make them *look* better. A blurred image can be sharpened to a degree, which generally means that fuzzy edges are made sharper. No new information can be revealed, though, *unless we have knowledge of specific details of how the image was blurred or distorted*, and even then getting more information is not always possible. Figure 8-10 shows that a motion blur in an image can be reduced using a knowledge of the direction and speed of motion.

When the Hubble Space Telescope was first placed into orbit, it produced poor images because the mirror had been built to the wrong specifications. Knowing what the mirror actually looked like permitted the images to be mathematically corrected (Figure 8-21). This is done through a complex process called *deconvolution*. Basically we observe what the distortion is on a single pixel and assume the same distortion happened at *all* pixels, then *undo* it.

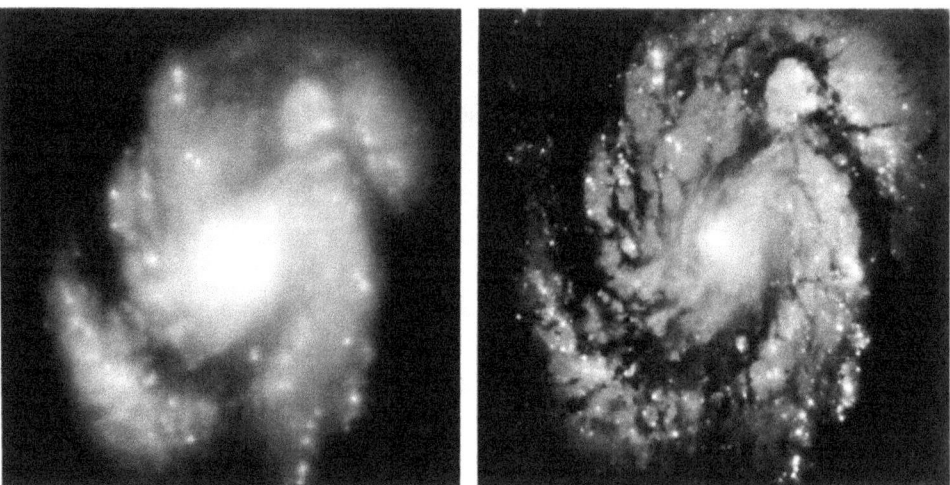

Figure 8-21. *The Hubble Space Telescope images before image correction (Left) and after (Right)*

Space in Abstract Composition

The rules of composition apply to all 2D visual artworks, including generative ones. Generative works can begin with an existing image, and that image is somewhat fixed and has already had some composition rules applied to it. There are composition forms that we can apply to more abstract artworks, the ones we simply make up in our heads. These are arrangements of visual elements that we can apply to our generative works, although not through an algorithmic process.

Cruciform Composition

This is an arrangement that uses intersecting lines and shapes that are organized loosely into a cross shape. It's not about religion. We use it to create a sense of *stability* and *balance*. There is a power in the geometry of the cross, and that is used to support the theme and evoke specific emotions.

CHAPTER 8 SPACE

Figure 8-22. *Example of cruciform composition (Parker 2025, "Tesseract")*

The work in Figure 8-22 (*Tesseract*) is a watercolor that was scanned and edge-enhanced for contrast.

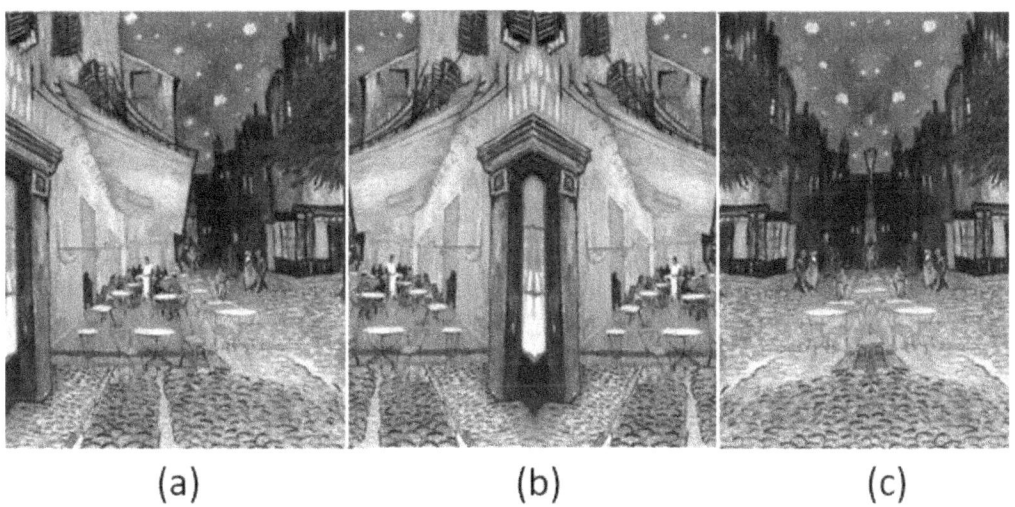

Figure 8-23. *(a) The Café Terrace, Van Gogh (1888), an asymmetrical composition. (b) The left half of the painting, duplicated. (c) The right side of the painting. The asymmetry is obvious*

333

CHAPTER 8   SPACE

Asymmetrical or Unbalanced Composition

Variously referred to as *asymmetrical*, or *unbalanced*, this arrangement creates visual interest and conveys tension. It is characterized by a departure from the usual symmetrical balance seen in many artworks, opting instead for an arrangement of elements that defies expectations. It often gives a sense of movement and instability.

Here the two sides of a composition are not the same or symmetrical but have an equal visual weight due to the equivalent amount of activity of each side: one large object in one part of the work can be balanced by multiple small objects on the other side, for example. We can also have an imbalance of negative and positive space throughout the work and balance the image by using dark values balanced by many light ones. The viewer's gaze is guided through the piece by this arrangement.

By placing visually heavier elements on one side of a painting or sculpture, artists can create interesting effects, and one can imply a sense of movement (Figure 8-23).

Horizontal Composition: High and Low

A horizontal composition creates a sense of calm and balance. These often use horizontal shapes that span the width of the canvas, and this leads to a feeling of stability. The term *high* refers to the placement of the horizontal elements near the top of the artwork, and low places them at the bottom. The high/low location of these horizontal elements has an impact on the viewer's emotional response to the artwork.

Figure 8-24 is an example (*Big Hill*).

Figure 8-24. *Horizontal composition (Parker 2025, "Big Hill")*

Vertical Composition

Vertical composition implies concepts like stability and growth. This style employs vertical elements that draw the viewer's eye upwards, often creating a sense of elevation or expansion. Vertical compositions can symbolize various themes, from the growth of living things like trees to the sense of being enclosed. There can be an implied religious message because of the viewer's gaze being drawn upwards. Figure 8-25 (*Gadget*) was created starting with a photo of a dog, which was then converted into a bi-level image. Vertical lines of random widths and positions were drawn over the background color, and vertical lines of different random widths and positions were drawn over the foreground color.

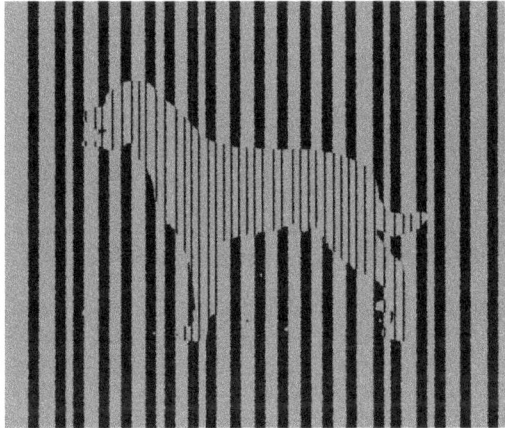

Figure 8-25. Example of a vertical composition (Parker, 2025, "Gadget")

Overlapping Frames

This is sometimes called *frame-in-frame* composition. It is an approach in abstract art that creates depth through a layering of objects. It involves the careful placement of shapes that intersect or enclose each other, forming an overall pattern that goes beyond any single layer. It allows artists to explore depth and relationships between objects. It can provide an interesting and complex visual appearance. The use of transparency, or not, is an important aspect of this style. It can define the depth of the individual layers.

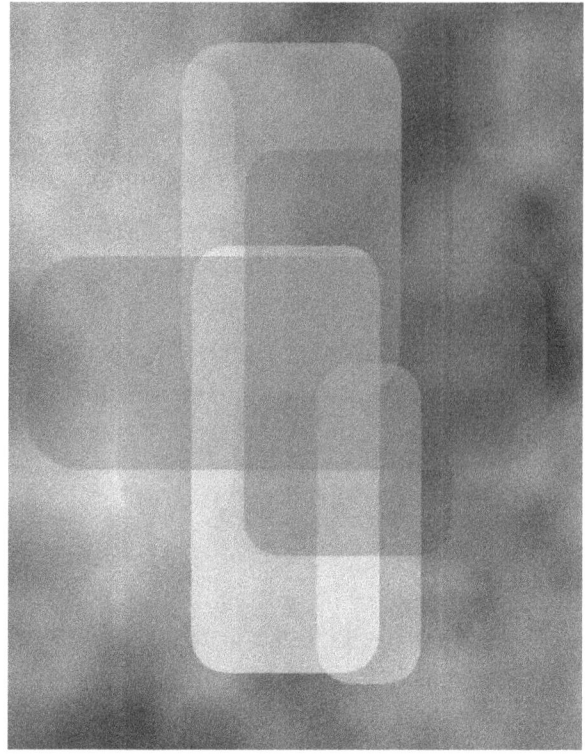

Figure 8-26. *Example of an overlapping frame composition (Parker, 2025, "Mirage")*

Figure 8-26 (*Mirage*) begins with a background of Perlin noise. Then rectangles with rounded corners were drawn in defined locations and using carefully selected fill colors with transparency.

Curvilinear Composition

The curvilinear composition in abstract art uses more organic forms. Lacking the rigidity of straight lines, it gives a more natural-appearing interpretation of shapes that imply calm, peace, and nature. Curves also imply movement, making them useful for conveying life and peaceful energy.

CHAPTER 8   SPACE

Figure 8-27. *Example of a curvilinear frame composition (Parker, 2025, "Photons")*

Figure 8-27 (*Photons*) draws an upper and a lower horizontal using a spline to connect points, where the lower part is a random variation of the upper (using **curveVertex**). Six of these are drawn with increasing Y coordinates and using colors that vary from top to bottom in a visually compatible way.

Constellation or Group Mass Composition

The *constellation* or *group mass* composition in abstract art refers to an arrangement where the many elements are grouped together to create a cohesive whole. This either creates a focal point or distributes mass of objects across the canvas. It can result in a complex visual experience. If the individual elements are placed carefully, the artist can explore space, connection, and relationships. The group mass composition is often characterized by the scattered but connected parts, which can invite the viewer to explore the relationships between them.

CHAPTER 8   SPACE

Figure 8-28. *Example of a group mass composition (Parker, 2021, "Patches")*

The example named *Patches* (Figure 8-28) draws a large number of rectangles of a specified color, with transparency, over a grey background. The locations and dimensions of the rectangles are random in specified ranges.

Diagonal Composition

Diagonal composition in abstract art is a powerful tool for creating a sense of dynamism and movement. By using diagonal lines and forms, artists can convey action, tension, and directional flow within their works. This compositional style is particularly effective in suggesting instability and change, contrasting with the stability often associated with horizontal and vertical lines.

CHAPTER 8   SPACE

Figure 8-29. Example of a diagonal composition (Parker, 2025, Vergo)

The work in Figure 8-29 (*Vergo*) was constructed using rectangles that were much larger than the drawing area. They start at a random location in the upper and/or right region or the upper left and are filled with a pastel color. Random, rare rectangles are drawn with a black outline.

Golden Section or Golden Ratio

The *Golden Section* or *Golden Ratio* is a mathematical relationship that has been used in art for centuries to create aesthetically pleasing compositions. Mathematically it is approximately 1:1.618 and is found in nature frequently. It is most commonly connected with the *Fibonacci* sequence, in which each number is the sum of the previous two. Starting with the sequence 1,2, then the next value is 1+1=2, then 2+1=3, then 3+2=5, then 8, 13, 21, and so on.

CHAPTER 8   SPACE

Figure 8-30. Example of a golden section composition (Parker, 2025, "Navrical")

Artists believe it gives a sense of harmony in visual designs. In abstract art, it can be applied as an algorithm for the placement of elements within a composition, thus creating a natural sense of equilibrium and focus.

In the example image in Figure 8-30 (*Navrical*), an image of mountains serves as a background. In the foreground is a living room with a large window looking over the mountains. In the left upper part of the window, the large window is broken up into smaller ones based on the golden section, and each is tinted in a different color.

Centered Composition

Centered compositions place the focus and center of mass in the center of the canvas, as opposed to the usual offset or rule of thirds. This can give a sense of balance in an abstract artwork within the artwork. It can create a feeling of equilibrium and stability. A centered composition draws the viewer's eye to the middle of the painting, where the connection to the surrounding shapes and colors forms a pattern to be explored.

CHAPTER 8   SPACE

Figure 8-31. Example of a centered composition (Parker, 2025, "Marigold")

Marigold (Figure 8-31) Requires 25 images of painterly brush strokes that have been thresholded. One is expanded and used as a background. Then, 242 times, a brush stroke image is selected, rotated, colored, and then drawn in a position that increases in distance from the center with each iteration.

Radiant or Radiating Composition

Radiant or radiating compositions in abstract art use lines and forms that emanate from a central point, creating a sense of energy and focus. This compositional style often suggests movement and expansion, drawing the viewer's eye towards the center and then outward along the radiating elements. It can be used to convey a range of themes, from the idea of a dynamic universe to the concept of cyclicality and motion.

CHAPTER 8   SPACE

Figure 8-32. *Example of a Radiant composition (Parker, 2025)*

The artwork in Figure 8-32 (*Radiant*) draws a collection of triangles all having a common vertex at one point, in this case (400, 300), based on the rule of thirds. The triangles vary in central angle and color, using constrained randomness. Colors are tints of the base color (128, 120, 200). This process is repeated three times using different base colors (220, 220, 0) and (220, 90, 220). Finally, three concentric circles are drawn in those three colors using the same center. There is a 1% chance that a triangle outline will be drawn in black.

Balanced Composition

Balanced composition in abstract art refers to the harmonious arrangement of forms, colors, and textures that creates visual equilibrium. This balance can be achieved through symmetry, repetition, or the strategic distribution of visual weight across the canvas. It plays a crucial role in engaging the viewer and guiding their eye through the artwork, often resulting in a composition that feels stable and aesthetically pleasing.

CHAPTER 8   SPACE

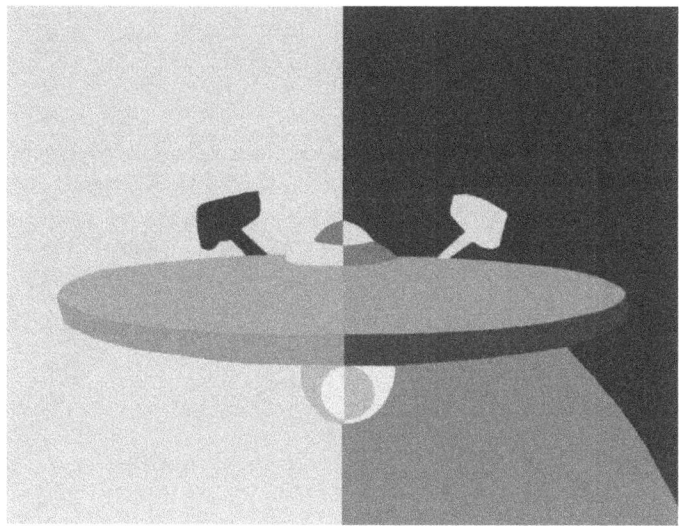

Figure 8-33. *Example of a balanced composition (Parker, 2025, "Enterprise")*

The image in Figure 8-33 began with a photograph of the starship Enterprise from the famous television program. In an image editor, it was divided into obvious portions by color and split into a left and right part. Each symmetrical part was colored in a contrasting tone to produce the result.

3-Spot or Triangular Composition

The 3-spot, or triangular, composition in abstract art is a design principle that relies on the placement of three key elements in a triangular arrangement. This compositional style offers both stability and dynamism, guiding the viewer's eye through the artwork and creating a sense of coherence and balance.

CHAPTER 8   SPACE

Figure 8-34. *Example of a triangular composition (Parker, 2025, "Incircle")*

Figure 8-32 could be thought of as a triangular composition, but the example selected for the example here (Figure 8-34, *Incircle*) uses the paradigm specifically. In three selected locations, a triangle is drawn, then the circle that is tangent to all three sides, then another triangle is inscribed in that circle, and this is repeated until the triangles become too small. One large transparent circle is drawn that connects the three other triangle centers.

Tunnel Composition

Tunnel composition in abstract art is a technique that creates an illusion of depth and perspective, guiding the viewer's eye through a tunnel-like passage within the canvas. This approach often uses central, receding forms surrounded by framing elements, creating a sense of three-dimensionality and leading the viewer into an imagined space beyond the physical boundaries of the artwork.

CHAPTER 8   SPACE

Figure 8-35. *Example of a tunnel composition (Parker 2025, "Nowhere")*

The tunnel effect in Figure 8-35 (*Nowhere*) is actually drawn using 2D graphics only. A set of 35 rectangles are drawn without outlines but filled with increasingly dark green and a transparency of 100. Each rectangle drawn is 0.98 the size of the previous one and is offset by 10 pixels in each dimension in each iteration. What we see is actually the collection of rectangles drawn overtop of one another, offset by a small amount each time.

L or Rectangular Composition

The L or rectangular composition in abstract art is a technique that uses L-shaped or rectangular arrangements to guide the viewer's eye through the canvas. This compositional style can create a sense of structure, depth, and spatial harmony, allowing for a dynamic interplay between form and space.

CHAPTER 8   SPACE

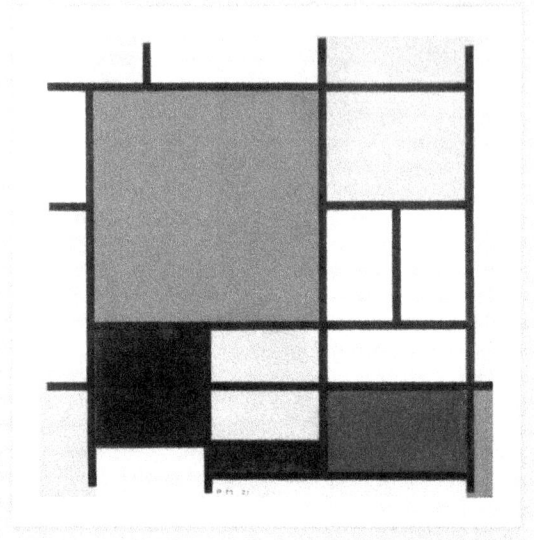

Figure 8-36. *Composition in red, yellow, blue, and black. Piet Mondrian*

Piet Mondrian was famous for this compositional style, and Figure 8-36 is one of his more famous paintings.

Pattern Composition

Pattern composition in abstract art is characterized by the repetition and rhythm of patterns, creating a rich visual experience through systematic yet dynamic arrangements. This compositional style often involves the meticulous application of motifs, exploring themes of order, chaos, and the interplay between them. Patterns in abstract compositions can vary in complexity and style, ranging from geometric forms to more organic shapes, and are used to create depth, movement, and texture within the artwork.

CHAPTER 8   SPACE

Figure 8-37. *Example of a pattern composition (Parker 2025, "Arctic Passage")*

The work *Arctic Passage* in Figure 8-37 uses a photo of an underwater scene as the basis and draws a million 100x12 rectangles at random positions and orientations on top of it. The rectangles are filled using the color at the center of the rectangle, with a transparency of 130 added to the RGB thus obtained.

O or Circular Composition

O or circular composition in abstract art focuses on the use of circular forms, which can symbolize various concepts such as wholeness, continuity, and infinity. Circular compositions often create dynamic visual experiences by drawing the viewer's eye around the canvas in continuous motion. These compositions can evoke the rhythmical and cyclical patterns found in nature and the universe, making them powerful tools for abstract expression.

CHAPTER 8   SPACE

Figure 8-38. *Example of a circular composition (Parker 2025, "Superposition")*

The artwork in Figure 8-38 (*Superposition*) draws cubes in a circular pattern. Three sets, each in a different color, are drawn in 3D and viewed slightly off center. Each cube is rotated to be aligned along its axis. The entire set of objects is drawn over a background made to look like the inside of a cube.

S or Compound Curve Composition

The S or compound curve composition uses smooth flowing curves, helping create a dynamic visual experience. These compositions can suggest natural forms and movements. The overlap and interrelationships of curves can suggest depth, adding to the visual complexity of the artwork.

Figure 8-39. *Example of a compound curve composition (Parker 2025, "Sunrise, Isla Mujeres")*

Figure 8-39 began by defining a single closed, curved shape. This was drawn 250 times in random locations in the upper portion of the drawing area. The curve was rescaled and rotated each time it was drawn and was filled with red. Then the same was done 300 times, drawing the shape in the bottom half of the image and filling it with blue.

Compositional Rules That Make Sense

These are good ideas, not hard and fast rules. Taken from the writings of the late Keene Wilson (https://www.keenewilson.com/page/1349/composition)

1. Make sure all the elements of a picture have a purpose.
2. Animals and people should be facing and looking inwards.
3. To push contrast to its limit, maintain a clear demarcation between the lights and the darks.
4. Give the eye something to look at after it has explored the main subject.

CHAPTER 8　SPACE

5. Avoid duplicating forms, lines, movement, and size. This will make them compete and conflict with each other.
6. Avoid grouping animals and people in even numbers. In case you wish to depict a pair, change their size and position.
7. Lean objects inwards and avoid lining them parallel to the frame.
8. Avoid straight lines unless they are quite short. Disguise them or modify them to curves.
9. Never divide a painting into equal parts, as it will look contrived. The horizon line should not bisect the painting.
10. "X" forms are unpleasant.
11. Do not close the viewer out; invite him in. Depict an open door rather than a closed door.
12. Keep the corners subdued with little texture and the values dark.
13. Avoid equal shapes or sizes of masses. Parallel curves are often a discord.
14. Foreground detail with heavy painting, smooth painting in distance.
15. To feature an extremely bright or intense color, include some of the main color in surrounding colors.
16. Horizontal structural lines evoke quiet; diagonal ones, vitality.
17. Composition is not a problem if there is a variety of interesting shapes and sizes with the negative as interesting as the positive.
18. Elements with axes or contours parallel to the sides of the frame tend to be more static.
19. Designs lack unity if an object is nearer to the edge of the composition than to other objects.
20. Keep detail suppressed in outer masses.
21. Arrange forms so as to diminish in size toward the inside of the canvas rather than reverse.

22. The total space between grouped objects should be less than the space surrounding them.
23. Breaking the rule is more interesting than doing the expected.
24. Shakespeare preferred the "untidy, damaged and unresolved to the neatly arranged, well made and settled." https://www.nybooks.com/articles/2004/10/21/the-death-of-hamnet-and-the-making-of-hamlet/?lp_txn_id=1043512
25. Placing two important lines so that they would meet at a right angle has the effect of strengthening the design and locking it together.
26. Don't run lines into corners.
27. All parts relate more easily if connected by at least a few lines.
28. Avoid lines of thrust, such as trees, leading out of the painting.
29. Breaking up lines can make them feel lighter.
30. A figure or something moving (or which can move) leads the eye in that direction.
31. Curving movements tend to move in and out of the picture space.
32. It is good to have a lead-in to painting (row of bushes, lamp cord, road).
33. If the focal point is brought forward as a light against dark, then movement should be directed with lights. If the focal point is a dark movement with darks.
34. Gradation creates movement, like a curved line.
35. Repoussoirs – large masses used as stops to prevent the eye from moving outwards.
36. The more curves you have, the more life (movement) you put into your design. The most important thing you can do when drawing a living form is to curve the length of the form.
37. Block the eyes movement where you want; don't let the eye move too fast.

38. The eye follows the longest line first.

39. Large masses at the sides of a picture can act as stops (repoussoirs) or can lead the eye in.

40. Diagonals convey movement and excitement. They are generally preferable because they aren't parallel to the frame.

41. Try to include a vertical, horizontal, and diagonal movement. One should predominate in length.

42. Contour lines should not be straight; rather, they should just give a sense of direction.

43. When including elements that usually move, indicate their movement without permitting them to look posed.

44. Avoid starting the visual path from a corner.

45. If vanishing points are beyond the confines of the picture, the artist disguises perspective lines to keep the eye in the picture.

Summary

Space refers to areas on a canvas and the physical relationships between objects on that canvas. In many situations an artist is provided with a scene or object to represent, and in those cases these relationships are provided by the scene. When creating a scene from one's imagination, there's a lot more flexibility. The use of space and placement of objects is often called *composition*. *Positive* space consists of the shapes or objects of interest, and *negative* space is the space between them. When representing 3D space, there are compositional tricks that assist us: occlusion, size, height, and color are just a few. *Deep* and *shallow* space refers to the degree to which the third dimension is used. The *rule of thirds* is a guide to placing important elements on the canvas.

Digital image space is virtual or imaginary. We can do whatever we like. We can invent shapes and extra dimensions, shift colors, and play games with perspective. The concept of spatial frequency refers to a hierarchy of details, where low frequencies refer to large areas and high frequencies to details. Artists often paint low frequencies first and then move to higher ones. There are a great many ways to use space in abstract compositions (cruciform, unbalanced, horizontal, and so on).

Library Code

bck	- Create a new image filled with Perlin noise.
embed	- Take an image and create a colored boundary around it.
getLeft	- Get an image comprising the left part of the given image.
getLower	- Get an image comprising the lower part of the given image.
getRight	- Get an image comprising the right part of the given image.
getUpper	- Get an image comprising the upper part of the given image.
getLowerLeft	- Get an image comprising the lower left of the given image.
getLowerRight	- Get an image comprising the lower right of the given image.
getThirds	- Get one of the specified thirds of an image.
getUpperLeft	- Get an image comprising the upper left part of the given image.
getUpperRight	- Get an image comprising the upper right of the given image.
left	- Are the given coordinates on the left of the drawing area?
lowerLeft	- Are the given coordinates in the lower left of the drawing area?
Lower	- Are the given coordinates in the lower part of the drawing area?
lowerRight	- Are the given coordinates in the lower right of the drawing area?
right	- Are the given coordinates on the right of the drawing area?
setLeft	- Copy one image to the left part of another
setLower	- Copy one image to the lower part of another
setUpper	- Copy one image to the upper part of another
setRight	- Copy one image to the right part of another
setQuadrant	- Copy an image to one specified quadrant of another.
setThirds	- Copy an image to one-third section of another.
Transp	- Make the bright pixels of an image transparent;
Thirds	- Draw lines in an image showing the thirds.
upperLeft	- Are the given coordinates in the upper left of the drawing area?
upper	- Are the given coordinates in the upper part of the drawing area?
upperRight	- Are the given coordinates in the upper right of the drawing area?

CHAPTER 8 SPACE

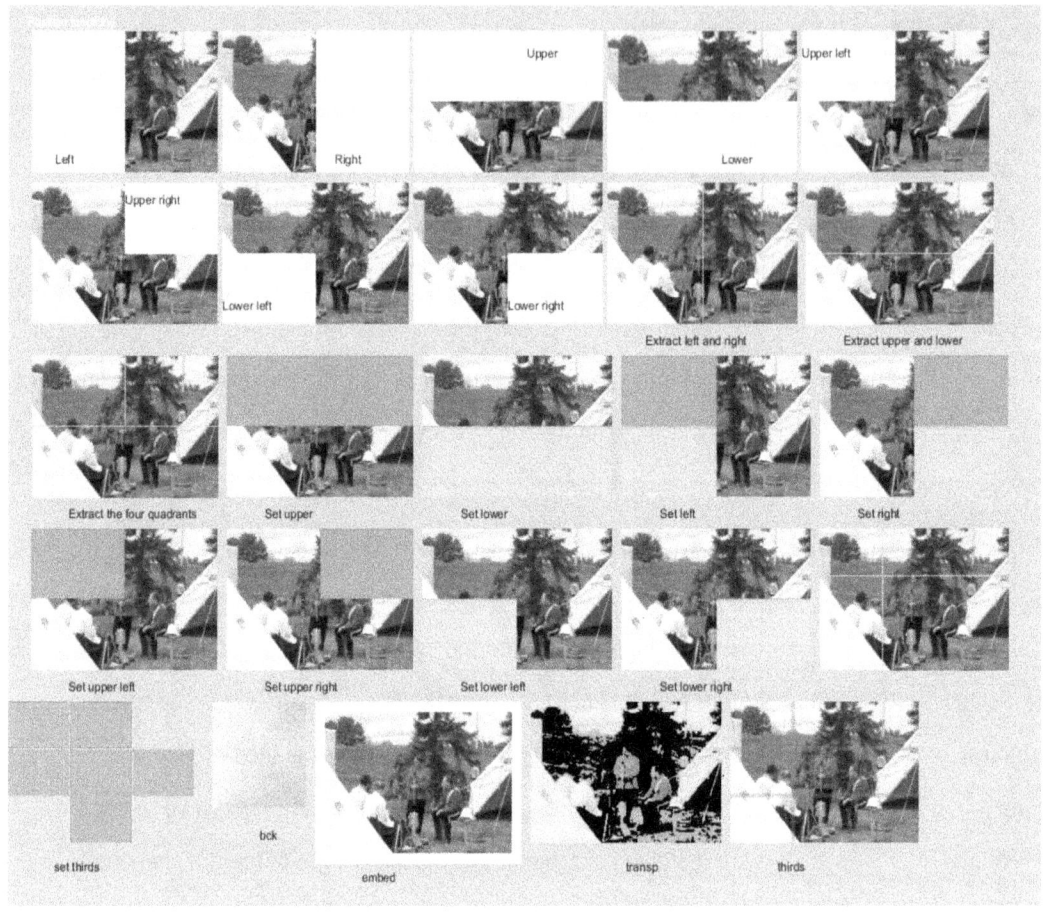

CHAPTER 9

Dynamism

Dynamic artworks are ones that can change with time or by using some observation of the surroundings. This is a novel feature of generative art. Paintings and drawings could not respond to the environment, nor could they change visually in any measurable way. A dynamic artwork is, at its minimum, one that can change with time. We might call this an animation, which literally means to bring life to something. Additionally, the advent of modern electronics technology makes it possible for an artwork to *see* and *hear* and for this to respond visually to colors, music, people, and motion in the volume that surrounds it. We won't discuss the details of the electronic sensors that are needed for some of these works, only the visual response of the work.

Animation

Animation, in a technical sense, is the creation and presentation of images in a rapid sequence so that the result to the human eye appears to be a set of moving objects. The vision system carries a recollection of the previous image; this is called the *persistence of vision*. Some time is needed to process an image, and the brain keeps it for a fraction of a second while processing it. This time can be between 1/10 and 1/15 of a second. When two images are shown to the eye such that an object in one image is in a different position in each image, and if that distance is small enough and the time between images is small enough, the object appears to have moved rather than being re-drawn.

CHAPTER 9   DYNAMISM

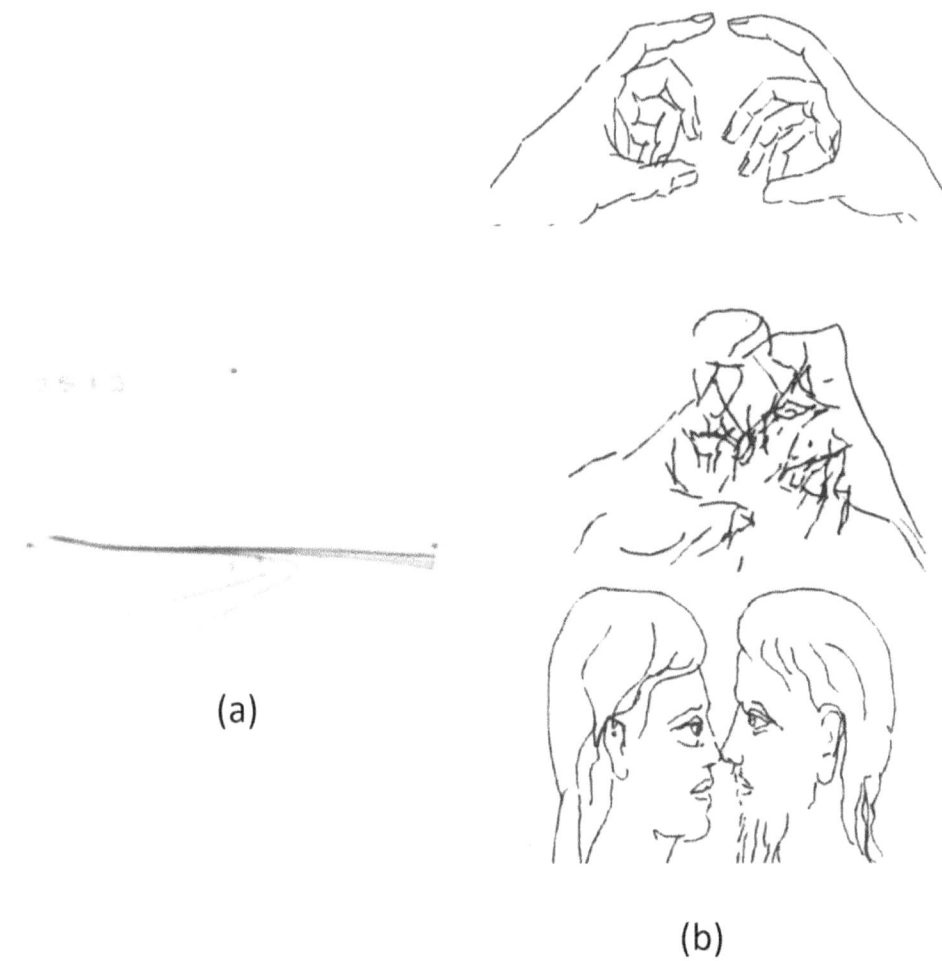

Figure 9-1. *(a) A frame from the first computer-generated animation. (b) Three frames from metadata showing an interpolated transition between hands and faces*

Cartoons on television and at the movies are animations, and they use renderings of complete scenes presented as images. Originally these scenes were drawn by hand by an artist and then painted and photographed, but these days they are nearly always rendered by computer. The first computer-generated animation may well have been a simulated drive along a highway from Stockholm toward Nacka, Sweden, in 1960. Indeed, most early computer animations were done for technical and not artistic reasons. It was done by drawing actual data on the screen of an oscilloscope for each frame, photographing it, and then playing the image sequence back at the appropriate speed (Figure 9-1a).

An early example of *procedural* animation, when the frames are created by the computer, is the film *Metadata* by Peter Foldes (National Film Board of Canada). The important (key) frames were drawn on a computer, and then the images were *morphed* or *interpolated* to create the illusion that the objects were changing shape from one to another (Figure 9-1b).

What we call a *procedural* animation is produced by a computer program that is simulating the objects and their positions and interactions. Some animations (frame by frame) simply read in the images and display them in sequence, which produces perfectly acceptable results as well. Both kinds can be artworks.

Time

Time is critical in animation. We don't know what time actually is, but we all observe it passing, and it appears to pass at the same rate for us all. We can define an *event* as "something that happens" at some point in time. This could be a doorbell ringing, the arrival of an email, or a raindrop striking your nose. Anything at all. And there is a time interval between any two events. Animations seek to quantize and display that. There are a couple of aspects of time that are useful to define.

Absolute time is measured as the time since the creation of the universe. In real life, this would be a rare thing to use. This has an absolute moment that we can call the origin, a known fixed zero point. We'd measure absolute time as the time since from the beginning of the animation itself, which would represent the zero time.

Relative time is the time we usually refer to, and it is what we are used to. The concept of 4 PM depends on knowing a particular day and that we start at 12 midnight. 4 PM is now defined as a certain amount of time after the local reference zero time. Another choice could be to define zero time as the time we wake up in the morning.

Duration is a measure of the time distance between two events. It can represent how long something has been going on: the time from the beginning to the end of an event or the time distance between two events.

CHAPTER 9 DYNAMISM

We measure time in minutes and seconds, and on a larger scale using days, weeks, and so on. An animation can be viewed in minutes, so that's the *scale* of our work. An animation's scale can be defined by its *duration* and its *frame rate*, which is the number of frames that are displayed in one second. The total duration of an animation is the number of frames it contains multiplied by the rate at which they play:

duration = number of frames / frame rate

In space, things have a natural scale, and that applies to time as well. Events in daily life generally occupy seconds or minutes, but on a geological scale, events can take millions of years. Time in an animation is fluid. We can compress or expand the apparent time as we like, but for things to seem real, they must occur on the same scale as they do in our world. This means that the time needed for a person to take one step forward should be the same in reality as it is in an animation.

In the same way that a pixel is a sample of 2D space, an animation frame is a sample of the scene over a period of time. A TV camera captures the frame every 1/30 of a second, and what happens in between is unknown. When drawing frames, though, nothing happens between frames unless we estimate is and we know everything about the beginning and ending scene. When an artist designs an animation, it's common to draw rough sketches of what happens at each discrete moment. This is a storyboard and is used in films as well.

One such design is shown in Figure 9-2. It is a person walking spread over a period of 0.8 seconds. The frame number and time of each frame are seen along the bottom, and the positions of the character are defined at each time. This is only half of a step, but it shows the idea. In many cases there are multiple objects moving in complex ways, and this is a great way to see what is happening.

The images in a storyboard are drawings or other still images and are not actual animation frames. These are often used in development meetings, often called *scrums*, where a team of artists or production staff get together to share ideas on the project. Each person presents their ideas by posting each frame on a wall and then moving from drawing to drawing, explaining the scene or even acting the parts. When the presentation is complete, the team assesses the scene, perhaps deleting items or adding new parts, or removing the scene altogether.

CHAPTER 9 DYNAMISM

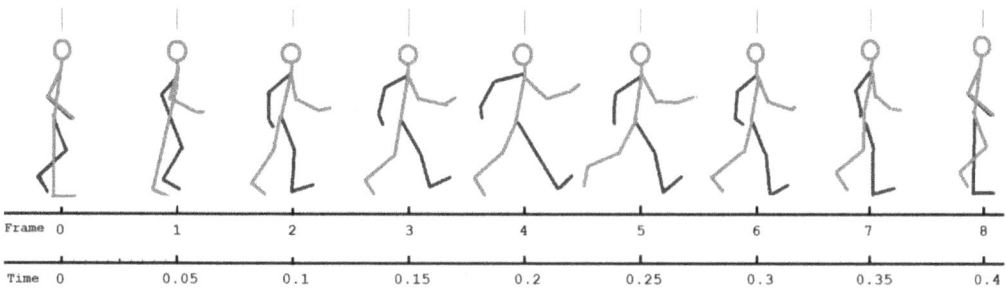

Figure 9-2. *A set of frames of a stick man walking. This set represents half of a complete step (one leg)*

Frame-by-Frame Animation

Performing the animation in this case is the easy part. The images (frames) exist as image files. An example of a small set of frames appears in Figure 9-2, and it represents a human gait. The simplest animations just display these images in sequence at a rate of 30 per second. In these situations the frames reside in image files having names that are consecutive in some way, like "frame000.png," "frame001.png," and so on.

The computer does not do very much work because the frames, where the art is, were provided by the artist. The computer only displays existing artwork.

A program that does this is:

```
PImage img;
int frame = 0;
void setup ()
{
  size (1000, 800);
  frameRate (10);
}
void draw ()
{
    background(100, 100, 100);    // Clear the screen
    img = loadImage ("frame"+frame+".png");
    image(img, 0, 0); // Write current frame (image) to screen
    frame = (frame+1)%10;     // Index for the next frame
    image (img, 0, 0); //width-img.width/2, height-height/2);
}
```

359

CHAPTER 9   DYNAMISM

Figure 9-3. *A sequence of images that show a human gait (walking) for a frame rate of 10 per second*

The frames exist in files named "frame0.png," "frame1.png," and so on.

Creating Animation Frames

Animation frames should be drawn so that the difference in position of objects between two adjacent frames accurately reflects the motion that one would observe in the time between those frames. The more space between the consecutive positions, the faster the object is moving: that's rule #1. Of course, there will be many objects in the scene that move simultaneously, and drawing those properly can be a challenge. There are basically two systems for drawing animations by hand: *straight ahead* and *key frame*.

Straight Ahead Animation

When using this scheme, the artist draws one frame after another in the correct sequence. Usually there is some way to compare the two frames, either digitally or using transparent sheets laid over top of each other, so that the movement between the frames can be clearly seen while they are being drawn. Accuracy is critical, because it is quite difficult to insert frames or correct one after a sequence has been created.

A good example is stop-frame animation, where the animator photographs a frame of a scene, then moves some of the objects, and photographs the scene again. Flip books are also examples of straight-ahead animation. The most important examples are the original animations from the 1950s and 1960s, like *Bugs Bunny*, the *Flintstones*, and most of the "Saturday morning" cartoons. The first Disney films were constructed that way as well.

CHAPTER 9   DYNAMISM

Advantages of straight-ahead animation are that it is artistic, is unencumbered by rules, and is great when there is a lot of activity. However, it puts a lot of pressure on the animator/artist, who must maintain a consistent style. It is hard to correct, and certain specific timings, like lip sync, are difficult.

Figure 9-4 shows some frames from a simple straight-ahead animation. The inspiration is a famous photograph by Harold Edgerton at MIT in 1964. The full animation here consists of 27 frames, each hand-drawn in pencil.

Key Frame Animation

Most animation these days is done using this design method. The action is defined by a set of key drawings, or *keyframes,* that represent places where the action changes. The time difference between these keyframes is known, and so the number of frames between them (called *tweens*, appropriately) is also known. The designer of the work does the keyframes, and other artists can fill in the tweens. This leads to a rather industrial approach, where a team of artists can work effectively on the same animation.

This makes it simple to synchronize key moments in specific frames, and it is easier to maintain consistency in the shape and size of objects. However, when multiple artists work on the same animation, there can be style changes between sections.

Figure 9-4. *Animation of Harold Edgerton's photo of a bullet piercing an apple. It's an example of straight-ahead animation*

CHAPTER 9   DYNAMISM

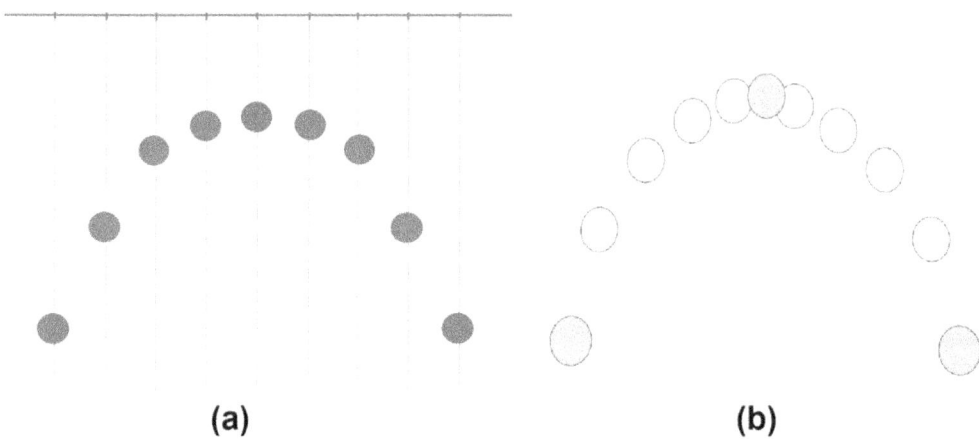

Figure 9-5. *(a) Key-frame sequence of a ball tossed in the air. This sequence does not account for the nonlinearity of gravity. (b) A better (more accurate) set of frames*

Figure 9-5 shows an animation sequence of a ball thrown upwards. The key frames are at the beginning and end of the toss and at the moment when the ball reaches its peak and starts to fall back (Figure 9-5). The tweens fill in the positions between those frames. There is a right and a wrong way to draw these. The wrong way shows the ball moving an equal amount of slowing between each frame (Figure 9-5a). In fact, gravity begins to slow the ball as soon as it is thrown. It decelerates according to the laws of physics until it reaches its peak and then accelerates as it falls back. The distance between the ball images differs between each frame (Figure 9-5b). Gravity or any constant force causes objects to move faster and faster with time. However, the important thing is that it has to *look* right, not *be* right. Sometimes the extra effort needed to make it correct is not worth it.

Rotoscoping

This is a technique involving drawing the same frame repeatedly or tracing over an existing frame many times. Each time we do this, it creates one frame. Because humans can't draw the same thing twice in exactly the same way, this produces a vibrating effect. We can also trace over photos or drawings to give a more accurate rendering.

CHAPTER 9 DYNAMISM

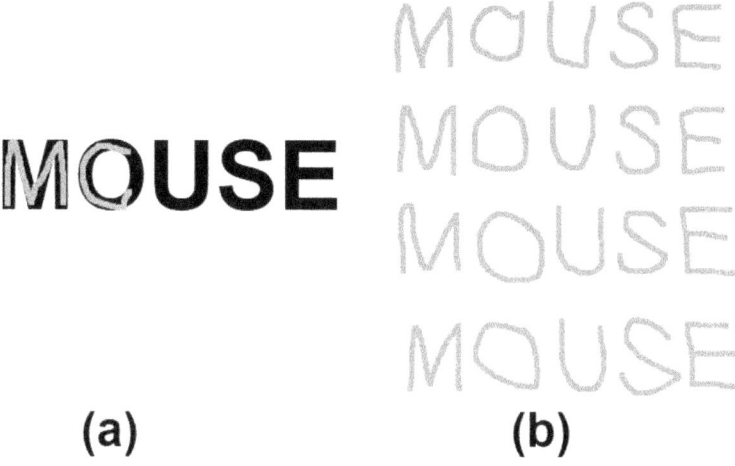

Figure 9-6. *(a) The image while using the tracing tool. The pixels being set in the result are drawn in green. Typing any character saves the tracing and clears the screen so we can do another one. (b) Four examples of tracings, each different*

The tool provided with the book displays an image and allows the user to draw over it with the mouse. When the left button is down, pixels will be drawn as the mouse moves. Typing the "q" key causes the program to quit, but any other key saves the image in a new file and clears the screen so another frame can be created. These can be displayed in the usual frame-by-frame manner (Figure 9-6).

Procedural Animation

Procedural animation using a computer program to keep track of objects and move them to create animation frames. Objects are software entities that have a visual representation (icon), and the entity can change position (move) and be drawn in that new location. The most common example of this is what we see in a computer game. Objects move about on the screen under the control of the game program, sometimes as directed by the player. What goes on in a game program is quite complex, but simple examples can be created.

363

CHAPTER 9 DYNAMISM

A simple example is that of a moving circle on the screen. The circle has an (**x,y**) location and a (**dx, dy**) speed, where dx is the number of pixels the circle moves in the x direction in one frame, and similarly for **dy**. Within the draw function we change (x,y) by (dx,dy) each time the circle is drawn:

```
void draw ()
{
  background (255);
  circle (x, y, 10);
  x = x + dx;
  y = y + dy;
}
```

This does draw a circle that seems to move, but it sooner or later moves off the canvas and can no longer be seen. The circle is still drawn each time draw is called and uses computer cycles but is drawn in a place where we can't see it. That seems wasteful, so we have some options: we could *restart* from some position on the canvas, or we could *wrap* the canvas so that if the circle moved off the right side it would appear on the left, or we could bounce the circle off the canvas boundary. Let's do the bounce.

Here's what a bounce does, in terms of an algorithm: if the circle starts to move off the right side, then we want it to make it move left so it stays on the canvas. This means changing the direction of x motion to be left, which is the opposite of what it currently is. In the code we have, this means setting dx to be **-dx**. In fact, the same code will also make the circle move right if it starts to leave the canvas on the left. Symmetrical code works for y if the circle moves off the top or bottom.

```
void draw ()
{
  background (255);
  circle (x, y, 10);
  x = x + dx;
  y = y + dy;
  if (x<0 || x>=width)
    dx = -dx;
  if (y<0 || y>=height)
    dy = -dy;
}
```

If we wish to wrap the canvas, then when the circle exits on the right, we move it to the far left of the canvas, setting x to 0, and the same for y.

```
void draw ()
{
  background (255);
  circle (x, y, 10);
  x = x + dx;
  y = y + dy;
  if (x<0) x = width;
    else if (x>=width) x= 0;
  if (y<0) y = height;
    else if (y>=height) y = 0;
}
```

We could draw multiple moving circles by extending x, y, dx, and dy into arrays and doing to each array element what we have been doing to the simple variables. We have not got a complex animation of circles moving in many directions, depending on the initialization, and never leaving the canvas (Figure 9-7a).

The moving and bouncing circle reminds us of the game *Pong*. This code is in fact at the heart of that game. In *Pong* there is only one circle, and it only bounces off the top and bottom of the canvas. If it hits the left or right side, then a point is scored, and the ball is placed at the center of the canvas. There are also two paddles, one on the left and one on the right, that can move up and down, and a circle can bounce off a paddle as well.

Let's implement this. First, we start with the code having one bouncing circle and change the bounce into an increase in a score and a restart from the middle:

```
if (x<0)
{
  rightScore = rightScore + 1;
  x = width/2; y = height/2;
  dx = -dx;
} else if (x>=width)
```

CHAPTER 9 DYNAMISM

```
{
  leftScore = leftScore + 1;
  x = width/2; y = height/2;
  dx = -dx;
}
```

Now we should draw the paddles. There is a left and a right. On the left, place the paddle **poff=25** pixels from the left canvas boundary. The paddles will move up and down and stay in the canvas and are **psize** pixel-sized. We add this code:

```
 line (poff, lpaddle, poff, lpaddle+psize);   // Left paddle
 lpaddle = lpaddle + dl;
 if (lpaddle+psize >= height || lpaddle<=0)   // bounce paddle
      dl = -dl;
// right paddle draw
 line (width-poff, rpaddle, width-poff, rpaddle+psize);
 rpaddle = rpaddle + dr;
 if (rpaddle+psize >= height || rpaddle<=0)   // bounce paddle
      dr = -dr;
```

Now the ball moves and the paddles move. One last thing: the ball should bounce off the paddles. The left paddle is **at x=poff** between **y=lpaddle** and **y=lpaddle+psize.** So if the circle has a **y** value in that range and overlaps with the paddle in the x direction, it should bounce, which means set **dx** to **-dx**.

```
if (y>=lpaddle && y<lpaddle+psize & x>poff-5 && x<poff+5)
     dx = -dx;
if (y>=rpaddle && y<rpaddle+psize & x>width-poff-5 && x<width-poff+5)
     dx = -dx;
```

Of course the actual game will allow the player to control the paddles, but we don't need to do that for this example. Figure 9-7b shows this game and adds a simple background.

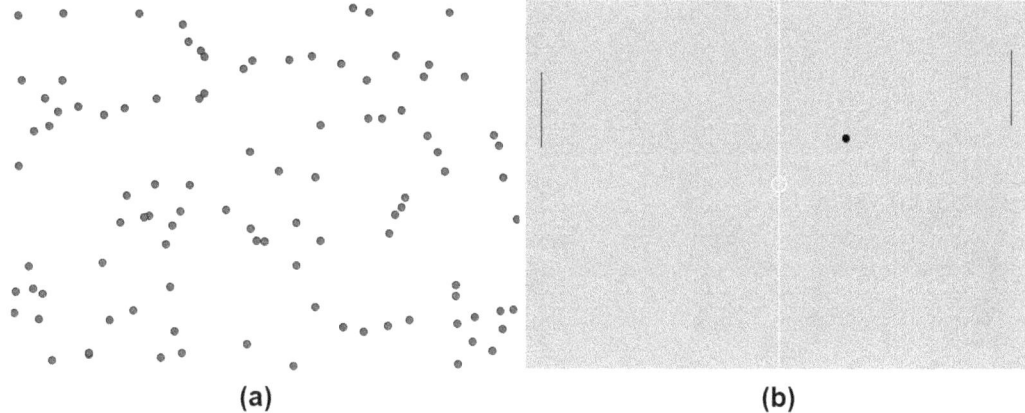

Figure 9-7. *(a) 100 circles moving in various directions. (b) The Pong game that uses very similar code*

Chroma-Key

This process is sometimes called the *green screen* process because it involves performing action in front of a green background, then extracting the foreground objects and placing them over a different background. Knowing that the background has a specific, uniform color makes the process of extracting the foreground easier, or at least one would expect so. Unfortunately, it's not as easy as it sounds. When the image is captured, the green values can vary from pixel to pixel because of noise and lighting. In addition, the image should be saved in a form that does not distort the color (i.e., not JPEG).

Figure 9-8 gives an example. The image of the stork has been captured over a green background, but it was saved as a JPEG file and has artifacts. We want to draw it over the background of the birdbath, but the obvious way of extracting the stork image – looking for pixels that are not (0,255,0) – does not work at all well, nor does using the hue value of 80 that we found in most of the green region (Figure 9-green-b) because it leaves green pixels near the edge of the bird. This kind of problem is very typical. It's nearly impossible to use a threshold on the green values to eliminate this.

CHAPTER 9   DYNAMISM

(a)   **(b)**   **(c)**

Figure 9-8. *(a) The two starting images, the green screen and the background. (b) Using a simple hue threshold does not eliminate all of the green pixels. (c) Identifying green pixels using the method in the text works much better*

A simple fix, which cleans it up but is not perfect in general, uses a threshold on all three color channels. We examine all pixels in the image, and for any pixel **p,** see if it is sufficiently green:

```
if ((green(p)-red(p)>delta && green(p)-blue(p)>delta))
 // pixel is a background pixel
```

This says that, first of all, the green channel is larger than the red or blue. It also says that it has to be larger by the amount **delta** or more for it to be green, where we can specify **delta** to be anything that works well. When we use delta = 7, we get the result in Figure 9-green-c. This method is not perfect, but it eliminates much of the problem in most images and all of it in some.

There are commercially available tools that will correct this problem, such as *Adobe Premiere*, using the Hue vs Hue adjustment, or the same adjustment in DaVinci Resolve.

Responsive Art

The idea of an artwork that could respond to changes in its environment is relatively new. The implementation of such works depends on modern electronics technology, because these works involve a *sensor* of some kind that can detect a change. This could be something that detects light intensity, color, sound, motion, or even temperature or air pressure. The sensor converts the input into an electronic signal and sends it to the computer, where it is used in an artwork. We're going to start at the point where the computer receives the input, because describing the electronics of the sensors would require much more detail than is appropriate here.

What kind of art are we talking about? It will consist of a display, a computer, and a sensor or sensors. The sensor sends a number to the computer every small interval that represents a measurement – let's say color. It senses the dominant color in the room it is in and returns a number **Z** between 0 and 100, where this is the hue value. This number, when received by the computer, controls the color of the work on the screen so that it changes as the color in the room changes. Why would the room change color? Because the viewers in the room wear different colors of clothing.

A simple work based on this would consist of rectangles moving from the center of the display in random directions, which change color as the value of Z changes. In the case of this text example, the value of Z depends on the horizontal mouse position. Figure 9-9 shows some frames from this, but of course you'll have to use your imagination (or visit the website) to see the dynamic color changes.

The color being drawn depends on the color value from the sensors (variable **Z**) between 0 and 100 as follows:

```
x = color ((z/100.0)*256, 200, 200);
fill (x);
```

where the color components are hue, saturation, and intensity, not RGB.

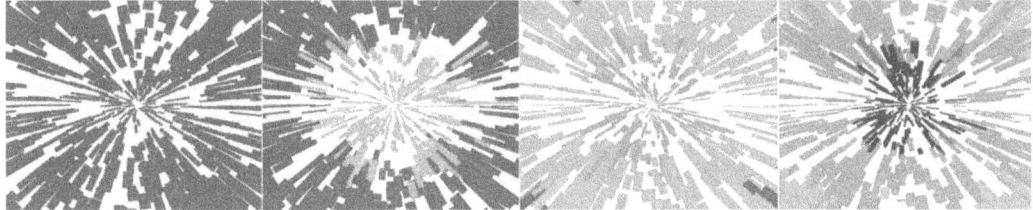

Figure 9-9. *Left to right, the animation frames change color as changes in ambient room color are detected*

This is the only aspect of the work that depends on the surroundings, yet it has a huge impact on the appearance. The sensor could just as easily return the distance to a particular person looking at the work or the average of distances of many people. Distance sensors are cheap and easily available. Audio sensors are too and can return the local intensity of sound or the intensity of certain frequencies. Almost any sensor could be made to return a value between 0 and 100, as used in this example.

When creating art of this kind, it is critical to consider its intended location. Historically paintings were intended to be displayed in a particular location, and they were painted with that in mind. Later, art became more "portable" as mass reproduction allowed it to be reproduced and displayed anywhere. When designing an artwork to be responsive to its environment, it is once again critical to know where it will be displayed. A piece that changes based on color or number of viewers is more suited to being in a gallery, where such things change frequently. A piece that is intended for someone's home might change based on sound, subtle changes in light, or motion.

The typical sensors can detect light intensity, color, sound level and sound frequency, movement, distance, touch, temperature, moisture, direction, acceleration, and some specific chemicals like CO and CO_2. These are the possible *modifiers*.

What aspects of the artwork can change depending on the input from the sensors? It very much depends on the essentials of the work and would be a core part of the design. Linguistically, the thing being modified is called the *head*, which is the term we'll use here. Why that term? Well, "red balloon" is a noun phrase, and the modifier is "red," and the *head* is "balloon," the thing being modified. In a verb phrase like "walk quickly," "quickly" is the modifier, and "walk" is the *head*.

Color

Color is an obvious choice for the head, as we used in **Figure 9-resp1**. A sensor can detect colors, and the program can either use tints of that color in the work or use complementary or split complementary colors. This is suitable in places where the ambient color changes relatively frequently.

If the sensor detects *sound*, it is common for high pitches to be mapped onto blue shades, and lower frequencies slide down to the reds.

When using *distance* (proximity), we can recall that more distant objects seem bluer than nearby ones and map distance to the red-blue spectrum that way. Or we could change things up and go some other direction, as long as it gives the desired effect.

Temperature is pretty obvious. Low temperatures are commonly mapped onto blues in most applications, and high ones to reds.

With *motion* we have interesting choices. Motion toward the artwork would correspond to proximity. The speed (change in x, y, z coordinates) can be tinted blue if approaching and red if receding, which corresponds to the way physics recognizes motion. In side-to-side motion, many people would associate a red color with faster movement and blue with slower.

Speed

High *light intensities* would usually correspond to high speeds, and vice versa. As mentioned before, red *colors* would correspond to fast speeds. *High sound levels* would usually be rendered as fast speed, and *high pitches* as well.

Movement in the scene could be made to correspond to movement in the artwork. If the viewers, for example, are moving slowly, then the objects in the work would do the same. This means that the work appears to respond in an obvious way to the viewers, which is usually a good thing. *Direction*, on the other hand, is a choice. Objects can move in a similar direction to the viewer or the opposite direction. Both choices attract attention. Rotation in the objects can vary according to measured speed and direction too, and there's really no way to decide on what is best in the absence of knowing what the objects in the work are.

High *temperatures* would correspond to fast motion, of course. An object can be made to stop when *touched*, as detected by a touch screen or mouse, or can be made to avoid a touch by moving away from it.

Shape

Humans don't have general perceptual connections between sensations and shapes. Are red shapes different from blue ones in some way? How is speed connected to shape? There's pretty little to go on. There are some general ideas we can use:

- If we sense fast motion, then we can add sides to a polygonal shape. This means that in the limit, very fast motion implies a circle. High-pitched sounds have the same implication.

- We normally prefer that motion in a particular direction implies that the shape is oriented in that direction. It could be thinner in the direction of motion than at the other end (*aerodynamics*).

- Distant shapes are smaller than nearby ones.

Detect light intensity, color, sound level and sound frequency, movement, distance, touch, temperature, moisture, direction, and acceleration

Video Cameras

A video camera provides a sequence of images at a particular known rate. This is a large amount of information, because the usual rate is 30 frames per second. Multiply this by the image size, let's say 1000x900 pixels to be conservative, and we get 27 million pixels to consider every second. Not only that, but recognizing objects within an image is, in general, an unsolved and difficult problem. What can we really do with a camera?

Anything that we've done with any image so far we can do with each frame of a video, if we can do it within 1/30 of a second. In fact, we actually only need to process each image in 1/20 of a second, and it will still look pretty good. We have to do things in real time because this is an artwork in a gallery, and people will be looking at it change in real time.

Summary

Dynamic artworks are ones that can change with time or by using some observation of the surroundings. When individual renderings are presented to a human quickly enough, changes in the position of objects are perceived as motion. This is the basis of all animation, films, and television. People are pretty good at seeing motion, and small errors in an animation can be jarring. When doing frame-by-frame animation, we draw each image (frame) showing motion as displacements, and then the computer can read and display the frames without much effort. *Straight-ahead* animation proceeds from frame to frame in sequence, whereas *keyframe* animation uses locations where action changes as keyframes and then fills in the in-between frames. Rotoscoping is a technique involving drawing the same frame repeatedly or tracing over an existing frame many times.

Procedural animation involves using a computer program to keep track of objects and move them to create animation frames. This is the standard these days when creating animations. Chroma-key uses a known color as a background and draws objects and a real background over that, replacing the color with image pixels. Art can be made to respond to its surroundings by using sensors that detect changes in light, color, sound, or any measurable data. The artwork then changes position, size, speed, or color based on what those measurements are.

Stand-alone Demo Programs

Pong	- The pong game with moving circle and paddles.
Resp1	- Animation of moving colored rectangles (Figure 9-9)
Green	- Example green screen code.
Extract	- Interactive extraction of lines using the mouse.
Morph	- Given two files of line coordinates, morph one to the other.

APPENDIX I

Math for Generative Art

The math in this book is high-school level. Most students will have studied it at some point, and some liked it and retained it better than others. What I present here is a review of the most important items from the perspective of the material we covered.

Most Important: Essential Trigonometry

Many times we have needed a few of the simplest formulas from trigonometry to accomplish our task. The "tri" in trigonometry means triangle; trig is all about triangles and the relationships between angles and the lengths of sides. I'll not deal with the *why* of things; I'll only show the needed calculations.

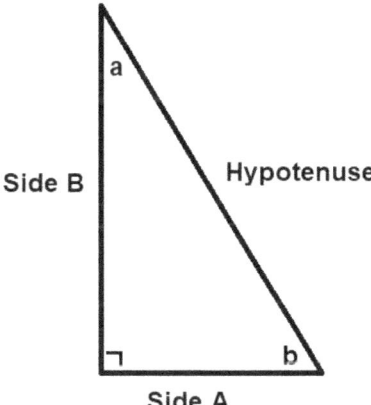

Figure I-1. *The model right triangle with angles and sides labeled*

In fact, we're mainly interested in what we call *right triangles*, which are triangles where one of the angles is 90 degrees. There can only be one such angle because the sum of the angles in a triangle is always 180 degrees. Two right angles in a triangle would sum to 180, and there would be no possibility of a third angle, so we don't have a triangle anymore.

We'll arrange the triangle so that the right angle is in the lower right corner. We can do that for any right triangle by rotating and flipping it. Those operations don't change the angles. So here's the model right triangle, we'll use the one in Figure I-1. The names **a** and **b** label the two angles that are not 90 degrees. The side named **A** is opposite angle **a**, and side **B** is opposite angle **b**. The hypotenuse is what we call the side opposite the 90-degree angle. At the right angle we make a little box to show it is 90 degrees – it's just a little visual aid we use.

We probably all remember *the Pythagorean theorem*:

$$A^2 + B^2 = \mathbf{hypotenuse}^2$$

This isn't critical here except maybe as a reminder of your high school days, as context for what follows.

We have been using coordinates for locating pixels and lines and things, and we can do that here too. If we place the triangle so that the right angle is at location (0,0), then angle **b** can be represented by the point **(b_x, 0)**, and angle **a** is at **(0, a_y)**. This is the situation in Figure I-2, and as one example we've given values to **b_x** and **a_y**: **b_x = 20, a_y = 30**.

Angles are measured in *degrees*, where one degree is 1/360 of a circle, or radians, where there are 2π radians in a circle. of a circle. In other words, there are 360 degrees in one complete circle, or rotation, and 2π radians. Mathematicians are the people who use radians. Everyone else is more familiar with degrees. Nonetheless, programming languages often use radians, as we'll see.

APPENDIX I MATH FOR GENERATIVE ART

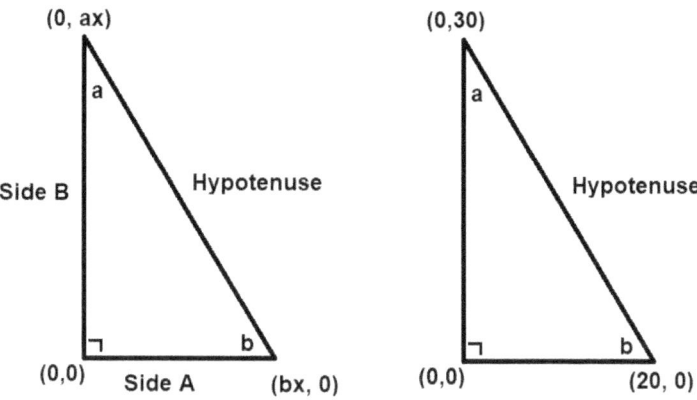

Figure I-2. *The model right triangle placed at the origin. This simplifies calculations. The triangle on the right is one example, having specific values for **bx** and **ay***

The critical fact is this: ***there is a fixed relationship between the angles in a triangle and the lengths of the sides.*** This relationship is contained in two functions: ***sine*** and ***cosine***. These functions have unique values for any angle given, independent of the length of the sides. The value of **sine(30)** is always the same.

On the other hand, the 30-degree angle can occur in many triangles of different sizes (Figure I-3). The angle does not determine the size of the triangle. However, if the angles stay the same, then as one side gets larger than the others must also. To determine the size of the triangle, we need to know the size of at least one side. The fixed relationship we talked about is as follows:

$$B = H*sine\ (b)$$

where **H** is the length of the hypotenuse and **B** is the length of side B. If we know any two values of **B**, **H**, and **b**, we can find the other:

$$sine\ (b) = B/H\ (= opposite/hypotenuse)$$
$$B = H*sine\ (b)$$
$$H = B/sine(B)$$

where do we get the value of the sine from? From a table that someone calculated previously, or from a calculator that probably just uses such a table. Because the sine of an angle is always the same given the angle, this is possible. We could even find the cosine values by measuring the sides of a triangle as the angle changes if we wanted to. Calculators are really the best way, though.

377

APPENDIX I   MATH FOR GENERATIVE ART

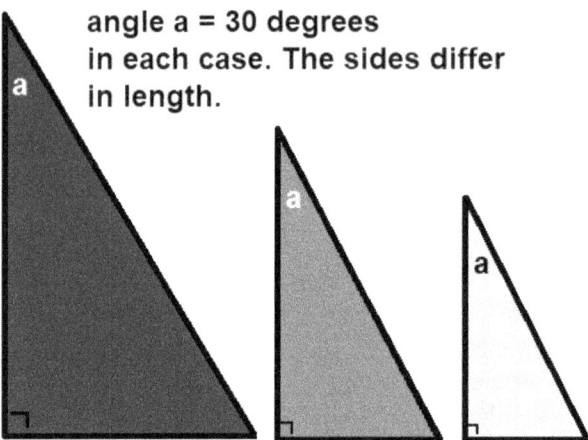

Figure I-3. *The size of a triangle can vary while the angles stay the same*

Going back to Figure I-2, we know two sides of the triangle. The hypotenuse[2] is $(20^2+30^2)= (400+900) = 1300$. So the hypotenuse is sqrt(1300), or 36.05. Sine(a) is opposite/hypotenuse = 20/36.05 = 0.55. We have a table of sines for all angles – look for the angle, and we find the sine. Here is a part of that table:

$$\sin(33°) = 0.544639$$
$$\sin(34°) = 0.559193$$
$$\sin(35°) = 0.573576$$

Thus, the angle a is between 33 and 34 degrees. The sum of the angles in a triangle is 180 degrees, so the angle b is 180-90-34, or about 56 degrees.

This is called the *arc sine*, or the *inverse sine*. Given an angle θ, **arcsin(sine(θ)) = θ.** There is also an *inverse cosine* (*arc cosine*), of course.

In a similar way, we find that:

$$\textbf{cosine (b) = A/H (= adjacent/hypotenuse)}$$
$$\textbf{A = H*cosine(b)}$$
$$\textbf{H = A/cosine(b)}$$

APPENDIX I   MATH FOR GENERATIVE ART

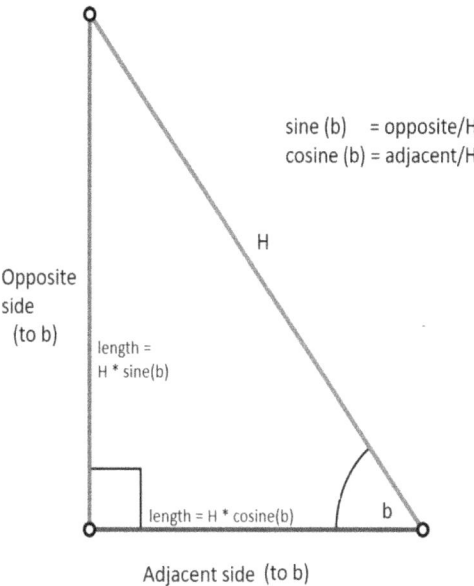

Figure I-4. Sine and cosine defined using opposite and adjacent angles, for angle **b**

A way to remember this is:

sine = opposite/hypotenuse

cosine = adjacent/hypotenuse

where *opposite* is the side opposite to the angle, and *adjacent* is the one next to it – the one that is not the hypotenuse or the opposite. This means that:

sine (a) = A/H

cosine(a) = B/H

sine(b) = B/H

cosine(b) = A/H

Now: why is this so important? Because it permits us to calculate *points* (pixel coordinates). The first time we did this was in Chapter 2, "Line," while drawing jagged lines. If you recall, we have divided a line into- N sections, and zig-zag between them. However, first we need to find the coordinates of the endpoints of each section of an arbitrary line. If the line has angle θ to the horizontal and endpoints **(x0,y0)** and **(x1, y1)**, we have the situation seen in Figure I-5a.

379

APPENDIX I MATH FOR GENERATIVE ART

We have three things and want to know where the points are that break the line into N (in this case N=4) equal portions. If the line is horizontal, that's easy: let **d = (x1-x0)/4** and the points are **(x0,y0), (x0+d,y0), (x0+2*d, y0), (x0+3*d,y0), (x1, y0)**. But the line is at an arbitrary angle θ. How do we do it now? Figure I-5 shows how. The idea is to make right triangles starting at **(x0,y0)** and use the trigonometry formulas to find successive x,y values.

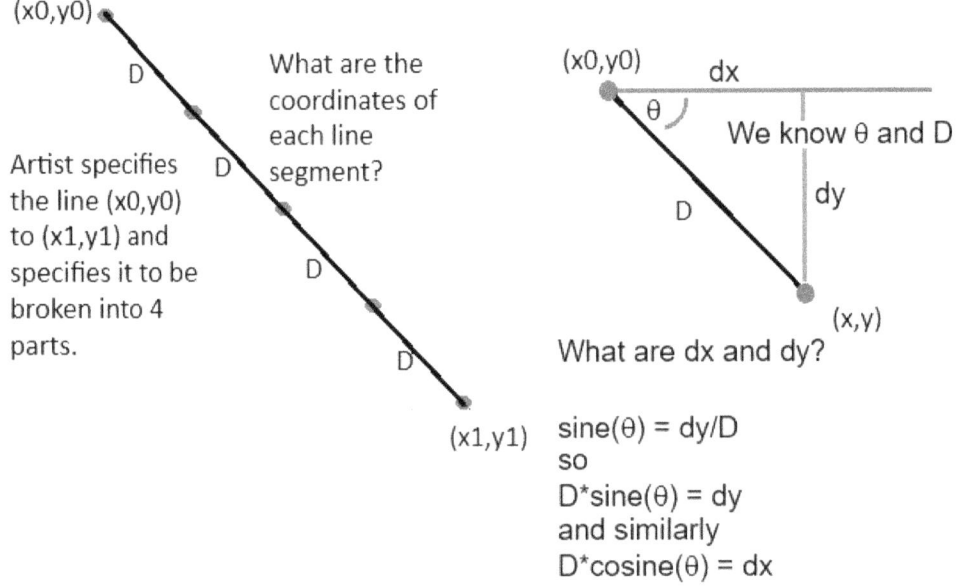

Figure I-5. *Breaking a line into N (=4) parts*

In the figure, we know θ and **D**, which is the distance between **(x0,y0)** and **(x1,y1)** divided by N. We want to know **(x,y)**, the coordinates of the first endpoint on the line. Make a right triangle from **(x0,y0)** to **(x,y)**. Given the angle θ, we know that **cosine (θ) = dx/D** and **sine(θ) = dy/D** (Figure I-5b) if we start at **(x0,y0)**. So we now know the values of **(x,y)** as **x0+dx, y0+dy.** The next point will be at **(x0+2*dx, y0+2*dy)** because the values of **dx** and **dy** are constant for this line.

The trick, if it's a trick, is to construct a right triangle for the situation where we know two of the parameters we need: the angle and a side. In the example of Figure I-5, we know the angle and the length **D**. How do we know the angle? Interesting question.

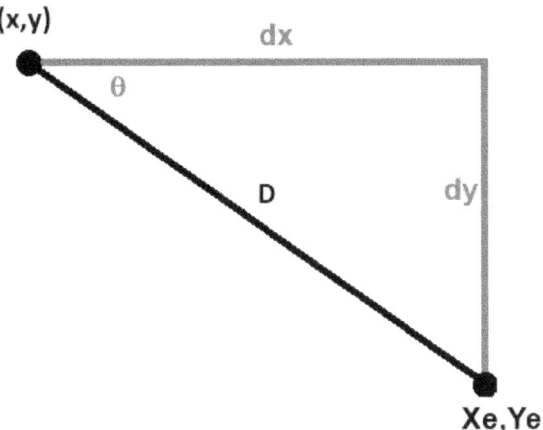

Figure I-6. *Drawing a line of known length given a starting point and an angle*

Given **(x0,y0)** and **(x1,y1)** as endpoints, we can make a new right triangle! The distance between **(x0,y0)** and **(x1,y1)** is the hypotenuse. The X distance is **(x1-x0)** and the Y distance is **(y1-y0)** (Figure I-5b). From this, **sine(θ) = dy/D**. If we know the sine of an angle, then because *sine* always gives the same value for the same angle, we must know the angle!

Another situation that happens frequently is to draw a line of length **D** starting at point **(x,y)** with angle **θ**. The line begins at **(x,y)**, and **D** is the length of the hypotenuse, as in Figure I-6. What is the end point **(Xe, Ye)**? With what we now know, it's easy! We know that **cosine(θ) = dx/D**, or in other words, **dx = D*cosine(θ)**. Also **dy = D*sine(θ)**. So we know that **(Xe,Ye) = (x+dx, y+dy)**. This right triangle relationship is one of the most useful in mathematics.

One final useful thing is that if we know **dx** and **dy**, the angle is unique, and we can find it. The function arc**tangent(dy/dx)** is the angle given by a change in **x** of **dx** and a change in **y** of **dy**. If we know **dx** and **dy** and not the length **D**, then the angle still must be arc**tangent (dy/dx)**. If **dx** is 0, then the line is vertical, but **dy/dx** is not computable. We need to treat this as a special case.

In *Processing* the functions we actually use are:

sin(x) - The sine of angle x.

cos(x) – the cosine of angle x.

tan (y/x) – tangent of y/x.

acos(z) – Arc cosine of z (angle for which z is the cosine).

asin (z) - Arc sine of z (angle for which z is the sine).

atan(z) - Arc tangent of z (angle for which z is the tangent).

atan2 (dy,dx) - Arc tangent of dy/dx (angle for which dy/dz is the tangent, allowing **dx** to be 0).

In conclusion, to use this sine/cosine relationship, we need to find a right triangle within our problem for which we know an angle and a length.

Analytic Geometry – Lines

A line in mathematics is a set of points that extend in each direction indefinitely. Between each two points there is another one. The *equation of a line* is a formula that, when given one of the x or y coordinates of a point on the line, can give the other. There are many forms of such an equation, but one of the most common is the point-slope, which is:

$$Y = mx + b$$

The values of **m** and **b** are constants for any line and are called the *parameters* of the line. The parameter **m** is the *slope* and indicates the angle or direction that the line appears to point. The parameter **b** is called the *y-intercept* and is the point where the line crosses the Y=0 axis. If **m = 0,** then the line is horizontal. To draw the line or find **y** given **x**, we must know those parameters.

The slope is defined as the change in **y** divided by the corresponding change in **x**. If the line (segment) runs from the point (x_0, y_0) to (x_1, y_1) then the slope is $(y_1-y_0)/(x_1-x_0)$. For a line between **(0,0)** and **(2,2)**, the slope is 2/2 = 1. We call the change in y *dy*. In math the Greek letter *delta* means *change*, so this is really *delta Y*, but *dy* can be printed using most devices. Similarly, the change in x is **(x1-x0) = dx**. Figure I-7 shows some values of slope m and what they look like in a graph.

In that same figure, we can see that the value of **b** is the Y value where the line crosses the Y axis. How do we find that point? Most like segments we draw have a start point and end point (x_0, y_0) and an end point (x_1, y_1). The slope **m = (y1-y0)/(x1-x0).** Now that we know that, use the values **(x0,y0)** and **m** to find:

$$b = y_0 - m \cdot x_0$$

Now we have the complete equation, and any point that satisfies this equation (i.e., for which it is true) is a point on the line. We could use (x_1,y_1) just as well, and the same value for **b** would be found. If the origin of the coordinate system is at the upper left, which is (0,0), then the following code would draw the line:

```
float xi, xj;
for (int i=0; i<width; i+=1)
{
  xi = i;
  yj = (m*i + b);
  circle (xi, yj, 1);
}
```

If the origin is at some point (cx, cy), then the code would be changed just a bit:

```
for (int i=-width; i<width; i+=1)
{
  xi = i+cx;
  yj = (m*i + b)+cy;
  circle (xi, yj, 1);
}
```

The function **psLine** will draw a line given the slope and intercept.

Note that for a vertical line the value of dx=0. This means that we can't calculate the slope, because we'd be dividing by zero. This can be coded as a special case, or we could assign a very large value, such as 100 or 100, to slopes with small values of **dx**.

There are a few things about the equation of a line that are important to note. First, a line that is perpendicular to the line **y=m+b** has a slope of **-1/m**. This can be handy. Also, all lines with the same slope are parallel to each other. If we have two lines:

$$y = m_0*x+b_0$$
$$y = m_1*x+b_1$$

and if m_0 is not equal to m_1, then they must intersect. Where? At the point where both equations are the same. So let: (algebra …)

$$y = m_0*x+b_0 = m_1*x+b_1$$
$$m_0*x = m_1*x+b_1 - b_0$$
$$m_0*x - m_1*x = b_1 - b_0$$

$$(m_0 - m_1{}^*)x = b_1 - b_0$$

$$x = (b_1 - b_0) / (m_0 - m_1)$$

This is the value of **x** at the point of intersection. Now just solve for **y** using either equation (the result has to be the same).

$$y = m_0{}^*(b_1 - b_0) / (m_0 - m_1{}^*) + b_0$$

Interpolation

Interpolation is the estimation of a value of some *function* between two known points. Let's start with a straight line. If the start point is (10,10) and the end point is (30,10), then the middle of the line is (20,10). Pretty simple. If we divide that horizontal line into 10 parts, we get (10,10), (12,10), (14, 10) … (30,10). For a division of the line into N=10 portions, we find a delta X (dx or change in X) of (30-10)/10 = 20/10 = 2, so each step from (10,10) has a change in X of 2.

Let's make this a little more complicated. If the line is not horizontal, then both X and Y will change as we go from the beginning to the end of the line. Let's use (10, 10) to (30, 50) as the line endpoints. If there will be 10 portions as before, we find that **dx** = 2, as before. But now there is a **dy** that is not 0: **dy = (50-30)/10 = 2**. For each step in the X direction of **dx**, there is a step in the Y direction of **dy that is proportional to the slope of the line**. Given this, what is the value of this *function* (a line), which is the value of **y**, when x=13? That's what interpolation is, and in this case it is a *linear* interpolation because we're assuming that the function is a line.

Each step in the x direction, dx, along the line has a corresponding step in y that is dx multiplied by the slope, or dx *(y1-y0)/(x1-x0). This means that for a value of x between x0 and x1, the change in y coordinate that corresponds is (x-x0) *(y1-y0)/(x1-x0). This is a change from y0, so the value of y corresponding to x is y0+(x-x0) *(y1-y0)/(x1-x0).

The value x=13 is a distance of 3 pixels from x0=10. The formula above gives y at that point as 30 + 3*1 = 33.

If, instead of using actual coordinates, we want to cut the line into smaller pieces and find the (x,y) coordinates at those points. Using the same start and end points, let's divide the line into 20 equal parts and find the (x,y) coordinates at each. We know that the slope m=(y1-y0)/(x1-x0) and the intercept of this line is b = y0 – m*x0, and dx is (x1-x0)/20.

The first point is obviously the start point at x=x0. The second has x = x0+dx, and the y value is m*x+b. We do calculate this for location i as:

$$x = (i * dx) + x0$$
$$y = m*x + b$$

We can define a linear interpolation function that we'll call **lerp**. The value of **lerp (a, b, z)** is the value of the linear function between **a** and **b** at the position defined by **z**, where **z** is between 0 and 1. The value of **lerp(10, 20, 0.5)** is the midpoint between 10 and 20, which would be 15. *Processing* has just such a function built in.

Pretty simple, really. But what if the function is *not* linear? Let's imagine a function like $y = x^2 - 15$. We want to interpolate this function between two **x** locations as before, but it's not linear. A change in **x** is not reflected in a proportional change in **y**. It turns out that any complex curve can be represented as a collection of straight lines if we use enough of them. Here are the values of the function $y = x^2 - 15$ between -5 and 5:

X	$x^2 - 15$
-5	10
-4	1
-3	-6
-2	-11
-1	-14
0	-15
1	-14
2	-11
3	-6
4	1
5	10

APPENDIX I   MATH FOR GENERATIVE ART

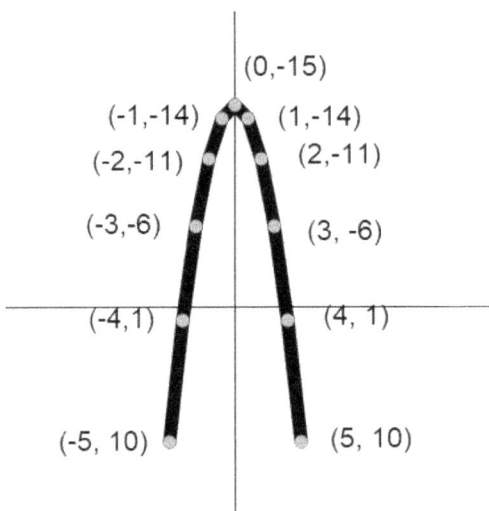

Figure I-7. *The function y=x²-15 approximated by straight lines*

We can draw the curve represented by this function by connecting the coordinates with straight lines: (-5,10) to (-4,1) is the first line, (-4,1) to (-3, -6) is the second, and so on. The effectively does a linear interpolation between two points on the curve. Obviously, the closer together the points are, the more accurate, the curve will represent the function.

Summary

These three mathematical concepts and processes are quite important to the material in this book. There are many other things you should know about: the function (equation) that represents a circle, for example. The distilled concepts are as follows:

1. A *function* returns a value given a parameter or parameters. The function **y = f(x) = x²-15** is one example. Given an **x** value, one can find a corresponding **y** value.

2. The term **dx** represents a small change in x. "Small" is defined any way you like but is usually relative to some other value, like a function value. The value of dx could be 0.1, and we can change a value x by this amount repeatedly to accomplish some task: we'd get values **x, x+dx, x+2*dx,** …

3. A function **f(x)** is *linear* if a small change in **x** gives a consistent change in **y**. This means that if **y=f(x)** and **y+dy = f(x+dx)** then **f(x+2*dx) = y+2*dy**.

4. Trigonometry is important because if we know an angle and the length of a side of a right triangle, we can find the rest. Useful for drawing lines at specific angles and finding the **dx** and **dy** for some existing points.

5. Most simple shapes have functions that define them. A circle and an ellipse are easy to draw from their function.

It is important to remember that angles can be measured in degrees or radians. It normally does not matter, but one must be consistent. *Processing* uses radians by default, so if you wish to find the sine of 25 degrees, you have to convert it into radians: **sin (degrees(25))**.

APPENDIX II

Programming in Processing

Some people think programming is hard and involves too much math. It's more a language *and* a way of thinking about a problem. Writing a computer program requires two things: you must understand the *syntax* (structure) of the programming language you are using, and you must be able to break your problem into small parts, each of which can be expressed directly using that language. *Processing* is just one programming language, but it was designed for artists to use, and it has many operations that draw things onto an area of the screen that we'll refer to as the canvas.

Processing can be downloaded to your computer for free from the website https://processing.org/download?processing. The current version (4.4.4 at the time of writing) can be downloaded with one click. This is an *MSI* file that can be executed and will install the language on your computer. Versions for *Windows*, *MacOS*, *Linux*, and the *Raspberry Pi* exist. On Windows, installing Processing will create a directory **C:\Program Files\Processing** where the system has been placed.

Double-click on Processing.exe in this directory and the window seen in Figure II-1 will pop up on your screen. This is where you enter your program and execute your *sketch*, which is what processing calls your code. The menus on top of the window are typical of most programming systems:

File allows you to save and open files.
Edit has options for the display (e.g., size) and text editing.
Sketch allows you to run and stop the program.
Debug makes it simple to find error in your code.
Tools allows you to create fonts, import libraries (i.e., Other people's code that is useful), and change display options, like color.

The circle with a triangle icon will run your program when clicked on, and the circle with a square icon will halt it.

APPENDIX II   PROGRAMMING IN PROCESSING

Now click the mouse in the window and type:

circle (50, 50, 20);

and then click on the *Start* button. This is actually a *Processing* program, albeit a simple one. It should draw a circle with a center at (50,50) and a diameter of 20 pixels. What this looks like on the screen is seen in Figure II-2. Processing opens another window (the canvas) and draws what you asked it to draw in that area of the screen.

Figure II-1. *The initial Processing window*

The size of the canvas can and should be changed to suit your artwork. The default, as in Figure II-2, is 100x100 pixels. It is changed by using the command (called a *function*) **size**:

size (1000, 800);

This specific command sets the drawing area to 1000 pixels in the X direction (width) and 800 pixels in the Y direction (height).

All of the basic shapes can be drawn using a single command, or function. Drawing a rectangle:

```
rect(100,120, 30, 60);
```

This draws a rectangle with the upper left corner at (100, 120), having a width of 30 pixels and a height of 60.

```
ellipse (100, 120, 30, 60);
```

draws an ellipse with the upper left at (100, 120) and a width of 30 and height of 60 pixels.

```
line (100,100, 200, 200);
```

Draws a line between the points (100,100) and (200,200). There are functions for drawing single points, triangles, and polygons.

Numbers and Variables

Drawing things gets tedious if you have to specify numbers to the functions. What we can do is to create a variable, which is a name that can contain a value, and use that instead. Consider the rectangle:

```
rect(100,120, 30, 60);
```

We can specify the upper left corner, width, and height using these variables, and then we can change them as the program executes. This is actually a pretty advanced topic in computer science, but if you have some high school math, it makes perfect sense. If the variable named **x** has the value 100, the variable named **y** has the value 120, the variable named **w** has the value 30, and the variable named **h** has the value 60, then the rectangle can be drawn using the function call:

```
rect(x,y, w, h);
```

APPENDIX II   PROGRAMMING IN PROCESSING

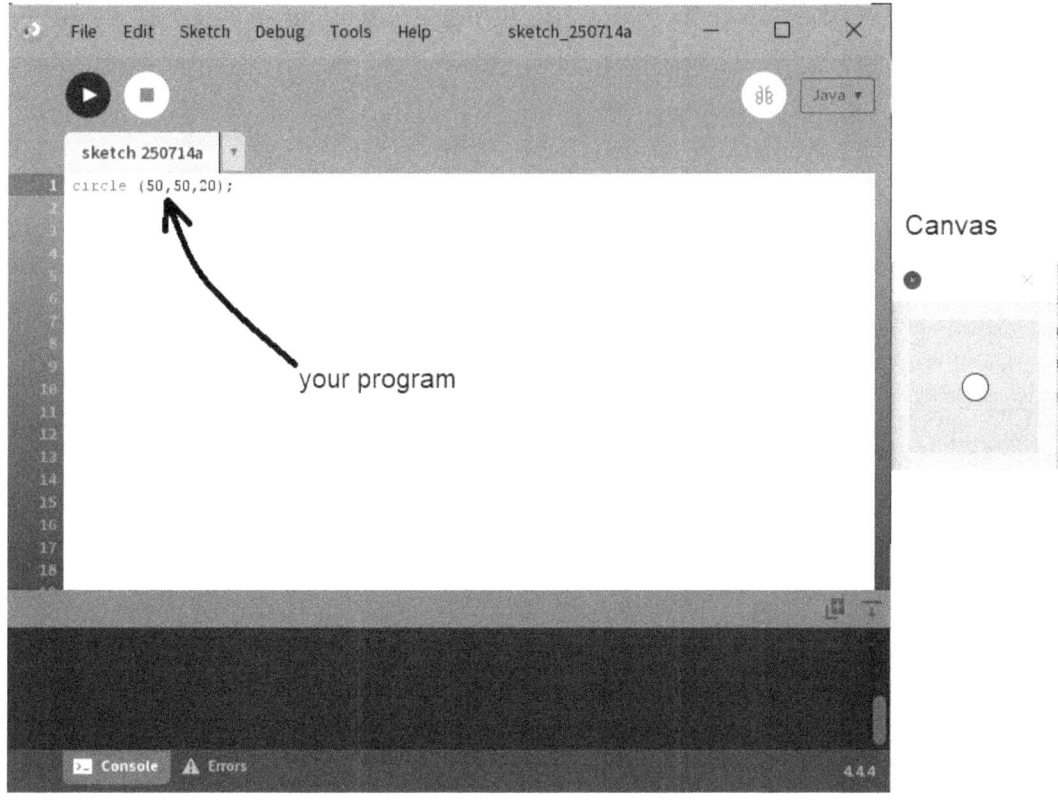

Figure II-2. *A Processing window containing a program and the corresponding canvas. The color of the sketch window is an option and does not matter*

We can make this happen as follows:

1. First, we have to define the names we're using. They are **x**, **y**, **w**, and **h**. *Processing* must be told that these names are variables, and it must be told what *type* they are. The types for now are **int** (which is short for integer) and **float** (which is short for floating point). An **int** is a simple number with no fractional part, like 1, 2, 3, 0, or -12. A **float** is a decimal fraction like 1.5 or 3.14159. We can define these variables in a *statement* called a declaration:

   ```
   float x, y, w, h;
   ```

   We must do this before the names are used so that *Processing* knows how they can be used.

2. Next, we need to give values to these variables. This is done in statements that are called assignment statements, because they assign a value to a variable.

   ```
   x = 100;
   y = 120;
   w = 30;
   h = 60;
   ```

Only now can we draw the rectangle using these variables (Figure II-3). The complete program is:

```
float x, y, w, h;
size (1000, 800);
x = 100;
y = 120;
w = 30;
h = 60;
rect(x,y, w, h);
```

The advantages of using variables are generalizability and modifiability. To illustrate this, let's add some code to the program to draw another rectangle 20 pixels to the left of one we just drew. All we need to do is add 20 to x and then draw the rectangle again:

```
x=x+20;
rect(x,y, w, h);
```

This shows what we can do with variables when we think of them as numbers. We can add, subtract, multiply, and divide variables that are **int** or **float**. Here are some legal ways to modify variables:

```
x = x*10+20;
x = y+x;
x = y/12.0;
```

The text to the left of the "=" is called an *expression*, and calculating it will result in a number that we assign to the variable. If you have read through Appendix I, you will see some trigonometric and other functions that are important to us, and *Processing* has those too:

APPENDIX II   PROGRAMMING IN PROCESSING

y = sin(x)	- Assign the sine of x to y.
y = cos(x)	- Assign the cosine of x to y.
y = sqrt(x)	- Assign the square root of x to y.
y = atan2(a, b)	- Assign the inverse tangent of b/a to y.

And so on. There are many such functions that you can look up in the *Processing* manual https://processing.org/reference/.

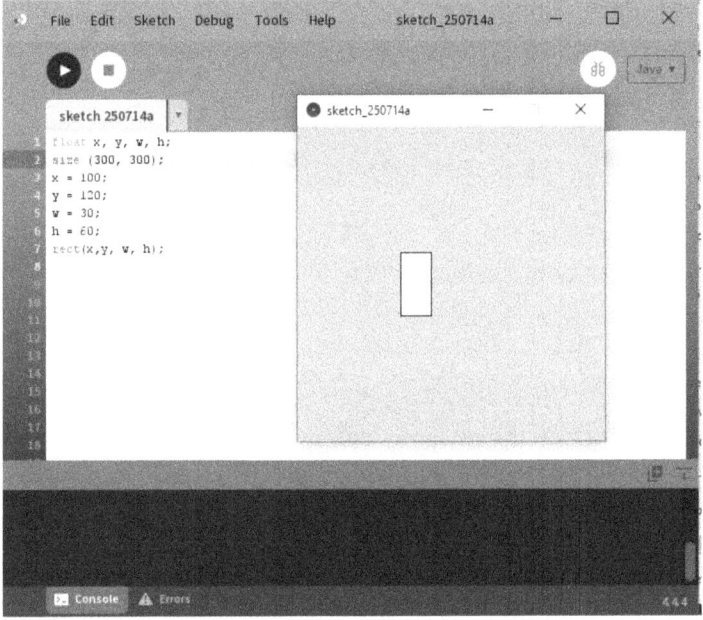

Figure II-3. *Complete program to draw a rectangle using variables*

It is important to note that a program is a sequence of *statements* and that they are usually executed one after the other in the order they are specified.

Color

A **color** is a type in processing that specifies a color value as its red, green, and blue components. A pixel value is always a color. We can declare a color as:

```
color circleColor;
```

A color can be specified as its three components, RGB, as:

```
circleColor = color(128, 200, 90);
```

The color for the background of the drawing area is specified as:

```
background(128, 128, 128);
```

for a middle grey background. For any grey color the three RGB components will be equal, so we can specify that simply as **background(128)** if we like. The color drawn by lines and outlines is set using:

```
stroke (r, g, b);
```

The color used to fill shapes is:

```
fill (circleColor);
```

For example, in most situations, the color components are *floats*, and we can get them out of a **color** variable as follows:

```
float r, g, b;
color c;
...
r = red(c);
g = green(c);
b = blue(c);
```

Statements

A statement in processing is a collection of characters that matches a template in the language syntax. The meaning of a statement varies depending on the syntax (structure). So, an assignment statement has the structure:

variable '=' expression ';'

The semicolon is used to terminate the statement and separate it from the next one. Are there other kinds of statements? Sure.

Groups/Blocks

We can group statements together using braces "{" and "}". Statements that occur between two braces are treated as one statement, even though they are still executed in sequential order within the braces.

So the statements:

```
{
    x = 20;
    y = 30;
}
```

are structurally treated as one statement.

IF Statement

The **if** statement is used when we want to make a decision about what code to execute next. Normally we execute statements in the order of appearance. The **if** statement can change that. Here is one form of this statement:

If (expression) statement1;

The statement **statement1** is executed only if the expression evaluates to a value we call **true**. This has a new type: **boolean**. A boolean expression or variable can only have one of two values: **true** or **false**. These mean exactly what you might think. The **expression** in the **if** statement should resolve to the type boolean. We have a set of operators that are most often used in such expressions, and they compare two things. Can ask if two numbers **a** and **b** are less than ('<'), greater than ('>'), equal ('=='), not equal ('!='), less than or equal ('<=') or greater than or equal ('>=') to each other. The statement:

```
if (a < 100) b = 12;
```

Will set **b** to 12 if and only if **a** is less than 100. We can use braces to execute many statements if the expression is true:

```
if (a < 100)
{
  b = 12;
  a = 10-0;
}
```

If the expression is **false**, none of those statements are executed. However, we can use **else** to execute things when the expression is false:

```
if (a < 100)
{
  b = 12;
  a = 10-0;
} else
{
  b = 13;
  a = -10;
}
```

Now if the expression **a<100** is false, we execute the code after the **else** part, and the result is different.

WHILE Statement

A great thing about computer programs is that they can do things over and over again and not get bored. They do this using *looping* structures, the simplest being the **while** statement. The syntax is:

```
while (expression)
{
  statements;
}
```

This executes the statements in the braces until the *expression* becomes **false**. This means that at least one of the statements in the loop must change the result of the expression, or the loop will execute forever. An example is the loop:

```
x = 10;
while (x < 100)
{
  circle (x, 100, 10);
  x = x + 11;
}
```

This code draws nine circles, each 11 pixels apart. The loop changes the value of **x** so that it draws circles at x=10, 21, 32, 43, 54, 65, 76, 87, 98. When **x** becomes 109 in the next time through, 109 is NOT less than 100, so the loop stops repeating, no circle is drawn, and the statement following the loop would be executed next.

FOR Statement

The **for** statement repeats a set of statements for a specific number of times and/or until an expression becomes **false**. The simplest and most common form is:

```
for (i=start; i<=end; i=i+1)
{
  statements;
}
```

which will execute the statements for each value of **i** from **start** to **end**, incrementing I by 1 each time. A loop that executes 10 times for values of **i** from 1 to 10 is:

```
for (i=1; i<=10; i=i+1)
{
  statements;
}
```

This allows us to specify any number of iterations in a general way. These loops can be nested:

```
for (i=0; i<10; i++)
  for (j=0; j<10; j++)
    statement;
```

will execute the **statement** 100 times. The inner for loop that increments **j** from 0 to 9 executes 10 time for values of **i** from 0 to 9. The most common use of this kind of nested loop is to examine all pixels in a region or an image:

```
// Variable x represents an image
for (i=0; i<width; i++)
  for (j=0; j<height; j++)//   examine pixel at x[i,j];
```

A **for** statement is not really required by *Processing*, because it can be implemented as a **while** loop. The following **while** and **for** loops are the same:

```
i = 1;                  for (i=1; i<=10; i=i+1)
while (i <= 10)         {
{                          statements;
  statements;           }
  i = i + 1;
}
```

Arrays

An array is a collection of values having the same type. Let's say that we want to have 100 integers, in ascending order from 0 to 99. This can be declared as an array of integers named **values**:

```
int values [];
```

This array can, at this point, be made to hold any number of integers. To make it hold 100 integers:

```
values = new int[100];
```

This is admittedly a strange syntax. We can declare values and give it 100 locations in the same statement:

```
int values[] = new int[100];
```

The characters "[" and "]" are called *brackets* and are characteristic of an array. Here **values** has 100 integers, and to access the first one, we use the name **values[0]**. The first element of an array is always indexed by 0, and so the 100 elements are **values[0]** .. **values[99]**. The index is an integer and can be an expression.

```
i=2;
values[i+1] = 9;
```

This makes **values[3] == 9.**

Now, to complete the task of creating 100 integers in ascending order from 0 to 99, we can use a **for** loop:

```
for (int i=0; i<100; i++)
  values[i] = i;
```

Images

An *image* is a built-in type in *Processing* called **PImage**. These are often loaded into *Processing* as files but can be created and drawn into. To read one from a file, first declare a variable:

```
PImage img;
```

Now read it using the *Processing* function **loadImage("in.png")**, when the file in this case is named "in.png." Any name can be specified, but the file must exist in the same directory as the program file:

```
img = loadImage ("in.png");
```

Now the image's pixels have been made a part of the variable **img**. We can display it on the drawing area using:

```
image (img, x, y);
```

where **(x,y)** specifies the position of the upper left corner of the image within the drawing area. It is often, but not always, (0,0). Let's say that the file "in.png" holds the image of the painting "nighthawks" (right). Reading and displaying this image is done as follows (Figure II-5):

```
PImage img;
img = loadImage ("in.png");
image (img, 0, 0);
```

APPENDIX II PROGRAMMING IN PROCESSING

Figure II-4. *The painting **Nighthawks***

Figure II-5. *The **Nighthawks** painting displayed by our Processing code*

The result is Figure II-4. The image is 480 by 261 pixels as stored in the file, so that is how large we made the canvas. We can find out how large the image is using the variables **width** and **height**, which are part of the **PImage** type. The value of **img.width** in this instance is 480 but in general will always be the width of the image saved in **img** in pixels. Similarly, **img.height** is the height of the image in pixels. A **PImage** can be thought of as an array of pixels in terms of how it is organized.

401

APPENDIX II PROGRAMMING IN PROCESSING

The value of **img.get(x,y)** is the value of the pixel, which is a **color**, at location **(x,y)** – column **x**, row y. The operation **img.set (x,y,c)**, where **c** is a color, will set the value of the pixel at **(x,y)** to the color **c**.

Using a nested **for** loop, we can copy every second pixel both vertically and horizontally to the upper left corner. This basically bakes a smaller copy of the original (every second pixel) and displays it in the upper left:

```
PImage img;
color c;

size (480, 261);
img = loadImage ("in.png");
image (img, 0, 0);

for (int x=0; x<width; x=x+2)
{
  for (int y=0; y<height; y=y+2)
  {
    c = img.get(x,y);
    set (x/2, y/2, c);
  }
}
```

The result is Figure II-6.

Figure II-6. The **Nighthawks** image is displayed, and then every second pixel is displayed in the upper left corner, effectively making the image ½ of the original size

Functions

A *function* is a name that you give to some code that you wish to execute many times, not necessarily in a loop. A variable is a name you give some value you wish to keep, and a function is basically the same for code. A function can have a value; a function that has no value is called a void function. So, for example, a function that would draw a circle in the center of the drawing area could be written like this:

```
void centerCircle ()
{
  circle (width/2, hcight/2, 5);
}
```

Whenever we want to draw such a circle, we simply type:

```
centerCircle();
```

This is not as general as we'd like but is just the first example. We can give the function some variables to use as parameters. For instance, let's say we wish to specify just the color of the circle. Then we could define the function to be:

```
void centerCircle (color f)
{
  fill (f);
  circle (width/2, height/2, 5);
}
```

When we call this function, we give it a color:

```
centerCircle (color(0,0,0));
```

and it will now draw a circle of the given color at the center of the screen. The variable **f** is defined within the parenthesis of the function declaration and is called a *parameter*. It acts just like any other variable inside of the function, but its value was given from outside of the function. We can have any number of parameters, and they must be given to the function in the order specified in the original declaration.

Parameters can be of any type and are passed as *values* to the function. This means that if they are modified within the function, that modification will not be reflected in the program that called it. So if we have:

```
int x = 2;
increment (x);
void increment (int z)
{
    z = 9999;
}
```

After the call to the function **increment**, x still has the value 2.

Static vs. Dynamic Processing Programs

The programs shown so far are in what *Processing* calls *static* mode. This means that the program starts executing at the top, and statements are executed sequentially until the final statement, with function calls not considered. The usual mode is *dynamic* mode. In this mode, the program is divided into two major parts: an *initialization* part and a *drawing* part.

The initialization part is accomplished in a function that the user must write named **setup**. Within this function we can create the drawing area, read images, set constants, and initialize arrays. *Processing* calls is set up only once, when the program first starts running. Here is a simple example:

```
void setup ()
{
    size(640, 480);
    fill (0,200, 0);
    stroke (0);
}
```

This creates a drawing area that is 640 by 480 pixels in size and sets the fill and stroke colors, which are effectively constants used by the rest of the program. It does not draw anything, although it could.

Now we can define the function that draws our artwork, or whatever we want to draw. This function is conveniently named **draw**, and *Processing* calls it many times each second. Here is a simple example of a **draw** function:

```
void draw ()
{
    background (255);
    fill (0,200,0);
    rect (100, 100, 200, 100);
}
```

Figure II-7. *Result of dynamic program to draw a green rectangle*

This will draw a green rectangle with a black outline at location (100,100) (Figure II-7). And it will do this many times each second, which you can't really see because it always draws the same thing in the same place.

The background statement sets the background color to, in this case, *white*, but also does one other important thing: it erases what has been drawn so far. In this case you can't see that because it always draws everything the same way every time. So, let's use the fact that draw is called many times each second to make a small animation. Instead of drawing the rectangle always at (100,100), we can draw it at (x,y) and then change the value of x each time draw is called (Figure II-8). We will make the rectangle green:

```
int x=100, y=100;
void draw ()
{
    background (255);
    fill (0,180, 0);
    rect (x, y, 200, 100);
    x = x + 1;
}
```

An Art Example

When we are creating artworks, we would never start by sitting in front of the keyboard and starting to write code. We first need to figure out what we want to do by creating a visual idea in our head. We should then write down how we could draw this in a human language, which means we need to make an *algorithm* for drawing our artwork. Finally, we would translate that algorithm into a program by breaking up the complex parts of the description into simpler ones until all parts can be represented as computer code. Let's show that process.

APPENDIX II   PROGRAMMING IN PROCESSING

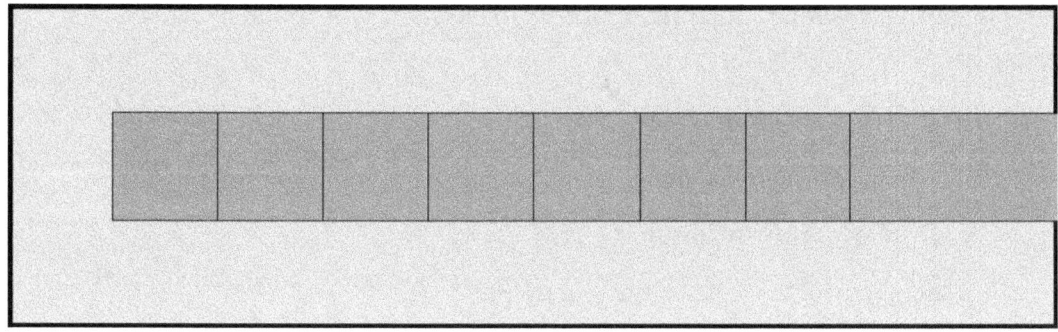

Figure II-8. *If the green rectangle changes position each time draw is called and we do not clear the screen using **background**, then all of the previously drawn rectangles will be visible*

Figure II-9. *A tunnel, the prototype example of our artwork*

As an example, let's draw a tunnel-like image where we start with a specific color along the nearest (outside) part of the tunnel, and which gets darker at interior parts, which are farther away from us. Something like the image in Figure II-9. Our final work will be in color.

407

APPENDIX II   PROGRAMMING IN PROCESSING

For general reference, the first algorithm to describe ANY problem using a computer is:

1. Initialize, including input.
2. Solve the stated problem
3. Print or output the result

This seems trivial but is just a starting point.

From the idea of Figure II-9, we can see that we will be drawing rectangles of differing colors and decreasing sizes, centered on the middle of the drawing area. The area is square in the figure but does not have to be. We can refine our algorithm by figuring out what variables we might need and then initializing them in step 1.

```
// 1. Initialize
int x=0, y=0;                     // Position of upper left of a rectangle
int w, d;                         // Size of the rectangle
float r=255, g=255, b = 255;      // Color of the rectangle
size (500, 500);                  // Drawing area is 500x500 pixels
```

We might need other variables depending on the method we use to do the drawing.

Step 2 is the complicated one. We can break it up into smaller parts. First, we need to draw a rectangle. It has a current size, position, and color, and these values can change. Nonetheless, the situation is:

```
// 2.1 Solve the stated problem. Version 1.
fill (r, g, b);
rect (x, y, w, h);
```

This just draws one rectangle at (0,0) to (width, height) that is filled with white, but it is a beginning. Let's change the fill color so that we can actually *see* the rectangle:

```
// 2.1 Solve the stated problem. Version 2.
fill (r, 0, 0);
rect (x, y, w, h);
```

This draws a red rectangle filling the entire drawing area.

What we want is a sequence of rectangles of decreasing size, centered, and becoming lighter in color. This means reducing the width and height of the rectangle, as specified by **w** and **h**, by some amount in each iteration. By how much? We can specify any amount we like, but **w** and **h** must be greater than or equal to 0. If we decrease **w** and **h** by an amount **delta** each time the size decreases by **delta*2** each iteration, and we can have no more than **N = (width/delta)** iterations before that happens, assuming width and height are equal.

We use a **for** loop to draw these **N** rectangles:

```
// 2.3 Solve the stated problem. Version 3.
  delta = 20;
  N = (width/(delta));

  for (int i=0; i<N; i++)
  {
    fill (r, 0, 0);
    rect (x, y, w, h);
    w = w-delta;
    h = h-delta;
  }
```

This draws N rectangles of the same color, one over the other. This means that we won't be able to see anything except the fill color. Add a statement at the end to read:

```
r = r - 10;
```

and now the red component decreases by 10 for each time this code executes. The result can be seen in Figure II-10.

Figure II-10. *Multiple rectangles drawn by version 3 of our program*

APPENDIX II   PROGRAMMING IN PROCESSING

This is still not quite what we want. The color is changing, and the rectangles are shrinking, but the rectangles are not centered in the drawing area. We need to change the position **x, y** each time. By how much? Well, the rectangles change in size by **delta** each iteration. If we increase **x** and **y** by **delta/2**, this should keep the rectangles centered.

So version 4 is:

```
delta = 20;
N = (width/delta);

// 2.3 Solve the stated problem. Version 4.
r = 255; x = 0; y = 0; w = width; h = height;
for (int i=0; i<N; i=i+1)
{
  fill (r, 0, 0);
  rect (x, y, w, h);
  w = w-delta;
  h = h-delta;
  r=r-10;
  x = x + delta/2;
  y = y + delta/2;
}
```

The result is Figure II-11.

Figure II-11. *The **for** loop version of the program that yields what we want*

This uses a **for** loop. When coding in dynamic mode, remember that **draw** is called 10 times per second. We can replace the **for** loop by drawing a new single rectangle each time draw is called, modifying the needed variables each time. The main difference is that we don't use **N** iterations but instead check the value of **w** each time. We keep drawing until **w** becomes smaller than 0, when we are obviously done; we can't have a negative width. The final dynamic version of this program is:

```
int x=0, y=0;
int delta = 20;
float r=255;
int w=0, h=0;

void setup ()
{
  size (500, 500);
  w = width; h = height;
  noStroke();
}
void draw ()
{
  if (w > 0)
  {
    fill (r, 0, 0);
    rect (x, y, w, h);
    w = w-delta;
    h = h-delta;
    r=r-10;
    x = x + delta/2;
    y = y + delta/2;
  }
}
```

The resulting image is the same as that in Figure II-11.

References

Chapter 1

Special reference:
John Berger (1972) **Ways of Seeing**, Penguin Books, UK.

This is a seminal work that changed who many people viewed art. It is based on a television series consisting of four-30 minute episodes that was created as a response to the British *Civilization* series. This book is a must read, but at least watch the videos. These could be found as of December of 2024 at:

`https://www.youtube.com/playlist?list=PL2SCoeb8QMtWWD5_7tiYBRWqq_ooZ2oR3`

Andrew Dixon (2018). **Art: The Definitive Visual Guide, New Edition**. DK; 2 edition. ISBN-13: 978-1465474759

Norman Koren (2007). **Introduction to Resolution and MTF Curves,** `http://www.normankoren.com/Tutorials/MTF.html`

Micael F. Marmor (2006). **Ophthalmology and Art: Simulation of Monet's Cataracts and Degas' Retinal Disease**, JAMA Opthamology, 124(12):1764-1769.

J. R. Parker (2010) **Algorithms for Image Processing and Computer Vision,** Wiley; 2 edition, ISBN-13: 978-0470643853

M. Pearson, M (2011) Generative Art: A Practical Guide Using Processing. Manning Publications; 1st edition.

L. Zhaoping (2014) **Understanding Vision: Theory, Models, and Data,** Oxford University Press, `https://doi.org/10.1093/acprof:oso/9780199564668.001.0001`

RGB Color chart `https://www.rapidtables.com/web/color/RGB_Color.html`
Computer vision Art Gallery `https://computervisionart.com/`
Download Processing `https://processing.org/download?processing`
Midjourney AI - `https://www.midjourney.com/home`
Craiyon AI - `https://www.craiyon.com/`

REFERENCES

Chapter 2

Adrrian Bowyer and John Woorwark (1983) **A Progremmer's Geometry**, Butterworth-Heinemann Ltd; Reprint edition. ISBN-13 978-0408012423

J. E. Bresenham (1965). **Algorithm for computer control of a digital plotter**, IBM Systems Journal. **4** (1): 25–30. *doi*:https://doi.org/10.1147/sj.41.0025

Edwin Catmull, Raphael Rom, (1974). **A class of local interpolating splines**. In Barnhill, Robert E.; Riesenfeld, Richard F. (eds.). *Computer Aided Geometric Design*. pp. 317–326. doi:https://doi.org/10.1016/B978-0-12-079050-0.50020-5.

James D. Foley, Andries van Dam, Steven K. Feiner, and John F. Hughes (2013) **Computer Graphics: Principles and Practice** (3rd Edition). Addison-Wesley Professional. ISBN-13 978-0321399526

Freeman, Herbert (June 1961). **On the Encoding of Arbitrary Geometric Configurations**. IRE Transactions on Electronic Computers. EC-10 (2): 260–268. doi:https://doi.org/10.1109/TEC.1961.5219197

Lyche T, Manni C, Speleers H (2018). **Foundations of spline theory: B-splines, spline approximation, and hierarchical refinement.** In: Lyche T, Manni C, Speleers H (eds) *Splines and PDEs: from approximation theory to numerical linear algebra*, vol 2219 of Lecture notes in mathematics. Springer, Berlin

Marchand-Maillet S, Sharaiha YM (2000) **Binary digital image processing — a discrete approach**. Academic Press, Maryland

Isabella Meyer (2022). **Paul Klee – Modernist, Colorist, Theorist, and Innovator**(Updated February 10, 2024) `https://artincontext.org/paul-klee/`

James Parker (1988). *Extracting vectors from raster images*, Computers & Graphics, vol. 12, pp. 75-79.

James Parker (2022) **Randomness in Generative Art: Drawing Like a Person**, Academia Letters, `https://api.semanticscholar.org/CorpusID:245939262`

T. Y. Zhang and C. Y. Suen(1984) **Fast Parallel Algorithm for Thinning Digital Patterns**, Communications of the ACM, Volume 27 Number 3, March

Chapter 3

Edmund Optics (2021). **Contrast:**
`https://www.edmundoptics.com/knowledge-center/application-notes/imaging/contrast/`

R.W. Floyd, L. Steinberg, **An adaptive algorithm for spatial grey scale**. Proceedings of the Society of Information Display **17**, 75–77 (1976).

N. Ikonomatakis; K. Plataniotis,; M. Zervakis, and A.N. Venetsanopoulos, (1977) **Region growing and region merging image segmentation.** 13th International Conference on Digital Signal Processing Proceedings, 1997. DSP 97. 1997 Volume 1

Chase Jarvaois (2012) **Photography Knowledge 101: What the Hell is SEPIA?** `https://www.chasejarvis.com/blog/sepia-what-the-hell-is-it/`

Rolf G. Kuehni, *(2003). Color Space and Its Divisions: Color Order from Antiquity to the present. New York: Wiley.* ISBN 978-0-471-32670-0

S. Kumar (2019) **A straightforward introduction to Image Thresholding using python.** `https://medium.com/spinor/a-straightforward-introduction-to-image-thresholding-using-python-f1c085f02d5e`

Haim Levkowitz; Gabor T. Herman, (1993*). GLHS: A Generalized Lightness, Hue and Saturation Color Model. CVGIP: Graphical Models and Image Processing. 55 (4): 271–285.*

Manahattan Distance: `https://iq.opengenus.org/manhattan-distance`.

Parker, J.R. (1993) **Practical Computer Vision Using C**, Wiley, New York.

J.R. Parker (2011) **Algorithms for Image Processing and Computer Vision**, Wiley, New York.

Alvy Ray Smith (1978*). Color gamut transform pairs. Computer Graphics. 12 (3): 12–19.*

Henry Trussel, (1979) **Picture Thresholding Using an Iterative Selection Method.** IEEE Transactions on Systems Man and Cybernetics 9(5):311 - 311

Chapter 4

Arthur S. Allen (1921) **The Application of the Munsell Color System to the Graphic Arts,** *The Art Bulletin* 3.4: 158–61.

Tawrin Baker, et al. (2015) **Introduction: Early Modern Color Worlds**, *Early Science and Medicine* 20.4/6: 289–307.

Faber Birren. (1976) **Color Perception in Art: Beyond the Eye into the Brain**. *Leonardo* 9.2: 105–10.

Kenneth E. Burchett (2002) **Color Harmony**, *Color Research & Application* Vol. 27.1 (2002): 28–31.

REFERENCES

Paul Centore (2012) **An open-source inversion algorithm for the Munsell renotation**, *Color Research and Application,* volume 37, pp 455-464. https://api.semanticscholar.org/CorpusID:56374046.

S. Cochrane (2014). **The Munsell Color System: A scientific compromise from the world of art**. *Studies in History and Philosophy of Science* Part A, 47, 26-41. doi:10.1016/j.shpsa.2014.03.004

N. Ikonomatakis; K. Plataniotis; M. Zervakis, and A.N. Venetsanopoulos, (1977) **Region growing and region merging image segmentation.** *13th International Conference on Digital Signal Processing Proceedings*, 1997. DSP 97., 1997 Volume: 1

Chase Jarvaois (2012) **Photography Knowledge 101: What the Hell is SEPIA?** https://www.chasejarvis.com/blog/sepia-what-the-hell-is-it/

Rolf G. Kuehni, (2003). **Color Space and Its Divisions: Color Order from Antiquity to the present**. *New York: Wiley.* ISBN 978-0-471-32670-0

S. Kumar. (2019) **A straightforward introduction to Image Thresholding using python.** https://medium.com/spinor/a-straightforward-introduction-to-image-thresholding-using-python-f1c085f02d5e

Haim Levkowitz; Gabor T. Herman, (1993). **GLHS: A Generalized Lightness, Hue and Saturation Color Model.** *CVGIP: Graphical Models and Image Processing. 55 (4): 271-285.*

Manahattan Distance: https://iq.opengenus.org/manhattan-distance.

A. H. Munsell (1915). **Atlas of the Munsell color system**.

A. H Munsell (1929). **Munsell book of color: defining, explaining, and illustrating the fundamental characteristics of color**.

These are hard to find and expensive if you *can* find them. Check the online *pocket* edition at https://munsell.com/color-blog/vintage-book-of-color-pocket-edition/

J.R. Parker (1993) **Practical Computer Vision Using C**, Wiley, New York.

J.R. Parker (2011) **Algorithms for Image Processing and Computer Vision**, Wiley, New York.

Nathan Gossett and Baoquan Chen (2004), **Paint Inspired Color Mixing and Compositing for Visualization**, *IEEE Symposium on Information Visualization*, October 10-12, Austin, Texas, USA

Alvy Ray Smith, *(August 1978).* **Color gamut transform pairs**. *Computer Graphics. 12 (3): 12-19.*

Chapter 5

Paula D. Beck (2014) **Fourth-Grade Students' Subjective Interactions with the Seven Elements of Art: An Exploratory Case Study Using Q-Methodology.** Long Island University. Print.

Abraham A. Davidson (1966) **Cubism and the Early American Modernist**. Art Journal 26.2: 122-65.

Z. Kelehear (2010) **Pass the Crayons: Leadership, Art Production, and Communities of Practice.** International Journal of Education Policy & Leadership 5.10. Print.

Galina Pasko et al. (2011) **Ascending in Space Dimensions: Digital Crafting of M.C. Escher's Graphic Art**. Leonardo 44.5: 411-16. Print.

Gerald Silk (2013) **In and out of Shape: The Art of Reva Urban**. Woman's Art Journal 34.2 (2013): 21-28.

George Stiny, and James Gips (1971) **Shape Grammars and the Generative Specification of Painting and Sculpture**. The Best Computer Papers of 1971. Ed. Petrocelli, O.R. Philadelphia: Auerbach. 125-35.

Chapter 6

Armi L., Ershad S.F.(2019). **Texture Image Analysis and Texture Classification Methods- A Review**, International Online Journal of Image Processing and Pattern Recognition

Brodatz, P. (1966). **Textures: A Photographic Album for Artists and Designers.** Dover Publications. ISBN: 0486216691.

Gatto, Joseph A. (2000) **Exploring Visual Design: The Elements and Principles**. Davis Publications, Worcester, Mass.

Haralick, R.M. and Shapiro, L.G., **Computer and Robot Vision**, Addison-Wesley, Reading, MA. 1992.

He, D.C and Wang, L. (1990), **Texture Unit, Texture Spectrum, And Texture Analysis**, IEEE Transactions on Geoscience and Remote Sensing, vol. 28, pp. 509 - 512.

Julesz, B., **Textons, the Elements of Texture Perception, and Their Interactions**, Nature, Vol. 290, No. 12, March, 1981. Pp. 91-97.

Laws, K.I., **Rapid Texture Identification**, SPIE Image Processing for Missile Guidance, 1980. Pp. 376-380.

REFERENCES

Madasu V.K., Yarlagadda P.(2007). **An in depth comparison of four texture segmentation methods,** IEEE. DOI 10.1109/DICTA.2007.83

Peet, F.G., Sahota, T.S., *Surface Curvature as a Measure of Image Texture*, **IEEE Transactions on Pattern Analysis and Machine Intelligence**, Vol. PAMI-7, No. 6, November, 1985. Pp. 734-738.

Pratt, W. K., **Digital Image Processing** (2nd. Edition), John Wiley & Sons, New York. 1991.

Rosedahl, L., Eckstein, M. and Ashby, F. (2018) **Retinal-Specific Category Learning**, *Nature Human Behaviour*, 2018, 2, 500-506.

Stewart, M. (2006). ***Launching the imagination: a comprehensive guide to basic design***. 2nd ed. New York: The McGraw-Hill Companies, Inc., 2006. ISBN 0-07-287061-3

Wirth M.A. (2004). **Texture Analysis**. Boca Raton, FL: CRC Press.

Yogi, C. (2023). **Texture Segmentation.** Medium. https://medium.com/aiskunks/texture-segmentation-c7796fb1b65a

Create textures that can be tiled:
https://www.imgonline.com.ua/eng/make-seamless-texture.php
https://galaxy.ai/ai-texture-generator
https://aitexturegenerator.com/
Brodatz texture images - https://www.ux.uis.no/%7Etranden/brodatz.html

Chapter 7

Canessa, A., Gibaldi, A., Chessa, M., Fato, M., Solari, F., Sabatini, S. (2018) **Data from: A dataset of stereoscopic images and ground-truth disparity mimicking human fixations in peripersonal space.** https://datadryad.org/stash/dataset/doi:10.5061/dryad.6t8vq Visited 2024-11-25.

Corker-Marin, Quentin; Adzhiev, Valery; and Pasko, Alexander. (2017) **Cubification and Animation of Artistic Shapes**, *SCA '17*, July 28-30, 2017, Los Angeles, CA

Glassner, Andrew S. (2000) **Cubism and Cameras: Free-form Optics for Computer Graphics**, *Microsoft Research MSR-TR-2000-05*.

Kelly, Rachel and Chakravorty, Dibya (2023) **The 10 Most Popular 3D File Formats.** https://all3dp.com/2/most-common-3d-file-formats-model/

Pyke, Randall (2019) **The Mathematics of Perspective Drawing: From Vanishing Points to Projective Geometry.** https://www.sfu.ca/~rpyke/perspective.pdf

REFERENCES

Data set of stereoscopic images. Mar 16, 2018 on Dryad. https://doi.org/10.5061/dryad.6t8vq

Free tutorials for modern Opengl (3.3 and later) in C/C++
http://www.opengl-tutorial.org/beginners-tutorials/tutorial-5-a-textured-cube/

Chapter 8

Abbot, E. (1884) **Flatland: A Romance of Many Dimensions**, Seeley & Co. of London. http://www.alcyone.com/max/lit/flatland/

Dixon, Andrew (2018). **Art: The Definitive Visual Guide**, **New Edition**. DK; 2 edition. ISBN-13: 978-1465474759

Dietrich, Frank (1986). **Visual Intelligence: The First Decade of Computer Art (1965-1975)**, *Leonardo,* Vol. 19, No. 2, pp. 159-69, 1986

Koren, Norman (2007). **Introduction to resolution and MTF curves,** http://www.normankoren.com/Tutorials/MTF.html

Iwatni, Tori (Designer) (1980). **Pac-Man**, video game, Namco.

Pajitnov, Alexey (Designer) (1988) Tetris., video game. Andromeda Software, Nintendo.

Wilson, Keene (2018) **Composition - Instruction, Notes and a Tutorial for the Advanced Artist** *Derived from numerous resources including notes from: Karl Gnass, Vadim Zang, Nathan Fowkes, Victor Casados, Carol O'Connor, Bill Perkins, Nicole Duet and others* (https://www.keenewilson.com/page/1349/composition) Mr. Wilson is now deceased.

A cool example of four dimensions. **Marc ten Bosch** https://4dtoys.com/
https://youtu.be/0t4aKJuKP0Q

PacMan, play online. https://www.pacman1.net/

Tetris, play online. https://play.tetris.com/

Carl Sagan on multiple dimensions.
https://www.youtube.com/watch?v=nwR8cVKVgCE

REFERENCES

Chapter 9

Laybourne, K. (1998) **The Animation Book**, Three Rivers Press, New York N.Y.

Parker, J. R. (2020) **Generative Art – Algorithms as Artistic Tool**. Uproute/Durvile Publications Ltd. Calgary, Canada

Parent, Rick (2002) **Computer Animation: Algorithms and Techniques**, Morgan Kaufman Publishers, San Francisco.

Pocock, L. and Rosebush, J. (2002) **The Computer Animator's Technical Handbook**, Morgan Kaufman Publishers, San Francisco.

Webster, C. (2005) **Animation- The Mechanics of Motion**, Focal Press, Oxfprd U.K.

White, Tony (1988). **The Animator's Handbook – Step-by-Step Techniques for drawn Animation**, Watson-Guptill Publications, New York N.Y.

Williams, Richard. (2001) **The Animator's Survival Kit. A manual of Methods, Principles, and Formulas for Classical, Computer Games, Stop Motion, and Internet Animators**. Faber and Faber Ltd, London, U.K..

First computer animation. `https://www.theautopian.com/the-first-realistic-computer-animation-was-a-drive-down-a-highway-in-1961/`

Metadata, Peter Foldes 1960. `https://www.nfb.ca/film/metadata_en/`

Harold Edgerton, *.30 Bullet Piercing Apple.* `https://mona.unk.edu/mona/harold-edgerton-mona-collection/`

DaVinci Resolve (has a free download) - `https://www.blackmagicdesign.com/products/davinciresolve`

Appendix II

Jim Parker (2022) **An Artist's Guide to Programming: A Graphical Introduction**, *No Starch Press, 248 pages, Paperback.*

James R Parker (2019) **Generative Art: Algorithms as Artistic Tool,** *272 pages, Paperback.*

Jeffrey L. Nyhoff, Larry R. Nyhoff (2017) **Processing: An Introduction to Programming,** *CRC Press. 544 pages. eBook, Paperback.*

Matt Pearson **(2011) Generative Art,** *Manning Publications. 300 pages. Paperback.*

Daniel Shiffman (2015) **Learning Processing, Second Edition: A Beginner's Guide to Programming Images, Animation, and Interaction,** *Morgan Kaufmann. 564 pages. Paperback.*

Index

A

Absolute time, 357
Abstract composition
    asymmetrical/unbalanced, 334
    balanced composition, 342, 343
    centered compositions, 340, 341
    constellation/group mass
        composition, 337, 338
    cruciform composition, 332, 333
    curvilinear composition, 336, 337
    diagonal composition, 338, 339
    forms, 332
    golden section/golden ratio, 339, 340
    horizontal composition, 334
    L/rectangular composition, 345, 346
    O/circular composition, 347, 348
    overlapping frames, 335, 336
    pattern composition, 346, 347
    radiant/radiating compositions,
        341, 342
    S/compound curve composition,
        348, 349
    3-spot/triangular, 343, 344
    tunnel composition, 344, 345
    2D visual artworks, 332
    vertical composition, 335
Additive color, 139, 182
Algorithm, 25, 32, 33
Ambient light, 300
Anaglyphs, 289–290
Analogous colors, 165
Analytic geometry, 382–384

Animal vision systems, 3
Animation
    cartoons, 356
    chroma-key, 367, 368
    computer-generated, 356
    frame-by-frame, 359, 360
    persistence of vision, 355
    procedural animation, 357
    responsive art, 368–372
    time, 357–367
    vision system, 355
Animation frames
    consecutive positions, 360
    key frame, 361, 362
    rotoscoping, 362, 363
    straight ahead, 360, 361
Arbitrary photographic image
    conversion, 79
Arbitrary thickness, 76
Arbitrary viewpoint, 274
Arc
    connecting arc, 54–56
    curves, 53
    definition, 52
    ellipse, 52–54
    function, 52
    radians(x), 53
    splines, 57–59
    start, 52
    stop, 52
    vase drawing, 59–64
arc function, 54, 56

INDEX

Arc sine, 378
Area, 209
Arrays, 399, 400
Artistic variations, 3
Artworks
    algorithm, 406
    background, 407
    general reference, 408
    for loop, 410, 411
    rectangles, 408–410
    size, position, and color, 408
    tunnel-like image, 407
    visual idea, 406
Artworks
    for loop, 409
ASCII art, 246
ASCII characters, 248
Assignment statements, 393
Asymmetrical/unbalanced composition, 334
Averaging, 65, 128
Axis of symmetry, 63

B

Balanced composition, 342, 343
beginShape(), 58, 271, 272
Biological vision systems
    cones types
        in Dogs and cats eye, 4
        in human eye, 4
        in turtles eye, 4
    human eye, 4
    light frequencies or wavelengths, 5
    optical portion, 3
    qualia, 5
    retina cells, 4
    RGB combination, 5

Blobs, 197–199, 220
Boundaries, 104, 108
    adjacent pixels, 113
    definition, 134
    digital analysis, 111
    parameter image, 113
    pixel locations, 111
    pixels, 112
Bounding box, 211, 226
Brackets, 399
Bresenham's algorithm, 39
Brightness, 8, 86, 88, 93, 142, 182
Brute force, tracing lines, 72–73

C

Calibration, 244
camera() function, 287
Camera coordinates, 260
Canny algorithm, 116
Canny edge, 116, 117
Cartoons, 356, 360
Catmull-Rom spline, 57, 272
Centered compositions, 340, 341
Chain coding algorithm, 74, 76
Character/value rendering, 244
Chroma, 143, 150
Chroma-Key, 367, 368, 372
Circle, 18
    definition, 188
    drawing, 189, 190
    drip, 189
    mathematical equation, 189
    smoke, 189
    square root, 191
    standard processing function, 188
    symmetrical, 191
Circularity, 210

Closed curves
    begin-end shape, 196
    curveVertex spline, 196
    definition, 195
Closed curves
    blobs, 197–199
    invented shapes (*see* Invented shapes (Midcentury Modern))
    natural organic shapes, 200–202
    organic shapes, 197
    splat, 199, 200
CMYK color model
    Albert Munsell, 149–151
    color coordinate system, 148
    conversion, 148
    description, 148
    mixtures, 149
    Munsell digital tool, 151–153
    subtractive mixing, 149
Coding and images
    declaration, 12
    file format, 13
    functions, 14
    individual pixels accessing, 13
    loadImage operation, 13
    myImage, 12
    pixel location, 13
    pixel size specification, 14
    pixel value setting, 13
    programming, 12
    2D array, 12
    type color, 13
Color, 370, 394, 395
    in art, 137
    artist, 137
    components, 9
    and edges, 173, 174
    numerical values, 9
    percentage, 8, 139
    perceptual concept, 182
    primary, 138
    quantization level, 9
    in reality, 137
Color channels, 144, 146, 166, 168, 172, 368
Color constancy, 175
Color from value
    colorization, 156
    DEM, 154
    gray, 153, 154
    LUT, 154
    space images, 155, 156
Colorization, 156
Color pairings
    analogous colors, 165
    complementary colors, 163
    palettes/color groupings, 162
    split complementary colors, 163, 164
    triadic colors, 164, 165
Color perception, 175, 176
Color psychology, 175–177
Color representations
    blue, 137
    color perception, 140
    conventional RGB value, 139
    gradient, 138
    HSB, 141–143
    percentage, 138
    RGB numerical values, 139
Color temperature
    digital implementations, 157
    in lighting, 156
    visual effects, 158
    warm/cool hues, 156

INDEX

Color variations
  from basic color, 158
  computer monitors, 158
  Pantone®, 158
  shades, 160, 161
  tint, 159, 160
  tones, 161, 162
Complementary colors, 163, 370
Composition, 309, 311, 313
Compression algorithm, 98, 320
Computer cycles, 364
Computer vision, 2, 6, 180, 185, 209
Cones, 4
Connecting arc, 54–56
Constellation/group mass composition, 337, 338
Constructivism, 23
Contouring, 90, 91
Contrast
  brightening and contrast expansion, 92, 93
  definition, 91
  histogram equalization, 93–95
  histogram specification, 95, 96
Convex area, 210, 215, 216
Convex deficiency, 217
Convex hull
  collection of points, 214
  convex area, 215, 216
  convex deficiency, 217
  convex perimeter, 216
  creation code, 215
  definition, 214
  Jarvis' March, 214
  start point, 214
Convexity
  convex hull (*see* Convex hull)
  template matching, 218
Convex perimeter, 216
Coordinates in 3D
  camera coordinates, 260
  object coordinates, 260–262
  OPP, 275–279
  perspective projection, 274, 275
  perspective projection/perspective transformation, 260
  perspective transformation, 262–267
  processing, 267–274
  projecting, 259
  screen coordinates, 261
  system in 3D computer graphics system, 260
  world coordinates, 260
Cosine, 377, 379
Cruciform composition, 332, 333
Cube
  box, 269
  complex 3D objects, 271–274
  drawing basic objects, 269–271
  in 3D space, 325
  implicit surfaces, 269
  P3D, 267
  rendered using Processing 3D primitives, 268, 269
  sets of coordinates, 267, 268
  setup function, 267
  sphere, 269
  tessellation, 269
Cubic interpolation, 235, 236, 239
Cubic noise, 253
  cubic interpolation, 237
  definition, 236
  interpolated interval, 237
  interpolated sequence, 237
  interpolation function, 236

linear interpolation, 237
2D interpolation, 238
Cubism
  ambientLight, 306
  beginShape(), 305
  Cezanne's *Still Life with Apples*, 303
  cubist version, 305
  illumination, 306
  pointLight, 306
  spotlight, 306
  texturing, 305
  transformation, 304
  triangles, 304
Curve, 30
Curved lines, 81
  arc (*see* Arc)
curveVertex(), 58, 205, 272, 274, 337
Curvilinear composition, 336, 337

D

Dashed lines, 40, 41
DDA Algorithm for drawing lines, 38, 39
Declaration, 12, 32, 392
Deconvolution, 331
Deep and shallow space, 317, 318, 352
Degree of agreement, 218
Degree of random activity, 21
Diagonal composition, 338, 339
Diffuse reflection, 300, 301
Digital camera, 3, 7
Digital differential analyzer (DDA), 38, 39
Digital elevation model (DEM), 154
Digital image space
  characteristics, 318
  dimensions, 318
  distorted for convenience, 320, 321
  generative artists, 318
  generative artwork, 322
  inaccurate, 319, 320
  malleable, 321
  mind-boggling, 318
  photograph/painting, 326
  relationships and values, 318
  relative, 322
  tesseract, 322–326
Direction, 30, 57, 72, 371
Discrete geometry library, 195
Disparity, 286–287
Distance transform, 78
Dithering, 118, 121–124
draw function, 364, 405
Drawing part, 404
Drawing general straight lines
  algorithms, 33
  endpoints specifying, 35
  intercept, 35
  pixels, 36
  point P_0, 34
  program and algorithm, 37
  slope-intercept equation, 34, 35
  two-point equation, 34
  variations, 35
Drawing operations
  circle, 18
  ellipse, 18
  line, 17
  rectangles, 18
  sample, 19
Drawing surface, 20–21
drawpixel function, 48
Drip, 189
Dynamism
  animation (*see* Animation)
  generative art, 355

INDEX

E

Edges
    Canny edge, 116, 117
    definition, 113
    detection schemes, 115
    horizontal edge, 114
    neighboring pixels, 114
    Sobel edge, 115, 116
    template/2D computational pattern, 114
    values, 114
    vertical edge, 114
Egyptian wall painting, 257, 258
Electronic sensors, 355
Electronic vision systems, images
    artists perception, 6
    collection of numbers, 6
    digital camera, 7
    3D scene, 6
    image format, 6
    individual light sensors, 7
    two-dimensional array, color values, 6
Elevation projection, 283, 284
Elevation views, 283
Ellipse, 18, 53
    axis length, 191
    mathematical definition, 191
    mathematical formula, 191
    Processing, 193
Empty canvas, 310–314
endCurve(), 58
endShape(), 58, 272
Equal distance algorithm, 169
Equilateral triangle, 187
Equation of a line, 382
Expression, 393, 396–398
Extracting curves from pixels, 73, 74, 76
Eye coordinates, 264, 265

F

Facing angle, 264–266
Features
    applications, 209
    definition, 209
    objects recognition, 209
    scale-dependent
        area, 209
        length, 210
        object recognition, 209
        perimeter, 210
        width, 210
    scale-in dependent
        signature, 211–213
    scale-independent
        compactness, 210
        rectangularity, 211
    selection, 209
Fixed viewpoint, 274
Flat renderings, 257
Flat shading, 301, 307
Float, 392, 393
for loop, 399, 400, 402, 409–411
Form, 257
    perspective, 257
    projections, 257
    See also Third dimension (3D)
Forms of straight line
    dashed lines, 40, 41
    jagged/zig-zag, 43–47
    textured, 47–49
    thick lines, 43
    variable thickness, 49–52
Four-dimensional cube, 323
for statement, 398, 399
Frame-by-frame animation, 359, 360, 372
Frame-in-frame composition, 335, 336

Frame rate, 358
Functions, 403, 404

G

Gamma correction/gamma transformation, 92
Generative AI tool Midjourney, 21
Generative art, 355
    advantage, 80
    algorithms, 25–26
    art of the algorithm, 24
    autonomous, 24
    constructivist art, 23
    definition, 23, 28
    vs. generative AI, 24
    interactive/dynamic, 24
    machine (computer), 24
    randomness, 25
    visual elements, 24
Generative art design, 25–28
Geological scale, 358
Geometric shapes
    circle, 188–191
    ellipse and oval, 191–195
    parameters, 186
    polygon, 187, 188
Geometric transforms in 3D
    rotation, 280, 281
    scale, 280
    translation, 280
Ghost/green screen, 219
GIMP, *see* Gnu Image Manipulation Program (GIMP)
gluLookAt(), 264
Gnu Image Manipulation Program (GIMP), 231
Golden section/golden ratio, 339, 340

Gouraud shading, 301–303
Gradients, 118, 138, 180
Gravity, 362
Gray-level histogram, 88–90, 100
Gray value, 118
Gray values, 77, 97, 104, 106, 153, 161
Green screen process, 367, 368
Grunge maps
    definition, 248
    distressed paper texture, 248
    implementation, 250
    Photoshop/Gimp, 251
    Processing, 249
    Processing tint() function, 250
    transparency, 250
    transparency (alpha) value, 249
Grunge maps, 248, 253
Grunge textures (*see* Grunge maps)

H

Halftones, 118–121
Half-toning (*see* Dithering)
Hamlet algorithm, 25
Hard edges, 117
Helix function, 272, 273
Hermann Grid Optical Illusion, 331
High key, 86
Histogram equalization, 93–95
Histogram specification, 95, 96
Horizontal composition, 334
Horizontal edge, 114
Horizontal line, 30
HSB color cone, 143
HSB color model, 142
HSB system, *see* Hue, saturation, and brightness (HSB) system
Hubble Space Telescope, 331, 332

Hue, 141, 174, 182
Hue *vs.* Hue adjustment, 368
Hue, saturation, and brightness (HSB) system, 141
Human-based textures, 229
Human color perception, 138
Human drawn lines stimulation
    computer scientist, 65
    connecting points, 65
    degree of creativity, 64
    endpoint changes, 68
    Euclidean distance, 65
    freehand drawn rectangles, Paint, 65
    lthresh variable, 65, 66, 70
    newlength/llength, 66
    probability, 67
    random number, 67
    random variation, 67
    vpct varaible, 70
    vpct variable, 67
Human visual system, 223, 327, 330
Hypercube, 322, 325
Hypotenuse, 376–379, 381

I

if statement, 396, 397
Illumination models
    ambient light, 300
    diffuse reflection, 300, 301
    flat shading, 301
    gouraud shading, 301–303
    incidence angle, 299
    reflection angle, 299
Image color changing, 15, 16
Image pairs, 287–289
Images, 400–403

Implicit surfaces, 269
Individual algorithm, 78
Initialization part, 404, 405
Integer arithmetic, 90, 91
Interpolation, 151, 233, 384–386
int variables, 393
Invented shapes (Midcentury Modern)
    iconography, 202, 203
    N-Flower drawing, 203, 204
    the pole, 206
    shape and color, 202
    zoop, 204, 205
Inverse sine, 378
Isometric projection, 282, 284
Iterative Selection algorithm, 101

J

Jagged/zig-zag line, 43–47
JPEG and *GIF* formats, 320

K

Key frame animation, 361, 362

L

Land effect, 175
LBP, *see* Local binary patterns (LBP)
Length, 36, 39, 186, 210
Library code, 157, 222, 307
Line, 17, 210
    definition, 29
    horizontal, 30
    straight/curved, 30
    straight line drawing, 33–35
    types, 30

vertical line drawing, 31–33
line3d(), 274
Linear interpolation, 234
Linear interpolation function, 385
Line function, 269
Line generation algorithm, 38
Lines
    essential, 81
    forms, 81
Lines of variable thickness, 49–52
Local binary patterns, 252, 253
Local binary patterns (LBP), 252, 254
Local thresholds, 102–104
Logarithmic transformation, 92
Lookat coordinates, 264, 265
Look-up table (LUT), 153, 154
Loops, 32
Low key, 85
L/rectangular composition, 345, 346
LUT, *see* Look-up table (LUT)

M

Malleable, 321
Mammals vision system, 2, 3, 251
Marilyn Monroe image
    averaging, 128
    background, 130
    filled contours, 132–134
    fuzzy boundaries, 128
    histogram, 128
    manipulations, 127
    median filters, 128, 129, 131
    Paint, 132
    thresholding, 129
Maya/3D Studio Max, 296
Mean, 108

Mean filter, 109
Measure of convexity, 217
Median, 108, 109
Median cut, 169–172
Median filter, 128, 129, 131, 173
Median filtering, 182
MeshLab program, 299
Midjourney AI, 21, 23
Mixing, 143, 144, 146–148
Mondrian's Geometrische Komposition, 207
Monet's Water Lilies, 165
Movement, 4, 371
Multiview orthographic, 283
Munsell Book of Color, 152, 153
Munsell color, 182
Munsell color chart, 150, 151
Munsell digital tool, 151–153
Munsell notation, 149
Munsell renotations, 151

N

Natural organic shapes, 200–202, 220
Natural textures, 253
    brightness/contrast, 229
    definition, 229
    degree of randomness, 229
    tiled textures, 230, 231
Neural networks, 252
NightCafe AI, 23
Numbers and variables, 391–393

O

Object
    basic shapes, 186
    definition, 1, 185

INDEX

Object (*cont.*)
    multiple views, 1
    shapes and colors, 2
    three–dimensional, 186
    visual appearances, 1
Object coordinates, 260
    shapes, 261, 262
Object recognition, 185, 186
OBJ files, 297–299
O/circular composition, 347–348
Octaves, 239
One-dimensional cube, 323
1D interpolation, 235
One-point perspective (OPP)
    and computer graphics, 276–279
    cube, 276
    vanishing point, 275
One threshold per pixel, 102
OpenGL, 263
Optical illusion, 327, 330
Organic shapes, 197, 220
Orthographic projection, 282–284
Orthographic transformation
    graphics systems, 282
Oval
    code function, 193
    drawing method, 195
    egg-shaped, 193
Overlapping frames, 335–336

P

Paint, 24, 65, 80, 144
Paper-and-pencil geometry, 276
Parallel coordinate projections
    definition, 282
    orthographic projection, 282–284
    vanishing point, 282

Parameters, 382, 404
Pattern composition, 346, 347
Patterns identification
    artistic representation, 206
    artworks, 206
    edges/boundaries, 208
    extracting shapes,
        images, 207, 208
    features (*see* Features)
    geometric shapes, 207
    Mondrian painting, 207
Perimeter, 210, 215, 216, 220
Perlin noise, 253
    code presentation, 241
    Internet, 239
    noise patterns, 240
    Processing noise function, 240
    red component, 242
    scale/step value, 241
    2D and 3D noise, 241
    uses of, 242
    video games, 242
    visual objects, 239
Persistence of vision, 355
Perspective function, 267
Perspective image, 284
Perspective projection,
    259, 260, 274, 275
Perspective transformation, 260
    aspect ratio, 263
    camera, 264, 265
    default values, 265
    eye coordinates, 264, 265
    geometry, 262
    lookat coordinates, 264, 265
    near and far clipping planes, 263
    non-animated applications, 264
    OpenGL, 263

point, 264
processing language, 263
unit vector, 264
vertical field of view (fov), 263
viewing position, 263
viewpoint, 265–267
width and height of drawing surface (w and h), 263
Photocells, 7
PImage, 12, 290, 400, 401
Pix, defined, 123
Pixel coordinates, 379
Pixel directions, 74
Pixels, 177
coordinates, 29
definition, 29, 81
identification, 81
location, 30
Pixels per inch (PPI), 10
Pixel value
between 0 and 255, 86
brightness(), 88
color value, 86
contouring, 90, 91
contrast (*see* Contrast)
functions, 87
gray-level histogram, 88–90
NTSC pixel, 87
PAL pixel, 88
size, 86, 87
specific encoding schemes, 87
weighted average, 88
Point-slope, 382
Polygon, 187, 188
Polygonalization/triangulation, 296
Polynomial equations, 219
Pong, 365, 367

Positive and negative space, 314, 315
PPI, *see* Pixels per inch (PPI)
Primary colors, 138
Procedural animation, 357, 363–367, 372
Processing
array, 399, 400
color, 393, 395
debug, 389
double-click, 389
edit, 389
files, 389
functions, 403, 404
images, 400–403
initial window, 390
installing, 389
MSI file, 389
numbers and variables, 391–393
programming systems, 389
size, 390
sketch, 389
statement, 395–399
static *vs.* dynamic, 404–406
tools, 389
Processing language
drawing operations, 17
function line(), 40
if and for statements, 33
PImage, 12
random, 21
specific functionality, 20
syntax, 11
Processing tint() function, 250
Programming language, 11
psLine, 383
P2D, 261
P3D, 261
Pythagorean theorem, 376

431

Q

Qualia, 5
Quantization, 167, 169
    definition, 124
    equal numbers of pixels, 125
    histogram, 125
    N levels, 124
    threshold, 126
    value, 124

R

Radiant/radiating compositions, 341, 342
Randomness
    appearance of reality, 21
    random number generator, 22
    size and color, 22
    statistical tests, 22
Random number generator, 22
readObj program, 298, 299
Real image, 106, 318
Real-world boundaries, 234
Rectangles, 18
Rectangularity, 211
Red-green color blindness, 140
Reflection, 230
Region-finding method, 177–180, 182
Region growing, 180, 207, 208
Regions, 104, 106, 117
Regular polygon, 187
Relative time, 357
Resolution
    color/value, 10
    definition, 9
    grey value, 11
    PPI, 10
    printing and scanning processes, 11

Responsive art
    color, 370
    frames, 369
    head, 370
    modifiers, 370
    portable, 370
    rectangles, 369
    sensors, 368–370
    shapes, 371
    speed, 371
    video cameras, 372
RGB colors combination, 139
Rhomboid leaf, 202
Right triangles, 376, 381
Rotoscoping, 362, 363, 372
Rule of thirds, 312
RYB color model
    computer implementations, 144
    mixing, 146–148
    RGB to RYB conversion, 144–146
    subtractive color systems, 144
RYB colors mixing, 146–148

S

Sample data, 28
Saturation, 8, 142, 182
saveStrings() function, 248
Scene
    definition, 185
    labeling regions, 185
S/compound curve composition, 348, 349
Screen coordinates, 261
Scrums, 358
Seeing, 1
Sensible locations, 312
Sepia toning, 180–181
Shades, 160, 161

Shading
    characters, 243, 244, 246
    color values and gray-level
        intensities, 243
    definition, 223, 242
Shapes, 371
    definition, 186, 219
    closed (*see* Closed curves)
    geometric (*see* Geometric shapes)
    integrals, 185
Signature
    curve, 212
    definition, 211
    line length, 211
    object identification, 212, 213
    shape identification, 212
    The match, 213
Sine, 377, 379
Sine/cosine relationship, 382
Skeletal pixel, 77
Skeleton, 77
Sketches, 312
Slope, 34, 382, 383
Smoothing, 107, 172, 173, 182, 207
Sobel edge, 115, 116
Sobel edge detector, 173
Space
    in abstract composition, 332–349
    composition, 309
    compositional rules, 349–352
    deep and shallow, 317, 318
    description, 309
    digital images, 318–326
    elements, 309
    empty canvas, 310–314
    positive and negative, 314, 315
    spatial relationship, 309
    3D space, 315, 316
    2D canvas, 309
    and vision
        analysis and rendering, 326
        visual response, 326–331
Space images, 155, 156
Spatial frequency, 327–331
Speeds, 371
Splatters, 199, 200
Splines, 57–59
Split complementary colors, 163, 164
3-spot/triangular composition, 343, 344
startCurve(), 58
startPoint function, 55
Statements
    groups/blocks, 396
    if statement, 396, 397
    for statement, 398, 399
    syntax (structure), 395
    while statement, 397, 398
Static *vs.* dynamic processing
        programs, 404–406
Stop-frame animation, 360
Straight-ahead animation, 360, 361
Straight line, 30, 34
strokeWeight(t) function, 49
Subtractive, 143, 144, 146, 147, 182
Subtractive color mixing, 143
Symphony (algorithm), 25
Syntax (structure), 389
Synthetic textures, 253
    color variations, 232
    controlled randomness, value noise,
        233–235, 239–242
    cubic noise, 236–239
    description, 232
    grass texture, 232
    random directional parameters, 232
    simple texture elements, 233

INDEX

T

Temperature, 370
Temperatures, 371
template array, 120
Template matching, 218
Tessellation, 230, 269
Tesseract, 322–326
Textons, 223, 253
Texture
    definition, 223, 253
    degree of random variation, 223
    identification, 251, 252
    painters, 223
    property, 224
    scale, 224
    traditional artists, 224
Textured line, 47–49
Texture mapping, 224, 225
Textures in 3D
    building, 293–295
    mapped image, 292
    mapping, 293
    mapping triangles, 295–296
    normalized, 292
    normalized coordinates, 292
    perspective projects, 293
    PImage variable, 290
    prism, 290, 293–295
    vertex function, 290–292
The Creation of Adam, 315
The pole, 206
The Voyager space probes, 155
Thick lines, 43, 77
Thinning algorithms, 77, 78
Thinning method, 78
Third dimension (3D)
    coordinates (*see* Coordinates in 3D)
    cubism, 303–306
    geometric transforms, 280, 281
    illumination models, 299–302
    parallel projection, 282–284
    scene or object in, 257
    textures, 290–293
    three coordinates and convert them into the 2D canvas coordinates, 258
    vs. 2D, 258
    vanishing point, 284, 285
    viewpoint, 258, 259
Three-dimensional cube, 323
3D Euclidean distance, 174
3D models
    FBX, 297
    Maya/3D Studio Max, 296
    OBJ, 296–299
    polygonalization or triangulation, 296
    STL, 296
    3DS, 297
    3D scanner, 296
3D object, 118
3D renderings
    graphics library, 276
3D space, 315, 316
3D viewing
    anaglyphs, 289–290
    disparity, 186–187
    geometry, 286
    image pairs, 287–289
Three-dimensional system, 169
Three-pixel-thick lines, 76
Thresholding, 129
    black and white boundary, 98
    brightness value, 97
    definition, 97

pixel values, 98
value selection, 99
　gray-level histogram, 100
　mean value, 99
　pixel classes, 101, 102
variation in values, 98
Thresholding algorithm, 103
Threshold selection method, 103
Tiled textures, 230, 231
Time
　absolute time, 357
　animation frames, 360–363
　define, 357
　design, 358
　duration, 357–359
　frame-by-frame animation, 359, 360
　Procedural animation, 363–367
　relative time, 357
　scrums, 358
　set of frames, 359
Tints, 159, 160
Tones, 161, 162
Tracking, 156
Traditional texture mapping, 227, 228
Transparency
　definition, 166
　implementations, 166
　value, 166
　weighted average, 166
Triadic colors, 164, 165
Trigonometry, 375–382
Tunnel composition, 344, 345
Tweens, 361
Two-dimensional cube, 323
Two-dimensional interpolation, 235, 238
Two dimensions (2D)
　drawing, 258
　vs. 3D, 258

2D canvas, 309
2D coordinates
　vanishing point, 279

U

Unit coordinates, 267
Unit vector, 264
Unpredictability, 21

V

Value
　definition, 134
　high key, 86
　line and color, 85
　low key, 85
　pixel (*see* Pixel values)
Value gradient, 117
Value noise, 233
Vanishing point, 275–279, 282, 284, 285, 306, 307
Variables, 12, 393
Vertex function, 271, 290
Vertex operation, 227
Vertical composition, 335
Vertical edge, 114, 115
Vertical line drawing
　code and algorithm, 33
　consecutive pixels, 33
　drawPixel(), 32
　function, 31
　loop, 32
　vline, 31
Video cameras, 372
Video game/VR environment, 266
Visual art, 25
Visual effects, 79

Visual response
   brightness, 8
   color, 8 *See* Color
   resolution, 9–11
Visual response and space
   blurred image, 331
   deconvolution, 331
   frequency ranges, 328
   Hubble Space Telescope, 331, 332
   large regions, 328
   optical illusion, 327, 330
   physical system, 327
   response curve, 329
   spatial frequency, 327–331
   virtual artist, 330
Visual system, 3
vnoiseCubic function, 239
vnoiseLinear function, 235
Void function, 403

W, X, Y

Weighted average, 88, 161
while statement, 397, 398
White pixels, 118
Width, 210
World Coordinates, 260

Z

Zfar, 277–279
Zmax, 278, 279
Znear, 263, 277
Zoop, 204–206

GPSR Compliance

The European Union's (EU) General Product Safety Regulation (GPSR) is a set of rules that requires consumer products to be safe and our obligations to ensure this.

If you have any concerns about our products, you can contact us on

ProductSafety@springernature.com

In case Publisher is established outside the EU, the EU authorized representative is:

Springer Nature Customer Service Center GmbH
Europaplatz 3
69115 Heidelberg, Germany